Emerging Markets and the World Patent Order

Emerging Markets and the World Patent Order

Edited by

Frederick M. Abbott

Edward Ball Eminent Scholar Professor of International Law, Florida State University College of Law, USA

Carlos M. Correa

Professor and Director, Centre for Interdisciplinary Studies on Industrial Property and Economics (CEIDIE), Law Faculty, University of Buenos Aires, Argentina

Peter Drahos

Professor, Regulatory Institutions Network, The Australian National University and Chair in Intellectual Property, Queen Mary, University of London, UK

Edward Elgar

Cheltenham, UK • Northampton, MA, USA

Published by
Edward Elgar Publishing Limited
The Lypiatts
15 Lansdown Road
Cheltenham
Glos GL50 2JA
UK

Edward Elgar Publishing, Inc.
William Pratt House
9 Dewey Court
Northampton
Massachusetts 01060
USA

A catalogue record for this book
is available from the British Library

Library of Congress Control Number: 2013944960

This book is available electronically in the ElgarOnline.com
Law Subject Collection, E-ISBN 978 1 78347 125 6

FSC www.fsc.org MIX Paper from responsible sources FSC® C013056

ISBN 978 1 78347 124 9 (cased)

Typeset by Servis Filmsetting Ltd, Stockport, Cheshire
Printed and bound in Great Britain by T.J. International Ltd, Padstow

Contents

Contributors

Frederick M. Abbott is Edward Ball Eminent Scholar Professor of International Law at Florida State University College of Law, USA.

Denis Borges Barbosa is at the Catholic University of Rio de Janeiro, Federal University of Rio de Janeiro – Institute of Economics (PPED), Argentina.

Carlos M. Correa is Professor of International Trade Law and Intellectual Property and Director of the Centre for Interdisciplinary Studies on Industrial Property and Economics (CEIDIE), Law Faculty, University of Buenos Aires, Argentina. He is Special Advisor on Intellectual Property and Trade of the South Centre, an intergovernmental organization located in Geneva, Switzerland.

Peter Drahos is a Professor in Law and the Director of the Centre for the Governance of Knowledge and Development in the Regulatory Institutions Network (RegNet), College of Asia and the Pacific, at the Australian National University, Canberra. He currently holds a Chair in Intellectual Property at Queen Mary, University of London, UK.

Mohammed El Said is a Reader in International Trade and Intellectual Property Law, Lancashire Law School, University of Central Lancashire (UCLAN), UK.

Carsten Fink is Chief Economist at the World Intellectual Property Organization.

Padmashree Gehl Sampath is Chief, Science and Technology Section at UNCTAD, Division for Technology and Logistics, Geneva, Switzerland.

Konstantinos Karachalios is Managing Director, IEEE-Standards Association, New York, USA.

Rajeev Kher is Additional Secretary, Trade Policy Division, Ministry of Commerce and Industry, Government of India.

Jakkrit Kuanpoth is Associate Professor and Head of Postgraduate Studies, Faculty of Law, University of Wollongong, Australia.

Andre Kudlinski is Director of Pharmaceuticals, Department of Trade and Industry, Pretoria, Republic of South Africa.

Tetyana Payosova is a Research Fellow, Institute for International and European Economic Law, University of Berne, Switzerland.

Pedro Roffe is a Senior Associate, Innovation, Technology and Intellectual Property Programme, International Centre for Trade and Sustainable Development, Geneva, Switzerland.

Susan K. Sell is Professor of Political Science and International Affairs, Department of Political Science, The George Washington University, Washington, DC, USA.

Yoshiyuki Tamura is Professor of Law, Hokkaido University Graduate School of Law, Japan.

Geertrui Van Overwalle is Professor of Intellectual Property Law, Centre for Intellectual Property Rights, Law Faculty, University of Leuven, Belgium. She is also Professor of Patent Law and New Technologies, Tilburg Institute for Law, Technology and Society (TILT), Tilburg University, The Netherlands.

Yousuf A. Vawda is Associate Professor and Academic Leader: Public Law, University of Kwazulu-Natal, South Africa.

Haiyang Zhang is a PhD Scholar at Crawford School of Public Policy, the Australian National University, Canberra.

Wei Zhuang is a PhD candidate at the University of Geneva, Switzerland. She is an Associate Fellow with the Centre for International Sustainable Development Law and a scholarship holder and visiting researcher at the Max Planck Institute for Intellectual Property and Competition Law.

Acknowledgements

This book completes a process initiated with the convening of a meeting of experts in the fields of intellectual property, economics, political science and trade at Florida State University College of Law in Tallahassee, Florida in April 2012. The participants were invited to prepare and circulate draft papers prior to the meeting, and to develop those papers into book chapters following it. In addition to the authors of the chapters, we would like to acknowledge the valuable presentations and participation in the meeting by Professors Nick Drager (McGill), Justin Hughes (Cardoza), Mingde Li (China Academy of Social Sciences) and Arti Rai (Duke). Antony Taubman (WTO) joined the meeting for an enriching presentation via video conference from Geneva.

The co-editors of this book were ably aided by research assistants Sabina Kania (FSU JD Candidate), Veronica La Roca (UBACyT Fellow), and Dr. Kylie McKenna (RegNet, Australian National University) and we thank them for their help.

The co-editors wish to thank Florida State College of Law for its hosting and financial support for the meeting. Special thanks are due to Dean Donald Weidner and Assistant Dean Catherine Miller.

Our thanks also to friends at Edward Elgar Publishing, Luke Adams (publisher, Law), Victoria Nicols (editorial assistant), Chloe Mitchell (desk editor) and Virginia Williams (copy editor).

PART I

Introduction

1. Emerging markets and the world patent order: The forces of change

Frederick M. Abbott, Carlos M. Correa and Peter Drahos

1 BACKGROUND

The world is always changing. The international system for the regulation of patents reflects these changes. The world of the 1870s and 1880s when the Paris Convention for the Protection of Industrial Property was negotiated, the world of the 1970s when developed and developing countries clashed over a New International Economic Order, the world of the late 1980s and early 1990s when the World Trade Organization (WTO) Agreement on Trade-Related Aspects of Intellectual Property Rights (TRIPS) was negotiated, and the world of 2013 each present a unique historical context. In this book, we do not intend to recap the historical development of the international patent system, including its relationship to the multilateral system for the regulation of trade. Instead we intend to focus on the world of today and the forces that are influencing the evolution of the international patent system. In particular, our focus is on the influence of the so-called "emerging market" economies.

Emerging economies such as Brazil, China and India had approached the international patent regime as importers of patented technology, worried about the cost and development implications of adopting the patent standards of developed countries. In many cases they joined key treaties of the patent regime comparatively late. For example, India joined both the Paris Convention and the Patent Cooperation Treaty (PCT) in 1998 and made full use of the transitional provisions available to it under the TRIPS Agreement. China joined the Paris Convention in 1984 and the PCT in 1994. Brazil was an early joiner of the patent regime, being one of the original signatories to the Paris Convention in 1883 and becoming a member of the PCT in 1978. That said, Brazil historically was a resister of pro-patent policies within the regime. Another important emerging economy, Russia (as the Soviet Union) developed in the twentieth century an alternative regulatory model to the patent system in the form of the system of inventors' certificates.

Today these countries have large domestic markets. Based on GDP data China is the second largest economy in the world, with Brazil, Russia and India coming in at sixth, ninth and tenth respectively.[1] As the United Nations Conference on Trade and Development's (UNCTAD) annual world investment reports have documented, these emerging markets have become important sources of foreign direct investment (FDI) inflows and outflows. Together the BRICS – Brazil, Russia, India, China and South Africa – represented about 25% of world GDP in 2010.[2] Our interest in emerging markets and the BRICS in particular is not in their influence as market powers, but rather as regulatory leaders within the patent regime.

Regulatory leadership does not necessarily follow market power. Japan emerged as a dominant economic power in the 1980s and yet its influence on the evolution of global regulatory standards has been remarkably weak.[3] More precisely, we are interested in seeing to what extent the BRICS are emerging as regulatory innovators within the patent regime. Even if they are not innovators in the sense of introducing new standards and models of patent regulation, they may nevertheless be adaptive managers of existing standards. The history of national patent systems is characterized by enormous diversity in terms of both administration and standards relating to things such as patentable subject matter, infringement and duration of protection. This diversity, at least on the face of it, suggests that states have engaged in a process of steering their systems to suit their industrial context. A third possibility is that some countries might be engaged in a process of simple modeling of standards set elsewhere. Simple modeling might be a prelude to adaptive management. A country might adopt a modeling strategy as a way of learning about the patent system before it begins the harder task of managing it for its own context. To some extent this may be the story of China. It is in a process of modeling the rules of the game because it sees itself as having the capacity to win significant benefits under those rules.

---

[1] *See* The World Bank, "Gross Domestic Product 2011", *World Development Indicators Database*, Washington, DC, The World Bank, 15 April 2013, http://databank.worldbank.org/databank/download/GDP.pdf.

[2] Adjusted for purchasing power parity (PPP). *See* BRICS, *The BRICS Report: A Study of Brazil, Russia, India, China, and South Africa with Special Focus on Synergies and Complementarities*, New Delhi, Oxford University Press, 2012, p. xiii.

[3] John Braithwaite and Peter Drahos, *Global Business Regulation*, Cambridge, Cambridge University Press, 2000, p. 27.

As we will see, there are few examples of regulatory innovation within the patent systems of emerging markets. Brazil's separation of examination power for pharmaceutical patents between its patent office and its drug regulatory authority ANVISA is one example. Perhaps the creation of a disclosure obligation standard for genetic resources and related traditional knowledge by some countries (for example China and Brazil) might also count as innovative since such a standard has not been part of Western patent law systems. There are some clear examples of adaptive management such as India's careful drafting of exclusions from the meaning of invention in Section 3 of its patent law, as well as its continuing commitment to pre-grant opposition at a time when Europe and the USA have put the emphasis on post-grant opposition. The chapters in this book dealing with the Middle East and the Association of Southeast Asian Nations (ASEAN) also suggest that some simple modeling is going on or perhaps just muddling through as small countries without much to gain from the patent system copy patent standards as part of a compliance strategy aimed at obtaining trade deals.

1.1 The Emerging Markets

During the second half of the twentieth century, from an economic development and "political systemic" standpoint, countries were largely referred to in three broad categories. The "developed" or "industrialized" countries referred to most of Europe, Japan, the United States of America (USA), Australia, New Zealand and other members of the Organisation of Economic Co-operation and Development (OECD). A second group of countries were characterized by a "communist" political and economic ideology, and functioned as "command economies" under the direction of centralized authority. The "developing countries" referred to a large and disparate group in terms of GDP per capita and comparable indicators, but were neither sufficiently economically developed to be grouped with the "industrialized" countries nor were they command economies. Regions as disparate as most of Africa, East Asia, Latin America and the Middle East were comprised of developing countries.

In the late 1980s, the political economy within the command economy countries shifted, markedly and rapidly in the case of Russia, and at a more measured pace in China. By the year 2000, the "communist bloc" had largely vanished, with China remaining as the only major command economy, and even then of a much different economic character than during the second half of the twentieth century. The process of economic liberalization that took place in China resulted in a tremendous economic boom. By the early 2000s, it had become difficult to characterize China as a typical "developing country" because of its high rate of GDP growth and its increasing influence in world markets, although based on per capita income and poverty levels China remains a developing country. Today China is seen by some as leading the creation of a distinctive model of authoritarian capitalism, one that will challenge the ascendancy of the neo-liberal model.[4]

Similar growth spurts took place in Brazil and India. The geographic size, natural resource endowment and political influence of Russia made it an increasingly attractive investment destination, despite a rather uncertain internal political environment. These four countries took on the acronym BRICs and have been labeled "emerging markets". Later, they were termed the BRICS as South Africa came to be seen as part of the group. There is no "neat division" that places a country within the category of an "emerging market". Indonesia is sometimes referred to as an emerging market. Surely the label can be applied elsewhere.

The emerging markets have changed the negotiating dynamic within the world trading system. The governments of these countries are not passive "takers" of initiatives proposed by the developed countries.[5] Negotiating initiatives put forward by the developed countries at the WTO and World Intellectual Property Organization (WIPO) have been stalled for more than a decade as developing countries refused to adopt them, and insist on their own agendas. Largely as a consequence of this, the principal negotiating forums are bilateral and regional, where negotiating partners can be selected on the basis of likely outcomes and strategic value, and on the perceived vulnerability of the other side. The emerging markets have recognized the economic and political power inherent in access to large and growing consumer markets that are attractive to multinational business.

1.2 The International Patent System

The Paris Convention of 1883 established the basic ground rules of the international patent system, represented by the principles of national treatment and independence, and a right of priority intended to facilitate system-wide patent protection.[6] The Paris Convention was not and is not

[4] *See, for example*, William H. Thornton and Songok Han Thornton, *Toward a Geopolitics of Hope*, New Delhi, Sage Publications, 2012.

[5] *See* Susan K. Sell, "The Geo-politics of the World Patent Order", Chapter 3 in this book, and Peter Drahos, *The Global Governance of Knowledge: Patent Offices and Their Clients*, Cambridge, Cambridge University Press, 2010 (hereinafter "Drahos, *Global Governance*").

[6] *See generally* Frederick Abbott, Thomas Cottier and Francis Gurry,

a "harmonization" exercise in terms of substantive patent law. The development of the European Patent Convention of 1973 and establishment of the European Patent Office (EPO), and the very recent adoption by the EU of the EU Patent Regulation (and EU Patent) represent the highest level of multi-nation harmonization of patent law, but in the rather unique context of European integration. The WTO TRIPS Agreement negotiated from 1986–93 introduced substantive "approximation" of patent law on a broad multilateral basis, though without covering all of the issues relevant to patent law (such as oppositions, employee inventions, etc.), and leaving considerable flexibility to individual WTO member countries.[7] Since the conclusion of the TRIPS negotiations, the developed countries, encouraged by the multinational business community, have pressed for closer harmonization of substantive international patent law, including with the proposal of a Substantive Patent Law Treaty (SPLT), seeking to limit the use of flexibilities in the TRIPS Agreement.

Although substantive harmonization at the multilateral level has not been realized, there have been a number of successful efforts toward creating a more harmonized international patent system. The Patent Cooperation Treaty (PCT) concluded in 1977 provides a mechanism for using the same patent application to file in numerous countries, and with an international examination report encourages similar assessment of patenting criteria.[8] The Patent Law Treaty (PLT) limits national variations in the format of patent applications. As or more important than these "hard law" treaties have been increasing levels of cooperation between national patent offices, including technical training and support, which encourages examiners to follow the same criteria in assessing patent applications, largely regardless of the underlying basic patent law. While the potential obstacles to a single global patent are probably too great for serious diplomatic effort today, a longer-term drive toward that objective appears implicit in the trend of concluded agreements.

Another major push toward substantive harmonization takes place in the context of bilateral and regional negotiations on intellectual property agreements, free trade agreements and investment treaties.[9] Here the

---

International Intellectual Property in an Integrated World Economy, New York, Aspen Publishers, 2011, pp. 59–107, 165–316.

[7] *See* UNCTAD-ICTSD, *Resource Book on TRIPS and Development*, Cambridge, Cambridge University Press, 2005; Carlos M. Correa, *Trade Related Aspects of Intellectual Property Rights: A Commentary on the TRIPS Agreement*, Oxford, Oxford University Press, 2007.

[8] *See* Drahos, *Global Governance*, p. 184.

[9] *See* Susan K. Sell, "The Geo-politics of the World Patent Order", Chapter

participating countries select their own negotiating partners or groups, bypassing the unwieldy multilateral Geneva environment. The Anti-Counterfeiting Trade Agreement (ACTA)[10] and negotiations on the Trans-Pacific Partnership Agreement (TPP)[11] are extensions of this push. A difference that has recently characterized the emerging markets is their reluctance to participate in negotiations with the EU or USA when intellectual property subject matter would be on the agenda. Significantly, none of the BRICS are part of the TPP negotiations, which, if concluded, would lead to the largest trade bloc in the Asia-Pacific region. A chapter on intellectual property in the TPP containing TRIPS-plus standards is a core negotiating objective of the USA. India is an exception to the extent that it has negotiated with the EU, but intellectual property rights (IPR) issues have been a major obstacle to concluding an agreement. However, the EU and USA have successfully recruited a significant number of developing (and developed) countries in bilateral and regional agreements, which cover patent subject matter. The standard template USA bilateral free trade agreement (FTA) attempts to conform patent law in the counterpart country to the substantive standards in force in the USA, and arguably provides in some respects even stronger patent protection than under domestic USA law.[12] It also provides an investor to state dispute settlement mechanism that can be used to challenge patent legislation and local court decisions as violations of international law on takings of property.[13]

---

3 in this book; Mohammed El Said, "IP Policy and Regulation in the Arab World: Changes, Challenges and Opportunities", Chapter 15 in this book; Jakkrit Kuanpoth, "Patents and the Emerging Markets of Asia: ASEAN and Thailand", Chapter 14 in this book.

[10] *See* Pedro Roffe, Xavier Seuba and Ricardo Melendez (eds.), *The Plurilateral Enforcement Agenda: The Genesis and Aftermath of ACTA*, Cambridge, Cambridge University Press, forthcoming 2013.

[11] *See, for example*, Office of the United States Trade Representative, "TPP Negotiations Shift into Higher Gear at 16th Round" [Press Release], 13 March 2013.

[12] *See, for example*, Frederick M. Abbott, "Intellectual Property Provisions of Bilateral and Regional Trade Agreements in Light of U.S. Federal Law", *UNCTAD-ICTSD Project on IPRs and Sustainable Development*, Issue Paper No. 12, February 2006.

[13] *See, for example, Eli Lilly and Company v. Government of Canada*: "On November 7, 2012, Eli Lily and Company, a US-based corporation, served the Government of Canada with a Notice of Intent to Submit a Claim to Arbitration under NAFTA Chapter 11. Eli Lilly and Company is alleging that the invalidation of its Strattera pharmaceutical patent by Canada is inconsistent with Canada's commitments under NAFTA." "Cases Filed Against the Government of Canada: Eli Lilly and Company v. Government of Canada",

The interest of the developed countries in promoting strong patent protection and harmonization reflects the mercantile interests of these countries, and their export and foreign direct investor communities. It is not surprising that countries with industries investing in new technologies seek to prevent third parties from relying on that technology to manufacture and market competing products. The "flipside" of this coin is that preventing others from using new technologies results in higher prices for consumers, and when public and social interests are at stake (e.g., in the field of public health) this can impose a significant cost on developing countries.[14] Moreover, precluding others from using patented technologies may impede follow-on technological development in developing countries (the type of imitation practiced by the USA during Britain's Industrial Revolution).

While agents of multinational business promote claims that implementing a strong patent regime will benefit developing (and even least developed) countries, leading economists have traditionally been wary of such claims.[15] Economists who have studied the international patent system in depth have concluded that the value of a patent system for a country will depend on the level of economic development and other country- and region-specific factors, as well as the specific industry to which it is applied.[16] As Haiyang Zhang points out in his chapter, the economic evidence for the developmental effects of the patent system is ambiguous at best. Countries at earlier stages of technological development are likely to benefit more from open access to patented technologies than they are from local development of internationally competitive new patent-dependent technologies. Only when the country has reached a sufficient

---

Foreign Affairs and International Trade Canada, Ottawa, ON, 2013, http://www.international.gc.ca/trade-agreements-accords-commerciaux/topics-domaines/disp-diff/eli.aspx?lang=eng&view=d (accessed 4 May 2013). Also, Notice of Intent to Submit a Claim to Arbitration Under NAFTA Chapter Eleven, Eli Lilly and Company, Disputing Investor, and The Government of Canada, Disputing Party, 7 November 2012.

14 *See* Andre Kudlinski, "Harmonizing the National Policies for Healthcare, Pharmaceutical Industry and Intellectual Property: The South African Experience", Chapter 12 in this book, for discussion of impact of patents on pharmaceutical pricing in South Africa, and for discussion of role in technology transfer.

15 *See* Edith Tilton Penrose, *Economics of the International Patent System*, Baltimore, MD, Johns Hopkins Press, 1951, pp. 101–07, 162–9, reprinted in Abbott, Cottier and Gurry, *International Intellectual Property in an Integrated World Economy*, pp. 135–41.

16 *See* Keith E. Maskus, *Private Rights and Public Problems: The Global Economics of Intellectual Property in the 21st Century*, Washington, DC, United Book Press, 2012.

level of economic development may the benefits from encouraging local innovators by means of patents exceed the economic and social costs of paying patent rents to multinational providers of goods and services. Even then, developing (and developed) countries must be careful to avoid damaging social welfare interests by allowing prices of essential goods to rise beyond the means of the population. There is also the possibility that even if one becomes a temporary net winner from the patent system, the system itself may not be the best way to retain innovation primacy. A combination of market competition, the use of other intellectual property rights and public good spending may be a more powerful combination. Moreover, in many instances patents may block rather than promote innovation.[17]

Despite this perspective of economists, there is a new wave of mercantilist theory promoting the idea of a new world order in which patents have become the new "value asset" that stimulates economic progress.[18] The more patents accumulated by a country and businesses, the more economically successful it will be. Using this premise, the adoption of a strong patent system is encouraged as a means of promoting rapid economic development. Conversely, the absence of strong patent protection will doom a country to falling behind in the development race.[19]

The idea of patents as ends in themselves in promoting economic progress seems to capture the imagination of journalists, including finan-

---

17 *See, for example*, Yochai Benkler, "A Political Economy of the Public Domain: Markets in Information Goods vs. the Marketplace of Ideas", in Rochelle C. Dreyfuss, Diane L. Zimmerman, and Harry First (eds.), *Expanding the Boundaries of Intellectual Property: Innovation Policy for the Knowledge Society*, Oxford, Oxford University Press, 2001, p. 271; and Michele Boldrin and David K. Levine, "The Case Against Patents", *Federal Reserve Bank of St. Louis* Research Division, Working Paper 2012–035A, September 2012, http://research.stlouisfed.org/wp/2012/2012–035.pdf.

18 *See, for example*, Global Intellectual Property Center, U.S. Chamber of Commerce, "Measuring Momentum: GIPC International IP Index", first edn., Washington, DC, Global Intellectual Property Center, December 2012, including scoring of patent regimes based on strength of enforcement and absence of flexibilities, finding BRICS countries deficient.

19 *For example*, Global Intellectual Property Center, "Measuring Momentum", p. 4, stating:

> No country aspires to be on the bottom of the jobs-supply chain. Promoting IP means protecting domestic innovators and creators, attracting world leading research and development, and creating and sustaining high-quality future jobs. The GIPC Index provides a clear and objective roadmap for nations to compete in a global economy, which is fueled by innovation, investment, and jobs.

cial reporters.[20] The idea also seems to have gained currency in some emerging markets like China where personal and financial success is measured by the number of patents one secures.[21]

The idea that countries at earlier stages of economic development will benefit from imitating the technological accomplishments of more advanced economies is dismissed as the thinking of a bygone era,[22] as FDI and technology transfer will presumably act as substitutes for internally generated local development. One is reminded here of the "thinking" that precedes every international financial crisis in which it is said that asset bubbles represent the dawn of a new era of constant growth in capitalism. There is little in the way of empirical evidence to support this new way of thinking. China is the country that most recently leap-frogged up the development curve and it did so with a weak patent system that encouraged local imitation of foreign-generated technology. Before China, Japan, as the chapter by Yoshiyuki Tamura in this volume makes clear, followed the same strategy. India was able to develop a vibrant pharmaceutical industry, often called "the pharmacy of the developing countries", in the absence of pharmaceutical product patent protection. But, perhaps this is the point. It may be that the new thinking is precisely designed to discourage the emergence of another China to challenge the existing organization of multinational business.

2 THE SITUATION IN THE EMERGING MARKETS

We have assembled chapters from each of the countries of the BRICS acronym that describe and analyze the state of the patent regime in 2013. Our intention is to look at a "snapshot" of the situation today, and what it may tell us about how the future of the international patent order will unfold, and with what potential consequences. Should we be recommending some modification or alteration in the current path, however modest? Is there some lesson or lessons to be drawn by developing countries or by the industrialized world?

To preview our conclusion, a review of the situation in the BRICS countries suggests that the international patent system should remain in a

---

[20] *See, for example*, Clive Cookson, "Patent Proof of Rising Innovation", *Financial Times*, 19 May 2011, http://www.ft.com/intl/cms/s/0/bfd85ce6–8111–11e0–9360–00144feabdc0.html#axzz2OyCRzhlf (accessed 4 May 2013).

[21] *See* Wei Zhuang, "Evolution of the Patent System in China", Chapter 9 in this book.

[22] *See* Global Intellectual Property Center, "Measuring Momentum".

"multispeed" mode for the foreseeable future, and that international patent law harmonization is not on the immediate horizon. Just as the United States and European Union placed considerable value on internal autonomy in the development and application of IP law, Brazil, China, India, Russia and South Africa also value autonomy. The potential wildcard is that multinational corporate interests may exert sufficiently strong lobbying pressure that government autonomy in these countries is challenged. But, these pressures and counter pressures have been at work since the mid-1800s, and it is hard to see why there would be a dramatic change now.

We have discerned a trend among emerging market countries in deployment of financial and other incentives to induce local production of technologically sophisticated products. There also has been some movement toward issuing or threatening compulsory patent licenses for excessive prices or failure to work locally, though so far activity of this type has been limited. Industrial policy intended to promote local production appears to challenge one of the tenets of the multinational business community's patent lobbying premises, that is, that granting local patents will result in increased licensing opportunities, transfer of technology and local production. Emerging market policymakers seem to have concluded that passive reliance on patents to induce technology transfer and local production is not working, and that a more direct approach is required. It is interesting to view this trend in historical perspective. When Article 5A(2) of the Paris Convention was adopted by the Hague Conference in 1925, it expressly recognized that failure to work was an acceptable ground for granting compulsory licenses, providing only a minimum timeframe prior to which such a license might be issued.[23] "Import substitution" policy was quite popular in Latin America in the 1970s and 1980s, and while compulsory licensing was not actively used, other means of compelling technology transfer were tried. By the 1990s, import substitution policies did not seem to be working to induce economic development. The Washington Consensus was in part a reaction to import substitution policies, and the TRIPS Agreement arguably places at least a modest constraint on compulsory licensing for failure to work since Article 31 requires compliance with a number of conditions for the granting of a compulsory license.[24]

---

[23] Article 5A of the Paris Convention has gone through a number of revisions. The main substantive addition regarding compulsory licensing occurred in 1925, but further clarifying elements were subsequently added to this Article. *See* G.H.C. Bodenhausen, *Guide to the Application of the Paris Convention for the Protection of Industrial Property as Revised at Stockholm in 1967*, Geneva, World Intellectual Property Organization, 1969, pp. 67–73.

[24] Article 27.1 of the TRIPS Agreement prohibits discrimination between

This trend toward local production is consistent with some recent work suggesting that technological development is a holistic process that incorporates elements of education and training, employment opportunity and infrastructure support, and that the social and economic welfare of a country will be limited if one or more of these components is lacking.[25] In this regard, the treatment of patents within a country will depend on how they fit within the framework for increasing local production opportunities. If the availability of patent protection can be successfully used to induce foreign investors to build facilities within a country, that will be one option. But, if the foreign investor cannot be induced to participate adequately in the local economy, compulsory licensing may be a way to accomplish a similar objective. China, for example, has been extraordinarily successful in attracting FDI. The fact that it has not issued compulsory licenses over the last two decades suggests it is attaining its goals for the transfer of technology in other ways. It is interesting that Edith Penrose was critical of using compulsory patent licensing to encourage local production on grounds that it would lead to a misallocation of global resources, i.e., a proliferation of less efficient producers. It may be that Penrose did not foresee how reliance on imports might limit the availability of employment and learning opportunities and ultimately harm the development process.

2.1 Brazil

Brazil adopted a patent statute in 1809, and was among the initial signatories and adherents to the Paris Convention in 1883/84.[26] By the 1930s the value of the patent system was being questioned, and by the 1960s Brazil had become a leading critic of the international patent system as it then

imported and locally produced products. However, as the WTO dispute settlement panel noted in *Canada – Patent Protection of Pharmaceutical Products*, Report of the Panel, WT/DS114/R, 17 March 2000 (the Canada-Generics case), "discrimination" is a pejorative concept reflecting distinction without justification (at para. 7.94). There are a substantial number of circumstances under which a requirement of local working of the patent may be justified.

[25] Frederick M. Abbott, *Trends in Local Production of Medicines and Related Technology Transfer*, Geneva, World Health Organization (WHO), December 2011, http://www.who.int/phi/publications/Trends_in_Local_Production_of_Medicines.pdf; Massachusetts Institute of Technology, *Production in the Innovation Economy*, Cambridge, MA, MIT Research Initiative, http://mit.edu/pie/research/index.html (accessed 4 May 2013).

[26] *See* Denis Borges Barbosa, "Patents and the Emerging Markets of Latin America – Brazil", Chapter 8 in this book.

operated. This critical perspective characterized Brazil's participation in the TRIPS negotiations. For complex internal and external political reasons, when Brazil reformed its patent law in 1996 it included some significant TRIPS-plus elements (such as by foregoing the pharmaceutical patent transition and providing for pipeline patenting of drugs). Since the late 1990s, Brazil's internal and external patent policy has been influenced by competing internal and external demands. Brazil has been a leader in pursuing the development agenda at WIPO.

Brazil presently is focused on improving the capacity of its patent office (INPI) to process applications as it seeks to address a significant backlog. INPI is working cooperatively with other patent offices in Latin America to improve cooperation in the region. It is taking steps to improve the judicial mechanisms under which patents are enforced and challenged. As Brazil has acted to strengthen its domestic patent system, applications and grants continue to be dominated by foreign inventors. The reasons for the ongoing relative shortfall in patenting activity by local inventors are not so clear. It might be noted that Brazilian private sector enterprises traditionally have not invested heavily in R&D. While patenting by domestic inventors has not been increasing relative to countries such as China, nationals seemed to predominate in filings for plant variety protection (PVP).[27] Denis Borges Barbosa in his chapter points out that the successful use of the PVP system by Brazil has a lot to do with Embrapa, the agricultural agency established by the Brazilian government in 1973. Embrapa has been key to developing thousands of technologies and plant varieties that have seen Brazil go from being a food importer to a major food exporter.[28]

The Brazilian government continues to maintain a significant social welfare focus that acts as a buffer to strong mercantile policies in the patent area. This can be seen, for example, in the involvement of ANVISA, Brazil's health regulatory authority, in pharmaceutical patent application assessment, an important example of regulatory innovation by one of the BRICS. Brazil has been one of the few countries to use compulsory licensing to address pharmaceutical pricing issues, in terms of both threatening and granting such licenses.[29] Brazil also maintains a

---

[27] However, it should be noted that Brazilian subsidiaries of foreign-based companies may be considered "domestic" in the data provided.

[28] On the importance of Embrapa in transforming Brazil's agricultural sector, *see* BRICS, *The BRICS Report*, pp. 106–08.

[29] *See* Frederick M. Abbott and Jerome H. Reichman, "The Doha Round's Public Health Legacy: Strategies for the Production and Diffusion of Patented Medicines Under the Amended TRIPS Provisions", *Journal of International Economic Law*, vol. 10, no. 4, 2007, pp. 949–52.

specific sectoral program that promotes local production of pharmaceutical products.[30]

In December 2010, the government of Brazil adopted the so-called "Buy Brazil Act" that gives substantial preferences in government procurement to products produced in Brazil and that otherwise reflect investments in Brazil (including in research and development (R&D)).[31] Brazil is not party to the WTO Government Procurement Agreement. Although this legislative initiative is not specifically linked to patents or compulsory licensing, it reflects a trend among emerging markets not to rely on stimulating domestic R&D and innovation merely by providing patent protection, but to take a more proactive role in channeling resources toward local production, with anticipated gains in local employment, integration with educational institutions, etc. Another example of where Brazil has been successful in stimulating local technological innovation without relying on the patent system has been its bio-fuel program. Launched in the

---

[30] *See* Frederick M. Abbott, "Comparative Study of Selected Government Policies for Promoting Transfer of Technology and Competitiveness in the Colombian Pharmaceutical Sector", *United States Agency for International Development*, Programa MIDAS, 2007.

[31] The European Commission Market Access Database describes the Act as follows:

> In 19 July 2010, the Brazilian government amended Law No 8666 with a provisional measure ("Medida Provisória" MP 495) giving preference of up to 25% to Brazilian-owned firms under specific conditions to achieve economic growth, national technological innovation and employment. Both houses of the Brazilian Congress passed the so called "buy Brazil act" law 12.349/10 of 15 December 2010. The new rules discriminate competing foreign-owned firms as these "buy national" preferences are given to products: 1) made in Brazil; 2) made or provided by Brazilian corporations, and 3) made or provided by corporations that have invested in research and technology development in Brazil. The margin of preference depends on a market study with criteria such as job creation and income generation, effect on the collection of taxes and development and technological innovation made in Brazil. However, the government can disregard preferences if there is no local production or capacity to provide the services in Brazil.
>
> . . .
>
> The new law gives Brazil the possibility for specific strategies to support Brazilian production such as in the information and communication technology (ICT) sector. Federal agencies and parastatal structures have to give preferences to locally produced ICT products and services based on non transparent criteria.
>
> European Commission, "Market Access Database", http://madb.europa.eu/madb/barriers_details.htm;jsessionid=C2D50B91C2D44F06B8B0612153A45E9F?barrier_id=970031&version=3 (accessed 4 May 2013).

1970s, this import substitution program has benefited from government-supported research and subsidies.[32]

Brazil appears to be moving gradually toward a more strongly protective patent regime, with particular interest shown by its domestic biotechnology industry. But, as noted above, offsetting internal social policy interests temper that movement.

As an emerging market actor, Brazil's most notable influence on the international patent system over the past several years has probably been its willingness to employ compulsory licensing to influence pharmaceutical pricing. In this regard, Brazil has stood as an example to developing countries considering the same course of action. The participation by ANVISA in the review of patent applications reflects Brazil's willingness to experiment with alternative methods of protecting the public interest. Brazil has also been active in promoting the development agenda at WIPO. It has also been an influential supporter of a disclosure obligation standard in patent law in fora such as the WTO. While the Brazilian patent office is investing to improve its capacity, and judicial capacity to assess patent claims is also improved, so far Brazil's policy perspective regarding patents is somewhat ambiguous. A "stronger" patent policy is pursued by the national patent office (INPI), while at multilateral fora Brazilian delegates argue for a more flexible patent policy.

2.2 China

China has embraced patenting as evidence of technological progress, but the correlation between increased patent applications and genuine innovation remains rather inconclusive.[33] In recent years, the volume of domestically-based applications to the China Patent Office has increased dramatically. However, the preponderance of these applications is for utility model and design patents, and not for "invention patents". About 15% of patents granted in China are for inventions, with utility models and designs accounting for the balance. In addition, the level of technical progress so far evidenced by the granted invention patents is argued to be rather limited, as reflected in a low rate of renewal. The percentage of Chinese-owned patents at the USPTO (United States Patent and Trademark Office) and EPO remains rather low in comparison with the main countries of origin.

Notwithstanding what may be a modest start, as China continues to

---

32 *See* BRICS, *The BRICS Report*, pp. 108–10.

33 *See* Wei Zhuang, "Evolution of the Patent System in China", Chapter 9 in this book.

invest in R&D, there seems little doubt but that this will lead to an increase in meaningful technological accomplishments. China has been increasing its spending on R&D by about 20% per year since 1999 with the aim of reaching a total of 2.5% of its GDP by 2020.[34] But, we should be careful to distinguish the cart and the horse. Investing in innovation and patents are different things. China will become more internationally competitive in high technology fields because the government has set about to do that, and is devoting very substantial financial resources to this endeavor. But, can and will patent law get credit for the accomplishments? No doubt proponents of strong patent protection will make that claim, but the Chinese government does not seem to be relying on strengthening of the patent system to create a high technology environment. Of the major revisions to China's patent law of 1984, only one has occurred since China became a member of the WTO in 2001, the revision of 2008. The other revisions were to some degree influenced by China's need to satisfy key WTO members on intellectual property issues as part of its accession to the WTO.[35] As Wei Zhuang shows in her chapter, this 2008 revision represents a balanced approach to patent reform. Certainly the strengthening of compulsory licensing and the introduction of a disclosure obligation for genetic resources would give patent lobbies in the USA such as the Biotechnology Association some cause for concern.

There are persistent reports that Chinese enterprises are penetrating US and European industry computers and databases to "appropriate" technological information, including the latest technologies.[36] Although this approach involves new tools, it is a more sophisticated approach to reverse engineering and/or piggybacking on the R&D investments of other countries and their enterprises that has propelled countries over development hurdles for centuries. Negotiation of the WTO TRIPS Agreement was intended to curtail some of this imitation. Yet it would appear that China is not content to rely on the potential innovation-inducing properties of patents to develop indigenous technology in the "slow lane".

China has recently amended its patent law to facilitate use of "flexibilities", signaling government recognition that strong patent protection

---

[34] The Royal Society, *Knowledge, Networks and Nations: Global Scientific Collaboration in the 21st Century*, London, The Royal Society, 2011, p. 19.

[35] For an analysis, *see* Andrea Wechsler, "China's WTO Accession Revisited: Achievements and Challenges in Chinese Intellectual Property Law Reform", in Christoph Hermann and Jörg Philipp Terhechte (eds.), *European Yearbook of International Economic Law 2012*, vol. 3, Springer, 2012, pp. 125–58.

[36] *See* Richard A. Clarke and Robert K. Knake, *Cyber War*, New York, HarperCollins Publishers, 2010.

raises potential technological and social roadblocks. There are indications that the Chinese government is preparing to issue compulsory licenses on several medicines for the treatment of hepatitis B, tuberculosis and HIV/AIDS.[37] China is also increasing its focus on competition law, though this is in its early phases.

As home-grown Chinese enterprises become more export-oriented, patent applications in foreign markets are increasing. China may join the USA, EU and Japan as a strong mercantile patent promoter. This assumes that China follows the pattern familiar to the developed economies, and seeks to take advantage of a strong technological portfolio by earning patent rents. But, this is speculation. While China has been relatively quiet in multilateral discussions of patent policy (as compared, for example, with Brazil and India), whether this reflects a subtle movement into the developed camp or an interest in reserving a more nuanced approach is not clear. Time will tell.

Whatever role the patent system will play in China's future development strategy we should be clear that it is FDI, along with China's management of that FDI, that accounts for its current economic and technological success. China today is the second largest recipient of FDI flows and has been the largest developing country recipient for the last 18 years.[38] Supporters of the patent system might argue that China's adoption of the patent system has been responsible for this FDI inflow. We can begin to assess the plausibility of this claim by means of the following null hypothesis: the opening up of China's internal market of 1.3 billion people made no difference to FDI flows.

We have elsewhere noted a trend toward government policies encouraging local production. As China is a leading recipient of FDI inflows and has become a manufacturing base for a large part of global multinational business, it seems fair to posit that Chinese government policy has been directed toward encouraging local production as part of its overall development strategy.

2.3 India

India faces similar pressures to Brazil and China to compete globally in technological development, but is showing less of an inclination to pursue a strong patent approach. This appears mainly a result of domestic social

---

37 Wei Zhuang, "Evolution of the Patent System in China", Chapter 9 in this book, note 93.

38 BRICS, *The BRICS Report*, p. 128.

pressures, for example with respect to access to medicines. It may also reflect the democratic nature of the Indian governing system, and the relatively incremental approach to change. Although a few high profile pharmaceutical cases have dominated the IP news coming out of India, that probably is not a good reflection of the situation at the patent offices, which are issuing many patents. India is not yet experiencing strong growth in domestically owned patent applications, though it is highly competitive in certain technological fields such as computer software development (where barriers to entry are relatively low). Because of the heavy involvement of the public and the Parliament in patent law, it would appear that India is unlikely to opt for a globally harmonized approach, absent some very strong incentive.

The chapter by Rajeev Kher explores and reflects the complexity of the internal and external forces influencing patent law development in India.[39] On the one hand, India is one of the central emerging market economies and sees itself as a future technological leader. The government remains a substantial contributor to R&D efforts, reflecting its historical pattern. The private sector is changing, but individual enterprises are fairly unaccustomed to investing substantial parts of their revenues back into R&D. There remains a private R&D shortfall, and the way to encourage domestic R&D is not clear. One potential avenue is to assure relatively strong IP protection, and there is an influential part of the government encouraging that direction. On the other hand, India has a very large poor population that is dependent on social programs, which even so are not well-funded. The budget is always strained. Therefore, measures that encourage private R&D through the assessment of patent rents on the public and private sectors create difficulties, and need to be offset in one way or another. There is no evident "easy answer" to balancing the interests in private capital formation for R&D investment, and public needs in terms of access to new technologies. A balance must be struck, and internally India is constantly struggling to find the right balance. What does seem clear, however, is that India is not interested in having its course charted by Europe or the United States.

India also seems to have an important capacity for price innovation. In the context of patents the price performance and export success of its generic industry has attracted much attention, but price innovation is part of a deeper pattern in Indian industry. For example, Tata Chemicals have produced a water filter that can provide a family with safe drinking water for $0.65 a month and in 2010 the government released a prototype of a

---

39 Rajeev Kher, "India in the World Patent Order", Chapter 10 in this book.

laptop costing $35.00.[40] India's combination of cheap but highly trained scientific labor, and a huge population of poor people is an endogenous driver of the development of low-cost products. It also means that there is less need to follow a US-EU patent system that produces technologies most Indians cannot afford.

India also provides us with a rare example of regulatory innovation by a member of the BRICS that has had an effect on international patent administration. In response to European patent claims relating to the neem plant and US patent claims concerning turmeric the Indian government set up a taskforce in 2000 to track the extent of misappropriation of Indian traditional medicinal knowledge.[41] India designed a traditional knowledge resource classification system that shares structural similarities with the International Patent Classification system. It is a proprietary database that the Indian government makes available to other patent offices on the condition that these offices use it only for patent searching and they only disclose so much as is essential as part of their reporting processes.[42] As a result of all this India's traditional knowledge systems are much better integrated into the patent-searching systems used by the world's major patent offices.[43] Like Brazil and China, India has been a supporter of a disclosure obligation standard for genetic resources.

The year 2013 will be considered a significant one in terms of the way in which Indian patent law evolves over the medium term. The Supreme Court has rendered an important decision on a case involving interpretation of Section 3(d) of the Patent Act (that incorporates an assessment of enhanced efficacy for pharmaceutical inventions claiming a modification of a known compound),[44] and the Supreme Court is also likely to hear

---

[40] BRICS, *The BRICS Report*, p. 123.

[41] A brief description of the history of the taskforce as well as the data produced by it can be found at the website of the Department of Ayurveda, Yoga & Naturopathy, Unani, Siddha and Homoeopathy in a document entitled "Traditional Knowledge Digital Library" available at http://indianmedicine.nic.in/showfile.asp?lid=316.

[42] A copy of the agreement allowing the European Patent Office access to the TKDL is available at http://www.spicyip.com/docs/TKDL-EPO.pdf.

[43] For a description of the cooperation between WIPO and India on the TKDL see WIPO, "WIPO and India Partner to Protect Traditional Knowledge from Misappropriation", 22 March 2011, http://www.wipo.int/pressroom/en/articles/2011/article_0008.html.

[44] *Novartis v. India*, Supreme Court of India, Civil Appeal Nos. 2706–2716 of 2013 (Arising Out of SLP(C) Nos. 20539–20549 of 2009), decided 1 April 2013. *See* Frederick M. Abbott, "The Judgment in Novartis v. India: What the Supreme Court of India Said", *Intellectual Property Watch* (Inside Views), 4 April 2013.

a challenge to the first compulsory license on a pharmaceutical product issued under the Patent Act.[45] In the *Novartis* case, the Supreme Court backed the Patent Controller in his rejection under Section 3(d) of a claimed drug modification for which enhanced therapeutic efficacy was not demonstrated. If the Indian courts likewise affirm the grant of the compulsory license, this should give the government confidence in charting its own path in the implementation of patent law standards.

India has in the first week of January 2013 announced the development of legislative proposals that would sharply restrict imports of information technology products; essentially demanding that multinational electronics companies produce information technology goods within India.[46] Although there is some question as to whether the Indian government intends to follow through and implement such import restrictions and local production demands, a legal emphasis on local production would constitute a break with or repudiation of "WTO orthodoxy" and might signal a new trend in emerging market approaches to existing imbalances in economic power. The underlying premise of the WTO legal system is nondiscrimination among imported and locally produced products, and first-best global economic development through comparative advantage/specialization. Local production requirements differentiate in favor of domestically produced goods, essentially mandating the creation of local employment opportunities.[47] Russia, as noted below, has adopted policies in the pharmaceutical sector directed toward requiring local production of medicines, suggesting the possible emergence of a pattern among emerging market countries.

2.4 Russia

Since the early 1990s and the quasi-opening up of the Russian economy to competitive market forces, the Russian patent system has transitioned from state awards of inventors' certificates to implementation of

---

45 *Bayer v. Union of India, Intellectual Property Appellate Board*, OA/35/2012/PT/MUM, 4 March 2013.

46 Amol Sharma, "India: Tech Import Restrictions Are for Security", *The Wall Street Journal*, 9 January 2013, http://professional.wsj.com/article/SB10001424127887324081704578231262464225242.html?mg=reno64-wsj.

47 The United States has, in fact, initiated consultations with India alleging that certain programs requiring the use of domestically produced solar cells and solar modules are inconsistent with, inter alia, the Agreement on Trade-Related Investment Measures (TRIMS). *India – Certain Measures Relating to Solar Cells and Solar Modules*, Request for Consultations by the United States, GIU1023; GISCMID96I1; GITRIMSID135; WTIDS456I1, request dated 6 February 2013.

TRIPS-compatible legislation.[48] The system of inventors' certificates will disappear into history's alleyways, but we should also note that the Soviet Union at various stages in the second half of the twentieth century outperformed OECD countries in terms of economic growth and innovation.[49] Russia will now have to play the innovation game under the rules of the patent world order.

Russia's economic opening up post-dates China's for all practical purposes, and the influence of multinational corporations in the operation of the domestic patent system has probably yet to be felt. Business R&D in Russia is only 29% of total R&D spending.[50] The Russian patent office (Rospatent) faces challenges similar to those of other emerging market economies in terms of investment by the government and personnel, but because Russia has a substantial scientifically trained labor force, this should not present a long-term issue (any more than in the US or Europe). Patent application filings by local inventors are relatively low in comparison with other emerging market countries like China. In the course of accession to the WTO, based on a decision of the Russian Supreme Arbitration court in April 2012, Russia has eliminated discrimination between patent fees payable by domestic and foreign applicants.

Until recently, Russia did not have judicial capacity in place to decide patent infringement and validity cases, but in 2011 legislation was adopted to create the Arbitration Court for Intellectual Property Rights (referred to as the "Patent Court") which as of 2013 has jurisdiction over federal executive authorities, as well as deciding private patent cases.[51] As this Patent Court is entirely new, it is premature to address its influence.

In the context of the WTO accession process, Russia was criticized by the EU, USA and others for failing to adequately protect IPRs. Most of such criticism was directed at the copyright sector and lack of protection for computer software and entertainment works. Russia was also faulted for failing to provide market exclusivity based on submission of regulatory data regarding pharmaceutical products. In the context of the accession negotiations, Russia has introduced regulatory data protection. It does not appear that Russia's patent system was a major factor in the enforcement discussions.

---

[48] *See* Tetyana Payosova, "Russian Trip to the TRIPS: Patent Protection and Public Health", Chapter 11 in this book.

[49] *See* Manuel Castells, *The Information Age: Economy, Society and Culture, Volume III: End of Millennium*, Oxford, Blackwell Publishers, 2000, pp. 5–67.

[50] The Royal Society, *Knowledge, Networks and Nations*, p. 32.

[51] Daria Kim, "Russia Establishes Specialised Court for Intellectual Property Rights", *Intellectual Property Watch*, 1 March 2013.

Russia is increasingly attracting foreign direct investment, and in this context it is a near-certainty that greater attention will be focused on Russia's implementation of its patent system, including the role of its courts.

As with other emerging market economies, Russia faces the challenge of achieving a balance between promoting investment in R&D and economic growth, on one side, and caring for a large population that includes many individuals dependent on public sector assistance. This challenge is particularly evident in the area of public health and access to medicines. Russia has adopted price controls on an extensive list of essential medicines (approximately 500). Russia has introduced a comprehensive program for the development of its pharmaceutical industry known as "Pharma 2020". There is a strategic goal to increase domestic production of pharmaceuticals as well as exports. To promote local production, the government has established additional price allowances for procurement from local enterprises of a total of 567 drugs under its national drug reimbursement program.[52] Russia is actively promoting the construction of pharmaceutical manufacturing plants in the country, and this has attracted substantial investments from Europe and Israel, and discussions are ongoing with Indian producers.

2.5 South Africa

Brazil, Russia, India and China constituted themselves as a formal group under the BRIC acronym in 2006. South Africa joined the BRICS in 2011 on the occasion of the group's third summit. South Africa is the only member of the group that is not a top ten economy. In addition, South Africa's economy remains strongly dependent on natural resource mining. While South Africa has a TRIPS-compatible patent law, its patent office has not conducted substantive examination of patent applications, leaving it to private parties to launch ex post grant challenges, of which there have been relatively few.

Notwithstanding the relatively low priority that patents have generally enjoyed in industrial development policy in South Africa, the country's patent system was the focus of a great deal of attention in the late 1990s and early 2000s. It was during this period that the USA and EU launched a challenge to the TRIPS-compatibility of provisions of the 1997 Medicines Act Amendments, a challenge that was pursued in the courts by

---

52 *See* Tetyana Payosova, "Russian Trip to the TRIPS: Patent Protection, Innovation Promotion and Public Health", Chapter 11 in this book.

multinational originator pharmaceutical companies. Ultimately, the challenge was withdrawn. But, the incident propelled developing countries to pursue the Doha Declaration on the TRIPS Agreement and Public Health at the WTO in order to prevent similar future attacks.

Notably, several originator pharmaceutical companies were found by South Africa's Competition Commission to have abused their dominant position by excessive pricing based on their patents, and this resulted in the negotiation of several "voluntary licenses" from the originator companies to local South African producers. This may have been the single most important invocation by a developing country of competition law in respect to patents.

There is an effort under way internally in South Africa to amend the Patent Act, including introducing substantive examination of patent applications.

South Africa is very actively pursuing local production of important medicines, including active pharmaceutical ingredients, to address large-scale ongoing demand for HIV/AIDS treatment.[53] The industrial policy program includes procurement preferences for domestically produced products. In addition, the South African Department of Trade and Industry is working with foreign direct investors to establish production facilities within the country. It is possible that compulsory licensing of patents will play some role in the development of the local production sector beyond that in place as a consequence of the Competition Commission action.

South Africa might be investing more in creating competition law regulatory capacity than the other BRICS. Its Competition Commission is increasing its enforcement capacity, particularly in the area of cartels.[54] This greater regulatory capacity may prove to be an important means for South Africa to control abuses of market competition by intellectual property owners. Andre Kudlinski in his chapter analyses the role of South Africa's Competition Commission in cases brought against GlaxoSmithKline and Boehringer-Ingelheim. Both involved patented antiretroviral medicines. Kudlinksi's views concerning the technical merits of these cases can be debated. What cannot be debated is the importance of developing countries creating competition law capacity to deal with structural effects of a large number of patents. This kind of capacity is

---

[53] *See* Andre Kudlinski, "Harmonizing the National Policies for Healthcare, Pharmaceutical Industry and Intellectual Property: The South African Experience", Chapter 12 in this book.

[54] BRICS, *The BRICS Report*, p. 153.

especially important in a country such as South Africa where patents are not examined and can be obtained by means of application and registration. It will also be important if patent offices move to a system of automatically recognizing the examination results of a small number of key offices. The work of the Federal Trade Commission in the USA in policing abuses of patents by the pharmaceutical industry is an example of where investing in institutional capacity in the competition law field has a long-term payoff. For the moment patent policy is not central to South Africa's development plans. It is focusing on other levers such as tariffs. But what it has done on patents in the health sector suggests that it will not be buying wholesale into any upward harmonization initiatives on patents coming out of the USA and EU.

3 DEVELOPING COUNTRIES OUTSIDE THE EMERGING MARKETS

Outside of the BRICS, there appears to be considerable pressure on and within developing countries to view patenting as emblematic of technological development. Efforts are directed toward increasing patent office capacity, reducing the time needed for patent grants, etc. However, movement toward strengthened patent environments in these regions confronts competing social demands, budgetary and personnel constraints. The picture is mixed.

3.1 ASEAN and Thailand

The Association of Southeast Asian Nations (ASEAN) is comprised of 10 countries with significantly different levels of economic development, and different social welfare concerns. Singapore and Brunei are among the world's wealthiest countries, while Cambodia and Myanmar are among the poorest. Nonetheless, the ASEAN countries have worked together on patent and other IP issues, mainly on a consultative basis and involving cooperation among the various patent offices in terms of sharing information on examinations. The ASEAN countries have not engaged in efforts to approximate or harmonize patent law, and the very different levels of development and political dynamic within the countries suggests that this will not take place anytime soon. Nevertheless, ASEAN could provide a forum to defend against political pressures from countries outside the region seeking to transpose externally developed patent norms ahead of a regional approach.

Thailand has adopted a TRIPS-compatible patent law, but its patent office confronts difficulties not uncommon to developing countries. There is a small number of patent examiners (17) expected to assess patent applications across the fields of technology. Because the pay scale for examiners is low, qualified technical personnel are very difficult to retain in competition with local industry.

Thailand issued three government use compulsory licenses in 2006–07 on antiretroviral (2) and anticoagulant (1) medicines in order to bring down prices, initially through importation.[55] When the licenses were issued, Thailand indicated that its medium-term objective was to produce the drugs locally. Its action was met by strong critical reaction, particularly from the European Commission, but also from the US government. Since Thailand was clearly within its legal rights under the TRIPS Agreement to grant the licenses, this incident showed that compulsory licensing continues to be highly controversial from a political standpoint. In 2008, Thailand issued four compulsory licenses on anticancer medicines.[56]

3.2 The Arab Middle East

Like ASEAN, the Arab Middle East region is comprised of countries with substantially different levels of economic development, social welfare systems and political perspectives. Many countries of the region were colonies of European powers, and patent laws modeled on European patent laws were in place for a long time.

More recently, countries of the Arab Middle East have come under pressure from the United States and European Union to include patent law within the framework of bilateral investment agreements, and to essentially move toward patent law harmonization with those countries. The EU has recently concluded a "patent validation" agreement with Morocco that reintroduces the concept of the "confirmation patent" by which the patent office of the Arab country agrees to grant patents based on grants made by the EPO.[57]

---

[55] *See* Abbott and Reichman, "The Doha Round's Public Health Legacy", pp. 949–57.

[56] The Ministry of Public Health and the National Health Security Office Thailand, "The 10 Burning Questions on the Government Use of Patents on the Four Anti-Cancer Drugs in Thailand", February 2008.

[57] *See* European Patent Office [Press Release], "Euro-Moroccan Partnership to Benefit the Patent System", 20 December 2010; "The EPO and Morocco Strengthen their Partnership on Patents", 20 June 2013, http://www.epo.org/news-issues/news/2013/20130620.html.

However, despite the commitments under bilateral agreements and the TRIPS Agreement, the patent offices of many Arab Middle East countries face problems common to developing countries, including lack of budget resources and lack of technically qualified examiners. There are problems with transparency in terms of information on patents granted.

There are recent studies showing that prices of pharmaceuticals within countries like Jordan have increased as a consequence of commitments under bilateral agreements. However, at least part of this effect is based on commitments to grant market exclusivity rights based on registration, and not exclusively on newly granted patents. A more complete assessment of the effect of the patent provisions in bilateral agreements will take some time.

It is interesting to note that Dubai has launched a major biotechnology research-pharmaceutical manufacturing park.[58] Saudi Arabia is also investing heavily in attracting pharmaceutical manufacturing by offering tax and other incentives, and major multinational originator companies have announced plans to build manufacturing facilities in that country.[59]

4 REACTION IN THE DEVELOPED COUNTRIES

In addition to considering the impact that emerging market implementation of patent law may have on the international patent system, it is also important to consider how the leading industrialized countries (e.g., the USA, EU and Japan) will react to stronger high-technology competition from home-grown emerging market companies. One clear response is pressure to conform both emerging market and other developing country market patent law to trilateral standards. As Drahos has pointed out, such pressure takes place not only at the level of bilateral and regional trade agreements such as the Trans-Pacific Partnership, but also (and arguably more importantly) at the level of patent office cooperation and training.

---

[58] pharmaceutical-technology.com, "DuBiotech, United Arab Emirates", London, 2012, www.pharmaceutical-technology.com/projects/dubiotech/ (accessed 4 May 2013).

[59] *See* Sara Gambrill, "Saudi Arabia Emerges as Pharma Manufacturing Hot Spot", *Life Science Leader*, 2012, http://www.lifescienceleader.com/magazine/current-issue-3/item/3916-saudi-arabia-emerges-as-pharma-manufacturing-hot-spot, (accessed 4 May 2013); Elizabeth Broomhall, "Pharmaceutical Firm to Build Plant at KAEC", ConstructionWeekOnline.com, 30 June 2010, http://www.constructionweekonline.com/article-8784-pharmaceutical-firm-to-build-plant-at-kaec/ (accessed 4 May 2013).

In this regard, there is pressure to conform domestic patent law in accordance with the mercantile interests of the major capital exporting countries.

A second level of reaction takes place in the internal markets of the trilateral capital-exporting countries. We see adoption of domestic laws and implementing actions directed toward limiting penetration of imports from emerging markets. These limitations include increased focus on enforcement of patent and other IPRs at the border, anti-counterfeiting initiatives, and an emerging attention to cybersecurity in ways that could be understood to constitute trade barriers. There is also a growing web of private enforcement of intellectual property rights that draws in global payment services such as American Express, Discover, MasterCard, PayPal and Visa.[60] The loss of payment services has the potential to affect many businesses in developing country markets. The heightened attention to protection of domestic markets can be seen in the European Union, for example, in relation to new rules making it more difficult to import pharmaceutical products.[61] The recent example of US blocking of acquisitions by China's Huawei in the telecommunications field shows the role of cybersecurity in economic competition. Most of these actions are not specifically "patent-directed", but are arguably a reaction to increased competition from high-technology products from the emerging markets. Both the USA and the EU already have in place legislation allowing IPRs enforcement at the border.[62] This is not to suggest that the trilateral countries do not have legitimate enforcement concerns in the interest of protecting public health and safety and national security. The difficulty for everyone concerned regards separating the wheat from the chaff.

As emerging market companies increase their patenting in the home markets of the trilaterals, there will almost by definition follow enforcement actions in those markets based on those patents. We have recently witnessed patent-based conflict between Apple Computer and Samsung in the USA and European markets, and this could be the prelude to

---

[60] *See* "2012 U.S. Intellectual Property Enforcement Coordinator Joint Strategic Plan 2012", whitehouse.gov, June 2012, p. 2, www.whitehouse.gov/sites/default/files/omb/IPEC/ipec_two-year_anniversary_report.pdf (accessed 4 May 2013).

[61] *See, for example*, Directive 2011/62/EU of the European Parliament and of the Council of 8 June 2011 amending Directive 2001/83/EC on the Community code relating to medicinal products for human use, as regards the prevention of the entry into the legal supply chain of falsified medicinal products.

[62] See Frederick M. Abbott, "The United States Response to Emerging Technological Powers", Chapter 18 in this book.

an enlarged arena for combat among well-capitalized patent owning enterprises that encompasses emerging market exporters. If current patenting patterns hold, Chinese enterprises will be significant factors in the USA and EU patent litigation fields. Geetrui Van Overwalle in her chapter explores this potential phenomenon in the context of the EU, and suggests that increased attention to patent quality may be necessary to prevent a flood of market impediments and counterproductive litigation.

5 CHANGING GLOBAL INTEREST PATTERNS

5.1 A Global Elite

In the early 1980s the chaebols that dominated South Korea's economy had very little interest in patents. If we fast forward to the patent litigation over smartphones between Apple and Samsung currently raging across at least nine jurisdictions, it is safe to say that interest in patents amongst South Korean multinationals has increased. During the patent litigation between Samsung and Apple it was reported that Samsung had about 28,000 granted US patents. If we assume an average cost range of between US$10,000 and US$20,000 to obtain these US patents, then Samsung paid out somewhere between $280 million and $560 million to obtain this patent portfolio. Of course, Samsung has also taken out patents in the other major markets such as Japan and Europe, as has Apple. Our point is that, as multinationals interested in keeping barriers to markets that they dominate high, both Samsung and Apple have a common interest in supporting the patent system. Once one masters the cost and complexity of the patent system, thereby becoming a member of an exclusive club, there is little reason to revolt against the system that supports one's status. If the BRICS spawn multinational networks of production and distribution of the kind represented by Apple and Samsung, then it seems a reasonable assumption that the convergence/harmonization pressures on the patent system will increase. Of course, while multinational elites may benefit from this convergence, it is still an open question as to whether states and the majority of their citizens will. Tax transfer games can easily deprive treasuries of their share of patent rents.[63] More fundamentally, can a globalized patent system deliver appropriate and affordable innovation to

---

[63] *See* Peter Drahos, "Rethinking the Role of the Patent Office from the Perspective of Responsive Regulation", Chapter 5 in this book.

the world's poor, who vastly outnumber the world's rich? As we observed earlier, price innovation in what Schumacher called "intermediate" technologies[64] is more likely to benefit the billions of poor people in the world.

The rise of the emerging market economies has lifted a significant part of their populations into a new middle class that is fueling a global consumption boom. At the same time, it has also created a new "super-elite" of the extraordinarily wealthy in each of the emerging market countries.[65] The super-elite controls a disproportionate share of the national economy and tends to have a significant influence on government. There is an existing class of extraordinarily wealthy individuals in the USA, Europe and Japan. For the USA, the concentration of wealth in the hands of a small percentage of the population has increased dramatically over the past decade.[66]

It is interesting to consider whether the super-elite across continents share more in common with each other than with the country where they reside, and whether this should influence how we think about the development of government policies in the emerging markets. It is possible that interests in the preservation of wealth among a few individuals will have a disproportionate impact on government policies, including patent policies. Patents are wealth preservation mechanisms. Theoretically, this argues toward convergence of patent law.

5.2 Small and Medium Enterprises

Small- and medium-sized enterprises (SMEs) are frequently referred to in debates on improving the efficiency of patent applications and grants. Inefficient patent administration systems are costly to navigate. Streamlining will reduce expenses and make the international patent system more accessible to SMEs.

Drahos has provided data showing that patenting is concentrated among highly capitalized companies in a small number of industrial sec-

---

[64] *See* Ernst Friedrich Schumacher, *Small is Beautiful: Economics as if People Mattered*, New York, Harper and Row, 1973.

[65] *See* Chrystia Freeland, *Plutocrats: The Rise of the New Global Super-Rich and the Fall of Everyone Else*, New York, The Penguin Press, 2012; P. Sainath, "Gates, Buffet & the Art of Giving", *The Hindu*, 12 March 2011, http://www.thehindu.com/todays-paper/tp-opinion/article1530591.ece.

[66] *See, for example*, Joseph E. Stiglitz, *The Price of Inequality: How Today's Divided Society Endangers Our Future*, New York, W.W. Norton & Company, 2012; Warren E. Buffett, "Stop Coddling the Super-Rich", *The New York Times* [op. ed.], 14 August 2011.

tors.[67] Arguably these companies will benefit most from streamlining of the system by which patents are granted and maintained.

Moreover, while SMEs might be able to secure patents under a more closely integrated administrative system, enforcement of patents in disparate geographic locations will remain beyond the means of most SMEs.

5.3 The Individual Consumer

Where does the individual consumer fit within this overall framework? Who is looking out for these interests? Here we will make reference to the continuing importance of competition law and its enforcement as a partial antidote to further integration of the international patent system. This observation is not a new one, as Edith Penrose made a similar suggestion in the 1950s. We revert also to suggestions each of us have made in the past. More rigorous standards of patent application assessment is necessary;[68] regional approaches to patent examination may help with allocation of resources;[69] non-governmental organization and general public attention to IP matters remains essential from a political standpoint.[70]

6 CONCLUDING OBSERVATIONS

The implementation of patent law in the emerging market countries is having an impact on the international patent system. First, it is apparent that the principal emerging market economies are not strictly adhering to the patent regimen of the USA, Europe and Japan, but are instead adapting patent law to their own unique environments. As we have seen this is more a story of adaptive management of existing standards than it is an innovation of new standards and models. Much of this adaptation of

---

67 Drahos, *Global Governance*.

68 *See* Carlos M. Correa (ed.), *A Guide to Pharmaceutical Patents*, vols. 1 and 2, Geneva, South Centre, 2008.

69 *See* Frederick M. Abbott, Ryan Abbott, Wilbert Bannenberg, and Marianne Schürmann, "Regional Assessment of Patent and Related Issues and Access to Medicines: CARICOM Member States and the Dominican Republic", *Health Research for Action Final Report*, Vol. I – Main Report, 31 December 2009, pp. 57–69; Drahos, *Global Governance*.

70 *See* Frederick M. Abbott, "Innovation and Technology Transfer to Address Climate Change: Lessons from the Global Debate on Intellectual Property and Public Health", International Centre for Trade and Sustainable Development, ICTSD Programme on IPRs and Sustainable Development, Issue Paper No. 24, 2009.

patent standards has been concentrated in the public health sector. Second, to the extent that these emerging economies want to maintain the operating space within which to chart their own paths, they are unlikely to sign on to a strong global patent harmonization exercise. Third, the emerging economies have placed some priority on addressing social welfare within the context of the patent regime, such as by using compulsory licensing to provide access to medicines.

Perhaps the most interesting trend among the emerging markets is the building up of local technology-dependent industries through use of preferential procurement policies and other industrial policy mechanisms. While the domestic and international patent system may play a role in the shape of industrial development, it seems that the emerging markets have concluded that a patent system "does not a high-growth economy make". This does not truly represent a break from the industrial policy implemented by the USA, EU and Japan. The governments of each of these countries have used their vast resources to incentivize local R&D and production. For the USA, much of this has been done in the context of expenditures by the Department of Defense, and more recently by the Department of Energy. For Europe, Airbus Consortium R&D and local production was heavily supported by government subsidy. The Japanese government has invested heavily in its computer industries.

For countries that are pursuing an integrated industrial policy that focuses on the result, rather than the particular means used to accomplish the objective, patents are likely to remain a part of the industrial policy mix. This chapter does not suggest that emerging markets have discovered an alternative to patents. Rather, and not surprisingly, they appear to have concluded, despite simplistic arguments about patents and innovation, that they cannot simply rely on the patent system to build up a sound technological base and a competitive economy. Patents are a tool to be modified and used as the specific task requires. As the task changes, so may the terms of patenting.

On the issues of technology transfer and collaboration, as the chapter by Padmashree Gehl Sampath and Pedro Roffe shows, there are deepening networks of South-South cooperation, networks in which the BRICS appear to be playing an important leadership role. The more general point is that we should not be looking at the world through a simple core (the OECD)-periphery model (the South) when it comes to technology innovation and diffusion. A final point is that the BRICS today are a formal coalition with a wide-ranging interest in global governance arrangements. Some big ideas are beginning to come out of this coalition, such as the proposal for a multilateral bank to be run by the BRICS. No doubt this will have caused some smirks in the IMF's corridors. But with leaders like

Putin, the BRICS as a geopolitical group will not fear confrontation. The negotiation of TRIPS was an example in which a powerful alliance of a few (the USA, EU, with supporting roles from Japan and Canada) charted a course for the many. Two decades on from TRIPS the power of this few to dictate terms on intellectual property has clearly waned. Whatever the future of global patent governance arrangements, it will be partly decided by choices made within the BRICS.

PART II

Context

2. Intellectual property activity worldwide – key trends, facts, and figures

Carsten Fink*

In 2011, more patents were filed at the patent office of China than at any other office in the world. In the 100 years before 2011, only four patent offices had occupied this position – those of Germany, Japan, the Soviet Union and the United States (US). Before 2011, China already accounted for most filings of utility models, trademarks and industrial designs.

The rise of China is probably one of the most significant shifts in the international intellectual property (IP) system in recent history. However, it is not the only shift. The purpose of this chapter is to document the main trends, facts, and figures about intellectual property activity worldwide.[1] In doing so, it intends to provide the context in which firms take decisions on intellectual property and governments adapt intellectual property policies. Invariably, the shifting patterns of IP use described here have far-reaching consequences for knowledge creation, knowledge diffusion, industrial organization, technological progress, economic growth, policy formulation, and IP office operations. This chapter does not explore these consequences, but seeks to provoke others to do so.

Before proceeding, it is important to make the well-known caveat that IP statistics can only tell us so much about innovation and broader economic performance. Every IP title describes a different intangible asset. Studies have documented the skewed distribution of those assets. For example, relatively few patents yield high economic returns.[2] Clearly,

---

* The author is Chief Economist of the World Intellectual Property Organization (WIPO). The views expressed here are personal and should not be attributed to WIPO or its Member States.

[1] Readers interested in additional statistical background are advised to consult WIPO's World IP Indicators, available at http://www.wipo.int/ipstats/en/wipi/.

[2] Bronwyn H. Hall, Adam B. Jaffe and Manuel Trajtenberg, "Market Value and Patent Citations", *Rand Journal of Economics*, vol. 36, no. 1, 2005, pp. 16–38.

there is no one-for-one correspondence between the number of patents filed and the commercial value of the underlying inventions or their contribution to technological progress. In addition, institutional norms and filing practices differ in important ways between jurisdictions, complicating the comparison of statistics across countries. This does not imply that IP statistics have no use. IP activity correlates in meaningful ways with other measures of innovative activity – at the level of firms, industries, and economies. Indeed, IP statistics remain one of the few widely available indicators of innovation available to analysts. However, any prudent reader should keep the statistical limitations in mind when interpreting the trends and patterns presented here.

1 THE PATENT SURGE

Numerous studies have documented and analyzed the worldwide surge in patenting.[3] Figure 2.1 presents this surge since 1995, showing that patent filings worldwide doubled from around 1 million in 1995 to more than 2 million in 2011.[4] It also shows how the global business cycle has left its

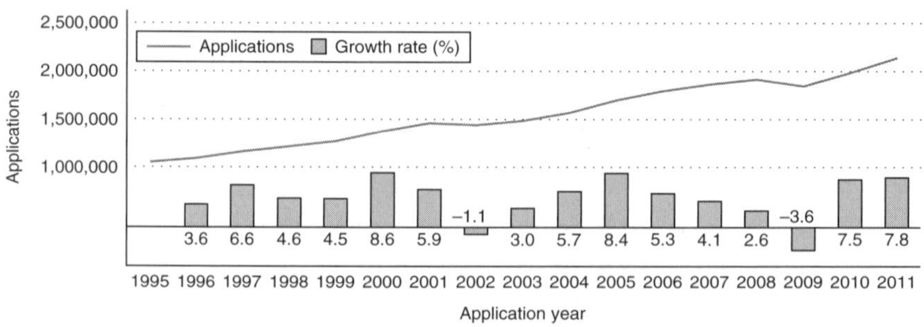

Note: The figures are based on a WIPO estimate covering 125 patent offices; they include direct applications and Patent Cooperation Treaty (PCT) national phase entries.

Source: WIPO Statistics Database.

Figure 2.1 Patenting worldwide, 1995–2011

3 See WIPO document PCT/WG/4/4 for a review.

4 The data underlying Figure 2.1 and most other statistics presented here come from the WIPO Statistics Database, which can be freely accessed at http://ipstatsdb.wipo.org/ipstats/patentsSearch.

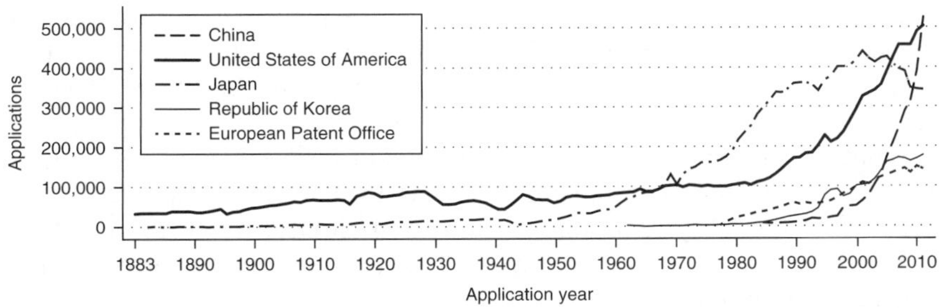

Source: WIPO Statistics Database.

Figure 2.2 The (really) long-term trend, 1883–2011

mark on patent activity: filings dropped in 2002 – following the dotcom bubble burst – and in 2009 – following the most recent financial crisis.

Figure 2.2 places the worldwide surge in patenting in a longer historical context and asks which patent offices account for the surge. Several broad insights emerge. First, the 1970s appear to have rocked the historical trend, with levels of patenting since that decade differing markedly from the relatively stable levels seen before. Second, the global patent surge has come in different waves, starting with Japan, followed by the United States, then Europe and the Republic of Korea, and most recently China.

The patenting rise of China, in particular, appears breathtaking – not only in the fact that China is still a middle-income economy, but also in how rapidly it has taken place. In the 20 years from 1991 to 2011, the number of patent filings increased more than 46-fold – from around 10,000 to more than half a million. Fast patenting growth in China also explains why global patent filings rebounded strongly in 2010 and 2011, despite weak world economic growth. From 2009 to 2011, China accounted for close to three-quarters of the growth worldwide.

China also remains the only non-high-income country to have emerged as a major patent filing origin. In particular, China's share of global patenting increased from 1.5 percent in 1992 to 24.6 percent in 2011; the share of all other low- and middle-income countries has remained steady at around 10 percent during this time period. Brazil and India have seen considerable increases in patenting over the last 20 years; however, their combined share in the world total stood at only around 3 percent in 2011. In addition, residents accounted for around three-quarters of patent filings in China in 2010, whereas non-residents dominate filings in most other low- and middle-income countries – including Brazil and India, where residents accounted for less than a quarter of all filings in 2010.

To conclude the discussion of Figure 2.2, a final noteworthy trend is the decline in Japanese patent filings since 2001. Whatever explains this decline, it shows that patent filing growth is not an inevitable force of nature.

What has driven the global patent surge? Do we live in an age of unprecedented technological opportunity or has there been an unprecedented embrace of the IP system, unrelated to technological fundamentals? One can gain at least some perspectives on these questions by decomposing aggregate filing figures.

To begin with, it is important to distinguish between first and subsequent filings. First filings capture the initial presentation of a new invention to a patent office – usually the applicant's home office. Subsequent filings are patent applications for the same invention – typically at the patent offices of other countries.[5] A study by the WIPO Secretariat estimates that first filings accounted for 48.3 percent of the growth in patent filings worldwide between 1995 and 2007 and subsequent filings for the remaining 51.7 percent.[6] In other words, roughly half of the patent surge during that time period was due to new inventions and the other half to greater internationalization – filings of the same inventions in more offices. The desire of applicants to see their patents protected in a larger number of countries thus emerges as the first key driver of the global patent surge.

What, in turn, has driven the growth in new inventions being presented to patent offices? One way to look at this is to ask to what extent the growth in first filings is rooted in underlying R&D investments. Figure 2.3 does so, though for reasons of data availability it focuses on resident filings rather than first filings.[7] It shows that over the last fifteen years, real R&D spending has outpaced growth in resident patent filings. At their face value, these trends imply a small decline in the productivity of R&D; each real dollar invested in R&D is associated with a declining number of patents.

---

5 Subsequent filings also include continuation and divisional filings at the office of first filing. However, with the exception of the United States, the share of continuation and divisional filings is small in most offices. See Annex A2 in PCT/WG/4/4.

6 See PCT/WG/4/4. Given the large contribution of China to overall growth over the past few years and the fact that Chinese residents account for most of the patent filings in China, the first filing share has most likely increased since 2007.

7 Data on first filings rely on patent family statistics, which only become available with a delay once patent offices publish patent applications. However, for most large offices, resident patent filings correlate closely with first filings. Indeed, the basic conclusions drawn in the text are the same as the ones drawn in PCT/WG/4/4, which employs first filing data.

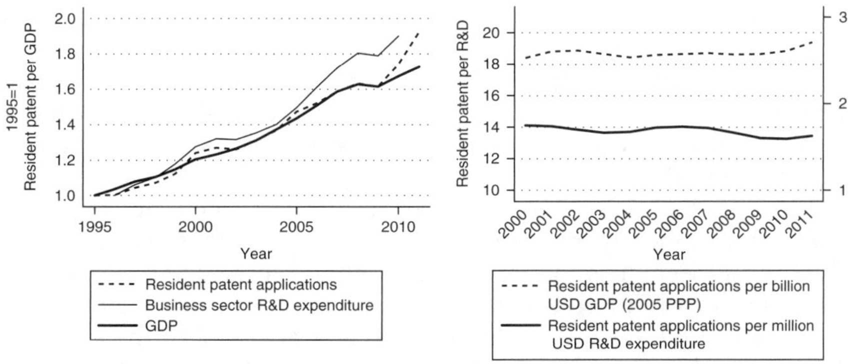

Source: WIPO Statistics Database.

Figure 2.3 Declining global R&D productivity?

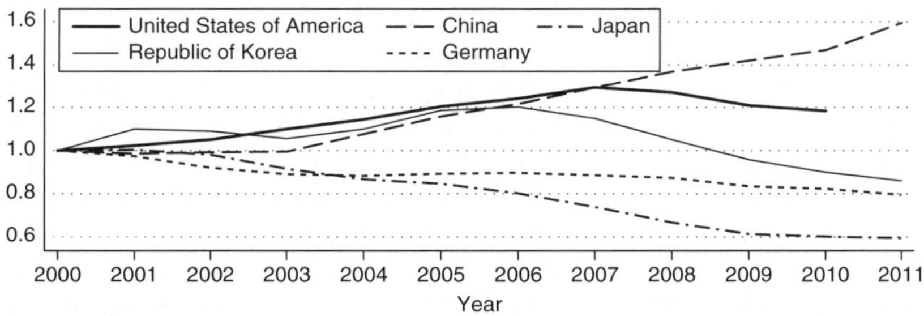

Note: As in Figure 2.3, R&D productivity is defined as resident patent applications per real R&D investments, with all time series expressed in index value with 2000 as the base year.

Source: WIPO Statistics Database.

Figure 2.4 Country trends in R&D productivity

In other words, once one decomposes the global surge into its base components, it looks much less spectacular; one sees growth in new inventions being presented to patent offices in line with underlying innovation investments, and those inventions then leading to a growing number of patent filings around the world.

However, this is where the descriptive analysis based on global data has to stop. The seemingly smooth decline in R&D productivity hides marked variation across countries. Figure 2.4 shows that the United States and

China have seen an upward trend in R&D productivity, whereas Japan and Germany have seen a downward trend.[8] In addition, there is marked variation in R&D productivity trends across sectors. Notably, certain complex technologies – including many information and communications technologies – have seen a rise in the propensity of patenting per dollar invested in R&D.[9]

Better understanding of the causes and consequences of the patent surge invariably requires micro-level investigations that analyze firms' filing strategies in relation to their innovation activities and competitive behavior. This is a fertile area for research and, as already pointed out, many insightful studies already exist. However, most of these studies have focused on the United States and a relatively narrow set of industries. It would be important to widen the set of countries and industries investigated to better reconcile micro-level findings with the global trends presented here.

2 GROWING USE OF OTHER IP RIGHTS

While most policymakers and scholars have focused on the surge in patenting filings, there also has been considerable growth in the use of other IP rights. Indeed, applications for utility models, industrial designs, and trademarks have seen even faster growth than those for patents. Utility model applications increased more than fourfold from 159,762 filings in 1995 to 670,665 in 2011; industrial design applications more than doubled from 290,787 filings in 2000 to 775,631 in 2011; and trademark applications also more than doubled from 1.8 million filings in 1995 to 4.2 million in 2011.[10]

More than in the case of patents, these marked filing increases over the last 15 years are predominantly a story about China. China already emerged as the largest recipient of utility model filings in 1994, of industrial design filings in 1999, and of trademark filings in 2001. In 2011, China accounted for 33 percent of global trademark filings, 67 percent of global design filings, and 87 percent of global utility model filings.

---

[8] PCT/WG/4/4 confirms these trends, looking at a longer time period and employing data on first filings.

[9] For example, see PCT/WG/5/4 and Bronwyn H. Hall and Rosemarie Ziedonis, "The Patent Paradox Revisited: An Empirical Study of Patenting in the U.S. Semiconductor Industry, 1979–1995", *Rand Journal of Economics*, vol. 32, no. 1, 2001, pp. 101–28.

[10] Due to missing data, consistent figures for industrial design filings worldwide are only available as of 2000.

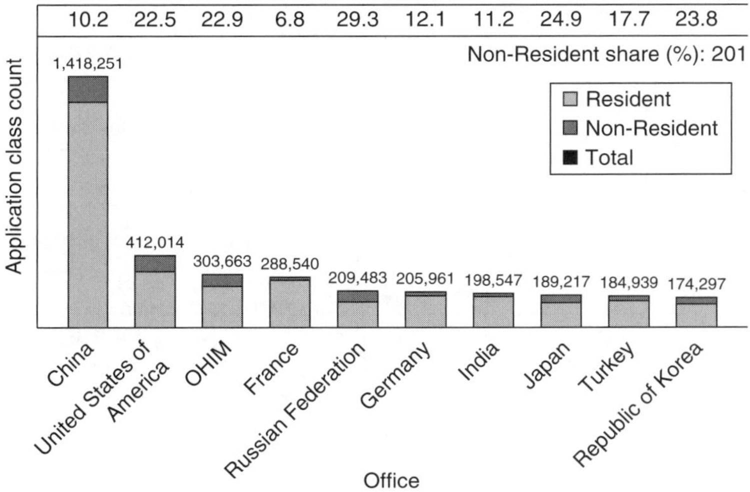

Source: WIPO Statistics Database.

Figure 2.5 Trademark application class counts for the top 10 offices in 2011

In the case of trademarks and industrial designs, these figures are skewed by the fact that China operates a single-class filing system (for trademarks) and a single-design system (for industrial designs). These systems invariably generate higher application counts compared with countries that operate multi-class and multi-design filing systems.[11] However, if one employs class and design counts rather than application counts, China still accounts for most filings (see Figures 2.5 and 2.6) – equivalent to 23 percent of the global total for trademarks and 53 percent for designs.

Economic research on these forms of IP is still in its infancy. Little is known about the fundamental drivers for greater use of these forms of IP. Internationalization is bound to be less important, given that non-residents account for smaller filings shares than in the case of patents. Understanding the root determinants of trademark and design filings is challenging, partly because of the nature of these rights and partly because of data availability.[12] Nonetheless, this is also a fertile area for research

---

[11] See Sections B and C of World Intellectual Property Organization, "World Intellectual Property Indicators", World Intellectual Property Organization, Geneva, 2012, pp. 97–148, http://www.wipo.int/export/sites/www/freepublications/en/intproperty/941/wipo_pub_941_2012.pdf (accessed 1 March 2013).

[12] Trademarks can protect anything from company names to product names,

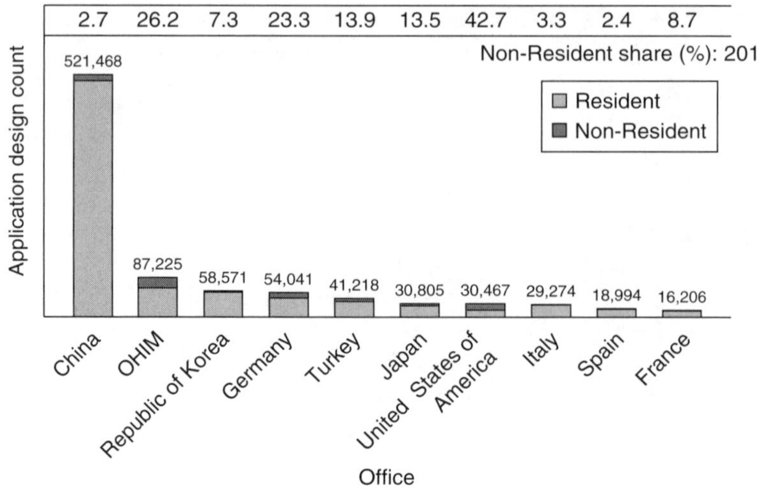

Source: WIPO Statistics Database.

Figure 2.6 Application design counts for the top 10 offices in 2011

and, indeed, the creation of new firm-level databases is enabling new investigation into these IP forms.[13]

3 CONCLUSION

How will future historians evaluate the shifting patterns of IP use described in this note? Will they largely see them as a reflection of the changing nature of economic activity – from the bricks-and-mortar economy to the intangible economy? Will they attribute them to the way IP policies and institutions have evolved? Will they see in them a fundamental shift in how firms produce intangible assets and compete in the marketplace? Will they see China as an exception of a middle-income economy intensively using

product designs, and advertising slogans. They are used widely throughout the economy. Industrial design rights only protect the aesthetic aspects of new designs; their functional characteristics are expressly excluded from the scope of protection. However, actual design innovation typically seeks to marry functionality with aesthetic appeal.

[13] See, for example, the studies on trademarks and designs undertaken by the UK IP office, available at http://www.ipo.gov.uk/pro-ipresearch.htm.

the IP system or will others have followed China's path? And how will they assess the impact of China's IP rise on the performance of the Chinese economy, and on the world economy at large?

Some may already have informed guesses to answer these questions. Yet, as the saying goes, the future is not what it used to be. Few people would have predicted today's global IP landscape some 25 years ago. However, one thing is certain: these are important questions that deserve serious study.

3. The geo-politics of the world patent order

Susan K. Sell

1 INTRODUCTION

The rise of dynamic emerging markets in Brazil, China, and India raise important questions about both the current and future world patent order. For the past thirty years industrialized countries, led by the United States, have made rules governing intellectual property and have spread their preferred systems of protection abroad. Beginning with bilateral deliberations in the 1970s and 1980s, continuing with the multilateral Agreement on Trade-related Aspects of Intellectual Property Rights (TRIPS) of 1994, the plurilateral Anti-Counterfeiting Trade Agreement (ACTA) and the ongoing Trans-Pacific Partnership (TPP) deliberations, industrialized countries with high standards of patent protection have made the rules that others have had to follow. Private rights-holders in the United States have profoundly shaped the intellectual property rules that the US government pushes abroad. Yet in the wake of the 2008 US and European financial crisis and the rapid economic rise of China and other dynamic emerging markets, will these rising countries remain rule takers or will they become rule makers in the world patent order? If they do become rule makers, what world would they prefer? Will the future world patent order look like more of the same, albeit with others in charge, or will these countries reshape the world patent order for fundamentally different purposes?

The answers to these questions are complicated. On the one hand, some countries, such as China, that have taken the rules are now seeking to use them to their strategic and competitive advantage. Many developing countries have established patent offices that institutionalize the Organisation for Economic Co-operation and Development's (OECD) pro-IP practices.[1] On the other hand, some countries, including China, Brazil, India,

[1] Peter Drahos, *The Global Governance of Knowledge: Patent Offices and their Clients*, Cambridge, UK, Cambridge University Press, 2010.

South Africa and Thailand, have selectively asserted their rights under TRIPS flexibilities and other treaties and conventions to retain important policy space that better serves their development needs. For example, India, China and Brazil pressed for a development agenda at the World Intellectual Property Organization (WIPO). China has adopted access and benefit sharing guidelines for their biodiversity. Thailand has issued compulsory licenses to produce affordable drugs. India has adopted strict patenting criteria for novelty to prevent the pharmaceutical practice of evergreening.[2] South Africa's Medicines Act included provisions for parallel importing to obtain affordable medicines. The Andean Community has adopted bans on pipeline and second-use patents.[3] It also has mandated use of TRIPS flexibilities and fought back against US TRIPS-plus Free Trade Agreement provisions.[4] These countries have actively resisted some aspects of the imposition of higher standards of intellectual property protection. They have stood their ground when forcefully challenged. While no longer merely passively taking the rules, none of these countries has yet stepped forward as a rule maker in intellectual property.

One might conclude that these countries' intellectual property preferences seem to be inconsistent – favoring high standards in some domains and more exceptions and flexibilities in others. However, rather than converging to OECD patent standards, they are likely to adopt more hybrid patent regimes. The United States has continued to press for one-size-fits-all policies and greater patent harmonization. Yet one size never truly fits all, and this particularly is the case in these dynamic and emerging economies.[5] Profound value divergence exists[6] because, while these up-and-comers are home to both real and potential innovations in particular sectors for which high standards of protection may be desirable,

---

2 Evergreening refers to the practice of firms extending patent life by switching from a tablet to a gel cap, for example, to get a new patent term, and the quest to obtain frivolous patents.

3 Laurence Helfer and Karen Alter, "The Influence of the Andean Intellectual Property Regime on Access to Medicines in Latin America", in Rochelle Dreyfuss and Cedar Rodriguez-Garavito (eds.), *Balancing Wealth and Health: Global Administrative Law and the Battle over Intellectual Property and Access to Medicines*, New York, Oxford University Press, 2013.

4 Helfer and Alter, "The Influence of the Andean Intellectual Property Regime".

5 Jerome Reichman and Rochelle Dreyfuss, "Harmonization Without Consensus: Critical Reflections on Drafting a Substantive Patent Law Treaty", *Duke Law Journal*, vol. 57, no. 1, 2007, pp. 85–130.

6 J. Janewa OseiTutu, "Value Divergence in Global Intellectual Property Law", *Indiana Law Journal*, vol. 87, 2012, pp. 1639–95.

they are also home to large populations of the desperately poor and uneducated who might be better served by a more lax approach to intellectual property. Therefore, one should not expect convergence reflecting a "Western" model, but rather one should expect hybrid models that reserve policy space to serve members of the "bottom billion" and thereby help to promote domestic political and social stability.[7] Divergence should be expected, given the diverse institutional legacies, variable sectoral strengths and weaknesses, trade dependence, and internal political dynamics.[8]

The section that follows briefly discusses intellectual property, the World Trade Organization (WTO) and the US preferences that have shaped the contemporary international patent system. The second section examines the practice of forum-shifting, in which participants move in and out of diverse forums in order to secure favored outcomes in intellectual property norm setting and rule making. The third section provides examples of developing countries' responses to the contemporary patent regime. It also discusses China's growing, yet checkered, embrace of OECD intellectual property practices for strategic advantage. Finally, the conclusion discusses implications for the future.

2 INTELLECTUAL PROPERTY, THE WORLD TRADE ORGANIZATION, AND US PREFERENCES

IP protection is supposed to provide incentives for producers to innovate, and for authors and artists to create cultural products. By offering exclusive limited rights, innovators and creators may get rewarded for their contributions. Many argue that without the incentives that property rights provide inventions and culture would be under-produced. Yet such rights also impede diffusion of the innovations, diffusion which benefits consumers and follow-on innovators. Policymakers must strike the right balance between the interests of producers, consumers, and follow-on innovators.

Intellectual property rights create scarcity in goods that are not formally scarce, and can increase the costs of goods. These rights can be abused to kill competition, secure monopoly power, and promote rent-seeking behavior. Many analysts argue that the scope and scale of IP protection that works for OECD countries is not appropriate for countries at

---

[7] Paul Collier, *The Bottom Billion: Why the Poorest Countries are Failing and What to Do About It*, New York, Oxford University Press, 2007.

[8] Dani Rodrik, *One Economics, Many Recipes: Globalization, Institutions, and Economic Growth*, Princeton, NJ, Princeton University Press, 2008.

earlier stages of development and net importers of IP-protected goods and services.[9]

International relations scholars frequently consider the distribution of state power as an important explanatory variable. After World War II, the United States emerged as the strongest economic power and was able to make the rules that other states had to follow. This structural power gave the United States substantial latitude to project its preferences abroad. Especially after the end of the Cold War, the United States pushed the spread of the so-called Washington Consensus and extolled the virtues of free trade, privatization, and liberalization. The majority of countries opened their markets and joined the WTO. During the Uruguay Round of Trade Negotiations that led to the WTO's establishment, the United States engaged in extensive bilateral negotiations to get developing countries to adopt new higher standards of intellectual property protection under threat of trade sanctions and denial of Generalized System of Preferences (non-reciprocal trade concessions) benefits.

The United States earned the reputation of being a trade bully, and many criticized its flouting of the multilateral GATT system by unilaterally acting as judge, jury, and executioner.[10] As part of joining the WTO, countries had to implement the TRIPS in their national laws. With the WTO and TRIPS, many countries expected the bilateral bullying to subside and for a rules-based multilateral approach to supersede the power-based bilateral bargaining. However, since TRIPS the United States has continued to push for TRIPS-plus standards through bilateral, regional, and plurilateral negotiations,[11] and has maintained steady pressure on developing countries to adopt higher standards.[12]

---

9 Ha-Joon Chang, "Institutions and Economic Development: Theory, Policy and History", *Journal of Institutional Economics*, vol. 7, no. 4, 2011, p. 481.

10 Jagdish Bhagwati and Hugh Patrick (eds.), *Aggressive Unilateralism: America's 301 Trade Policy and the World Trading System*, Ann Arbor, MI, University of Michigan Press, 1991.

11 Peter Drahos, "BITs and BIPs: Bilateralism in Intellectual Property", *Journal of World Intellectual Property*, vol. 4, no. 6, 2001, pp. 791–801; Kimberlee Weatherall, "ACTA as a New Kind of International IP Lawmaking", *American University International Law Review*, vol. 26, no. 3, 2011, p. 839; Eddan Katz and Gwen Hinze, "The Impact of the Anti-Counterfeiting Treaty on the Knowledge Economy: The Accountability of the Office of the U.S. Trade Representative for the Creation of IP Enforcement Norms through Executive Trade Agreements", *Yale International Law Online*, vol. 35, 2009, pp. 24–30.

12 Peter Yu, "The Rise and Decline of Intellectual Property Powers", *Campbell Law Review*, vol. 34, 2012, p. 541.

3 FORUM-SHIFTING

Powerful actors have engaged in horizontal forum-shifting, taking an issue from one forum and introducing it into another to secure better outcomes. The United States, dissatisfied with the World Intellectual Property Organization (WIPO)'s lack of enforcement capability, linked intellectual property to trade and inserted it into the General Agreement on Trade and Tariffs' (GATT) Uruguay Round negotiations in 1986. The trade-linkage allowed the United States to leverage access to its large market as a carrot or a stick to get its trading partners to adopt higher standards of intellectual property protection. This was a crucial horizontal shift, from one multilateral forum to another, and led to the enforceable TRIPS in the World Trade Organization (WTO).

Powerful countries also engage in vertical forum-shifting. When strong states have preferences that very few other states share, they often shift to vertical power-based negotiations in which weaker countries are more likely to acquiesce.[13] Beginning in the 1980s and throughout the Uruguay Round, the United States engaged in numerous bilateral negotiations with weaker states and threatened them with trade sanctions if they failed to adopt the strong intellectual property protections that the US rights-holders desired. This strategy helped the United States reduce resistance to the multilateral agreement. Developing countries initially saw their institutional choice as one of WIPO versus GATT, and they preferred the weaker one-state one-vote regime of WIPO. But the United States changed the game through its vertical forum-shifting of bilateral pressure and the choice became one of either US bilateral bullying, or a rules-based multilateral agreement, TRIPS, in the trade regime. Thus, the rules-based system became the more appealing option.

However, as the distribution of economic power shifts in the international system, one would expect that the re-alignment would become manifest in international institutions and bargaining dynamics. In intellectual property since TRIPS several emerging economic powers have become increasingly assertive. South Africa, Brazil, India, China and Thailand actively have challenged US efforts to push TRIPS-plus standards. They have engaged in horizontal forum-shifting, and have availed themselves of TRIPS flexibilities.

Developing countries engage additional forums to promote policy

---

[13] Eyal Benvenisti and George Downs, "The Empire's New Clothes: Political Economy and the Fragmentation of International Law", *Stanford Law Review*, vol. 60, 2007, pp. 595–631.

space for development and approaches to intellectual property that reflect their preferences. The first developing country-led horizontal forum shift came during the HIV/AIDS pandemic. A number of developing country governments linked intellectual property and access to essential medicines in the World Health Organization (WHO). Linking intellectual property protection to public health brought the WHO into the mix, and ultimately led to the 2001 Doha Declaration on the TRIPS Agreement and Public Health[14] and the *only* amendment proposed to TRIPS, the so-called "paragraph 6" provisions in 2003. This amendment is designed to enable the export of generic medicines produced under compulsory licenses to countries needing them.[15]

Many bio-diverse developing countries have complained of bio-piracy, in which multinational firms, research groups, universities and individuals take traditional knowledge and genetic resources from their territory and then use that material to produce a patented good that could be quite profitable. Yet those who profit from acquiring such material do not share the benefits with the originating country. Bio-diverse developing countries pressed for provisions in the Convention on Biological Diversity (CBD) for prior informed consent and access and benefit sharing to combat this practice. It is more generous to bio-diverse countries than is TRIPS.

As a result of the horizontal forum-shifting deliberations on intellectual property take place, generally upon developing countries' demand, in an increasing number of multilateral institutions. These include the WTO, WHO, WIPO, CBD, the United Nations Economic and Social Council, the Food and Agriculture Organization, UNFCCC, UNCTAD, and the Office of the High Commissioner for Human Rights. The intellectual property rules in these different forums are neither consistent with each other, nor are they all consistent with TRIPS. For example, Laurence Helfer and Graeme Austin have examined the tensions and interfaces between the intellectual property regime and the human rights regime in great detail.[16] TRIPS remains the most important multilateral instrument because only the WTO has enforcement powers, but numerous developing

---

14 The World Trade Organization, "Declaration on the TRIPS Agreement and Public Health", WT/MIN(01)/DEC/2, 20 November 2001, http://www.wto.org/english/thewto_e/minist_e/min01_e/mindecl_trips_e.htm (accessed 9 February 2013).

15 Frederick Abbott, "The WTO Medicines Decision: World Pharmaceutical Trade and the Protection of Public Health", *American Journal of International Law*, vol. 99, 2005, p. 317.

16 Laurence Helfer and Graeme Austin, *Human Rights and Intellectual Property: Mapping the Global Interface*, Cambridge, Cambridge University Press, 2011.

countries have adopted provisions from other agreements into their national laws.[17]

Some of this horizontal forum-shifting, accompanied by increasing developing country assertiveness and an economic power shift, has led to multilateral stalemate. The Doha Round of trade negotiations is deadlocked. Sharp conflict erupted in the Cancun talks in 2003, in which several countries walked out over agricultural issues and amidst recriminations of broken Northern promises left over from the Uruguay Round. Progress remains elusive. Gridlock between developed and developing countries across a number of multilateral forums (WTO and WIPO) has chased the United States and Europe out of multilateral forums to pursue plurilateral, regional and bilateral routes to achieve their goals.

After the 2001 Doha Declaration on TRIPS and Public Health, the United States realized that it would be unable to secure TRIPS-plus patent protections in WTO because of the access to medicines controversies. So it shifted to a presumably friendlier forum, WIPO, to pursue progress on a Substantive Patent Law Treaty (SPLT) that aimed to harmonize TRIPS-plus standards.[18] However, this time the developing countries organized their opposition to the US position. Developing countries refused to resume negotiations on a SPLT unless the United States first took developing countries' concerns seriously.

India, Brazil, and the Andean Pact states had spent many years in the 1970s and 1980s resisting efforts at harmonization in an overtly pro-IP direction.[19] After developing countries rejected the SPLT a "Friends of Development" coalition, led by India, Brazil and Egypt, sought to advance the more development-friendly provisions within the broader intellectual property regime. These countries secured WIPO's approval for a "development agenda" in WIPO that would incorporate developing countries' concerns about intellectual property, including protections for traditional knowledge, farmers' rights, prior informed consent, and access and benefit sharing reforms – TRIPS includes none of these. The United States rejected their demands, insisting that WIPO was not a development organization. The development agenda drove the United States to vertically shift to the plurilateral level (ACTA) for IP rulemaking as developing countries asserted their interests against the United States' in the multilateral forums WTO and WIPO.

---

17 Helfer and Alter, "The Influence of the Andean Intellectual Property Regime".

18 Reichman and Dreyfuss, "Harmonization Without Consensus", pp. 85–130.

19 Susan K. Sell, *Power and Ideas: The North-South Politics of Intellectual Property and Antitrust*, Albany, NY, State University of New York Press, 1998.

The day after WIPO adopted the Development Agenda in October 2007, the United States, Japan and the European Union announced that they would commence plurilateral negotiations on ACTA. ACTA is not a trade agreement; it is an intellectual property agreement. It aimed to secure heightened intellectual property protection for the digital age. The United States negotiated ACTA with select trading partners (mainly OECD countries and countries already bound by TRIPS-plus agreements with the United States). ACTA is TRIPS-plus, incorporating features and provisions that the United States could not secure at the multilateral level.

In yet another vertical forum-shift the United States has engaged in the Trans-Pacific Partnership (TPP) negotiations with Australia, Brunei Darussalam, Canada, Chile, Malaysia, Mexico, New Zealand, Peru, Singapore and Vietnam. Most of these countries are already yoked to TRIPS-plus bilateral agreements. These secretive negotiations cover much more than just intellectual property, but the leaked intellectual property chapter has revealed rather extreme TRIPS-plus provisions.

The real targets of this agreement are not sitting at the negotiating table. China, Brazil, India, South Africa – none of them is present. The idea behind TPP is to secure a very high standard plurilateral intellectual property agreement, and then to invite others to enroll in it so that it will become the de facto new global standard. The United States knows that these important emerging economies would not agree to the intellectual property provisions that go beyond TRIPS and that would impose new and inappropriate standards for their development needs. As Reichman and Dreyfuss point out:

> What developing countries most need is a period of calm and stability in which to devise intellectual property strategies consistent with both the TRIPS Agreement and the needs of their own emerging national and regional systems of innovation. . . . Developing countries cannot succeed if, at the international level, a new round of multilateral intellectual property negotiations threatens to raise the technological ladder once again, before these countries even get a solid foothold on it.[20]

4 REACTING, RESISTING, AND PUSHING BACK

One of the earliest developing country reactions to TRIPS was the developing country and NGO mobilization in the late 1990s to protest US government and private sector pressure on South Africa in the midst of its

---

[20] Reichman and Dreyfuss, "Harmonization Without Consensus", p. 102.

HIV/AIDS pandemic. The US government and 39 brand-name pharmaceutical firms sued the South African government over its 1997 Medicines Act which would have allowed for parallel importation of more affordable patented drugs.[21] After prolonged social mobilization and the early disruption of then-Vice President Al Gore's presidential campaign, the US finally backed off and the firms dropped their lawsuit. Brazil has successfully used the threat of compulsory licensing brand name pharmaceuticals to get lower prices on HIV/AIDS drugs for its widely praised public health program. The controversy over patents and access to medicines ultimately led to the unanimous adoption of the Doha Declaration on TRIPS and Public Health in 2001, which affirmed the right of countries to adopt policies promoting public health. In response to pressure from developing countries, in 2005 WTO members agreed to make permanent an August 2003 waiver as an amendment to TRIPS to allow for compulsory licenses to be used for the export of drugs into countries that lack pharmaceutical manufacturing capacity.

In a strategy that Amy Kapczynski calls "counter-harmonization",[22] a number of developing countries have adopted laws that expand their options in intellectual property policy. To combat bio-piracy, China, India and the Andean states have adopted prior informed consent, access and benefit sharing, and requirements to disclose the origin of biological materials. India has introduced limits on patentable subject matter, has introduced a high inventive step requirement for patent grants, and has included pre- and post-grant opposition provisions, limits on injunctive remedies, and strong patent misuse standards. The Philippines adopted provisions of the Indian Patent Law (Article 3(d)) that help to prevent the pharmaceutical practice of evergreening (extending patent life by switching from a tablet to gel cap, for example, to get a new patent term) and the granting of frivolous patents.

Thailand, India, Malaysia, Indonesia, Zambia, Brazil and Ecuador have all availed themselves of TRIPS flexibilities by issuing compulsory licenses to increase access to medicines. Malaysia was the first country to actually issue a compulsory license, one of the TRIPS' flexibilities, to a local firm to import HIV/AIDS drugs from India in 2003.[23] In September

---

[21] Patrick Bond, "Globalization, Pharmaceutical Pricing, and South African Health Policy: Managing Confrontation with U.S. Firms and Politicians", *International Journal of Health Services*, vol. 29, 1999, p. 768.

[22] Amy Kapczynski, "Harmonization and its Discontents: A Case Study of TRIPS Implementation in India's Pharmaceutical Sector", *California Law Review*, vol. 97, 2009, p. 1574.

[23] Martin Khor, "Measure to Make Drugs Affordable", *The Star Online*, 22

2012 Indonesian President Dr. H. Susilo Bambang Yudoyono authorized government use of seven patents for HIV/AIDS and hepatitis B medicines.[24] Thailand has issued compulsory licenses for drugs for chronic diseases such as cancer and heart disease, much to the Pharmaceutical Research and Manufacturers' Association's dismay.

With the ongoing geopolitical power re-alignment, countries such as China, India, Brazil and Thailand are pushing back against the TRIPS-plus agenda. At the June 2010 TRIPS Council meeting China, along with India, Argentina, Venezuela and Mauritius, expressed concern over TRIPS-plus enforcement trends and ACTA. At the October 2010 TRIPS Council meeting, China suggested that ACTA might be incompatible with TRIPS.[25]

In 2010 India initiated WTO dispute settlement consultations with the European Union and the Netherlands over seizure of Indian generic drug shipments en route through the Netherlands to various developing countries. In a number of instances, Dutch customs authorities had seized Indian generic drug shipments as they passed through Schiphol airport and the Rotterdam port based on pharmaceutical firms' allegations that the shipments infringed on the firms' patents in the Netherlands, even though the drugs were never intended for distribution there. This practice raised fears that the real aim was to disrupt generic competition for brand-name pharmaceutical firms. The EU and India concluded an interim settlement under which the EU committed to halting this practice, but India reserved the right to return to the WTO in the event that the EU's policies and regulations did not change as promised.[26] (Initial ACTA proposals would have allowed or required seizure of goods in transit based on

---

October 2012, http://thestar.com.my/columnists/story.asp?file=%2F2012%2F10%2F22%2Fcolumnists%2Fglobaltrends%2F12206262&sec=globaltrends (accessed 9 February 2013).

[24] Public Citizen, "Indonesia Licenses Patents for Seven HIV & Hepatitis B Medicines", *Public Citizen*, 12 October 2012, http://www.citizen.org/PC-statement-on-compulsory-licensing-in-Indonesia (accessed 9 February 2013).

[25] Excerpt from China's intervention at the WTO TRIPS Council meeting held from 26–7 October 2010. Knowledge Ecology International, "ACTA: Intervention of China to the WTO TRIPS Council", Washington, DC, 2011, http://keionline.org/node/1001 (accessed 9 February 2013).

[26] Matthias Williams, "Update 2 – India, EU Heal Drug Seizures Dispute with Interim Agreement", *Reuters*, 28 July 2011, http://www.reuters.com/article/2011/07/28/india-eu-drugs-idUS (accessed 9 February 2013). In-transit shipments also were detained in Germany, France and the UK on grounds other than patent infringement (e.g., trademark infringement). Some of these shipments were either destroyed or turned away, never reaching their intended destination.

transit-country patents, though negotiators eventually abandoned this proposal.)

China is an interesting case because it exhibits a very broad range of behaviors in the intellectual property regime. First, as befits a developing country, it has adopted utility models or "petty patents" for incremental innovation. The Chinese hope that these types of patents will encourage indigenous innovation. Second, while widespread counterfeiting and copyright piracy remain, this is to be expected given the decentralization of enforcement authority and grinding poverty in many regions in China. Many Chinese simply cannot afford IP-protected products. Third, it has also embraced OECD intellectual property norms in important respects and has even begun mimicking the aggressive litigious behavior of the West for strategic competitive advantage.

China has implemented some innovative domestic IP policies and strategies for developing technological capabilities. Three important trends in this period have been capacity building initiatives, a sharp rise in Chinese patenting and IP litigation, and China's commitment to indigenous innovation. Despite China's huge trade surpluses with multiple trading partners, it captures very little of the value of the goods it assembles and sends abroad. For each Chinese-made Apple iPad that sells for US$499, China retains only about US$25, mainly labor costs.[27] Chinese leaders are eager to spur indigenous innovation to capture more value in licensing fees, royalties and more sophisticated and expensive exports.

Since joining the WTO in 2001 China has introduced new incentives for innovation and indigenous intellectual property development. In 2003 the government began to use invention patent filings as criteria for promotion and tenure in universities and provided patent subsidies to encourage domestic filing. Gross domestic spending on R&D surged from US$89.6 billion in 2000, to US$160.8 billion in 2012, amounting to 2% of China's gross domestic output.[28]

China adopted three important initiatives to promote more IP-intensive development. Its 2006 fifteen-year Medium- to Long-Term Plan for Scientific and Technological Development established priorities for industrial development in sectors such as pharmaceutical and agricultural biotechnology, civilian aircraft, clean energy, and new materials.[29] The

---

27 Peter Drahos, "The US, China and the G-77 in the Era of Responsive Patentability", *Queen Mary Journal of Intellectual Property*, vol. 2, no. 4, 2012, pp. 315–28.

28 Drahos, "The US, China and the G-77", pp. 344–5.

29 Richard Suttmeier and Xiangkui Yao, "China's IP Transition: Rethinking Intellectual Property Rights in a Rising China", The National Bureau of Asian

2008 State Council's National Intellectual Property Strategy highlighted the importance of IP as a strategic resource.[30] Its 2010 Five-Year Plan emphasized core technology development, and its 2010 National Patent Development Strategy underscored China's commitment to promote innovation. China has developed innovative capacity, inter alia, in genome sequencing of plants and insects, nanotechnology, and nuclear technology.[31]

China has invested in human capital to improve its intellectual property management and capacity. China increased the number of IP courts, trained judges in IP, and introduced a university IP curriculum. It has expanded its State Intellectual Property Office (SIPO) from 2,700 patent examiners in 2007 to roughly 6,000 in 2011. SIPO plans to increase the number of examiners to 10,000 by 2015.[32] SIPO is now the world's largest patent office.

Most benchmarks of success for China's various IP initiatives are quantitative. While quantity does not necessarily indicate quality, quantitative progress has been remarkable. In 2008 China became the eighth largest user of the Patent Cooperation Treaty (PCT). WIPO administers the PCT, collecting fees from firms that seek patent protection in multiple countries with a single international application. By 2011 China had jumped to fourth, behind the United States, Japan and Germany; between 2009 and 2010 alone Chinese PCT applications surged by 55.6%, and in 2011 PCT applications from China rose another 33.4%.[33] Between 2005 and 2010 patent applications to SIPO increased from 476,264 to 1,222,286; of these, Chinese applicants filed 1,109,228 applications whereas foreigners filed 112,858.[34] In 2011 residents of China filed the second largest amount of patent applications (a 41.3% increase) after Japan, and ahead of the United States.[35]

Research, Seattle, WA, NBR, July 2011, p. 8, http://china-us.uoregon.edu/pdf/IP_report.pdf (accessed 9 February 2013).

30 Suttmeier and Yao, "China's IP Transition", p. 3.

31 Yu, "The Rise and Decline of Intellectual Property Powers", p. 527.

32 Drahos, "The US, China and the G-77", pp. 6, 8.

33 World Intellectual Property Organization, "PCT Yearly Review: The International Patent System: Developments and Performance in 2010", World Intellectual Property Organization, Geneva, 2010, pp. 12–13, http://www.wipo.int/freepublications/en/patents/901/wipo_pub_901_2010.pdf (accessed 9 February 2013); World Intellectual Property Organization, "2012 PCT Yearly Review: The International Patent System", p. 27, Geneva, 2012, http://www.wipo.int/freepublications/en/patents/901/wipo_pub_901_2012.pdf (accessed 9 February 2013).

34 Suttmeier and Yao, "China's IP Transition", p. 13.

35 World Intellectual Property Organization, "Global IP Filings Continue to Grow, China Tops Global Patent Filings", World Intellectual Property Organization, Geneva, 11 December 2012, http://www.wipo.int/pressroom/en/articles/2013/article_0025.html (accessed 9 February 2013).

China has learned lessons the hard way, but has been a quick study. Getting burned by foreigners' strategic patenting and their aggressive patenting practices has taught China important lessons. While the patent system could be a tool to spur innovation, firms also deploy it as a strategic market weapon. Strategic patenting is not about stimulating innovation but rather about extracting maximum value from global value chains of production.[36] Foreigners often have charged very high licensing fees for mature, trivial, and even off-patent technology.[37] The Chinese have learned that foreign firms routinely use patenting strategies including "litigation threatening, alliance, and overcharging synchronously, to earn excess benefits".[38] Until 2007 China had no anti-monopoly legislation to protect itself against these abuses.[39]

Chinese firms have learned from litigation experience. A French electronics firm, Schneider Electronics, had competed with the Chinese firm, Chint, for European markets since the mid-1990s. Schneider sued Chint for IP infringement in 19 cases in Europe and six in China; in each case Schneider won injunctions against Chint. In 2006 Chint counterattacked with its utility model portfolio, suing Schneider for infringement. SIPO ruled in favor of Chint's patent as valid and enforceable.[40] In 2009 Schneider paid Chint $23 million to settle the lawsuit.[41] Chinese firms now routinely sue foreigners for Chinese-held utility model infringement. Foreign firms claim that these utility model infringement cases are difficult to fight and refer to utility models as "junk patents".[42] Chinese firms' strategic patenting suggests that they are learning to game the

---

[36] Drahos, "The US, China and the G-77", p. 10.

[37] Lan Xue and Zheng Liang, "Relationships Between IPR and Technology Catch-Up: Some Evidence from China", in Hiroyuki Odagiri et al. (eds.), *Intellectual Property Rights, Development, and Catch-Up: An International Comparative Study*, Oxford, Oxford University Press, 2010, p. 348.

[38] Xue and Liang, "Relationships Between IPR and Technology Catch-Up", p. 348.

[39] Michael Jacobs and Xinzhu Zhang, "China's Approach to Compulsory Licensing of Intellectual Property Under Its Anti-Monopoly Law", *Competition Policy International*, vol. 6, no. 2, 2010, p. 201.

[40] Jeffrey Duncan, Michelle Sherwood, and Yuanlin Shen, "A Comparison Between the Judicial and Administrative Routes to Enforce Intellectual Property Rights in China", *The John Marshall Law School Review of Intellectual Property Law*, vol. 7, no. 3, 2008, p. 536.

[41] James McGregor, "China's Drive for 'Indigenous Innovation': A Web of Industrial Policies", *US Chamber of Commerce, Global Intellectual Property Center*, Washington, DC, 2010, p. 27, http://www.uschamber.com/sites/default/files/reports/100728chinareport_0.pdf (accessed 9 February 2013).

[42] McGregor, "China's Drive for 'Indigenous Innovation'", pp. 26, 28.

system to extract rents just as OECD-based firms have been doing for decades.

In intellectual property China has emerged as the world's most litigious country.[43] Domestic litigation has surged, with most cases involving Chinese litigants suing other Chinese firms. Between 2003 and 2010, IP lawsuits in China rose from 9,000 to 42,902.[44] The Chinese firms Huawei and ZTE, competitors inside China, now sue each other for infringement in European markets.

China has gained impressive competence in intellectual property policy in a short time and is a skilled participant in the WTO. Highlights of China's participation include its effective performance in a landmark WTO copyright case, and its more assertive participation in the TRIPS Council and WIPO. Since joining the WTO China has been an observer in *every* dispute settlement case dealing with IP to learn first-hand how the system works. China has been a quick study and defended itself ably in a WTO copyright enforcement case. The WTO Panel's report[45] upheld most of China's practices. It has affirmed a considerable amount of policy discretion under TRIPS.

Developing countries may find a new leader in China, yet so far its multilateral engagement has been more supportive than leading and its preferences have been more reformist than radical. Competition between the BRICS will increase over time, but for now some of these countries have been effective champions for some developing countries' intellectual property concerns.

As China's, Brazil's, India's, and South Africa's power and participation grow they will seek greater institutional power, both for their own purposes and to advance a broader global governance agenda. They will be promoting reform rather than radical change. As Benvenisti and Downs suggest:

> It is . . . possible that the major developing democracies such as India, Brazil, South Africa, and South Korea could evolve into an anti-fragmentation coalition. . . . The size of their economies would . . . give the coalition considerable clout. Such a coalition . . . might be able to pressure major powers to reduce

---

[43] Suttmeier and Yao, "China's IP Transition", p. 13.

[44] Tony Chen, "Western Ways, Good and Bad: A Battle over a Patent for Viagra Gives a Glimpse of Several Trends", *Financial Times*, 21 July 2004, p. 10; Suttmeier and Yao, "China's IP Transition", p. 13.

[45] Panel Report, China – Measures Affecting the Protection and Enforcement of Intellectual Property Rights, WT/DS362/R, World Trade Organization, 26 January 2009 (adopted 20 March 2009), http://www.wto.org/english/tratop_e/dispu_e/cases_e/ds362_e.htm (accessed 9 February 2013).

their reliance on the tactics of regime shifting and threatening to retaliate in kind (for example, withdrawing from aspects of WTO's intellectual property regime).[46]

5 CONCLUSION

The 2008 financial crisis has exacerbated a perception that global economic power has shifted, and the United States may no longer impose its economic preferences on the rest of the world. US efforts to push for ever higher standards on IP will continue to meet with resistance. It seems that the US will have a hard time getting away with IP norm-setting business as usual. If the real targets of continued TRIPS-plus initiatives such as ACTA and TPP are not at the table, why would they go along with agreements that they were not party to? India, China, Brazil and South Africa are gaining relative economic muscle, and one should expect them to start flexing it in a variety of venues as they have begun to in recent years. As Kimberlee Weatherall points out, "if the negotiators do not change their approach, I wonder if it will end up being changed for them".[47]

By the same token, however, as higher standards of IP protection begin to make sense in select sectors one should expect these countries to adopt and enforce such standards accordingly. China has embraced strong IP protection in select sectors such as green energy in which it has innovative capacity. One should also expect selective enforcement of IP protection in these countries. While countries such as South Korea have moved through the imitation stage to the innovation stage and have fully embraced IP protection, India, China, Brazil and South Africa have huge and impoverished populations for whom strict IP protection may be destabilizing. Access to affordable medicines, educational materials, and employment opportunities will remain pressing concerns that these governments will need to address going forward. If governments have to choose between external pressure for strict enforcement and internal social stability, one should expect them to choose the latter.

---

[46] Benvenisti and Downs, "The Empire's New Clothes", p. 629.

[47] Kimberlee Weatherall, "Three Lessons from ACTA and its Political Aftermath", *Suffolk Transnational Law Review*, vol. 35, 2012, pp. 575–603.

4. Rethinking the patent system from the perspective of economics

Haiyang Zhang

1 RETHINKING THE PATENT SYSTEM FROM THE PERSPECTIVE OF ECONOMICS

Pro-patent policy makers generally propagandize the patent system as an effective institution to stimulate innovation, facilitate technology dissemination, promote trade, and enhance competitiveness.[1] However, by granting exclusive property rights, the patent system stimulates innovation, but it may also cause monopoly, which in turn results in the loss of social welfare and may impede the use and development of the patented technologies by others. Therefore, the overall role of the patent system in promoting economic development, especially for developing countries characterized by a generally low technology level, is rather ambiguous.[2]

Next, I briefly review the basic economic theories behind the patent system and the arguments for and against it put forward by many economists, followed by an introduction of some patent related economic studies and their implications for current patent institutions in developing countries. To conclude, I summarize some suggestions for policy makers in developing countries on designing and improving their patent institutions.

---

[1] Please refer to K. Idris, *Intellectual Property – A Powerful Tool for Economic Growth*, Geneva, World Intellectual Property Organization, 2003.

[2] M. Boldrin and D. Levine, "The Case Against Intellectual Property", *American Economic Review*, vol. 92, no. 2, 2002, pp. 209–12; P. Drahos, "Information Feudalism in the Information Society", *The Information Society*, 11, 1995, pp. 209–22; P. Drahos (ed.), *Intellectual Property*, England, Dartmouth Publishing Company Limited, and USA, Ashgate Publishing Company, 1999.

2 THE BASIC ECONOMIC THEORIES BEHIND THE PATENT SYSTEM

The core economics of the patent system, also applicable to some other intellectual property rights, is that it is an institution facing the inherent trade-off between encouraging innovation and suffering the consequences of potential monopoly. Like knowledge or information, an invention can be non-rival and non-excludable in its nature of consumption. The non-rival feature of knowledge implies that the amount of knowledge available to any user does not decrease when others use it, while the non-excludable character of knowledge means that once it is made public, we cannot exclude others from using it unless it is protected by a legal exclusive right. Although an invention sometimes can be excludable by keeping it as a secret, such as the secret recipe of Coca-Cola, there is a potential risk that such secrets may be easily discovered through reverse engineering or by other means.

A patent is a right granted by a government to the patent owner or owners to exclusively make, use, and sell that invention for a certain period of time, and, as an exchange condition, it is required to disclose the invention to the public. Thus, acquiring a patent or other intellectual property rights for a particular creation of knowledge is an example of making a non-rival and non-excludable good excludable. By granting the exclusive right on a patented invention, the patentee(s) can charge a higher price or enjoy a lower marginal cost while excluding others from doing so.

Since newly invented knowledge has the characteristics of non-excludability and non-rivalry, it is observed that the provision of such goods will be below the socially desired level due to the free-rider problem. That is, unless there are some incentives granted by the government. Entrepreneurs that expect profit from research and development may not be willing to take risks and invest in such activities since any rewards from doing so may dissipate due to imitation. In such a context, it is traditionally argued, perfect competition in the market of knowledge-based products does not allow innovators to recover their innovation costs such as R&D investment.[3] It is called innovation market failure summarized in Martin and Scott[4] and

---

[3] K. Arrow, "Economic Welfare and the Allocation of Resources for Invention", *NBER Chapters in the Rate and Direction of Inventive Activity: Economic and Social Factors*, National Bureau of Economic Research, 1962, pp. 609–26.

[4] S. Martin and J.T. Scott, "The Nature of Innovation Market Failure and the Design of Public Support for Private Innovation", *Research Policy*, 29, 4–5, 2000, pp. 437–47.

Colombo and Delmastro,[5] which mainly refers to the phenomenon of under-investment in innovation from the social standpoint. The patent system is a social institution intended to alleviate the negative impact caused by the innovation market failure by granting patent owners exclusive rights to make, use, and sell their inventions for a certain period of time. Nonetheless, some scholars argue that there is no general market failure for innovations as, in most industries, the cost of invention is low; or just being first in market confers a durable competitive advantage.[6]

Moreover, the exclusive rights given by patent law may cause monopoly, which is another sort of market failure. Basic economics indicates that monopoly harms social welfare at least from the static point of view. Although not all patents can cause monopoly, the market power associated with patents may impose social costs even as it encourages invention and commercialization. Accordingly, societies limit the power of patent grants not only in duration and scope, but also in disclosure requirements. Moreover, the potential for abusing the market power inherent in patent grants is considered anticompetitive.

3 DEBATE ON THE PATENT SYSTEM

Arguments for and against patents are not new, but still continue. At the time when the patent system was being established, those who were in favour of the patent system believed that it could stimulate inventions and creations, whereas some thought that the patent system was unnecessary because inventions were based on the inspiration of inventors and had little to do with incentives, and even when some inventions were induced by profit incentives, the profits obtained through selling first in the market were large enough to compensate for invention costs.

This debate may be intensified and complicated under the current context of economic globalization. The Agreement on Trade-Related Aspects of Intellectual Property Rights (TRIPS) was reached, during the Uruguay Round (1986–94) of negotiations on the reform of the world trading system, with a view to reducing or eliminating tensions due to

---

5 M.G. Colombo and M. Delmastro, "How Effective are Technology Incubators? Evidence from Italy", *Research Policy*, 31, 2002, pp. 1103–22.

6 H.V.J. Moir, "What are the Costs and Benefits of Patent Systems?", *Centre for Governance of Knowledge and Development Working Paper*, October 2008; R. Posner, "Why There Are Too Many Patents in America", *The Atlantic*, 12 July 2012, http://www.theatlantic.com/business/archive/2012/07/why-there-are-too-many-patents-in-america/259725/ (accessed on 15 January 2013).

cross-country differences in the treatment of intellectual property rights (IPRs). The TRIPS Agreement essentially imposes "minimum" standards for the protection of intellectual property on all member economies. For example, the term of patent protection is at least 20 years counted from the filing date and the patentable subject matter covers almost all fields of technology, including such areas as pharmaceuticals, agriculture, chemicals, food, and micro organisms where most developing countries used to provide no or little patent protection. Although the countries on the United Nations' list of least developed countries may delay implementing TRIPS in respect of pharmaceutical products until 1 January 2016, extended by the Doha Declaration, the standard on IP protection required by TRIPS is still rather high for most developing countries.

In such a context, some argue strongly that intellectual property rights including patents are necessary to stimulate economic growth, which, in turn, contributes to poverty reduction. By stimulating invention and development of new technologies, patents would increase agricultural or industrial production, promote domestic and foreign investment in technology research and development, facilitate technology transfer and improve the availability of medicines necessary to combat disease. Others argue equally vehemently the opposite: that patents do little to stimulate invention in developing countries, because the necessary human and technical capacity may often be absent. Patents are ineffective at stimulating research to benefit poor people because they will not be able to afford to buy the newly developed products at the patent price. Patents limit the option of technological learning through imitation and allow foreign firms to drive out domestic competition by obtaining patent protection and to service the market through imports, rather than domestic manufacture. Moreover, they increase the costs of essential medicines and agricultural inputs, affecting poor people and farmers particularly badly.[7]

Thus, the relationship between the patent system and economic development is extremely complex and the evidence is insufficient. Moreover, there seems to be a gap between the economic research and patent system design, especially in the case of China, which might have been caused by a lack of communication between economic researchers and the patent community, whose members are mainly scientists, engineers and legal professionals.

---

[7] UK Commission on IPR, "Integrating Intellectual Property Rights and Development Policy", The Commission on Intellectual Property Rights of the United Kingdom, 2002, http://www.iprcommission.org/graphic/documents/final_report.htm (accessed 17 January 2013).

4 WHAT WE KNOW FROM PAST ECONOMIC STUDIES AND WHAT WE DO NOT KNOW

It is generally noted that from the late 1960s the economic research focusing on patents has made some substantial achievements, symbolized by the optimal patent life model of Nordhaus.[8] Nordhaus[9] initiates an analysis of the optimal patent life by modeling the trade-off inherent in the patent system – a system that creates static losses by granting innovators temporary monopoly power in order to realize social gains by inducing greater innovative effort. Scherer[10] gives a geometric reinterpretation of Nordhaus' optimal patent model to make it more straightforward for understanding. In their models, the resolution of this trade-off leads to the economic justification for a finite length of protection, according to the argument that it is better to forego some innovations by restricting patent life in order to reduce deadweight loss on those that are realized. Generally speaking, the longer the patent protection term, the stronger is the incentive for innovation, but also the market power. According to Nordhaus[11] and Scherer,[12] theoretically, differentiated patent protection terms are better than a unified statutory patent life.

However, it is almost impossible for government to differentiate which inventions should be given longer or shorter patent life due to asymmetry of information and inherent uncertainty of invention. Thus, in the real world, patent length is almost statutorily the same, usually 20 years from the filing date for invention patents as regulated by TRIPS. Although it is difficult to differentiate statutory patent life individually, an annual patent maintenance fee system was created to let patent owners themselves decide whether they would like to pay the annual patent fees in order to keep their patents valid. The annual patent fee system, thus, may play an important role in balancing the trade-off between private and public interests on patented technologies. Some studies have confirmed that "renewal fees can influence the decision to renew patents and more valuable patents are

8 W. Nordhaus, *Invention, Growth and Welfare: A Theoretical Treatment of Technological Change*, Cambridge, MA, MIT Press, 1969.

9 W. Nordhaus, *Invention, Growth and Welfare: A Theoretical Treatment of Technological Change*, Cambridge, MA, MIT Press, 1969.

10 F.M. Scherer, "Nordhaus' Theory of Optimal Patent Life: A Geometric Reinterpretation", *American Economic Review*, 62, 3, 1972, pp. 422–7.

11 W. Nordhaus, *Invention, Growth and Welfare: A Theoretical Treatment of Technological Change*, Cambridge, MA, MIT Press, 1969.

12 F.M. Scherer, "Nordhaus' Theory of Optimal Patent Life: A Geometric Reinterpretation", *American Economic Review*, 62, 3, 1972, pp. 422–7.

usually held longer[13]".[14] However, it is unlikely to be the case for patents of real economic value as the current patent annual fees are not high enough.

Since it is technically and practically difficult to allow different statutory patent length across individual inventions and in reality governments usually fix a finite patent duration for all inventions, more follow-on research is concentrated on the optimal design of patent breadth (scope). The breadth of a patent refers to the patent scope in the sense of patent law. In principle, it is determined by claims made in an application and accorded by patent examiners to a patentee, defining the boundaries between what is protected and what is not. As most technologies are based on previous innovations, patent breadth becomes extremely important in balancing the incentives for the first-generation and following-on innovations.

There are two main opposing camps on how to balance the incentives for first-generation inventors of initial technologies and second-generation innovators of applied research and development. Scotchmer,[15] Chang,[16] Green and Scotchmer,[17] and Matutes, Regibeau, and Rockett,[18] argue that first-generation inventors of initial technologies should be given strong forward protection so as to overcome the diminishing return on R&D of the first inventor because second-generation improvements can be obtained by outsiders. However, broad forward protection can stifle second-generation products; affect the accessibility of patented knowledge embedded in the initial inventions; and thus slow down the rate of

---

13 A.S. Pakes, "Patents as Options: Some Estimates of the Value of Holding European Patent Stocks", *Econometrica*, 54, 1986, pp. 755–84; M. Schankerman and A. Pakes, "Estimates of the Value of Patent Rights in European Countries during the Post-1950 Period", *Economic Journal*, 96, 1986, pp. 1052–77; M. Schankerman, "How Valuable is Patent Protection? Estimates by Technology Field", *RAND Journal of Economics*, 29, 1998, pp. 77–107; J. Lanjouw, "Patent Value in the Shadow of Infringement: Simulation Estimations of Patent Value", *Review of Economic Studies*, 65, 1998, pp. 671–710.

14 Please refer to F. Cornelli and M. Schankerman, "Patent Renewals and R&D Incentives", *RAND Journal of Economics*, 30, 2, 1999, p. 197.

15 S. Scotchmer, "Standing on the Shoulders of Giants: Cumulative Research and the Patent Law", *Journal of Economic Perspective*, 5, 1, 1991, pp. 29–41.

16 H. Chang, "Patent Scope, Antitrust Policy, and Cumulative Innovation", *RAND Journal of Economics*, 26, 1, 1995, pp. 34–57.

17 J. Green and S. Scotchmer, "On the Division of Profits in Sequential Innovation", *RAND Journal of Economics*, 26, 1, 1995, pp. 20–33.

18 C. Matutes, P. Regibeau, and K. Rockett, "Optimal Patent Design and the Diffusion of Innovations", *RAND Journal of Economics*, 27, 1, 1996, pp. 60–83.

innovation, as emphasized by Merges and Nelson[19, 20] and Heller and Eisenberg.[21]

Scotchmer[22] finds that the incentive to file initial patents is especially weak when patent protection is narrow since a second-generation product is more likely to damage the first innovator's profit. As observed by Scotchmer,[23] in markets with cumulative research, patent protection cannot offer both the first and second innovators the full surplus from the second innovation. As a result, some distortion of incentives is unavoidable under a patent system: for at least one firm, the private reward for its innovation will fall short of the social value of that innovation. Green and Scotchmer[24] show that profit erosion can be mitigated by broadening the first innovator's patent protection scope and/or by permitting cooperative agreements between initial innovators and later innovators.

Chang[25] argues that an inventor would be reluctant to patent a "*stepping-stone*" innovation in the absence of broad protection since others can improve upon the imperfect technology disclosed by the patent and invent around it. However, he neglects the possibility that broad patent protection may deter the further improvement made by other firms if they have to get licenses from the patent holder, which may exceed the expected profit from improvements. Therefore, there is no straightforward answer as to whether broad patent protection will achieve such objectives as proposed by Chang.[26]

Matutes, Regibeau, and Rockett[27] concentrate on the patent protection of basic innovations, which can be used in wide areas. They argue that

---

19 R. Merges and R. Nelson, "On the Complex Economics of Patent Scope", *Columbia Law Review*, 90, 4, 1990, pp. 839–916.

20 R. Merges and R. Nelson, "On Limiting or Encouraging Rivalry in Technical Progress: The Effect of Patent Scope Decisions", *Journal of Economic Behaviour and Organization*, 25, 1994, pp. 1–24.

21 M. Heller and R. Eisenberg, "Can Patents Deter Innovation? The Anticommons in Biomedical Research", *Science*, 280, 1998, pp. 698–701.

22 S. Scotchmer, "Standing on the Shoulders of Giants: Cumulative Research and the Patent Law", *Journal of Economic Perspective*, 5, 1, 1991, pp. 29–41.

23 S. Scotchmer, "Standing on the Shoulders of Giants: Cumulative Research and the Patent Law", *Journal of Economic Perspective*, 5, 1, 1991, pp. 29–41.

24 S. Scotchmer, "Standing on the Shoulders of Giants: Cumulative Research and the Patent Law", *Journal of Economic Perspective*, 5, 1, 1991, pp. 29–41.

25 H. Chang, "Patent Scope, Antitrust Policy, and Cumulative Innovation", *RAND Journal of Economics*, 26, 1, 1995, pp. 34–57.

26 H. Chang, "Patent Scope, Antitrust Policy, and Cumulative Innovation", *RAND Journal of Economics*, 26, 1, 1995, pp. 34–57.

27 C. Matutes, P. Regibeau, and K. Rockett, "Optimal Patent Design and the Diffusion of Innovations", *RAND Journal of Economics*, 27, 1, 1996, pp. 60–83.

"in the absence of patent protection, an innovator who has made a significant breakthrough in technologies may delay its disclosure and would be tempted to get a head start in developing the applications of the new discovery before commercializing any product." Such a delay in disclosing the basic innovation and hence introducing the first application is socially undesirable both because it postpones the diffusion of the knowledge of the basic innovation and because it withholds desirable products from the market. Their main finding is that patent breadth rather than length should be used to induce early disclosure of fundamental innovations while still preserving firms' incentive to do R&D and suggest that broad patent protection should be applied on basic innovations.

On the other side, based on an empirical-historical examination of the course of technical advance in several industries, Merges and Nelson[28] argue that broad patent scope may increase incentives to invent for some pioneers, but any lessening of the patentee's potential reward by narrowing patent scope may not severely undercut the incentive to invent. However, broad patents diminish incentives for others to stay in the invention competition. In many industries the efficiency gains from the pioneer's ability to coordinate are likely to be outweighed by the loss of competition for improvements to the basic invention. Merges and Nelson[29] draw their basic conclusion: "Without extensively reducing the pioneer's incentives, the law should attempt at the margin to favor a competitive environment for improvements, rather than an environment dominated by the pioneer firm."

Merges and Nelson[30] reemphasize their view that broad and prospect-claiming pioneer patents may cut down on the diversity and creativity of the development when their holders try to uphold them in a cumulative research setting. Other parties are often more active or creative than the pioneer patent holder, but are obstructed if the pioneer's broad patent and bargaining about the terms of individual licenses proves to be difficult. There is no reason to believe that more narrowly drawn patents would have dampened the incentives of the pioneers and other early comers to the field. Even under a cumulative technology framework, superior design, production, and marketing rather than strong patent protection

---

28 R. Merges and R. Nelson, "On the Complex Economics of Patent Scope", *Columbia Law Review*, 90, 4, 1990, pp. 839–916.

29 R. Merges and R. Nelson, "On the Complex Economics of Patent Scope", *Columbia Law Review*, 90, 4, 1990, pp. 839–916.

30 R. Merges and R. Nelson, "On Limiting or Encouraging Rivalry in Technical Progress: The Effect of Patent Scope Decisions", *Journal of Economic Behaviour and Organization*, 25, 1994, pp. 1–24.

are the principal source of profit, and an inventor has a natural lead time advantage in incorporating his or her own invention into the product or process. Thus, Merges and Nelson[31] suggest that patent authorities should provide more consistently strict interpretation on patent scope, especially for basic technologies.

Heller and Eisenberg[32] show a famous "tragedy of anti-commons" phenomenon in biomedical research. Contrary to the "tragedy of commons" introduced by Garrett Hardin to explain why people overuse shared resources, a proliferation of patents on individual fragments held by different owners in biomedical research suggests a different tragedy, an "anti-commons" in which people underuse scarce resources because too many owners can block each other. Follow-on inventors may be confronted with obstacles raised by previous inventors, in terms of exclusive rights over knowledge or resources they might need to access. More patents may lead paradoxically to fewer useful products for improving human health.

Clearly, there are no simple conclusions on the optimal patent breadth. It is not necessarily optimal to protect the first innovation so broadly that every second-generation product infringes, nor so narrowly that a new product never infringes. In reality, an applicant usually wants to claim as much as he/she can, and then a patent office must decide what claims are allowable. While decisions regarding what to allow are constrained by a number of legal principles, and by the invention itself, in many cases a patent office has considerable room for discretion. Within that discretionary zone, the office must decide which claims should be admitted and which ones pruned back or rejected.

According to TRIPS, with some very limited exceptions, "patents shall be available for any inventions, whether products or processes, in all fields of technology, provided that they are new, involve an inventive step and are capable of industrial application" (TRIPS, 1994). However, under this general requirement, a national patent law can be flexible in recognizing what inventions can satisfy its standards for novelty, non-obviousness (an inventive step), and industrial applicability. For example, some inventions related to software or business methods are recognized as patents by the United States Patent and Trademark Office (USPTO), but they may be turned down by the Chinese Patent Office. This is due to the fact that Chinese patent examiners may interpret such inventions as lacking

---

31 R. Merges and R. Nelson, "On Limiting or Encouraging Rivalry in Technical Progress: The Effect of Patent Scope Decisions", *Journal of Economic Behaviour and Organization*, 25, 1994, pp. 1–24.

32 M. Heller and R. Eisenberg, "Can Patents Deter Innovation? The Anticommons in Biomedical Research", *Science*, 280, 1998, pp. 698–701.

industrial applicability or an inventive step according to Chinese Patent Law. Thus, we can see that patent breadth or scope is closely related to patentability requirements. Therefore, patentability requirements are an important and operational instrument for optimal patent design at a national level. However, there is a tendency to harmonize the substantive patent laws at an international level, which will further limit the discretionary power in patent examination in each nation.

One general conclusion we can draw is that different countries with different technological and economic strengths may treat differently the trade-off between promoting the diffusion of knowledge and rewarding innovators. For example, Sakakibara and Branstetter[33] find that before 1988 Japan had traditionally had a narrower patent scope than the United States since Japan had a comparative advantage on applied research and development.

Economic theories indicate that patents might be important incentives to induce private investment in producing new knowledge or knowledge-based products as new knowledge is non-rival and often non-excludable. To provide more empirical evidence on the role of patents in economic development, some economists try to empirically test the relationship between patents, trade and economic growth.

Basically, the protection strength of patents or other intellectual property rights (IPRs) affects international trade flows. If a nation strengthens its patent law, it could experience higher or lower imports. Foreign firms may face increasing net demand for their products due to strengthened patent protection, but they may also choose to raise their prices, often through a reduction of their sales in this nation's market. This is because of their greater market power in an imitation-safe environment. Maskus and Penubarti[34] find that strengthening patent protection has a positive impact on bilateral manufacturing imports into large developing economies, but a negative one on small ones. Fink and Primo Braga[35] further provide evidence regarding the effects of patent protection on international trade. They confirm a positive link between IPR protection and trade flows for

---

33 M. Sakakibara and L.G. Branstetter, "Do Stronger Patents Induce More Innovation? Evidence from the 1988 Japanese Patent Law Reforms", *RAND Journal of Economics*, 32, 1, 2001, pp. 77–100.

34 K.E. Maskus and M. Penubarti, "How Trade-Related are Intellectual Property Rights?" *Journal of International Economics*, 39, 1995, 227–48.

35 C. Fink and C.A. Primo Braga, "How Stronger Protection of Intellectual Property Rights Affects International Trade Flows", *World Bank Working Paper*, No. 2051, Washington, DC, the World Bank, 1999.

the aggregate of non-fuel trade, but do not find a significant positive relationship between IPR protection and high-technology trade flows.

Maskus[36] summarizes the predicted relationship between IPRs (here mainly referring to patents), foreign direct investment (FDI) and technology transfer. First, FDI and technology transfer are relatively insensitive to international differences in IPRs in sectors that have old products and standardized, labor-intensive technologies because FDI in those sectors is influenced more by factor costs, market sizes, trade costs, and other location advantages than by IP policies in this setting. Second, other things being equal, FDI that represents complex but easily copied technologies is likely to increase as IPRs are strengthened because patents, trademarks, and copyright increase the value of knowledge-based assets, which may be efficiently exploited through internalized organization. Third, to the extent that stronger IPRs reduce licensing costs, FDI could be displaced over time by efficient licensing. Finally, whatever the mode, the likelihood that the most advanced technologies will be transferred arises with the strength of IPRs. However, in reality, the transfer of high technologies may go well beyond the issue of intellectual property. National interests and politics may be the real block to the transfer of advanced technologies. For example, the United States has high-tech export restrictions on China.[37]

In fact, theoretical treatments of the effects of IPRs on technology diffusion bear mixed messages. In some cases, technology is transferred through imitation by firms in developing countries. When the global IPR system is strengthened by the adoption of minimum standards, imitation becomes more difficult as foreign patents are more seriously protected. The rate of imitation declines, and contrary to what might be expected, this decline slows down the global rate of innovation. If innovative firms expect slower loss of their technological advantages, they can earn higher profits per innovation, reducing the need to engage in R&D.[38] However,

---

36 K.E. Maskus, "The Role of Intellectual Property Rights in Encouraging Foreign Direct Investment and Technology Transfer", Prepared for the Conference Public-Private Initiatives After TRIPS: Designing a Global Agenda, Brussels, 1997.

37 Z. Shijian, "US High-tech Revival Blocks China's Industrial Climb", *Global Times*, 2 February 2012, http://www.globaltimes.cn/DesktopModules/DnnForge%20-%20NewsArticles/Print.aspx?tabid=99&tabmoduleid=94&articleId=694345&moduleId=405&PortalID=0 (accessed 17 January 2013); Z. Monan, "Relax High-tech Restrictions, *China Daily*, 8 May 2012, http://www.chinadaily.com.cn/opinion/2012–05/08/content_15231849.htm (accessed 17 January 2013).

38 J.A. Glass and K. Saggi, "Intellectual Property Rights and Foreign Direct Investment", *Journal of International Economics*, 56, 2, 2002, pp. 387–410;

this result is sensitive to model assumptions and may not hold up to alternative specifications. Indeed, Lai[39] finds that product innovation and technology diffusion are strengthened under tighter IPRs if production is transferred through FDI, rather than through imitation. However, we must be aware that this result is both country and model sensitive, which may be true for large FDI recipient countries, such as China, but may not hold for other countries.

The discussion so far has focused on a narrow interpretation of how IPRs influence foreign investment and technology transfer. However, strong protection of intellectual property rights plays a much larger role in signaling to potential investors. Because IP protection has taken on increasing importance to multinational enterprises, the adoption of stronger IP protection has become a primary device that governments in emerging economies take to indicate a shift toward a more business-friendly environment.[40] The objective is to attract more foreign investment through this signal. To date, there is little evidence supporting the responsiveness of investment to this signal, but in emerging economies there is a widespread and growing belief in its importance.

A few studies have investigated the impact of patent protection on cross-country economic growth. Gould and Gruben[41] estimate a growth model on a cross-section of up to 95 countries with data averaged over the period 1960–88, including an index measuring patent protection strength created by Rapp and Rozek[42] in their regression. They find patent protection has a significant positive impact on economic growth. Gould and Gruben[43] examine whether IP protection affects growth in open versus closed economies differently, by interacting their measure of IP protection

---

E. Helpman, "Innovation, Imitation, and Intellectual Property Rights", *Econometrica*, 61, 6, 1993, pp. 1247–80.

[39] E.L. Lai, "International Intellectual Property Rights Protection and the Rate of Product Innovation", *Journal of Development Economics*, 55, 1, 1998, pp. 133–53.

[40] K.E. Maskus, "The Role of Intellectual Property Rights in Encouraging Foreign Direct Investment and Technology Transfer", Prepared for the Conference Public-Private Initiatives After TRIPS: Designing a Global Agenda, Brussels, 1997.

[41] D.M. Gould and W.C. Gruben, "The Role of Intellectual Property Rights in Economic Growth", *Journal of Economic Development*, 48, 1996, pp. 323–50.

[42] R.T. Rapp and R.P. Rozek, "Benefits and Costs of Intellectual Property Protection in Developing Countries", *Journal of World Trade*, 24, 5, 1990, pp. 75–102.

[43] D.M. Gould and W.C. Gruben, "The Role of Intellectual Property Rights in Economic Growth", *Journal of Economic Development*, 48, 1996, pp. 323–50.

with three measures of a country's trade orientation. Their results suggest that IP protection can have a slightly larger impact on growth in open economies. Therefore, according to their findings, trade liberalization in combination with stronger IP protection enhances economic growth because it improves the competitive nature of markets and increases access to foreign technologies. However, this may also lead to displacement of local companies and even less economic growth.

Thompson and Rushing[44] estimate cross-section growth regressions, including 112 countries for the period 1970–85, and examine whether increased IP protection is more beneficial once a country has reached a particular level of development, as measured by initial GDP per capita. Their results indicate a break point at an initial level of $3,400 (1980 US dollars). For countries below this no relationship between IP protection and growth is found, but above it there exists a positive and significant relationship.

Thompson and Rushing[45] extend their analysis using a simultaneous equation model on a cross-section of 55 developed and developing countries over the period 1975–90. Their results once again suggest that patent protection only has a positive and significant impact upon total factor productivity (TFP) for the most advanced countries, with insignificant coefficients found for the full sample and the sample of developing countries.

Park and Ginarte[46] create an index of patent protection strength for 110 countries for the period 1960–90. The index is used to examine what factors or characteristics of economies determine how strongly patent rights will be protected. The evidence does indicate that more developed economies tend to provide stronger protection. But the underlying factors that influence patent protection levels are the country's level of research and development (R&D) activity, market environment, and international integration, which are correlated with its level of development. The results qualify, however, that R&D activity influences patent protection levels only after a nation's research sector reaches a critical size.

---

44 M. Thompson and F. Rushing, "An Empirical Analysis of the Impact of Patent Protection of Economic Growth", *Journal of Economic Development*, 21, 2, 1996, pp. 61–79.

45 M. Thompson, and F. Rushing, "An Empirical Analysis of the Impact of Patent Protection on Economic Growth: An Extension", *Journal of Economic Development*, 24, 1, 1999, pp. 67–76.

46 W.G. Park and J.C. Ginarte, "Determinants of Patent Rights: A Cross-National Study", *Research Policy*, 26, 1997, pp. 283–301.

Maskus and McDaniel[47] investigate empirically how the Japanese patent system has affected post-war growth in Japanese TFP. The post-war Japanese patent system before 1988 has been recognized as a mechanism for promoting technological catch-up and diffusion through incremental innovation. Given certain patent procedures, such as pre-grant disclosure, single-claim requirement, a first-to-file rule, and lengthy pendency periods, the Japanese patent system has enabled a channel of technology transfer through the application process. Maskus and McDaniel[48] find that technology diffusion through utility model applications had a positive impact on Japan's post-war productivity growth.

5 CONCLUSIONS AND POLICY SUGGESTIONS

The above overview of the patent system from the perspective of economics has underlined a series of practical issues that deserve policy makers' attention, especially for those in developing countries.

First, patent protection is a double-edge sword, with a positive and negative side. On the one hand, patents are effective in stimulating inventions, encouraging disclosure of new technologies, and facilitating market transactions over technologies, but on the other hand they may also generate costs to society partially due to the potential monopoly and barriers to free use of the patented technologies. Moreover, competitive rents, in the absence of patent protection, might be able to compensate innovators in certain circumstances. For instance, where first-mover advantages arising from seizing the market are important and the cost of imitation is high, patents may not be necessary to encourage such innovation. Generally speaking, an optimal patent system should be in a good balance between private and public interests.

Second, patentability requirements, such as novelty, non-obviousness, and industrial applicability, are important instruments to avoid the grant of unqualified patents that increase the social cost of the patent system. Moreover, strict application of such principles in patent examination is also an effective measure to prevent broad patent protection scope. However, there is some suggestion that this may deter further innovation and improvement.

---

[47] K.E. Maskus and C. McDaniel, "Impact of the Japanese Patent System on Productivity Growth", *Japan and the World Economy*, 11, 1999, pp. 557–74.

[48] K.E. Maskus and C. McDaniel, "Impact of the Japanese Patent System on Productivity Growth", *Japan and the World Economy*, 11, 1999, pp. 557–74.

Third, in the context of globalization, a nation often has limited leverage in making its own patent law and policy under TRIPS and other international patent agreements. For instance under trade-driven pressures of convergence, the statutory patent life must be at least 20 years and patent protection should cover almost all technologies, which may not be in the interests of most developing countries. It is important for developing countries to realize this point and cooperate with each other to collectively support their interests in international negotiations.

Fourth, econometric studies seem to support the theoretical importance of patent institution in promoting trade, attracting FDI, and facilitating technology transfer, including imports of goods at least under some conditions. However, the net impact on technology transfer to developing countries under the current international patent framework is still ambiguous and lacks concrete evidence.

Finally, cross-country analyses seem to show that intellectual property or patent protection has a positive and significant contribution to the economic growth in high-income countries, while for low- and middle-income countries, the net impact is ambiguous.

Therefore, in reality, the relationship between patents and economic development in developing countries is more complex than that in developed countries. In the short term, developing countries may suffer from being disadvantaged in filing competitive patents, and developed countries may take advantage of their technology advancement in securing their innovation and market power in developing countries. In the long term, it depends on many internal factors of developing countries, such as the size of internal market, domestic enterprises' competitiveness, and their government administration. Nonetheless, they have to learn fast and compete with multinational companies under an international framework that is in favor of stronger technology innovators.

REFERENCES

Arrow, K., "Economic Welfare and the Allocation of Resources for Invention", *NBER Chapters in the Rate and Direction of Inventive Activity: Economic and Social Factors*, National Bureau of Economic Research, 1962, pp. 609–26.

Boldrin, M. and Levine, D., "The Case Against Intellectual Property", *American Economic Review*, 92, 2, 2002, pp. 209–12.

Chang, H., "Patent Scope, Antitrust Policy, and Cumulative Innovation", *RAND Journal of Economics*, 26, 1, 1995, pp. 34–57.

Colombo, M.G. and Delmastro, M., "How Effective Are Technology Incubators? Evidence from Italy", *Research Policy*, 31, 2002, pp. 1103–22.

Cornelli, F. and Schankerman, M., "Patent Renewals and R&D Incentives", *RAND Journal of Economics*, 30, 2, 1999, p. 197.
Drahos, P., "Information Feudalism in the Information Society", *The Information Society*, 11, 1995, pp. 209–22.
Drahos, P. (ed.), *Intellectual Property*, England, Dartmouth Publishing Company Limited and USA, Ashgate Publishing Company, 1999.
Fink, C. and Primo Braga, C.A., "How Stronger Protection of Intellectual Property Rights Affects International Trade Flows", *World Bank Working Paper*, No. 2051, Washington, DC, The World Bank, 1999.
Glass, J.A. and Saggi, K., "Intellectual Property Rights and Foreign Direct Investment", *Journal of International Economics*, 56, 2, 2002, pp. 387–410.
Gould, D.M. and Gruben, W.C., "The Role of Intellectual Property Rights in Economic Growth", *Journal of Economic Development*, 48, 1996, pp. 323–50.
Green, J. and Scotchmer, S., "On the Division of Profits in Sequential Innovation", *RAND Journal of Economics*, 26, 1, 1995, pp. 20–33.
Heller, M. and Eisenberg, R., "Can Patents Deter Innovation? The Anticommons in Biomedical Research", *Science*, 280, 1998, pp. 698–701.
Helpman, E., "Innovation, Imitation, and Intellectual Property Rights", *Econometrica*, 61, 6, 1993, pp. 1247–80.
Idris, K., *Intellectual Property – A Powerful Tool for Economic Growth*, Geneva, World Intellectual Property Organization, 2003.
Lai, E.L., "International Intellectual Property Rights Protection and the Rate of Product Innovation", *Journal of Development Economics*, 55, 1, 1998, pp. 133–53.
Lanjouw, J., "Patent Value in the Shadow of Infringement: Simulation Estimations of Patent Value", *Review of Economic Studies*, 65, 1998, pp. 671–710.
Martin, S. and Scott, J.T., "The Nature of Innovation Market Failure and the Design of Public Support for Private Innovation", *Research Policy*, 29, 4–5, 2000, pp. 437–47.
Maskus, K.E., "The Role of Intellectual Property Rights in Encouraging Foreign Direct Investment and Technology Transfer", Prepared for the *Conference Public-Private Initiatives After TRIPS: Designing a Global Agenda*, Brussels, 1997.
Maskus, K.E. and McDaniel, C., "Impact of the Japanese Patent System on Productivity Growth", *Japan and the World Economy*, 11, 1999, pp. 557–74.
Maskus, K.E. and Penubarti, M., "How Trade-Related are Intellectual Property Rights?" *Journal of International Economics*, 39, 1995, pp. 227–48.
Matutes, C., Regibeau, P., and Rockett, K., "Optimal Patent Design and the Diffusion of Innovations", *RAND Journal of Economics*, 27, 1, 1996, pp. 60–83.
Merges, R. and Nelson, R., "On the Complex Economics of Patent Scope", *Columbia Law Review*, 90, 4, 1990, pp. 839–916.
Merges, R. and Nelson, R., "On Limiting or Encouraging Rivalry in Technical Progress: The Effect of Patent Scope Decisions", *Journal of Economic Behaviour and Organization*, 25, 1994, pp. 1–24.
Moir, H.V.J., "What are the Costs and Benefits of Patent Systems?", *Centre for Governance of Knowledge and Development Working Paper*, October, 2008.
Nordhaus, W., *Invention, Growth and Welfare: A Theoretical Treatment of Technological Change* (Cambridge, MA: MIT Press, 1969).
Pakes, A.S., "Patents as Options: Some Estimates of the Value of Holding European Patent Stocks", *Econometrica*, 54, 1986, pp. 755–84.

Park, W.G., and Ginarte, J.C., "Determinants of Patent Rights: A Cross-National Study", *Research Policy*, 26, 1997, pp. 283–301.

Posner, R., "Why There Are Too Many Patents in America", *The Atlantic*, 12 July 2012, http://www.theatlantic.com/business/archive/2012/07/why-there-are-too-many-patents-in-america/259725/ (accessed on 15 January 2013).

Rapp, R.T. and Rozek, R.P., "Benefits and Costs of Intellectual Property Protection in Developing Countries", *Journal of World Trade*, 24, 5, 1990, pp. 75–102.

Sakakibara, M. and Branstetter, L.G., "Do Stronger Patents Induce More Innovation? Evidence from the 1988 Japanese Patent Law Reforms", *RAND Journal of Economics*, 32, 1, 2001, pp. 77–100.

Schankerman, M., "How Valuable is Patent Protection? Estimates by Technology Field", *RAND Journal of Economics*, 29, 1998, pp. 77–107.

Schankerman, M. and Pakes, A., "Estimates of the Value of Patent Rights in European Countries during the Post-1950 Period", *Economic Journal*, 96, 1986, pp. 1052–77.

Scherer, F.M., "Nordhaus' Theory of Optimal Patent Life: A Geometric Reinterpretation", *American Economic Review*, 62, 3, 1972, pp. 422–7.

Scotchmer, S., "Standing on the Shoulders of Giants: Cumulative Research and the Patent Law", *Journal of Economic Perspective*, 5, 1, 1991, pp. 29–41.

UK Commission on IPR, "Integrating Intellectual Property Rights and Development Policy", The Commission on Intellectual Property Rights of the United Kingdom, 2002.

Thompson, M. and Rushing, F., "An Empirical Analysis of the Impact of Patent Protection of Economic Growth", *Journal of Economic Development*, 21, 2, 1996, pp. 61–79.

Thompson, M. and Rushing, F., "An Empirical Analysis of the Impact of Patent Protection on Economic Growth: An Extension", *Journal of Economic Development*, 24, 1, 1999, pp. 67–76.

Zhang, Monan, "Relax High-tech Restrictions", *China Daily*, 8 May 2012.

Zhou, Shijian, "US High-tech Revival Blocks China's Industrial Climb", *Global Times*, 2 February 2012.

5. Rethinking the role of the patent office from the perspective of responsive regulation

Peter Drahos[1]

1 INTRODUCTION

Patent offices, especially the world's largest patent offices, contribute to uncertainty. In 2011 almost 1 million patents were granted around the world, bringing the total number of patents in force to an estimated 7.88 million.[2] The hundreds of thousands of patents that are issued by patent offices every year produce a state of flux in the obligations of third parties in the marketplace. Each new patent generates exclusivity rights and corresponding obligations. Trade in these patents through assignment and licensing intensifies the flux. This flux generates uncertainty. The uncertainty has two basic sources. A company making product X cannot be sure that it has found all the patents relevant to product X in all the jurisdictions in which it is operating (completeness uncertainty) and, where it has found relevant patents, there are likely to be, at least for some patents, interpretive uncertainties – what does the patent cover and what does it not? Would the patent be upheld by a court? It is not only granted patents that are a source of uncertainty. Published patent applications also contribute (more than 2 million applications were filed worldwide in 2011).[3]

Uncertainty is no friend of property rights and efficiency. Mangling the poet Robert Frost's phrase one might say that 'good fences make good property rights'. Hayek describes law, liberty and property as being part of

---

[1] My thanks go to Fred Abbott, John Braithwaite, Carlos Correa and Konstantinos Karachalios for their constructive suggestions.

[2] World Intellectual Property Organization [WIPO], *World Intellectual Property Indicators*, Geneva, WIPO, 2012, p. 7.

[3] WIPO, *World Intellectual Property Indicators*, Geneva, WIPO, 2012, p. 6.

'an inseparable trinity'.[4] The task of law, as he saw it, was to draw boundaries using rules so that people would not interfere in each other's freedom and so could transact with each other with high certainty.[5] Hayek would probably be disappointed by the performance of today's patent system if he were to judge it by his goals of what law and property rights are meant to achieve.

Of course, there are efforts to deal with the uncertainty being generated by the world's patent systems. One only needs to spend a few minutes on the internet to realize there are many companies offering patent mapping or patent landscaping services. The World Intellectual Property Organization (WIPO) has started some patent mapping on important complex technologies such as vaccines for infectious diseases.[6] Where patent mapping reports are publicly available, they do reveal in detail the large scale of patenting going on. WIPO's report on vaccines revealed a group of almost 12,000 patent families (amounting to over 51,000 patents/published applications), with most of that activity taking place after the 1980s, in line with the general trend of increasing patent applications in the 1980s and 1990s.[7] There are clear limits to the usefulness of patent mapping. It may not resolve completeness uncertainty for a firm because patent applications may not contain vital information, thereby increasing their chances of not being found. One study of pharmaceutical patents in five developing countries found that a great proportion of pharmaceutical patents do not include the known generic name of the drug to which the patent relates in the title, abstract or claims.[8] Patent mapping also increases interpretive uncertainty (more patents to interpret). It also requires one to be able to manage complexity, meaning that one has to manage many component parts of a system.[9] In the US interesting business models have emerged in

---

4 F.A. Hayek, *Law, Legislation and Liberty*, London and New York, Routledge Classics, 2013, p. 102.

5 F.A. Hayek, *Law, Legislation and Liberty*, London and New York, Routledge Classics, 2013, p. 103.

6 WIPO, 'Patent Landscape Report on Vaccines for Selected Infectious Diseases', Geneva, WIPO, 2012, p. 20, http://www.wipo.int/export/sites/www/freepublications/en/patents/ (accessed 4 March 2013).

7 WIPO, 'Patent Landscape Report on Vaccines for Selected Infectious Diseases', Geneva, WIPO, 2012, p. 20, http://www.wipo.int/export/sites/www/freepublications/en/patents/ (accessed 4 March 2013).

8 See C. Correa, 'Pharmaceutical Innovation, Incremental Patenting and Compulsory Licensing', Research Paper No. 41, South Centre, Geneva, 2011, http://www.southcentre.org/index.php?option=com_content&view=article&id=1601%3Ap (accessed 8 April 2013).

9 I use the term complexity here to refer to systems in which there are many

response to patent uncertainty. The company RPX, for example, acquires patents from a variety of sources and then uses this portfolio to offer a protection service to its clients in exchange for an annual fee. In RPX's words, clients receive 'a license to every patent and patent right we own. We will never assert or litigate the patents in our portfolio'.[10] Companies like RPX exist because other companies developing products in complex technology fields such as information technology face patent landscapes involving thousands or tens of thousands of patents. A company like Apple or Google might see an advantage in paying for RPX's services because it removes some patents from circulation that might otherwise affect its product development strategies.

In this short chapter I want to focus on the part played by patent offices in the production of uncertainty and complexity. Clearly they play a crucial part since their decisions about patent applications determine the supply of patents to the market. More specifically, I want to ask and sketch answers to two questions. What ideal should guide a patent office when it comes to its regulatory duties? Is there a regulatory approach that can help implement this ideal?

2 THE PATENT SOCIAL CONTRACT

Elsewhere I have argued that the ideal that should guide patent offices is the patent social contract.[11] I do not want to repeat those arguments here, but for the purposes of answering my two questions I need to make the following points. The version of the patent social contract that I defend is the social value conception rather than the disclosure version. The patent applicant must deliver something of potential social value to society in exchange for which the applicant is entitled to a patent. Disclosure is not the essence of the bargain, innovation is. The not-so radical idea behind the patent social contract is that patents are meant to help society achieve higher levels of technological innovation than it otherwise would in the

---

known parts. This is a simple view of complexity and not to be confused with the application of complexity theory to social systems and institutions. For a discussion of the latter see J. McGlade and E. Garnsey, 'The Nature of Complexity', in McGlade, J., and Garnsey, E. (eds.), *Complexity and Co-Evolution: Continuity and Change in Socio-Economic Systems*, Cheltenham, UK and Northampton, MA, USA, Edward Elgar, 2006, p. 1.

[10] See http://www.rpxcorp.com/ (accessed 4 March 2013).

[11] P. Drahos, *The Global Governance of Knowledge: Patent Offices and their Clients*, Cambridge, Cambridge University Press, 2010.

absence of patents. We desire *technological* innovation because most of us believe it contributes to progress (I emphasize technological since there is considerable scepticism at present concerning the contribution of financial innovation to progress). Through the patent institution society is, as it were, contracting for a better future. That at any rate is the theory. As Chapter 4 in this volume by Haiyang Zhang shows, some economists are sceptical about whether in fact patent systems have lived up to this promise. Moreover, even if we have some evidence that a patent system has benefitted one or two countries it does not follow that it will benefit the more than 190 other countries in the world.

One of the chief virtues of focussing on the patent social contract is that it brings the role of a patent office into sharp focus. Under the contract, society deputizes the patent office to act on its behalf to ensure that the inventor upholds its end of the bargain and delivers something that is genuinely new in exchange for the grant of the monopoly. The patent office is society's agent and its primary obligations are towards society. Of course, these days most offices are funded out of the fees that they collect from patent applicants. But it does not follow from this that the terms of the patent social contract or the duties of the patent office under it are affected by the adoption of the user-pays principle. Pharmaceutical companies, for example, pay large fees to drug registration authorities when they submit medicines for marketing registration. But no-one can seriously argue that this in some way changes the obligations of a drug registration authority as an independent regulator when it comes to evaluating medicines for toxicity and efficacy. A widespread assumption of the regulation literature is that we achieve better regulatory outcomes when we have independent central banks, independent competition authorities, independent financial regulators and so on. In short, independence should be a primary virtue of regulators. Regulatory capture is generally seen as a bad thing.

We should also be clear that the patent office is a regulatory agency with regulatory powers. This is perhaps a description that is not applied often enough to patent offices. If we take as our starting point, as economists often do, the free market and ask whether it will optimally allocate resources to invention then, at least on some economic views, the answer is no.[12] Since invention information can usually be copied at less cost than its original costs of production, it follows it is better to be a copier than an originator. Under this logic everyone waits for everyone else to choose the role of originator, with the result that no-one so chooses. The patent

---

[12] For a discussion of this market failure view of the free market in the case of innovation see Chapter 4 by Haiyang Zhang in this volume.

system is a form of regulatory intervention designed to correct for this failure of the market. It is not the only form of regulatory intervention and moreover for some types of information discovery processes, such as those in basic science, the patent system has very little chance of working.[13]

Summing up, we can say that the patent office is chartered under the patent social contract to regulate markets in innovation, the overall regulatory goal being to increase innovation. As Carsten Fink points out in Chapter 2 in this volume and as is widely accepted, there is no simple linear relationship between intellectual property statistics and innovation. If a patent office has issued at the end of one year double the number of patents to residents compared to the previous year it does not mean that the country has become twice as innovative. The explanation for the doubling of the number of patents may be as prosaic as a change in the number of allowable claims per patent application. In fact, operating under a social contract in which it is intervening in innovation markets, a patent office should be aware of the possibility that by doubling the number of patents it may well be hampering innovation and so failing in its regulatory duty in much the same way as when an environmental regulator fails when it issues too many forestry logging permits, thereby damaging the forests it is obliged to protect. The basic point, which is perhaps not made often enough, is that the patent office is a regulator of the free market for innovation.

At this point in the argument someone might object that even if the patent office is a regulator it does not have the duties of a regulator. The task of a patent office, it might be argued, is simply to issue patents to the marketplace. The uses to which those patents might be put are not the affair of a patent office. We can label this view of the role of a patent office as 'some care, no responsibility'. Perhaps this objection might be accepted if the goal of a society was simply to increase the number of patents. But if the goal of society is to use the patent system to obtain more innovation then the duty of the patent office as a regulator is to consider the effects of a decision to continue intervening in the marketplaces of innovation through the supply of more and more patents. This is a direct responsibility under the patent social contract that the patent office cannot say belongs to other regulators such as a competition regulator. One can

---

[13] On the need for government to fund basic science see K. Arrow, 'Economic Welfare and the Allocation of Resources for Invention', in National Bureau of Economic Research, *The Rate and Direction of Inventive Activity*, NJ, Princeton University Press, 1962, p. 609, at p. 623. Prizes and contests have been much discussed by economists as a form of intervention. See S. Scotchmer, *Innovation and Incentives*, Cambridge, MA, The MIT Press, 2004, pp. 41–53.

draw a parallel here with the duty of a central bank regulator. Central banks have to make decisions about the supply of money, but they are not chartered for that purpose. Rather the goal of monetary policy has to do with the control of inflation and ultimately the financial stability and welfare of a country. Money supply is not a goal in itself but a means to a goal. No central bank would, for instance, continue to increase money supply irrespective of the impact on the market, unless it wanted to engineer a hyperinflation collapse of its economy. In a similar way, no patent office should say that its only task as a regulator is to issue more and more patents. Much like central banks, patent offices have to assess their market interventions with a great deal of care. Retreating into the splendid isolation of 'some care, no responsibility' is not an option for central banks and should not be one for patent offices.

The remainder of the chapter argues that responsive regulation offers a patent office some guidance as to how it might approach its regulatory task. My discussion is not intended to be exhaustive of the possibilities, but merely illustrative. Responsive regulation has been the most influential theory of the last two decades in regulatory scholarship and so it seems a worthwhile question to ask whether patent offices might gain something from it.[14] What follows is an analysis of what patent offices ought to do under the ideal of responsive regulation. As Fred Abbott observed in his comments on this chapter, much of what I argue for is a virtual antithesis of current trends. I am not especially optimistic about the capacity of patent offices to think creatively about reversing these trends. My study of patent offices revealed that they do not really have a conception of themselves as regulators with duties to the public. Instead I found that the main users of the system, multinational enterprises, were seen by offices as being their real clients. Of course, the heads of patent offices would probably strenuously deny that society had become invisible to their respective offices, but my study was more akin to a street life study in which I interviewed examiners and middle managers who spoke about the realities of the daily grind of meeting targets and quotas, as well as having to deal with pressures from attorneys anxious to secure patents for their clients. These kinds of conditions are breeding grounds for capitulation and capture.[15]

---

[14] The classic statement of the theory is I. Ayres and J. Braithwaite, *Responsive Regulation: Transcending the Deregulation Debate*, Oxford, Oxford University Press, 1992. For an account of the origins of the theory see J. Braithwaite, 'The Essence of Responsive Regulation', *UBC Law Review*, vol. 44, 2011, p. 475.

[15] J. Braithwaite, *Regulatory Capitalism: How It Works, Ideas for Making it Work Better*, Cheltenham, Edward Elgar, 2008, p. 134.

This does raise the question of what might lead to the kind of responsive institutionalism for innovation that I develop in this chapter (depicted in Figure 5.1 at the end of this chapter). This is a question about regulatory change, indeed global regulatory change that is well beyond the scope of my present analysis. But if significant change is to come to the patent system it will most probably be generated by a perceived pattern of crisis that gains a significant level of public recognition. Crisis and anxious mass publics have been recurrently important factors in globalizing new regulatory models. Often the crisis has been a single event such as the *Titanic*, Chernobyl, Bhophal, the *Torrey Canyon*, or a financial crash, but a pattern of regulatory failure can also bring mass concern into play, as shown by the influence of Rachel Carson's *Silent Spring* and Ralph Nader's *Unsafe at Any Speed*.[16] Over its history the patent system, which is meant to generate new knowledge as a public good, has been linked to some major public 'bads' – its adverse impact on free trade in the nineteenth century, its link to oligopoly market power that led to strong competition law responses beginning in the US and more recently its impact on innovation and various access problems, most notably access to medicines.[17] Public concern has impacted on the patent regime in the context of access to medicines, but for the most part the public 'bads' to which the system has been linked remain a matter of technical discussion, analysis and debate. More will be needed to capture public interest than debates over how to best estimate the social returns from the patent system. For the time being the system will lurch on in the direction of incremental reform under the watchful eye of the powerful industrial groups that have colonized the policy reform process.

Before moving on to discuss responsive regulation in more detail, the next section offers some brief observations about the implications for emerging markets of analysing a patent office's decisions as a form of regulatory intervention.

---

[16] J. Braithwaite and P. Drahos, *Global Business Regulation*, Cambridge, Cambridge University Press, 2000, p. 500.

[17] The literature on these topics is vast. For overviews see H.V.J. Moir, *Patent Policy and Innovation: Do Legal Rules Deliver Effective Economic Outcomes*, Cheltenham, UK, Edward Elgar, 2013; G. Ghidini, *Innovation, Competition and Consumer Welfare in Intellectual Property Law*, Cheltenham, UK, Edward Elgar, 2010; M. Boldrin and D.K. Levine, *Against Intellectual Property*, Cambridge University Press, 2008; A.B. Jaffe and J. Lerner, *Innovation and Its Discontents: How Our Broken Patent System Is Endangering Innovation and Progress and What To Do About It*, Princeton University Press, 2004.

3 PATENT OFFICES IN EMERGING MARKETS

Independent regulators are usually seen as producing better decisions than captured ones. If we look at the history of central banking, the evolution of independence of central banks from private and political control is one of the great achievements of twentieth century financial regulation.[18] Central banks have their origins in private entities that eventually became independent public institutions.[19] As mentioned above, my study of patent offices suggests that many developing country offices do not fit the mould of the independent regulator. Rather they are unduly influenced in their decision-making by a combination of the Trilateral Offices (the US Patent and Trademark Office, the European Patent Office and the Japanese Patent Office) and big business. An argument for the independence of a patent office should not be construed as an argument against cooperation. Cooperation amongst patent offices on matters such as data collection, information exchange and transparency of the patent system is important. The history of central banking is full of examples of the virtues of cooperation.[20] But the central banking story does suggest that it has to be cooperation amongst regulators with some scope for autonomous decision-making. One priority for all developing country governments should be to assess the independence of their patent offices.

Another priority for emerging markets should be to avoid buying into trade agreements that formally constrain the independence of their respective patent offices. The Agreement on Trade-Related Aspects of Intellectual Property Rights 1994 (TRIPS) leaves a government with considerable scope to preserve the autonomy of its patent office and therefore to regulate patent supply to innovation markets. TRIPS does not define invention, set a level of inventive step to be followed, prescribe a standard of usefulness, require a patent office to eliminate proven patent-quality-improving procedures such as pre-grant opposition, interfere in procedural innovation by a patent office or require a patent office to follow the decisions of another office on patent applications. However, bilateral agreements, as well as the

---

18 On the importance of this to financial regulation see J. Braithwaite and P. Drahos, *Global Business Regulation*, Cambridge, Cambridge University Press, 2000, ch. 8.

19 R.N. Cooper, 'Almost a Century of Central Bank Cooperation', *BIS Working Paper*, 198, 2006, p. 3, http://econpapers.repec.org/paper/bisbiswps/198.htm (accessed 8 April 2013).

20 For a discussion see R.N. Cooper, 'Almost a Century of Central Bank Cooperation', *BIS Working Paper*, 198, 2006, http://econpapers.repec.org/paper/bisbiswps/198.htm (accessed 8 April 2013).

work of the Trilateral Offices behind the scenes, are beginning to probe and constrain these areas of autonomous decision-making (see Chapter 15 by Mohammed El Said in this volume). Persistent global financial instability is seeing emerging markets begin to explore the logic of decoupling themselves from the effects of Western regulatory prescriptions for dealing with this instability. Part of this logic seems to be deepening cooperation amongst themselves (see Chapter 6 by Padmashree Gehl Sampath and Pedro Roffe this volume), as well as creating new institutions of cooperation such as the decision to establish a BRICS development bank.[21] This same decoupling logic should be applied by developing countries to looking at the implications of trade agreements for the regulatory autonomy of their patent offices. Independent central banks have proven crucial to helping the major developing countries cope with financial crises that originated in the US and EU. Developing countries should also be doing what they can to guard (or in some cases recapture) the independence of their patent offices.

4 RESPONSIVE REGULATION

Responsiveness as an ideal in law goes back at least to the tradition of legal realism.[22] The American Realists argued that legal institutions should be more responsive to both the diversity of social interests and the changing nature of those interests. The path to responsiveness was seen to lie in systems of legal decision-making that were more open to knowledge, and driven by purposes and outcomes rather than the formalistic reproduction of rules. A responsive law system 'perceives social pressures as sources of knowledge and opportunities for self-correction'.[23] Responsive regulation adopts the ideal of responsiveness. Epistemologically it is committed to working towards a greater knowledge and understanding of the business cultures it seeks to regulate.[24] Contextual understanding is crucial because the guiding idea of responsive regulation is that a regulator should assess

---

[21] See 'BRICS Bank Will Complement Other Multilateral Lenders: P. Chidambaram', *The Economic Times*, 1 April 2013, http://articles.economictimes.indiatimes.com/2013-04-01/news/38189713_1_brics-bank-asian-development-bank-world-bank.

[22] P. Nonet and P. Selznick, *Law and Society in Transition: Toward Responsive Law*, New York, Harper and Row, 1978, pp. 73–4.

[23] P. Nonet and P. Selznick, *Law and Society in Transition: Toward Responsive Law*, New York, Harper and Row, 1978, p. 77.

[24] J. Braithwaite, 'Responsive Regulation and Developing Economies', *World Development*, vol. 34, no. 5, 2006, p. 884, at p. 885.

how well actors are regulating themselves before it intervenes. Responsive regulation, however, does not defer to self-regulation. Nor is it driven by a rule-punishment model (if A breaches rule X then punishment Y). Instead it focuses on a set of regulatory options that will maximize the chance of A complying with rule X. These options such as self-regulation, deterrent penalties and punishment are well known, but what is distinctive about responsive regulation is its sequencing of these options in the form of a regulatory pyramid.[25]

The key idea behind the pyramid is that punishment and persuasion should be linked in a certain sequence that always begins with persuasion at the base of the pyramid and ends with the most punitive sanction at the apex of the pyramid. The assumption that lies behind this escalation sequence is that there are different actor types – rational, virtuous, irrational or incompetent. Dialogue will work with a virtuous actor, but not necessarily a rational actor that calculates compliance in cost-benefit terms. With such actors a regulator will have to resort to a level of deterrence that makes non-compliant behaviour too risky.

Located at the base of the pyramid are the tools of dialogue and persuasion (for example, guidelines, protocols and educational strategies). At this level of the pyramid actors are assumed to want to do the 'right thing'. As one moves up the pyramid, the tools of regulation begin to assume a more coercive character until, at the top of the pyramid, there is some form of incapacitation (this depends on the area of regulation but may involve imprisonment, suspension of trade, loss of licence and so on). Where the regulator is unsuccessful at the bottom of the pyramid, he or she can move up the pyramid to deploy more coercive tools. There is a presumption in favour of a regulator starting at the bottom of the pyramid with dialogic tools, even when dealing with serious breaches.[26]

A straightforward application of this classic enforcement pyramid model by a patent office would be to presumptively trust the information it received from a patent applicant, but then begin a process of escalation to other levels of the pyramid once it had suspicions that the applicant was gaming the system. One of the problems is that patent office procedures do allow applicants a lot of scope for manoeuvring. Still there is no reason why patent offices could not be much more active in using the various levels of an enforcement pyramid such as audits and the use of outside

---

25 J. Braithwaite, *Restorative Justice and Responsive Regulation*, Oxford, Oxford University Press, 2002, pp. 30–31.

26 J. Braithwaite, *Restorative Justice and Responsive Regulation*, Oxford, Oxford University Press, 2002, p. 30.

experts as a check on this manoeuvring, even in cases where they were unsuccessful in obtaining procedural reform.

Responsive regulation is a theory that has over the last two decades been refined through analysis and debate by scholars and practitioners, as well as through its adoption by regulatory agencies.[27] It has moved well beyond its origins in business regulation and enforcement to become a more generalized theory of regulation and governance that moves beyond the enforcement pyramid and compliance into deeper questions about how to achieve broader regulatory purpose, how regulatory learning takes place, and the links between institutional integrity and regulation.[28] It has become a theory of responsive institutionalism. In the section that follows I want to draw in particular on the approach of networked pyramidal governance that has emerged from an integration of responsive regulation with theories of networked governance in order to sketch a model of responsive institutionalism for innovation.[29]

5 THE PATENT OFFICE AS A RESPONSIVE REGULATOR

Unlike many regulatory agencies, a patent office does not have responsibility for a specific industry (as do, for example, mining inspectorates,

---

27 For the history see J. Braithwaite, 'The Essence of Responsive Regulation', *UBC Law Review*, vol. 44, 2011, p.475.

28 Examples of works that have moved it in this direction are J. Braithwaite, *Restorative Justice and Responsive Regulation*, Oxford, Oxford University Press, 2002; J. Braithwaite, *Markets in Vice, Markets in Virtue*, Australia, Federation Press, 2005; J. Braithwaite, T. Makkai and V. Braithwaite, *Regulating Aged Care: Ritualism and the New Pyramid*, Cheltenham, UK and Northampton, MA, USA, Edward Elgar, 2007; and V. Braithwaite, *Defiance in Taxation and Governance: Resisting and Dismissing Authority in a Democracy*, Cheltenham, UK and Northampton, MA, USA, Edward Elgar, 2009.

29 For this line of development see P. Drahos, 'Intellectual Property and Pharmaceutical Markets: A Nodal Governance Approach', *Temple Law Review*, vol. 77, 2004, p.401; S. Burris, P. Drahos and C. Shearing, 'Nodal Governance', *Australian Journal of Legal Philosophy*, vol. 30, 2005, p.30; J. Braithwaite, 'Responsive Regulation and Developing Economies', *World Development*, vol. 34, no. 5, 2006, p.884; P. Drahos, 'A Networked Responsive Regulatory Approach to Protecting Traditional Knowledge', in Gervais, D. (ed.), *Intellectual Property, Trade and Development: Strategies to Optimize Economic Development in a TRIPS Plus Era*, Oxford, Oxford University Press, 2007, p.385; and J. Braithwaite, T. Makkai and V. Braithwaite, *Regulating Aged Care: Ritualism and the New Pyramid*, Cheltenham, UK and Northampton, MA, USA, Edward Elgar, 2007, pp.315–17.

food standards agencies or media regulators). Much like a tax regulator, a patent office deals with many industries. These days it is hard to think of an industry unaffected by patents simply because high technology techniques are applied to most areas of primary production whether it is mining or the growing of food. A patent office does not supervise or regularly inspect companies for compliance with particular standards in the way, for example, chemical companies are inspected for compliance with safety and environmental standards. Nor does the patent office investigate companies in the manner of a corporate and securities regulator. The principal regulatory function of a patent office is to make patent supply decisions about various innovation markets. Its role, as I suggested earlier, can be likened to that of a central bank making decisions about money supply. As a regulator of innovation markets, a patent office is not faced by a compliance problem, but rather by an information and intervention problem. It has to have information about the aggregated effects of its interventions in various markets. This task is dynamic and continuously complex.

Patent offices through the very nature of their operations generate a selection bias. Those who want patents for their inventions go to a patent office and those who do not want patents do not. It is easy to assume from the number of patent applications coming to the major patent offices that innovation depends on patents. Under the patent social contract, the patent office's obligation is to help society make innovation gains. Decisions not to grant patents are just as important in the quest for innovation gains as are decisions to grant patents. The first principle of responsive regulation for a patent office operating under the patent social contract properly construed is to be an active gatherer of information about innovation markets.

Under the ideal of responsiveness, the principle of information gathering entails developing a process of organizational learning about the effects of patents on communities or networks of innovation that do not use patents. A patent office gathering information solely from patent-intensive networks of innovation simply compounds its problem of selection bias in learning about innovation. An example of where an innovation market can work without patents and did so for several decades before IBM led it into the patent era is the case of software.[30] The free revealing of technological information is a practice that even owners of large patent portfolios engage in at various times.[31] For example, Novartis, the Broad

---

[30] P. Drahos with J. Braithwaite, *Information Feudalism: Who Owns the Knowledge Economy?*, London, Earthscan, 2002, p. 170.

[31] For a discussion of free revealing in the innovation literature and its

Institute and Lund University announced the completion of a genome-wide map of genetic differences in humans and their relationship to type 2 diabetes in February of 2007 and made the results available to the global research community.[32] A responsive patent office would look carefully at cases where its grant of patents might affect innovation networks operating on the basis of free or largely free revealing. There is an obvious efficiency argument for not adversely affecting free revealing – information once in existence can be distributed at zero or marginal cost.

How might a patent office implement the principle of information gathering? One critical point here is that patent offices need to break away from a consultation model in which critics of patents are given a ritualistic hearing and then it is back to business as usual for offices.[33] Responsive regulation in this context means continuous engagement with and listening to those who can provide information about what is happening in innovation markets. This probably means establishing permanent working parties with a broad membership that well and truly moves beyond the usual suspects (patent attorneys, multinational patent owners and scientists or others who gain personally from patents) in certain crucial innovation markets such as biotechnology, clean energy technologies, nanotechnology, pharmaceuticals, software and so on. The Free Software movement is an example of a community that can provide patent offices with information about the effects of patents in the information technology market. Working parties on innovation markets would increase the information gathering capacity of an office and it would reduce the danger of regulatory capture, especially if standard protections against capture such as rotating memberships and public reporting are applied.

Establishing working groups in crucial innovation markets is one way in which a patent office can draw in networks to better manage the complex intervention problem that it faces. There are at least two other ways in which it can make use of networked governance to improve its performance as a responsive intervener. The first lies in forging networks of greater cooperation with other regulators and the second is to network pyramidal governance.

---

application to biotechnology see J. Hope, *Biobazaar: the Open Source Revolution and Biotechnology*, Cambridge, MA, Harvard University Press, 2008.

32 The data is available at http://www.broadinstitute.org/diabetes (accessed 4 March 2013).

33 On the dangers of participatory ritualism in regulation see J. Braithwaite, T. Makkai and V. Braithwaite, *Regulating Aged Care: Ritualism and the New Pyramid*, Cheltenham, UK and Northampton, MA, USA, Edward Elgar, 2007, ch. 7.

For a patent office important information about the uses and abuses of patents might come from other regulatory authorities. A good example of why it is important for a patent office to establish cooperative network relationships with a wide range of regulators comes from the field of tax. The use of patents in tax strategies has become a major problem for states.[34] For example, in the US the Republican Senator Chuck Grassley introduced a legislative provision to prevent corporations from 'reducing their tax bill by hundreds of millions of dollars each year by taking intellectual property of little to no value and donating it to a charity'.[35] A much greater problem has been the use of intellectual property rights in transfer pricing games by multinationals. The sale or licensing of intellectual property rights is used to shift income from high tax jurisdictions to low tax jurisdictions. The scale of the problem has grown in magnitude. In the US, the Senate Permanent Subcommittee on Investigation, which has been examining the problem for several years, reported in detail on Microsoft's transfer of intellectual property assets to subsidiaries in Puerto Rico, Ireland and Singapore.[36] The Puerto Rico transfer game saw US$21 billion shifted for a saving of $US4.5 billion in US taxes.[37] In the Irish transfer pricing game Microsoft transferred intellectual property to a Microsoft entity in Dublin that in 2011 reported profits of $4.3 billion on which it paid an effective tax rate of 7.3%. This worked out to a profit of $11 million per employee in this small Dublin office, a quite astonishing case of labour productivity.[38]

The issues are technical, but a basic problem for tax offices is that

---

[34] Something that Drahos and Braithwaite warned about. See P. Drahos with J. Braithwaite, *Information Feudalism: Who Owns the Knowledge Economy?*, London, Earthscan, 2002, p. 88.

[35] See American Jobs Creation Act of 2004, Public Law 108–357, 22 October 2004. Details are to be found at http://www.finance.senate.gov/newsroom/ranking/release/?id=83f6b20e-3327-4619-8b92-36ce643ef5fe (accessed 3 March 2013).

[36] The Microsoft case study is to be found in United States Senate Permanent Subcommittee on Investigations, 'Exhibit: Hearing on Offshore Profit Shifting and the U.S. Tax Code', 20 September 2012, pp. 19–23, http://www.hsgac.senate.gov/subcommittees/investigations/hearings/offshore-profit-shifting-and-the-us-tax-code (accessed 3 March 2013).

[37] United States Senate Permanent Subcommittee on Investigations, 'Exhibit: Hearing on Offshore Profit Shifting and the U.S. Tax Code', 20 September 2012, p. 2, http://www.hsgac.senate.gov/subcommittees/investigations/hearings/offshore-profit-shifting-and-the-us-tax-code (accessed 3 March 2013).

[38] United States Senate Permanent Subcommittee on Investigations, 'Exhibit: Hearing on Offshore Profit Shifting and the U.S. Tax Code', 20 September 2012, p. 11, http://www.hsgac.senate.gov/subcommittees/investigations/hearings/offshore-profit-shifting-and-the-us-tax-code (accessed 3 March 2013).

applying the principle of arm's length pricing to cross-border licensing transactions by multinationals involving intellectual property rights in the core technologies of those multinationals (generally patents) is difficult because, unlike in the case of common goods and services, finding comparable prices for those transactions is much harder.[39] Of course, the fact that these transactions involve many complex patents makes it difficult for tax offices to understand these arrangements in the first place. The networked governance version of responsive regulation recognizes that a regulator in managing systems complexity will need network partners that have information and capacities that the regulator does not have. Individual regulators are themselves part of complex systems (innovation systems, health systems, environmental systems etc.) about which they cannot have information omniscience. They confront a reality of nested complexity in which subnational, national, regional and global systems interact in a multitude of ways. For individual regulators the goal is to identify actors that have the best information about the particular problems that face the regulator. Staying with the example of patents and transfer pricing problems, it is clear that tax offices need patent offices as part of a tax office network aimed at disentangling transfer pricing arrangements. Some tax offices such as the Danish and UK offices have realized this and have begun to develop closer links with their respective patent offices.[40]

Tax offices clearly need patent offices, but equally patent offices need tax offices. As a responsive intervener in innovation, a patent office should be concerned to ensure that its supply of patents to innovation markets stimulates innovation and not tax strategizing. Information from a tax office about the uses to which individual multinationals are putting granted patents becomes a reason for a patent office to target the quality of its work not just in that sector, but with respect to particular multinationals. If, for example, patents are too easy to obtain, allowing a multinational to patent every minor step, then this simply increases the options for a multinational to use patents to move its income to offshore

---

[39] For a discussion of the technical issues see Written Testimony of William J. Jilkins, IRS Chief Counsel, accompanied by Michael Danilack IRS Deputy Commissioner (International) of the Large Business & International Division before the Senate Committee on Homeland Security and Governmental Affairs, Permanent Subcommittee on Investigations, Hearing on the Shifting of Profits Offshore by U.S. Multinational Corporations, 20 September 2012, http://www.hsgac.senate.gov/subcommittees/investigations/hearings/offshore-profit-shifting-and-the-us-tax-code (accessed 3 March 2013).

[40] OECD, *Dealing Effectively with the Challenges of Transfer Pricing*, Paris, OECD Publishing, 2012, p.23, http://dx.doi.org/10.1787/9789264169463-en (accessed 3 March 2013).

jurisdictions of tax convenience. In fact it would seem that patent offices have done more than their fair share over the last decade to assist multinationals (their most regular clients) in transfer pricing strategies. A study by JP Morgan reported the following:

> Many multinationals appear to be centralizing many of their valuable IP [intellectual property] assets in low-tax jurisdictions. The reality is that IP rights are easily transferred from jurisdiction to jurisdiction, and they are often inherently difficult to value.[41]

One might have added to the last sentence the words 'but easy to get'. It is not only multinationals in the information technology business that take advantage of patent-enabled transfer pricing games. Patent licensing strategies that allow companies to wash licences through low tax jurisdictions are invaluable to multinational pharmaceutical companies that would simultaneously like to present governments with high prices for pharmaceutical products but low profits for tax purposes.[42] Patents have become an integral part of a win-win game for pharmaceutical companies in which they obtain high product prices from governments but pay low taxes.

So far I have been suggesting that a responsive patent office should utilize network governance in various ways to increase its information about an innovation system before intervening in it with patent supply decisions. Although a patent office does not enforce the patents it issues, as an intervener in complex systems it can structure its decisions about intervention following the sequencing principles of pyramidal governance. Where, for example, it received information from a tax office about the persistent use of patents in transfer pricing strategies, it could target those companies and patent attorney firms responsible for using patents in this way for special attention. At the bottom of the pyramid, the first step would be warnings to these companies and their attorneys that their applications would now come in for special scrutiny. Special examinations teams could be formed to target applications from these companies. There is no reason why a patent office could not bring in outside experts to help in assessing these applications to make sure they really did meet the criteria of patentability. The concentrated use of resources in the form

---

[41] JP Morgan, 'Global Tax Rate Makers' (2012), cited in United States Senate Permanent Subcommittee on Investigations, 'Exhibit: Hearing on Offshore Profit Shifting and the U.S. Tax Code', 20 September 2012, p.9, http://www.hsgac.senate.gov/subcommittees/investigations/hearings/offshore-profit-shifting-and-the-us-tax-code (accessed 3 March 2013).

[42] This was pointed out to me by John Braithwaite.

of special teams to focus on crucial sectors is a strategy that has paid dividends for tax offices and could be used to much greater effect by patent offices.[43] The end game here for a patent office is to be pitching its smart networks against the smart networks of the multinationals that are using the system. Patent offices that rely on individual busy examiners rushing to meet quotas to make the call on patent applications will be intervening in innovation in ways that are deeply sub-optimal.

Ultimately, however, the pyramidal escalation by a patent office will not serve to improve the regulation of innovation unless a patent office is using the standards of patentability to target innovation as opposed to standards that lock in the roll out of more and more patents. A patent office in making patent supply decisions is engaged in standards-based regulation. The European Patent Office, for example, has to decide the inventive step requirement by reference to what is or is not 'obvious to a person skilled in the art'.[44] There are many examples of patent statutes conferring regulatory discretion through standards whether it is where to draw the line between discovery and invention, the application of the morality criterion, what it is to industrially apply an invention, whether a patent application has been sufficiently disclosed and so on. A patent office can only carry out its tasks as a regulator under the patent social contract using standards. It seems unlikely, for example, that a legislature can issue drafting instructions for rules codifying what is obvious to a skilled chemist that would have much relevance in a decade or two. When a regulator has to intervene on society's behalf in a complex system such as innovation, then standards linked to a clear view of societal purpose are the only feasible form of guidance for a regulator.

As Geertrui Van Overwalle argues in Chapter 16 in this book, patent offices have to 'revitalize' their 'vertical regulatory function'. If we go back to the core idea of responsiveness in law, it is about learning from social pressures and this by implication requires open organizational forms capable of detecting, analysing and responding to those pressures. Responsive intervention into a complex system requires a regulator to have open systems of information gathering, to be engaged in a creative process of finding ways to connect with the social pressures that form the basis of learning and opportunities for self-correction. The ideal of responsiveness requires a patent office, as a first step, to come to some genuine

---

[43] For a description of how tax offices have re-organized themselves to meet the challenges of transfer pricing see OECD, *Dealing Effectively with the Challenges of Transfer Pricing*, Paris, OECD Publishing, 2012, ch. 7, http://dx.doi.org/10.1787/9789264169463-en (accessed 3 March 2013).

[44] See Article 56 of the European Patent Convention.

understanding of innovation markets and networks of innovation. But the selection bias I mentioned earlier impoverishes the knowledge base of patent offices about innovation. One approach that I covered previously is for an office to constitute permanent working groups on innovation populated not by those few who gain from patents but by those capable of genuine reflective debate about the state of innovation in their particular technological area. These groups could help a patent office align standards of patentability, the inventive step standard in particular, with what technological communities in various sectors understand to be genuine innovation. This, of course, remains a pipe-dream. The major offices spend the bulk of their time servicing the needs of their multinational clientele, discussing ways in which to reduce the backlog of patent applications and speed up the granting of more and more patents. So, for example, they dream up fast-tracking initiatives for 'green' patent applications, not asking whether in fact their decision to increase patent supply to markets such as those in renewable energy will actually speed up innovation or diffusion of innovation in those markets.[45] Their assumption is always that more patents equal more innovation.

Pyramidal regulation has used theories of networked and nodal governance to articulate a partnership principle of regulation.[46] In deploying an enforcement pyramid, a regulator should look to network with partners who have information and capacities that the regulator does not. This part of responsive regulation was developed to answer the criticism that regulators, especially in developing countries, face capacity deficits of various kinds.[47] For example, a tax regulator in a developing country may not have the capacity to identify sophisticated tax evasion schemes, but it can help overcome that deficit by enrolling the aid of a large accounting firm like a KPMG or a Deloitte. As it happens, even well-resourced tax regulators have recognized how important external partners are to improving their regulatory capacity.[48]

---

[45] For a discussion of these initiatives see A. Dechezleprêtre, *Fast-tracking Green Patent Applications: An Empirical Analysis*, Geneva, Switzerland, ICTSD Programme on Innovation, Technology and Intellectual Property; Issue Paper No. 37; International Centre for Trade and Sustainable Development, 2013, http://ictsd.org (accessed 3 March 2013).

[46] J. Braithwaite, 'The Essence of Responsive Regulation', *UBC Law Review*, vol. 44, 2011, p. 475 at p. 476.

[47] J. Braithwaite, 'Responsive Regulation and Developing Economies', *World Development*, vol. 34, no. 5, 2006, p. 884 at pp. 889–94.

[48] OECD, *Dealing Effectively with the Challenges of Transfer Pricing*, Paris, OECD Publishing, 2012, ch. 7, http://dx.doi.org/10.1787/9789264169463-en (accessed 3 March 2013).

Networked pyramidal regulation recognizes the truth that regulatory capacity is not just a capacity of state agencies but is widely scattered amongst business and civil society actors of all kinds. It also builds on the insight of the early work on the tightly woven social networks that render apparently large worlds small – only a small number of steps are required to enrol strength to compensate for weakness.[49]

Patent offices have experimented with the partnership principle of regulation, a good example being the Peer to Patent pilot program begun by the USPTO in 2007.[50] Other patent offices such as the Australian, Japanese and UK offices also developed similar pilots.[51] The basic idea was that volunteer experts would have the opportunity to review patent applications placed on a website, posting any prior art they thought that a patent examiner should take into account in assessing the application. Responsive regulation would see this as first steps in the right direction. The idea of citizen experts being engaged in an assessment of innovation is in keeping with the separation of powers principle that underpins much of the deeper normative dimensions of responsive regulation and turns it into a theory of responsive institutionalism. The key, however, is whether patent offices will embrace the transformative potential of a model like peer to patent and this, as I have argued, depends on how they construe their duty under the patent social contract. A good start would be to rename these programs Peer to Innovation.

A responsive patent office would under the partnership principle look to engage with partners who could help it not to interfere in innovation initiatives that were flourishing without patents. For example, if an organization like the International Maize and Wheat Improvement Center (more generally referred to under its Spanish acronym, CIMMYT[52]) launches an open access initiative for bio-assets that it holds because it takes the view that this will speed up the innovation cycle, then a responsive patent office would look to make CIMMYT a network partner.[53] The goal of the partnership would be to make sure that any patents issued by the patent

---

49 The classic study is J. Travers and S. Milgram, 'An Experimental Study of the Small World Problem', *Sociometry*, vol. 32, no. 4, 1969, p. 425.

50 See http://www.uspto.gov/patents/init_events/peerpriorartpilotindex.jsp (accessed 4 March 2013). A second one-year pilot was started in 2010. There appear to be no further pilots planned.

51 Details of these can be found at http://www.peertopatent.org.au/main/aboutp2p (accessed 4 March 2013), http://www.iip.or.jp/e/e_p2pj/ (accessed 3 March 2013) and http://www.ipo.gov.uk/peertopatent.htm (accessed 4 March 2013).

52 Centro Internacional de Mejoramiento de Maíz y Trigo.

53 The initiative is called 'Seeds of Discovery'. See http://seedsofdiscovery.org/seed/how-we-work/sharing-bio-assets-and-benefits/.

office complemented the goals of the open access project – minimizing the possibility of IP claims in order to maximize the freedom to breed in the case of CIMMYT.

Projects like CIMMYT's Seeds of Discovery are public goods that ultimately depend on acts of trust for their successful constitution. If the scientists who contribute to these open access initiatives see others being able to capture private benefits from their contributions with relatively little effort because patent offices are making it easy to obtain patents, then it is a safe prediction that those scientists will stop contributing to those public initiatives. Open access databases are public goods that depend profoundly on social assets such as trust and volunteerism. Individuals have to volunteer their time to make contributions to the databases, others have to check those contributions for quality and yet others have to review the operation of the database if it is to become a genuinely useful public good. A patent office that presides over an irresponsible proliferation of patents that disrupts the social assets on which public good initiatives depend robs the society it is meant to serve.

A responsive patent office would find no shortage of network partners to help it understand the dynamics of innovation and the role of open access principles in those dynamics. The concerns about the impact of patents on science and innovation have been there for some time.[54] But some scientists have started to take practical steps to try and connect the patent system to the goal of innovation. One such initiative led by the molecular biologist Richard Jefferson focuses on the design of algorithms that will bring a global and freely available public transparency to the patent system instead of the pay-per-window transparency that feeds the patent information industry.[55]

6 CONCLUSION

The real world costs of the patent system continue to mount. Some economists have come to the conclusion it is time to do away with the system, but real world politics will keep this idea confined to scholarly corridors for a

[54] See The Royal Society, *Keeping Science Open: The Effects of Intellectual Property Policy on the Conduct of Science*, London, 2003 and more recently The Royal Society, *Science as an Open Enterprise*, London, 2012, http://royalsociety.org/policy/projects/ (accessed 3 March 2013).

[55] Described as the 'Lens' (formerly the 'Patent Lens') it is an 'open resource to serve innovation cartography'. At the moment it covers some 90 jurisdictions. See http://lens.org/lens/ (accessed 4 March 2013).

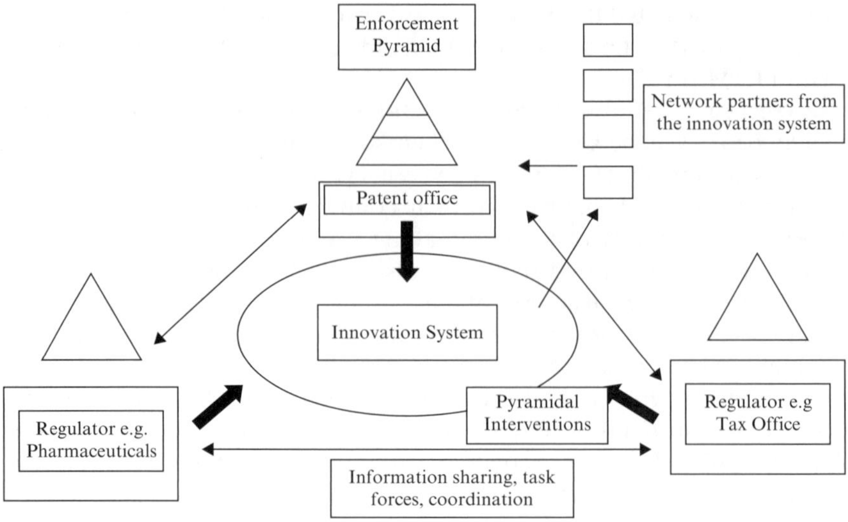

Figure 5.1 A model of responsive institutionalism for innovation

while longer.[56] The need for patent reform is on most people's lips, unless it happens to be a reform that affects their ability to use the system to extract monopoly rents. So everyone mouths reform proposals while continuing to use the system to play beggar-thy-neighbour games. The use of patents in transfer pricing strategies has made some in the US realize that even it sometimes ends up as a victim in these games. Patent offices go along with all this because they have convinced themselves and their political masters that more patents really do equal more innovation. And in any case patent size gives states full of techno-nationalist ambition something to measure.

It could be different. Patent offices could see themselves as custodians of a society's most precious resource – the creative and innovative potential of its people. On any rational construction of the patent social contract, that is their duty. Like central banks they could see themselves as responsible interveners in complex systems. They could use the power of small worlds to construct networks with regulators and other partners to learn about the problems of oversupplying markets with patents. The same small worlds would allow them to enrol non-state partners which had capacities they did not to help them with pyramidal intervention. Figure 5.1 is a

[56] M. Boldrin and D.K. Levine, 'The Case Against Patents', Working Paper 2012–035A, http://research.stlouisfed.org/wp/2012/2012–035.pdf (accessed 3 March 2013).

simple sketch of the kinds of networks that would produce a responsive institutionalism for innovation. Each regulator, in deciding on an intervention in the system or a deployment of its enforcement pyramid, would draw on the information and capacities in the network. In keeping with the separation of powers principle, rather than having the power of command over the system, the regulator would have the opportunity to cause the power of the network to coalesce into peaks of information synthesis and intervention. The same network could be used to check abuses of the patent system. A tax office, a patent office, a pharmaceutical prices regulator, a securities regulator, a competition regulator and so on could form a task force to go after those companies that were committing the worst offences. Each regulator could move against a target company deploying the pyramidal powers it had in a cascading strategy of networked enforcement. The aim would be to bring the company to the negotiating table to sign a corporate integrity agreement, an enforceable undertaking or whatever other instruments a jurisdiction had as part of its enforcement options. Patent offices could help to build this responsive institutionalism for innovation, but they won't; at least not any time soon.

6. The technology transfer debates and the role of emerging economies

Padmashree Gehl Sampath and Pedro Roffe

1 THE INTERNATIONAL TECHNOLOGY TRANSFER DEBATE

Discussions on technology transfer have now been ongoing in various international forums for over fifty years. It was first tabled as an international issue in 1961, articulated within a request to the United Nations Secretary General by some developing countries to commission studies to ascertain the role played by international treaties in promoting the protection of intellectual property rights in developing countries. With time, the debate has grown in proportion, not only becoming an important issue in a variety of international processes and institutions, but also gaining more prominence as a result of several reasons.

A first factor contributing to its growing relevance over time is the proliferation of demands on developing countries to improve their regimes of protection and enforcement of intellectual property rights (IPRs), which has been ongoing for some decades now. Developing countries have sought to respond to the ever-growing IPR stipulations by calling for a specific framework or obligations on the part of their trading partners on technology transfer that would promote their access to existing technologies. The most targeted effort to achieve such a framework was conducted in the context of the draft International Code of Conduct on Transfer of Technology (hereafter, the Code), which failed to materialize by the mid-1980s. However, despite the failure of those efforts, the fundamental issues raised fifty years ago still remain relevant and continue to influence and polarize international debates to a large extent in the current context.

A second factor that continues to focus attention on technology transfer is the fact that while the world has seen an increased shift towards the knowledge economy, many developing countries have been witnessing a concurrent widening of the technological divide. Particularly, since the beginning of the 1990s, there has been a remarkable shift in global relations, where knowledge has emerged as a key strategic asset. This has been accompanied by an ever-increasing service component in the global economy that relies on the acquisition of knowledge assets. Both these trends have led to a shift in focus from ownership of tangible to intangible assets as part of goods and services, and transactions globally. IPRs, especially markets for patents, copyrights and trademarks, have begun to dominate global commercial transactions, accounting for a large amount of GDP in western countries.[1] The proliferation of patents on software, databases, life forms and, most recently, business methods/financial innovations are apposite examples of this trend.

In parallel with these trends, the world has been witnessing a growing technological divergence in the developing countries themselves. Currently, we are faced with a reality where several developing countries, also often referred to as emerging economies, are well on their way to catching up (UNCTAD, 2012; Ocampo and Vos, 2009),[2] but a large number of other countries, particularly low income countries are struggling to promote technological change.[3] For these countries, technological marginalization remains a fundamental impediment to promoting sustainable development.

At the same time, however, all developing countries face some important common challenges, and technology and innovation are ubiquitous to framing developmental responses to these challenges. Common examples include questions of promoting food security and access to health care; but a serious look shows that this list is lengthy. Technological capabilities will determine how countries can deal with the challenge of sustainable development overall.

These factors no doubt render technology transfer as relevant an issue as it was fifty years ago. In many ways, this is attested to by the fact that debates on technology transfer continue to be a standard component of deliberations and negotiations in a variety of international forums. These can be divided into areas where there are pressing issues of delivering global public goods, such as climate change under the United Nations Framework Convention on Climate Change (UNFCCC), or public health negotiations under the aegis of the World Health Organization (WHO), and issues of technology access to promote catch-up processes of developing countries such as those within the existing trade and technology

---

1 For example, already as of 2001, the copyright industries contributed $535.1 billion to the US economy, accounting for 5.24 per cent of total GDP (Siwek, 2004). For similar trends on a global scale, see early estimates in OECD (2000).

2 Economic catch-up is commonly understood as the process of closing the gap between developing countries and their industrial counterparts.

3 It is estimated that the number of least developed countries has doubled over the past three decades.

negotiations in the World Trade Organization (WTO) and World Intellectual Property Organization (WIPO).

Since its introduction in international debates in 1961, the international political economy of technology transfer has evolved and several new developments have taken place. The first of these is related to our understanding of the processes and institutions that influence technological change. As opposed to the early 1950s, when technological access was mentioned in the same breath as industrial development, our understanding of how technological change occurs and what factors seem to play a role has vastly evolved. It is widely acknowledged now that technological change relies on the ability of countries to absorb, use and adapt existing technologies and these are shaped by dynamic capabilities of firms, sectors and countries (see McMillan and Rodrik, 2011). Trade and other modes of international exchange can often facilitate this process. Secondly, whatever the channel through which an existing technology is acquired, the acquisition of information concerning the technology is only one part of the process. The ability to learn, use and adapt the acquired technology is just as important, if not more so. Successful technology transfer is therefore deeply embedded in the ability of recipients to diffuse and use the technologies in question, which is shaped by what is known as the 'innovation system' of the country/sector in question.

Thirdly, a baton of newly industrializing countries, beginning with the East Asian economies, have helped to further our understanding of how technological learning takes place in different contexts. The process of catch-up that was initiated by the East Asian economies in the 1970s has been steady, although often punctuated. The past decade has seen the rise of a new group of developing countries, such as India, China and Brazil. The experience of these countries shows that numerous recipes exist to promote sustainable industrial development, and the question of when to grant IPRs (at which stage) in the development process is often as important an issue as whether to grant it and in what forms.

In the context of these developments, a fundamental issue that confronts us is whether we can continue to address the growing technological divergence amongst countries within a North-South context. Developing countries, including the emerging economies, still are not fully industrialized and need support in tackling issues of poverty reduction and inequality. In this context, the international discussions have witnessed the claims by developing countries for improving conditions for greater access to technologies for sustainable development.[4] But at the same time, there

---

[4] See the discussion in Gehl Sampath and Roffe (2012).

are vast differences in technological capabilities of countries in the South itself, thereby forcing a new thinking on how best to frame negotiations on how to achieve this important goal. Needless to say, a new framing of the technology transfer discourse needs to be cognizant of the changed reality of today's international context. This chapter seeks to analyze one such reality: the rise of several developing countries and what that might mean in furthering the cause of access to technologies and knowledge accumulation across the developing world.

2 EMERGING ECONOMIES: NEW GROWTH PROSPECTS, NEW INSIGHTS

Economists and policy advocates, seeking to find ways to jump-start industrialization in the developing world, advocated South-South trade and integration as an important means to overcome resource constraints and market size issues as early as the 1950s (see, for example, Myrdal, 1956; Lewis, 1979). Promoting South-South cooperation and regional integration was seen as an important means of promoting industrialization even up to the 1980s (ECLA, 1950; Prebisch, 1984). The 'vent-for-surplus' theory (see Shafaeddin, 2006, for instance) that is often advocated in the trade literature is based on the same perspective, arguing that there are large reserves of unutilized productive resources in developing countries, including labour, and these could be best allocated through increased South-South trade.

Despite the prevalence of these views, South-South relations have only now become a reality, with the rise of several developing countries that have the capability to trade in a wide variety of products, services and processes internationally. This section summarizes the key developments based on recent data in this regard.

2.1 The Rise in South-South Trade and Investment[5]

Recent data on trends in South-South trade show that intra-South trade has increased quite significantly since the mid-1990s. As of 1995, 38 per cent of imports of developing countries were sourced from other developing countries, and by 2010 this figure had exceeded 57 per cent. This general statement should not hide the fact that this trend responds principally to the growing role being played by emerging economies, particularly

[5] This section draws on UNCTAD (2012).

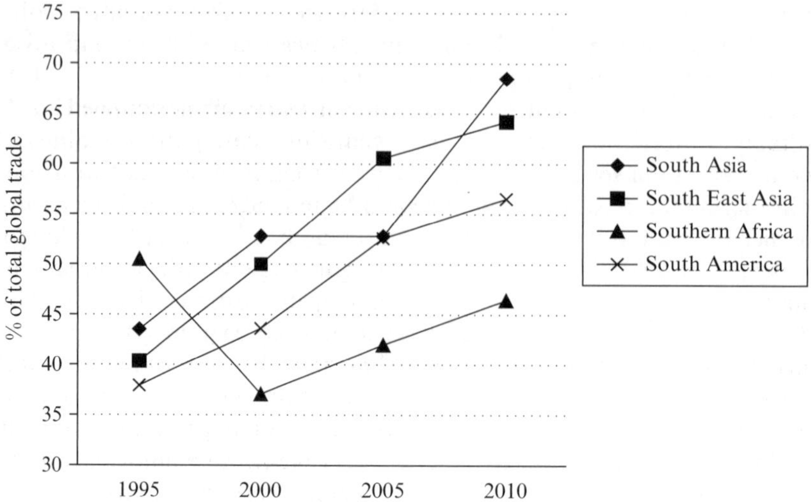

Source: UNCTAD (2012).

Figure 6.1 Evolution of South-South trade, 1995–2010 (as a percentage of total trade)

the East Asian countries and the BRICS, as the examination of investment flows shows.

A similar rise has been observed in FDI from emerging economies. Over the past two decades, the share of FDI from emerging economies has increased quite significantly, their share in global outflows rising from 15.2 per cent to 21.4 per cent in 2011. This rise has been all the more steep since the peak of the global financial and economic crisis in 2008. At the same time, the share of developed countries in total global FDI outflows has declined, from 93.1 per cent in 1980 to 70.7 per cent in 2010, compared with that of developing countries, which has risen from 5.73 per cent in 1980 to 24.62 per cent in 2010. The East Asian countries and China and India accounted for a large share of this rise.

This growing trade and investment trend among developing countries holds the prospect that it may also result in technology flows and transfer. Increased trade, particularly in capital goods, has been historically considered to be a very important means through which firms build technological capabilities. Imports of capital goods in economies that are not so technologically intensive signal investment in a variety of learning activities, including learning by doing and reverse engineering. Trade can also lead to furthering other means of technological exchange, including through customer-supplier-retailer relationships in value chains, reverse engineering and copying, interacting with foreign clients on design, standards and quality requirements, and collaborating in joint ventures.

Fostering these forms of learning effects through South-South trade and investment is a highly significant way to promote technological growth across the developing world. Sustained economic development that is built on productivity increases in a large number of developing countries does not rely on frontier innovations, but rather on the possibility to learn and build upon already existing technologies. Enabling this calls for increased trade and investment-related exchange in a range of sectors that together lead to overall industrial development. These range from manufacturing to services to marketing, managerial and financial services, as well as infrastructure activities.

Economic history as well as evidence from ongoing trade and investment studies indicates that learning effects contribute to increased absorptive capacity and the ability to adapt and apply existing technologies (in the forms of products and processes) by means of local innovations, and thus lead to a gradual increase in productivity in all sectors. Such growth is intrinsically tied to how production structures evolve and what kinds of factors, policies and institutions enable the diffusion of technological knowledge to domestic sectors and firms (Ocampo, 2004). Empirical work in this area reveals the relative weight of some factors in dictating the process of technological change and productivity growth. In particular, opportunities can arise as part of various international transactions, including technology spillovers from FDI (Benhabib and Spiegel, 1994; Pavitt and Soete, 1982), participation in global value chains (or production networks) or simply accessing technology through the import of capital goods.

Among these different channels, imports of capital goods and growing participation in global value chains may help local firms accumulate knowledge, not only of the kind related to technical aspects of production, but also of managerial, business and quality-related aspects. FDI and licensing can also have important implications for technology acquisition and learning in some contexts. However, to what extent this holds, and whether economic growth in the South and the resulting rise in South-South trade and investment do indeed lead to a surge in technological learning and innovation capacity, remain important questions, and are explored here.

2.2 Cases of South-South Technological Exchange

In practice, a wide range of collaborations can be identified in the current context. A more systematic review (see UNCTAD, 2012) shows that these

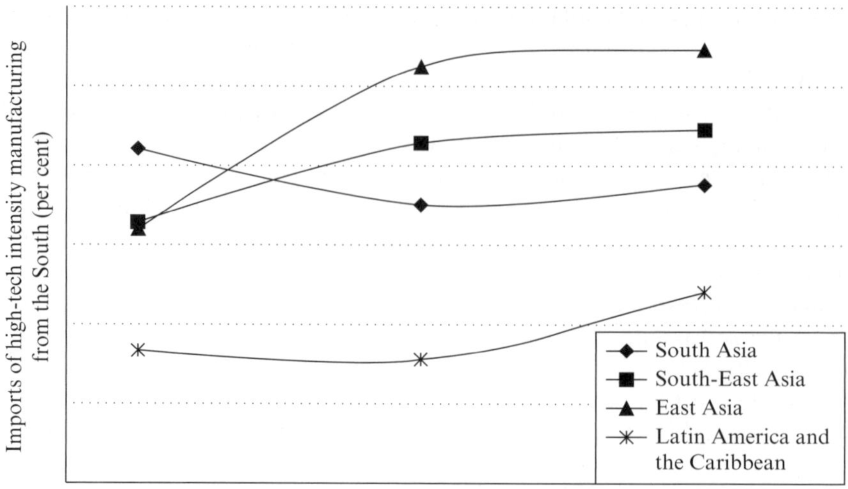

Source: UNCTAD (2012).

Figure 6.2 Imports of capital goods with high-technology intensity as a percentage of total imports from developing countries, by selected regions, 1995–2010

can be broadly classified as firm-level collaborations, government-driven collaborative ventures and intergovernmental initiatives, all of which have intensified over the past decade.

2.2.1 South-South value chains and production networks

Existing data and trends show that, along with growing trade, there has been a consistent increase in imports of high-technology-intensive goods in the South. A closer look at the growing technological intensity of South-South imports shows that, on average, over 53 per cent of all high-technology products imported by developing countries as a group was sourced from developing countries (Figure 6.2). The same is true for medium-technology-intensive goods as well, although the share of high-technology-intensive goods is higher.

A substantial share of these high-technology exports from the South is directed to developing countries. A country-level disaggregation shows that 60 per cent of Brazil's high-technology exports, 54 per cent of China's high-technology exports and 47 per cent of India's high-technology exports were imported by other developing countries.

A predominant factor explaining the technological import trends is the growth of production networks driven by some of the more technologically advanced developing countries. In addition, increasing domestic demand in some of the emerging economies – particularly China and India – due to their large populations and the increasing purchasing power of the growing middle class, is a factor explaining the surge in imports of technological products from other countries in the South into these economies. These imports, as data trends show, serve as inputs for the expanding economic activities and consumption patterns in these countries.

2.2.2 Firm-level collaborations and joint ventures

These broader economic trends are supported by some examples of firm-level collaborations. Typically, a large number of inter-firm ventures are between a technologically advanced firm (from an emerging economy) and a technology-seeking firm (typically based in another developing country). Motives for collaboration often vary. For the technologically advanced firms, motives include the search for cost efficiency by moving all or some of their production to other developing countries, as well as the search for new or expanded market opportunities in those countries or in regional groups. For those that seek technological collaborations in the recipient countries, the motivations for collaboration include their desire to enhance their technological capabilities in order to promote innovation, improve their competitiveness and meet public demand for specific products/services.

On a sectoral basis, technological collaboration is particularly prominent in the pharmaceuticals sector, renewable energy technologies, climate change and agriculture. Potential production barriers due to most developing countries' obligations to comply with provisions of the Agreement on Trade Related Aspects of Intellectual Property Rights (TRIPS) is a major motivating factor that drives their firms to expand production by collaborating with firms in least developed countries (LDCs) that are exempt from immediate compliance.

In the area of renewable energy, a large number of collaboration agreements exist to promote sharing of existing and successful renewable energy-based applications, and training and capacity-building for upgrading human resources. A few cases of joint R&D between firms are also evident. Such renewable energy-related technological exchange is often facilitated by intergovernmental organizations or multilateral or regional development banks.

A common feature observed across all these firm-level collaborations is that they are facilitated through targeted incentives granted by governments in developing countries. For instance, in the case of pharmaceuticals, investment incentives, tax rebates and purchase commitments have played a large role in the collaboration between Cipla Pharmaceuticals (India) and Quality Chemicals (Uganda). The same is true in a similar case of pharmaceutical collaboration between China and Ethiopia.[6] The TRIPS' waiver in favour of LDCs has also played a role in the case of the India-Uganda joint venture for the production of antiretroviral (ARV) and anti-malaria drugs. In renewable energy, the cases discussed show that, in addition to government incentives, market prospects have played a role in decisions by firms to enter into joint ventures. Indeed, market incentives play an important role in strategic choices of firms generally, as noted in the literature (see, for example, Taylor, 1994; DFID, 2009; Lanjouw, 2005).

3 CAN EMERGING ECONOMIES PROVIDE A NEW IMPETUS TO THE TECHNOLOGY TRANSFER DISCOURSE?

3.1 Understanding the Dynamics of Ongoing South-South Interactions

How do we understand and interpret ongoing South-South exchange? Existing data and case studies lend support to a few stylized conclusions. To begin with, South-South technology-intensive imports have received a significant boost over the past decade. Some emerging economies are able to manufacture several high-technology products at competitive (and often lower) prices, which is leading to a shift in imports of the South from developed countries to developing countries. Second, developing countries are increasingly participating in global value chains and production networks. Manufacturing activities of the South are gradually integrating into production networks and value chains, which are contributing to increasing the technological capabilities of firms in many developing countries.

The globalization processes of the 1990s have clearly contributed to facilitating this trend. Technological collaboration among developing countries is an aspect of the ongoing, progressively expanding

---

6 The Ethiopian company SEAA is a joint venture company in Ethiopia operating in the pharmaceutical sector. The joint venture involves three partners: one Ethiopian company, which originally focused on the import and distribution of pharmaceutical products in Ethiopia, and two Chinese companies, which specialize in the production of pharmaceutical products, medical devices, as well as equipment and machinery for pharmaceutical manufacturing. See UNCTAD (2011) for more details.

manufacturing in the South. However, as this discussion shows, many LDCs and developing countries that do not have some minimum level of technological capabilities have not been able to leverage the existence of or their participation in such value chains to upgrade technologically.

These trends in production and exports of technology-intensive goods and related value-added, as well as participation in value chains, need to be viewed in a more nuanced perspective of divergent capabilities of countries in the developing world. Imports of capital goods have long been recognized in the literature as a contributor to technological learning and capacity-building. Participation in value chains and FDI are other factors that could promote learning and capabilities-building through technological spillovers to local firms either directly through licensing and technology transfer or more indirectly through tacit know-how accumulation in local personnel. The impact of these channels on capabilities-building depends on the presence of some level of absorptive capacity within countries.

Country and context-specific factors such as education (particularly vocational and tertiary education), availability of capital (public and private), knowledge infrastructure (such as testing and design laboratories, public centres of excellence and universities), quality standards and quality control facilities are instrumental in promoting the absorptive capacity of firms to avail themselves of technological opportunities. New knowledge related to processes acquired by these means allows for increases in output, while knowledge related to new products helps local firms create newer markets or expand already existing markets. This leads to economies of scale and provides further scope for growth.

Developing countries, as much literature on the topic has noted, are very different in their levels of technological capabilities. In fact, the rise of some emerging economies particularly helps to portray the ever-widening technological divide in the South. A further illustration of this phenomenon is contained in Figures 6.3 and 6.4, which showcase two important indicators that reveal the differences in technological progress within the developing world.

On a general level, a country can import capital goods so long as it can pay for them. However, what remains important for productivity growth is how these imports are channelled effectively into generating future income. This brings us back to the issue of how firms and sectors are able to adapt and use technologies embodied in these imports to generate productivity growth. So long as this is possible and evident, it would lead to the conclusion that such imports of capital goods are contributing

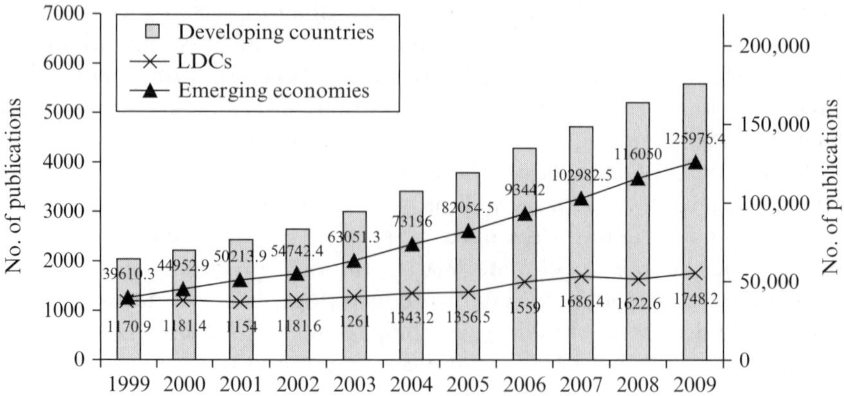

Source: Authors' own calculations.

Figure 6.3 Increase in scientific journal publications

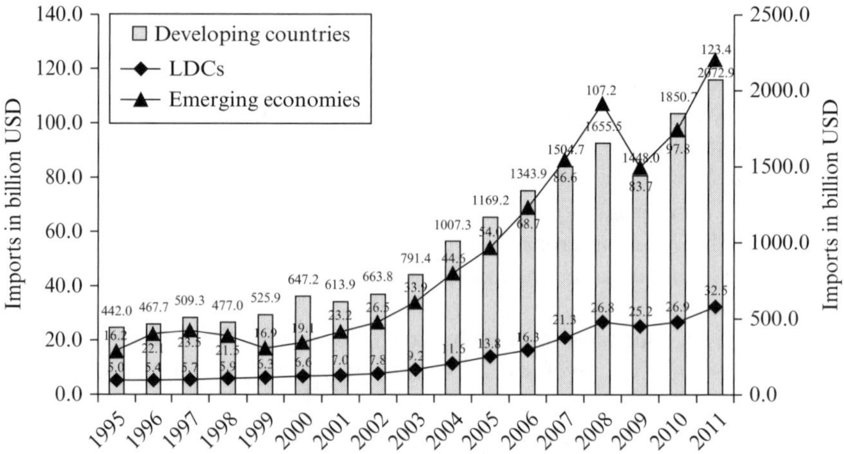

Source: Authors' own calculations.

Figure 6.4 Imports of capital goods with high skills and technological intensity

to building technological capabilities in developing countries. In this respect, two trends stand out. First, the trends show that countries with an already existing minimum level of technological capabilities are engaging in extensive trade in capital goods with other countries of the South. This points to the importance of some level of technological capacity to participate in capital goods trade, underscoring the fact that while any country could import capital goods, those that consistently participate in such capital goods trade are the countries where these imports feed into enhancing production capacities. This is underscored by the second trend, which shows a significant overlap between countries that import capital goods and those that export goods with technological content.

3.2 How Can Emerging Economies Facilitate Greater Technological Exchange?

The previous section leads to one important, critical conclusion: countries that are currently marginalized in global trade and technological exchange also risk being marginalized in South-South technological exchange. At first glance, one could argue that it is early to draw final conclusions, or that the impact is not all that severe. One valid question that needs to be raised is: how different is this from the traditional North-South dynamic that the current set of emerging economies have often characterized as being unfair, in the demand for better conditions and special treatment for technologically weaker economies? The emerging economies of today were avidly engaged for decades in articulating these fundamental issues at the global level.

Emerging economies are very important in several ways to help address the current global technological reality because the technology transfer discourse is in most ways different from the world in which it was conceptualized fifty years ago. A new North-South-South dynamic is beginning to emerge in most spheres of international relations. In the case of technology transfer, emerging economies will play a major role in determining the new global reality of technology exchange.

Currently, there are many positive indications that emerging economies could play an important role in shaping the new North-South-South reality of technology transfer in a constructive way.

First and predominantly, as data and trends show (Figures 6.3 and 6.4 above), the traditional sources of technology and knowledge in the South are not the exclusive domain of the North. The new emerging economies, through trade, FDI and licensing are competing with the traditional North in the supply of services and know-how to the traditional South. This is by itself an important development not only because it improves the availability of knowledge but also due to the fact that the emerging economies are in a better position to meet needs in a way that is adapted to conditions prevailing in the South.

In fact, the experiences of the emerging economies provide important lessons, not only with respect to how to overcome technological barriers in their own economic development and adopt policies for technological transformation, including IPR policies adapted to their development conditions. The proximity of these developmental experiences are very important and relevant for developing countries that are still grappling with ways to create harmonious and coherent local innovation and industrial policy environments. Recognizing this, both policy and scholarly analyses have begun to give greater attention to what lessons can be drawn for low income countries, particularly in Africa, from the East Asian experiences, and, more recently, from the experience of the Asian countries for other developing countries (see Stiglitz et al., 2012).

A second and perhaps more critical advantage of the South in the context of technological learning is that most of the emerging economies have followed a similar pathway in building their capabilities: from reverse engineering to incrementally innovating and then to research and development (R&D). In fact, most innovation analyses of the emerging economies show that the continuum through which these countries, their sectors and firms have progressed in their quest to build technological capabilities has been quite similar in nature. Developing countries also face a number of similar innovation constraints. Even within the developing countries that can be termed as emerging, while there are many sectors that are at the technological frontier globally, many other sectors or firms face routine constraints on innovation similar to those prevailing in other developing countries and LDCs. This raises more basic issues of promoting the technological absorptive capacities of their systems as a whole. Modes of learning and capability-building are also similar, with a focus on reverse engineering and incremental innovation.

Lastly, as is explicit in Boxes 6.1 and 6.2, the emerging economies take due account in their regular summits of the constraints of less developed countries in accessing technologies and of the need to address these questions through cooperative efforts to support development and stability in weaker economies. In this respect they have expressed their support for the efforts of those countries to accelerate the diversification and modernization of their economies, emphasizing that this should be done through infrastructure development, knowledge exchange and support for increased access to technology, enhanced capacity-building, and investment in human capital. This, as we have tried to emphasize here, is the proper way to facilitate access and enhance the dissemination of knowledge and technology.

BOX 6.1 NEW INTERGOVERNMENTAL INITIATIVES WITHIN EMERGING ECONOMIES

A wide variety of initiatives have taken root in the international and regional contexts over the past decade or so, demonstrating the emphasis on collaboration of emerging economies with other developing countries. Two such initiatives are the BRICS Summits and the IBSA (India, Brazil and South Africa) Initiative.

BRICS Summits: Greater cooperation among developing countries, including in the areas of science, technology and innovation (STI), is a central tenet of the BRICS, as emphasized at the 2012 summit in Delhi. The Delhi Declaration highlighted the need to promote science and technology and related knowledge exchange in the South.[7] Recognizing the broader relevance of knowledge sharing, paragraph 40 of the Delhi Declaration states that there is a pool of 'knowledge, knowhow, capacities and best practices available in our countries that we can share and on which we can build meaningful cooperation for the benefit of our peoples' (BRICS Summit, 2012).

The specific sectors for cooperation set out in paragraph 43 of the Declaration include the priority areas of food, pharmaceuticals, health and energy, as well as basic research in emerging interdisciplinary fields such as nanotechnology, biotechnology and advanced materials science.

At the 2013 BRICS Summit, the countries agreed to establish a BRICS Developmental Bank, to further their developmental partnership with other countries in the developing world.

The BRICS Summits also further collaboration amongst the BRICS countries, such as the Action Plan on Agriculture that was finalized in 2011.[8]

---

[7] Declaration of the Fourth BRICS Summit: BRICS Partnership for Stability, Security and Prosperity, 29 March 2012; available at: http://www.bricsindia.in/.

[8] The Plan was first formulated during the BRIC meeting of agricultural ministers in Moscow on 26 March 2010, and a consensus on its implementation framework was agreed at the first meeting of the BRICS Agricultural Cooperation Working Group in Beijing, China, in 2011.

The IBSA initiative: A trilateral initiative between India, Brazil and South Africa forged the New Delhi Agenda for Cooperation and Plan of Action, which aims to enhance trilateral trade and cooperation between the three countries. It includes technological collaboration in pharmaceuticals and health care, ICTs, civil aviation and defence.

Source: Based on UNCTAD (2012).

BOX 6.2 GOVERNMENTAL INITIATIVES IN EMERGING ECONOMIES: SOME EXAMPLES

These international initiatives are not isolated, and are conducted through regional, interregional and other institutional channels. The various legal initiatives can be viewed as part of a broader agenda setting in the policy arenas for the countries of the South. They are a reaffirmation of the growing recognition of the importance of greater collaboration on technology and innovation. In addition to these initiatives, a range of emerging economies have strengthened their national institutions in this regard. Some examples are provided here.

MEXICO: In 2011 the Mexican government issued the International Development Cooperation Law (LCID). This law institutionalizes for the first time a national system of international development cooperation within the Mexican public policy framework (SEGOB, 2011).[9] It explicitly highlights the need to engage in development cooperation activities in developing countries.[10] Similarly, China's South-South technological collaboration covers a variety of areas,

[9] Mandated by Constitutional Article 89, X, the LCID provides the government of Mexico with the necessary legal instruments to conduct both donor and recipient activities related to development cooperation actions and programmes between Mexico and other countries. It also provides for cooperation with international organizations through the exchange of resources, goods and educational, cultural, technical, scientific, economic and financial knowledge and experiences (Article 1).

[10] This includes cooperation in the areas of environmental protection and sustainable development, and the improvement of technical, scientific and cultural education through the collaborating entities, among other developmental issues (SEGOB, 2011).

including agriculture, oil and gas, and infrastructure development such as construction and telecommunications. Mexico has also been innovative in creating newer methods and instruments of development cooperation. One such instrument is the joint Mexico-Chile Fund that finances development projects in a number of countries in the region, including Ecuador, Bolivia and Uruguay.

INDIA: India also engages in South-South technological collaboration via the International Cooperation Division of the Ministry of Science and Technology. Cooperation projects are implemented through bilateral, multilateral or regional agreements for facilitating and strengthening interactions among governments, academia, institutions and industries in areas of mutual interest. India currently has bilateral science and technology cooperation agreements with several developing countries.[11] These focus mainly on the facilitation and enhancement of bilateral trade with other developing countries, and many have a technological learning component. A significant number of them take place in Africa (UNCTAD, 2012).

BRAZIL: The Brazilian Cooperation Agency (ABC), set up under the Ministry of Foreign Affairs at the end of the 1980s, became the primary institution to coordinate the country's technical cooperation programmes.[12] It is estimated that the largest share of Brazil's development assistance goes to 16 African countries,[13] although this is gradually expected to expand to include some Asian countries as well. The ABC's projects focus primarily on agriculture

---

[11] Countries include: Argentina, Bangladesh, the Bolivarian Republic of Venezuela, Brazil, China, Colombia, Croatia, Cuba, Egypt, Indonesia, the Islamic Republic of Iran, the Democratic People's Republic of Korea, the Lao People's Democratic Republic, Lebanon, Libya, Malaysia, Mauritius, Mexico, Mongolia, Mozambique, Myanmar, Namibia, Nepal, Oman, Peru, the Philippines, the Republic of Korea, Singapore, South Africa, Sri Lanka, Sudan, the Syria Arab Republic, Tajikistan, Thailand, Trinidad and Tobago, Tunisia, Turkey, Uzbekistan, Vietnam, Yemen, and Zambia.

[12] Brazil's development cooperation through the ABC has been expanding: between 2005 and 2009, it dispensed a total of $1.7 billion in technical assistance (IPEA et al., 2010).

[13] According to ABC (2010), these countries are: Algeria, Angola, Benin, Botswana, Cameroon, Cape Verde, Ghana, Guinea-Bissau, Kenya, Mali, Morocco, Mozambique, Nigeria, São Tomé and Príncipe, Togo and the United Republic of Tanzania.

(19 per cent), health (14 per cent) and education (11 per cent), as well as vocational training of relevance to industrial development in response to requests from countries in sub-Saharan Africa (World Bank and IPEA, 2011).

Source: Based on UNCTAD (2012).

It is against this background that efforts to foster technology transfer among the South needs to be strengthened, in an effort to maximize the benefits of the rise of the South for the entire developing world.

4 CONCLUSIONS

It is too early to say conclusively whether the new North-South-South dynamic will suffer from the traditional polarization in terms of conditioning technology transfer in return for enhanced protection and enforcement of IPRs, or simply granting IPRs in the hope of eventual technology transfer. What is clear, however, as Boxes 6.1 and 6.2 on emerging mechanisms of South-South technological cooperation show, is that emerging economies are expressly seeking to break away from the traditional emphasis on social sectors in development partnerships, with an emphasis on technological learning.

A second, potential outcome of growing South-South technological cooperation might be to promote a more nuanced, capacity-oriented approach to technology transfer benefit by answering from the outset a number of issues that have obscured the global debate on transfer of technology:

a. How can we better conceptualize technology transfer?
b. How is technology dissemination linked to technology transfer?
c. How can technology transfer be measured and assessed?
d. How can emerging economies in the South contribute to the responsibilities of developed countries in enhancing the technological and scientific base of least developed countries?

One failing of technology transfer approaches in the past has been that the focus has been on simply providing 'access' to technologies without facilitating aspects of such improved access, namely, promoting know-how exchange and the development of indigenous technological capabilities. The success of the technology transfer processes lies in how collaborations are structured around ground realities of technology acquisition and use processes. Emerging economies could help shift the focus of technology transfer from simply promoting 'access' to measuring its success based on increased collaborative ventures with technological know-how sharing at the enterprise level.

This role of emerging economies, no doubt, still needs to be reconciled with their demands for technology transfer in several forums internationally, including in climate change. One way to cushion and enable this dual role of emerging economies in the political economy of technology transfer would be to generate a broader understanding that the notion of technology transfer and technology dissemination may mean different things to countries at different stages of development, particularly in the South. For the more technologically advanced developing countries, it seems appropriate to assume that concerns related to promoting technology transfer under fair and competitive conditions are highly relevant. These are the broad issues that have permeated North/South debates in the past. While these are relevant to all developing countries, those that are yet to develop a threshold of innovation capacity are also likely to be interested in promoting local technological absorption capacity through scientific and technical collaboration as well. This is particularly true in the case of least developed countries, where technology transfer and dissemination needs to be viewed as a two-step exercise: (a) promoting local technological absorption capacity through scientific and technical collaboration; and (b) enabling enterprise innovation by sharing tacit know-how and technological expertise related to product and process development at the firm level.

Acknowledging the above distinctions could help to frame a new reality of transfer and dissemination of knowledge among developing countries and escape from the trap that has entangled multilateral discussions.

* *The views expressed in this chapter are the authors' personal views.*

REFERENCES

ABC, *Brazilian Technical Cooperation in Africa*, Brasília, Agência Brasileira de Cooperação, 2010.

Benhabib, J. and M. Spiegel, 'The Role of Human Capital in Economic Development: Evidence from Aggregate Cross-Country Data', *Journal of Monetary Economics*, vol. 34, no. 2, 1994, pp. 143–73.

Department for International Development (DFID), *Response to the International Development (Reporting and Transparency) Act 2006*, London, DFID, 2009.

Economic Commission for Latin America (ECLA), *The Economic Development of Latin America and its Principal Problems*, New York, United Nations, 1950.

Gehl Sampath, P. and P. Roffe, 'Unpacking the International Technology Transfer Debate: Fifty Years and Beyond', ICTSD, Geneva, 2012.
IPEA, SAE/PR, MRE and ABC, *Cooperação Brasileira para o Desenvolvimento Internacional 2005–2009*, Brasília, Instituto de Pesquisa Econômica Aplicada, 2010.
Lanjouw, J.O., 'Patents, Price Controls and Access to New Drugs: How Policy Affects Global Market Entry', NBER Working Paper No. 11321, Cambridge, MA, National Bureau of Economic Research, 2005.
Lewis, A., 'The Slowing Down of the Engine of Growth', 1979, http://ideas.repec.org/p/ris/nobelp/1979_002.html.
McMillan, M. and D. Rodrik, 'Globalization, Structural Change and Productivity Growth', *SSRN eLibrary*, 2011, http://papers.ssrn.com/sol3/papers.cfm?abstract_id=1866102 (accessed 29 March 2012).
Myrdal, G., *An International Economy, Problems and Prospects*, New York, Harper & Brothers Publishers, 1956.
Ocampo, J.A., 'Globalisation and the Development Agenda', in *Diversity in Development – Reconsidering the Washington Consensus*, The Hague, FONDAD, 2004, pp. 61–86.
Ocampo, J.A. and R. Vos, *Uneven Economic Development*, New York, United Nations Publications, 2009.
OECD, *Science, Technology and Innovation in the New Economy*, Paris, OECD, 2000, http://www.oecd.org/dataoecd/3/48/1918259.pdf.
Pavitt, K. and L. Soete, 'International Differences in Economic Growth and the International Location of Innovation', in H. Giersch (ed.), *Emerging Technologies: Consequences for Economic Growth, Structural Change and Employment in Advanced Open Economies*, Tübingen, Germany, J.C.B. Mohr, 1982.
Prebisch, R., 'Five Stages in My Thinking on Development', in G.M. Meier and D. Seers (eds.), *Pioneers in Development*, London and New York, Oxford University Press, 1984.
Taylor, M.S., '"Once-off" and Continuing Gains from Trade', *Review of Economic Studies*, vol. 61, 1994, pp. 589–601.
SEGOB (Secretaría de Gobernación) (2011), *Ley de Cooperacion International para el Desarrollo*, Cuauhtémoc, Diario Oficial de la Federacion.
Shafaeddin, M., *Does Trade Openness Favour or Hinder Industrialization and Development?*, Penang, Malaysia, Third World Network Trade and Development Series no. 31, 2006.
Siwek, S.E., 'The Measurement of "Copyright" Industries: The US Experience', *Review of Economic Research on Copyright Issues*, vol. 1, no. 1, 2004, pp. 17–25.
Stiglitz, J., A. Norman, K. Botchwey and H. Stein, *Good Growth and Governance in Africa: Rethinking Development Strategies*, Oxford and New York, Oxford University Press, 2012.
United Nations Conference on Trade and Development, *Local Production of Pharmaceuticals and Related Technology Transfer in Developing Countries*, New York, United Nations, 2011.
United Nations Conference on Trade and Development, *Technology, Innovation and South-South Collaboration*, New York, United Nations, 2012.
World Bank and IPEA, *Bridging the Atlantic: Brazil and Sub-Saharan Africa South-South Partnering for Growth*, Washington, DC and Brasília, 2011.

7. Development strategies of emerging economies in the era of climate change: Do patent statistics tell us anything?

Konstantinos Karachalios[1]

1 INTRODUCTION

Emerging or developing countries are being lauded[2] for their contributions to climate change mitigation. This has led some to question the carbon-intensive practices of the dominant Western development trajectory. This trajectory is based on the assumption that the linear path of the 'developed' economies is not only natural, but is the *only* means to achieving 'development'. It is, as Banerjee[3] argues, a 'unitary system of knowledge' that makes the search for alternatives not easy.

However, due to the urgency of the climate change problem,[4] the assumption that 'the benevolent (white) hand of the West will save the

[1] A version of this chapter was presented at the International Forum on the Geopolitics of Culture and Technology, São Paulo, 11–13 November 2010 when Dr Karachalios was a Scenarios Analyst at the European Patent Office. Although the EPO supported his participation in this event, Dr Karachalios is solely responsible for the opinions expressed herein: they are not necessarily shared by the EPO.

[2] A. Morales, 'China, Mexico Leading Fight on Climate Change with New CO2 Laws', *Bloomberg*, 14 January 2013, http://www.bloomberg.com/news/2013–01–14/china-mexico-leading-fight-on-climate-change-with-new-co2-laws.html (accessed 12 April 2013).

[3] S.B. Banerjee, 'Who Sustains Whose Development? Sustainable Development and the Reinvention of Nature', *Organization Studies*, vol. 24, no. 2, 2003, p. 144.

[4] S. Solomon et al., 'Contribution of Working Group I to the Fourth Assessment Report of the Intergovernmental Panel on Climate Change', *Cambridge University Press*, Cambridge and New York, 2007, http://www.ipcc.ch/publica tions_and_data/ar4/wg1/en/contents.html (accessed 10 April 2013); M.L. Parry et al., 'Contribution of Working Group II on the Fourth Assessment Report of the Intergovernmental Panel on Climate Change', Cambridge and New

Earth'[5] is being challenged. A key failing of the Western path is that it is dependent on the availability of energy sources and a significant increase in energy consumption per capita. The question this raises is how can emerging or developing countries be expected to follow this trajectory, without making the climate of the planet extremely hostile to humans?

This question was at the heart of the very tough negotiations within the United Nations Framework Convention on Climate Change (UNFCCC). The lack of a convincing answer contributed to the failure of the Climate Change Summit in Copenhagen (COP 15) in December 2009. A growing appreciation of climate science may mean that emerging countries do not seek to emulate the resource-intensive affluent living standards of Western cities. However, the achievement of the relatively modest aspirations of the Millennium Development Goals will nonetheless require a significant increase in energy per capita globally.

The question this chapter poses is whether emerging economies like China, India and Brazil are in a position to devise alternative, less carbon-intensive, models of economic development. Or do they remain trapped in a core-periphery relationship between themselves and OECD economies?[6] Drawing on an analysis of patents and clean energy, the chapter argues that emerging economies are limited in their capacity to initiate development alternatives, due to the lack of ownership of the technologies required for this to be achieved.

A telling example is evident in the current climate change and technology transfer debates. In these debates, drawing on international knowledge and the ability to invent our way out of the reliance on fossil fuels seems to be the only solution to the escalating global environmental risks and social problems. Information has been largely commoditised and has advanced to being the most valuable asset in those economies that are dominated by the power of intangibles. Moreover, in this setting, multinational 'flagship' corporations, not governments, are the key players regarding the generation, appropriation and control of valuable economic codified knowledge. This makes the deep and sweeping cultural re-calibration that is needed to catalyse a new approach to climate change less likely. Collaborative attempts by industry, for example the eco-patents commons by the World

---

York, Cambridge University Press, 2007, http://www.ipcc.ch/publications_and_data/ar4/wg2/en/contents.html (accessed 10 April 2013).

[5] A. Escobar, *Encountering Development: The Making and Unmaking of the Third World*, Princeton, NJ, Princeton University Press, 1995, p. 193.

[6] I. Wallerstein, 'The Rise and Future Demise of the World Capitalist System: Concepts for Comparative Analysis', *Comparative Studies in Society and History*, vol. 16, no. 4, pp. 387–415.

Business Council for Sustainable Development (WBCSD),[7] quickly hit limits. On the WBCSD website it is unambiguously stated: 'The Commons concept recognizes that some patents that provide environmental benefit may represent the jewels of a company's kingdom. Asking an enterprise or University to relinquish such key assets is not the objective of the Commons.' The desirable alternative is for developing countries to invent their own techno-fixes. Yet how can this be possible when so much of R&D depends on global networks? The next section of the chapter discusses recent findings from patent data on clean energy.

2 SOME NEW FINDINGS FROM PATENT STATISTICS

2.1 Study About Patents and Clean Energy[8]

A joint study by the United Nations Environment Programme (UNEP), the European Patent Office (EPO) and the International Centre for Trade and Sustainable Development (ICTSD) on the relationship between patents and the development and transfer of clean-energy technologies has yielded important insights, evidence and data. The final report includes findings from a comprehensive mapping of clean-energy technologies (CET), an in-depth analysis of the patent landscape for these technologies, and a survey of licensing activities in this field. A groundbreaking outcome of the project has also been the creation by EPO of a new system for providing easy-to-use information about patented technologies. Some results concerning innovation dynamics of emerging economies in the strategic sector of 'clean energy' are presented below.[9]

The analysis confirmed the general trend in other technology sectors, showing dominance by the OECD countries and similar ranking trends. An interesting exception is that while China features in the top five countries in terms of total patent filings, this is not the case for the claimed priorities in the CET sector. It is only tenth in solar photovoltaics (PV), and has a similar position in the biofuel sector. This indicates that, although

---

7 WBCSD, *Overview*, WBCSD, Geneva, http://www.wbcsd.org/work-program/capacity-building/eco-patent-commons/overview.aspx (accessed 10 April 2013).

8 K. Karachalios et al., 'Patents and Clean Energy: Bridging the Gap between Evidence and Policy', UNEP, EPO and ICTSD, Munich, 2010.

9 Not all patent documents were considered for this analysis; only a specific subgroup of patents that 'travel abroad', building a so-called 'patent family'. They are called 'claimed priorities'.

countries like India and China have become leading producers in the field of solar PV and are participating in global production chains, their intellectual property (IP) strategy is focusing only on the domestic market.

Compared to other emerging economies, China has the highest number of claimed priorities in CETs, predominantly in the area of solar PV. However, what is noticeable from the patent data is that Chinese companies have very little patenting activity in the area. Indeed, this trend is repeated with respect to the leading Chinese wind turbine manufacturers. This suggests that, while such companies are leading manufacturers and producers in the field, their IP assets are mainly domestically oriented and their export strategies are based on cost rather than innovation.

A similar story can be told for India, which appears just outside the top 20 patenting countries for aggregate activity in all examined CET categories. Patentees from India show the highest activity in solar PV. Most noticeable is that, in the area of wind power, patentees of Indian origin show little activity. This means that most patents recorded there are filed in the name of foreign companies' subsidiaries. The pertinent question that arises here is whether Indian parent companies still license these technologies.

The main patenting activity of Brazil lies in the area of hydro/marine and biofuels. However, compared with the rate of patenting in the leading countries, activity here is rather limited. For example, in absolute numbers, China has more patents for biofuels and as many patents in the area of hydro/marine as Brazil. Considering that Brazil is an ethanol-producing country, this suggests that Brazilian companies are focused more on the production process than on developing and exporting technologies for biofuels. This also raises the question of whether Brazilian companies are dependent on technology transfer in the area of biofuels.

2.1.1 Trends over time (decades)

The champions of today are not necessarily those of tomorrow. Our analysis shows that the ranking of countries in terms of their worldwide share of claimed priorities has changed over the last three decades. As an example, patent activity in Germany in wind technologies has outstripped other leading countries since 1998. In contrast, patenting in carbon capture and IGCC (integrated gasification combined cycle) have decreased significantly. In the area of geothermal technology, patenting in Germany started off strongly, and then saw a decline, before resurging in the last ten years.

In this context, of particular note is the emergence of patenting in China since 1998 in the fields of geothermal, solar PV (albeit, as mentioned above, mostly from non-Chinese applicants), wind, carbon capture and

IGCC. In geothermal technology China has made a significant entry into the field, virtually matching the patenting rates of the UK, Sweden and Italy. If these trends continue, China is likely to emerge as a key patenting arena in these fields.

As a contrast, patenting in India does not appear to be emerging to the same extent. Of all the technologies discussed above, solar PV is the only field where there is any activity. Interestingly, the patenting rates in solar PV by Indian companies between 1998 and 2007 are the same as between 1978 and 1987. This trend in patenting between 1978 and 1987 probably reflects the fact that the Indian government started a solar PV programme in the mid-1970s.

2.1.2 Patenting across countries

Unsurprisingly, most activity takes place between the top patenting countries, Japan, the US, Germany, the Republic of Korea, France and the UK. Japan and the US have the largest numbers of claimed priority patents, also filed in China. Germany, the UK, France and the Republic of Korea are the next largest patent filers in China, which is apparently considered an important market, but also a potential competitor.

Inventors from China on the other hand do not have a high number of CET patents filed first in China and then in any of the leading patenting countries. Indeed, most of China's patenting activity takes place at home. This trend reflects general patenting behaviour by China in all technology sectors.

Inventors from the US and Germany are the highest filers of claimed priority patents in Brazil. In comparison, inventors from Japan file very few patents in Brazil. Further, there are only two CET patents of Chinese origin that have subsequently also been filed in Brazil, indicating that emerging economies are not very much interested in each other in this context (no south-south filing).

A review of patenting trends in the areas of solar PV and solar thermal by 'Annex I countries' in 'non-Annex I countries'[10] reveals that China, the Republic of Korea and Taiwan are the biggest recipient countries for the examined patent flow, followed by Israel, Brazil, Mexico, South Africa and Morocco. Inventors from Japan are the most active filers of solar PV inventions in China, followed by the US and Germany. US inventors file the highest number of claimed priority patents in China in relation to solar

---

[10] For country taxonomy, see: United Nations Framework Convention on Climate Change, *Parties & Observers*, Germany, http://unfccc.int/parties_and_observers/items/2704.php (accessed 10 April 2013).

thermal. In contrast, India receives very few claimed priority patents in any of the CET fields examined.

2.2 Cross-national Inventors and Ownership of Patents

In the following, an additional analysis (not included in the aforementioned study about patents and clean energy) is presented. It aims to shed light on how innovation gains are appropriated in the context of internationalised R&D. The data is derived from EPO's aforementioned new technology information system[11] and the PATSTAT[12] statistics database.

First, all 'cross-national patents' (patents or patent applications with at least two countries of origin – applicant or inventor) from the subclasses Y02E (energy generation) and Y02C (greenhouse gas (GHG) capture and storage), including a total amount of approximately 600,000 documents, were retrieved. The result was some 25,000 patent documents with such cross-national inventor- or ownership (absolute numbers, not grouped according to 'patent families'). Then the countries were assigned to the applications in the proportion of their respective contribution (fractional counting), which allowed the percentage of inventor- and ownership per country to be calculated. Interestingly, for very few countries is the ownership percentage higher than the inventorship.

It is generally considered that patents with inventors from several countries indicate processes with a relatively high degree of scientific or technological cooperation or collaboration. In an ideal situation one might expect that the shares of co-inventor- and co-ownership would be more or less equal. However, as Table 7.1 shows, the reality is different. In many cases there is a significant deviation between these two indices.

Table 7.1 shows a list of the first 31 countries with the highest co-inventorship rate, sorted according to Delta, the percentage difference between applicants and inventors. When Delta is positive, then one can assume that a country appropriates efficiently IP generated through international collaborative processes. If it is negative, then this country may be failing to reap the benefits of the internationalisation of its R&D.

---

[11] European Patent Office, *Patent Information Services for Experts*, Munich, http://www.epo.org/searching/subscription/expert.html (accessed 10 April 2013).

[12] PATSTAT is a snapshot of the EPO master documentation database (DOCDB) with worldwide coverage, containing 20 tables, including bibliographic data, citations and family links. This database is co-developed by the EPO and the OECD Secretariat and is designed to be used for statistical research and requires the data to be loaded onto the customer's own database.

Table 7.1 Cross-national inventorship and ownership of energy and carbon-related patents[13]

Country	Applicants in %	Inventors in %	I/A	Delta
US	31.7	23.32	0.74	8.38
CH	6.89	3.66	0.53	3.23
KR	2.3	1.55	0.67	0.75
FR	6.19	5.56	0.9	0.63
FI	0.94	0.61	0.65	0.33
NO	1.11	0.79	0.71	0.32
TW	1.12	0.9	0.8	0.22
NL	3.28	3.17	0.97	0.11
SG	0.49	0.47	0.98	0.02
BE	1.43	1.41	0.99	0.02
SE	1.66	1.69	1.02	−0.03
ES	0.67	0.74	1.12	−0.07
PL	0.07	0.16	2.5	−0.09
BR	0.05	0.15	2.81	−0.1
NZ	0.13	0.23	1.77	−0.1
GR	0.05	0.17	3.18	−0.12
CZ	0.13	0.26	1.93	−0.13
UA	0.16	0.41	2.59	−0.25
ZA	0.1	0.48	4.68	−0.38
AU	0.74	1.15	1.56	−0.41
AT	1.23	1.87	1.51	−0.64
IN	0.12	0.85	6.92	−0.73
IL	0.57	1.3	2.28	−0.73
DK	1.48	2.26	1.53	−0.78
CA	5.47	6.38	1.17	−0.91
IT	1.23	2.28	1.86	−1.05
RU	0.37	1.66	4.53	−1.29
JP	4.75	6.05	1.27	−1.3
CN	0.72	2.19	3.05	−1.47
UK	4.7	7.22	1.54	−2.52
DE	13.64	18.27	1.34	−4.63

[13] US (United States), CH (Switzerland), KR (South Korea), FR (France), FI (Finland), NO (Norway), TW (Taiwan), NL (Netherlands), SG (Singapore), BE (Belgium), SE (Sweden), ES (Spain), PL (Poland), BR (Brazil), NZ (New Zealand), GR (Greece), CZ (Czech Republic), UA (Ukranian Republic), ZA (South Africa), AU (Australia), AT (Austria), IN (India), IL (Israel), DK (Denmark), CA (Canada), IT (Italy), RU (Russia), JP (Japan), CN (China), UK (United Kingdom), DE (Germany).

The countries where the rate of ownership is higher than the rate of inventorship (I/A < 1) are the US, Switzerland, Republic of Korea, France, Finland, Norway, Chinese Taiwan, the Netherlands, Singapore and Belgium.

As discussed before, international R&D projects are usually seen as an important means of knowledge and technology transfer. These data seem to indicate that there is indeed such transfer, but not always and not necessarily from industrially developed to developing or emerging economies. But this is by no means a north-south divide, the picture is quite mixed. The main countries that have more participation in inventorship than in ownership are Germany, the UK, China, Japan, Russia and Italy (Delta less than −1%), which means that inventors from these countries often fail to appropriate the results of the joint R&D, Germany and UK being the main 'donors'.

Further, South Korea (third best after the US and Switzerland), Taiwan and Singapore are on the positive side of this equation, but no developing country and none of the emerging economies, India, China, Russia, Brazil, and South Africa, is represented.

However, as indicated above, this is only a preliminary analysis. It has to be noted, for example, that the well-known 'headquarter effect', namely the fact that patent applications from subsidiaries abroad are filed from the headquarters in the home country, where the patent department is centrally located, may have to be considered. To get a more exact picture, the data needs further consolidation (e.g. grouping according to families, i.e. unique inventions). One could also look into specific sub-sectors (e.g. renewable energy sources, carbon capture, clean coal technologies, etc.), country/region combinations (US/EU/Japan with China/Brazil/ India), etc.

Finally, research on the ground must be done to look into the real causes of this phenomenon (e.g. contract clauses regulating input and output from collaborative transnational projects).

3 CONCLUSIONS AND SOME SUGGESTIONS

If the upstream stages in the knowledge chain (generation and appropriation) are essentially dominated by exclusive processes, then the end stage (diffusion) can hardly be inclusive. This is plausible if we assume maximising behaviour. The more powerful will dictate their terms and this is a common experience, even in international formally collaborative research projects. Consequently, the core-periphery relationship that characterises the global economy will continue to prevail. Unless clear and enforceable rules are established, technical knowledge will not be transferred from the ones that have more to the ones that have less of it, but from the ones that have less power to the powerful ones. Thus, the technology gap will not decrease, but increase, with the exception of new entrants who have a significant geopolitical and market leverage, and this not necessarily in the strategically important innovation fields[14] and categories.

Thus, logically, inclusiveness must start already in the way knowledge (and innovation) is generated. On a bilateral basis, the US, Japan and the EU are establishing – of course, separately from each other – scientific research funds with emerging economies like China, but this is not sufficient. It could even be seen as one more expression of competition among the trilateral block for shares of the new markets, rather than collaboration on the search for innovative low-carbon models of development.

3.1 Examples of Collaborative Platforms

John Barton and Keith Maskus have proposed an Agreement for Access to Basic Science and Technology, as a knowledge generation and diffusion platform, where both the input (scientific and technological capacities) and output (new scientific insights and basic technologies) should be shared by and be broadly accessible to the international community.[15] 'Basic' could be defined as knowledge that is important for our survival as a species and for some key global technology platforms. Of course, on top of such platforms there would be open competition for best technical solutions and implementations, patenting thereof etc.

Thinking further ahead, the current IP system could be adapted to support and also promote more cooperative practices. The EPO's 'Scenarios for the Future' (2007)[16] depicts such possibilities ('soft IP' for key platform technologies), but this is only one example. Other solutions are also possible, for instance Professor Jerry Reichmann's proposal for 'Compensatory Liability Regimes'.[17]

---

14 R. Silberglitt et al., *Global Technology Revolution 2020*, Santa Monica, CA, Rand Corporation, www.rand.org/pubs/technical_reports/TR 303 (accessed 10 April 2013).

15 J.H. Barton and K.E. Maskus, 'Economic Perspectives on a Multilateral Agreement on Open Access to Basic Science and Technology', The World Trade Forum, World Trade Institute, Berne, 2003, http://www.law.ed.ac.uk/ahrc/script-ed/issue3/barton-maskus.asp (accessed 10 April 2013).

16 See EPO, 'Scenarios for the Future', Munich, EPO, 2007, chapter 9, http://www.epo.org/news-issues/issues/scenarios/download.html.

17 Duke University, *Jerome H. Reichman*, Duke Law, http://www.law.duke.edu/fac/reichman/ (accessed 10 April 2013).

3.2 Role of IP Offices

What is the position and what is the role and potential of patent offices in this context? They are already institutions that play an important role in the technology knowledge chain, by implicitly regulating the border line between private property and public domain, through their examination practice and their legal decisions. Additionally, they have an obligation to disclose technical teaching about the invention to the public. Being public authorities, they should explicitly reinforce policies to protect and foster public interest in broader terms, in particular improving the quality of examination and transparency of disclosure.

The latter is very important, because, before starting to transfer technology, one must know which technologies exist and by whom they are owned and where. Thus, patent offices should provide easy-to-use registers, at least in key technology sectors, not only for climate change technologies, but also in such fields as ICT standards, essential medicines etc. Beyond delivering useful practical information, such registers could help also to remove current structural uncertainties. Today it is virtually impossible even for experts to get a comprehensive overview of what is patented by whom and where in very critical sectors. Thus, decision makers may start to assume that everything may be patented everywhere. I think this would be a very serious threat to the social acceptance of the patent system.

How could transparency improve? To use the words of a well-known scholar:[18]

> Turning patent offices from passive publishers into active diffusers of information requires patent offices to begin approaching their task much more like public libraries: finding creative ways to engage with very diverse user communities.

This does not mean going beyond their mandated tasks, but taking them at their word.

As the EPO's President recently said:

> 'For the patent system it may be necessary to revisit the basic patent social contract, its "raison d'être", which is contained in its very name. The word "patent" comes from the Latin verb patēre, which means to be open or accessible. The opposite of the adjective patent is latent, which comes from latēre,

---

[18] P. Drahos, *The Global Governance of Knowledge*, Cambridge, Cambridge University Press, 2010, p. 299.

meaning to lie hidden or escape notice. Ironically, many critics perceive this to be the consequence of the present patent system.'[19]

Finally, given the size and complexity of the challenges, patent offices must necessarily look outside their usual territories and the 'small IP family'. They must try to embed themselves, mentally and politically, within frameworks with broader social aims at the national, regional or international level. Taking this challenge seriously, the EPO established in the year 2007 with the aforementioned Scenarios project a new type of platform for a public dialogue around IP issues. Since then, its engagement in the context of climate change, in the patents and ICT standards debate,[20] in mapping patent landscapes for essential drugs, etc. are all pointing in the same direction. It can only be hoped that this trend will prove sustainable and that other patent offices and IP institutions may follow suit.

---

[19] B. Battistelli, 'Keynote Speech on Clean Energy Technologies and IP', German Patents and Trademark Office (DPMA), Munich, 22 July 2010.

[20] K. Karachalios, 'Whose Game? Standards and their Patents at 21st Century's Crossroads', ITU Workshop on ICT Standards and IPR, Geneva, http://www.itu.int/dms_pub/itu-t/oth/06/14/T06140000020002PDFE.pdf (accessed 10 April 2013).

PART III

The BRICS

Brazil

8. Patents and the emerging markets of Latin America – Brazil

Denis Borges Barbosa

Brazil is listed among the emerging markets, and is mentioned as a potential prime player in the intellectual property field. Although the country has a long history and has displayed a continued interest in its patent system, it should not be expected that Brazilian patent applications will flood the patent offices of OECD countries in the near future, as may be expected of Chinese and (to a lesser extent) Indian filings.

This study assesses the Brazilian patent system as it exists today under the 1996 law. The new players and the context are liable to change this system in the medium term. The value of patents in the development of Brazil is one of the most striking policy issues being discussed in the country, though patent legislation has been in force for over 200 years.

1 FROM A DIVIDED STANDPOINT TO A LOCAL-CENTERED PERSPECTIVE

A peculiar aspect of the patent system in Brazil is its long history. In 1809 King João VI of Portugal, fleeing from Napoleon, established the capital of the worldwide Portuguese Empire in Rio de Janeiro.[1] On April 23, 1809, he issued a royal decree[2] establishing a Patent Law, making this statute the fourth oldest of its kind in the world.

---

[1] The history of the Brazilian patent system is well documented. See L. M. Malavota, *A construção do sistema de patentes no Brasil: um olhar histórico*, 1st edn, Rio de Janeiro, Lumen Juris, vol. 1, 2011, p. 308; N. P. de Carvalho, *200 Anos do Sistema Brasileiro de Patentes: O Alvará de 28 de Abril de 1809*, Rio de Janeiro, Lumen Juris, 2009; N. P. de Carvalho, *A Estrutura dos Sistemas de Patentes e de Marcas – Passado, Presente e Futuro*, Rio de Janeiro, Lumen Juris, 2009. These authors indicate that the antiquity of the system did not translate into the patent tool having any particular importance in Brazilian development.

[2] Just for the Kingdom of Brazil and the region that eventually evolved into Uruguay, therefore excluding Portugal and other portions of the Empire.

By the time the Paris Convention was being negotiated, local opinion had changed regarding the value of restricting patents to those economic agents engaged in local production, as the 1809 and 1830 statutes did. According to such new sentiment, foreign patents should be accepted. Brazilian negotiators were active during the last stages of the diplomatic conference and before the Convention came into force. Brazilian law was revised to accept all foreign filings.

In opposition to this internationally oriented trend, over the next 40 years local resistance to the international industrial property system grew steadily. By 1934, Brazil started denouncing some minor treaties within the Paris Convention system. After the The Hague version of the Paris Convention, Brazil decided to cease updating it, holding on to the 1925 version, deemed to be the last pro-developmental one. (Brazil adopted the most recent version of the Paris Conventions in 1990 when the Agreement on Trade Related Aspects of Intellectual Property Rights (TRIPS) was on the verge of reaching its final wording.)

In 1961 Brazil's nationalist position took a more active stance when, at that year's UN General Assembly, Professor Guerreiro Ramos, the Brazilian delegate, challenged the purpose of the whole patent system for the developing countries. UN Resolution 1713, of December 19, 1961, mandated a review of the system from a developmental perspective. This was eventually done through a UN report.[3] Eight critical perspectives towards the value of intellectual property (IP) led Brazilian IP policy over the next decades.

2 A TURN AROUND

By the end of the Uruguay Round a different policy perspective came to prevail in Brazil. The new Industrial Property Code of 1996 incorporated most of the TRIPS requirements, and added to them. Brazil renounced most of the TRIPS transitional periods for developing countries that would have deferred the obligation to introduce pharmaceutical and chemical patents until January 1, 2005.

The new Code authorized such patents from May 15, 1997, and included the so-called "pipeline" provision that gave retroactive protection for previously published patents once granted abroad. This mechanism had been

---

[3] UN Department of Economic and Social Affairs, "The Role of Patents in the Transfer of Technology to Developing Countries at 5", UN Doc. E/3861/Rev. 1, UN Sales No. 65.II.B.1, 1964.

proposed by the US delegation to TRIPS, but was eventually rejected by consensus, as required by the negotiation rules.

A complete set of new laws covering all IP rights were provided for over the next few years, in some cases including TRIPS-plus provisions, even though Brazil was not bound by any bilateral or multilateral treaties requiring such extended protection.

However, while complying with and in many cases exceeding its international obligations, the build-up of the new Brazilian IP system was far from consensus-based or uniform. The choice of the pipeline mechanism, for instance, emerged from a deeply divided government: some ministries were and remained in favor of granting retroactive patents, whereas other agencies lobbied against this and all TRIPS-plus devices. Such divisions reflected societal questioning and contradictions.

The legal system in force reflects these competing interests. In the pharmaceutical and chemical field, the 1996 law was inordinately open to the interests of (mostly foreign) patent holders. In the biotechnological area, however, a quite distinct approach developed:

> Brazilian legal policy, with regard to both ABS and IPR, has been dictated by fear and political initiative. The fear is that of losing control of genetic resources and natural substances during the course of innovation processes: these are frequently long, involve many different stakeholders and make it difficult to identify the original natural items in the final outcome. The political initiative has involved reaffirming both Brazil's sovereignty over biodiversity with regard to third countries and the pre-eminence of state authorities with respect to its own citizens.
>
> At the same time, during negotiations on intellectual property – whether in the forum of the World Intellectual Property Organization (WIPO) or that of the World Trade Organization (WTO) – Brazil asserted its refusal to grant intellectual property rights (IPRs) such as patents to naturally occurring substances, even though rights on cultivars such as those defined by International Union for the Protection of New Varieties of Plants (UPOV) have been recognized nationally since 1997.[4]

3 TRIPS AS AN UNREQUITED PROMISE

Even though a complete overhaul of the Brazilian IP system occurred when the TRIPS Agreement entered into force, many authors believe that the treaty is not to be held responsible for all aspects of the system that are felt to be detrimental to local public policy.

---

[4] G. Filoche, "Biodiversity Fetishism and Biotechnology Promises in Brazil: From Policy Contradictions to Legal Adjustments", *The Journal of World Intellectual Property*, vol. 15, no. 2, 2012, pp. 133–54.

Much to the contrary, many aspects of present Brazilian IP policy reflect a growing sense that TRIPS came to be a reasonable basis on which to build an intellectual property system. Even though the treaty required Brazil (and almost all developing countries) to raise its level of protection to a level not necessarily compatible with local needs, the subsequent exercises conducted at bilateral and plurilateral fora sought levels much exceeding TRIPS. Compared to what came after, TRIPS was a moderate stance.

The post-TRIPS era especially frustrated the expectation that the Uruguay Round treaty would end all unilateral pressure to change and raise IP standards. Brazil had been the target of a series of unilateral sanctions by the late 1980s, and had stressed that preventing further sanctions was one of its clearest objectives in participating in the TRIPS negotiations:

> The fact that in some limited areas, especially in the public health sector, TRIPS has actually been used to achieve balance and poise does not change the overall issue. The unilateral thrust which TRIPS was meant to end just increased. It is reasonable to guess whether, in the absence of TRIPS, the situation would be the same.
>
> A very important aspect of this post-TRIPS era, by the way, is the denial of the multilateral promise. We were assured that unilateralism was over. All of us were members of the club, after paying the steep entrance fee. It was not so.[5]

Brazil conducted the negotiations for the proposed Free Trade Area of the Americas (FTAA) from this standpoint. The country's position in connection with the IP content of FTAA was: everything that Brazil had to bargain for in connection with its IP interests was already bargained for in TRIPS.[6] The FTAA has not been completed, and Brazil has not engaged in any other similar exercise.

The 2004 proposal by Brazil and Argentina of a development agenda for the World Intellectual Property Organization[7] may also be attributed at least in part to Articles 7 and 8 of TRIPS,[8] which made clear that developmental concerns and intellectual property interests should not be

---

[5] D. Borges Barbosa, "Counting Ten for TRIPS: Author Rights and Access to Information – A Cockroach's View of Encroachment", November 4, 2005, SSRN, http://ssrn.com/abstract=842564.

[6] D. Borges Barbosa, "TRIPS Art. 7 and 8, FTAs and Trademarks", March 9, 2006, SSRN, http://ssrn.com/abstract=889107.

[7] Found at http://www.wipo.int/ip-development/en/agenda/ (accessed August 1, 2012).

[8] A development agenda for intellectual property was precisely what Guerreiro Ramos proposed at the UN Assembly in 1961.

treated as antagonistic. The Uruguay Round, echoing prior discussions in the GATT (General Agreement on Trade and Tariffs) environment, created some sort of development agenda for the WTO (here compatible with prevailing trends in UN system), which was conspicuously absent in the WIPO environment.

The WIPO document initiating the development agenda stresses the stepping with the times nature of the exercise:

> Bearing in mind the internationally agreed development goals, including those in the United Nations Millennium Declaration, the Programme of Action for the Least Developed Countries for the Decade 2001–2010, the Monterrey Consensus, the Johannesburg Declaration on Sustainable Development, the Declaration of Principles and the Plan of Action of the first phase of the World Summit on the Information Society and the São Paulo Consensus adopted at UNCTAD XI;

4 MORE THAN A DIVISIVE ENVIRONMENT, A PLURALITY OF EMERGING ACTORS

In the last few years, the Brazilian IP environment, especially as regards the patent system, has been subject to a number of important legal and policy factors:

(a) Since 2006, Federal and state specialized IP courts have been instituted. As a result of this specialization, a more balanced judicial perspective has succeeded a previously excessively pro-holder tendency of the courts.[9] Brasilia's Superior Federal Court (STJ) aligned with lower Federal courts against the extension of patent terms or domestic application of TRIPS rules before the expiry of the January 2000 special transitional term for developing countries;
(b) A significant number of civil society non-governmental organizations (NGOs) and local industry trade associations (generics, seed producers) started to file suits and act as amici curiae in patent cases;
(c) The Ministry of Health now has an important role in IP matters:
    (i) In 1999 the Ministry of Health implemented a peer review system of patent examinations, whereby ANVISA (the Brazilian

---

9 Prior to specialization, a very high number of final court decisions in suits filed by foreign patent holders in Federal courts favored plaintiffs. After such specialization, this trend changed to a nearly 50/50 chance in favor of plaintiffs.

FDA) duplicates the Patent Office in assessing patent filings for pharmaceutical technologies. After an extended inter-agency battle over this double examination, a standstill agreement allowing for a common procedure was reached in May 2012[10];

(ii) In 2007, the Ministry of Health issued a compulsory license on an HIV drug after three failed attempts;

(iii) From 2007, utilizing its huge purchasing power, the Ministry of Health started to induce alternative suppliers of pharmaceutical products. This program relies (among other TRIPS-permitted devices) on statutory licenses provided in cases of dependent patents. From December 2010, public contract law changed to consider local technology development as an alternative to low prices (margin) in awarding contracts. In August 2012, such a program received further statutory enhancement whereby contracts resulting in transfer of technology to publicly held laboratories are dispensed from otherwise legally required tenders.

(d) Federal Policy in IP matters was centralized in the GIPI (Interdepartmental IP Steering Group); although the Brazilian Patent Office has resisted some general directives, GIPI helped to overcome many of the prior interdepartmental conflicts regarding IP;

(e) Since 2004 a new Innovation Law has multiplied the number of individual and institutional interested actors in a patent system encouraging local technology. Significant tax relief statutes are directed to local technology, patents and plant variety protection (PVP).

5 PATENTS AS A LOCAL DEMAND

Does its patent system actually serve Brazilian interests? A crucial aspect of public policies regarding patents in Brazil (as in many other countries) is the inbalance between local and foreign filings and patent grants.

---

[10] For a political science analysis of such double examination, see K. C. Shadlen, "The Political Contradictions of Incremental Innovation: Lessons from Pharmaceutical Patent Examination in Brazil", *Politics & Society*, vol. 39, 2011, p. 143, originally published online April 5, 2011, http://pas.sagepub.com/content/39/2/143. This study did not consider the May 2012 changes in the policy.

Brazilian Patent and Trademark Office (BrPTO) statistics[11] illustrate such a trend: taking all kinds of patents into consideration, local filings in 2010 represented only 25.86% of the total. Excluding utility models, the local filings represented only 20.68%. According to its 2012 data,[12] WIPO indicates that globally on average 62% of patent filings are local. It must be noted that utility models, which represent roughly one-third of all local Brazilian filings, have been plummeting in recent years: utility models dropped 36% in 2010 as compared with 2009. This represents the most severe loss within the 15 top patent offices (PTOs).

A comparison can be made here with plant variety protection (PVP). Resulting from a longstanding, successful research program funded mostly by the Brazilian government[13] and especially oriented to regional development,[14] PVP filings are much more locally oriented.[15] Thus, most PVP granted for cotton, beans (except soy) and wheat were filed by public or private entities domiciled in Brazil.

In view of the above, it seems that the Brazilian patent system is not as yet of major interest for local industries and researchers, at least as compared with the global average of filings by domestic users. This is a problem for Brazilian public policy. On the other hand, the data both on PVP registrations and its actual utilization may indicate that, at least in areas where technology is locally oriented and adequately funded, particular segments of the IP system (such as the PVP regime), may contribute to achieve local development objectives.

---

[11] Found at http://www.inpi.gov.br/images/stories/downloads/pdf/INPI_Relatorio_Comunicacao.pdf (accessed February 2012).

[12] http://www.wipo.int/freepublications/en/statistics/943/wipo_pub_943_2012.pdf, p. 13 (accessed August 1, 2012).

[13] "Finally, an extensive national agricultural research network that already has a proven track record, especially with soybeans, of successful varietal development and adaptation to tropical conditions", R. Schnepf et al., "Agriculture in Brazil and Argentina: Developments and Prospects for Major Field Crops", Agriculture and Trade Report No. WRS013, *Economic Research Service, USDA*, 85 (2001) at 61, http://www.ers.usda.gov/publications/wrs013 (accessed May 28, 2009).

[14] "Embrapa has managed to achieve success by focusing on customization and adaptation of plant varieties to local environments", D. Borges Barbosa and M. Lessa, "The New Brazilian Government Draft Law on Plant Varieties (Or. . . 'How a Developing Country May Want to Enhance IP Protection Because It May Actually Need It')", SSRN, June 6, 2009, http://ssrn.com/abstract=1415406.

[15] Data from National Service for the Protection of Cultivars, D. Aviani, http://www.sbmp.org.br/6congresso/wp-content/uploads/2011/08/1.-Daniela-Aviani-Panorama-Atual-no-Brasil.pdf (accessed August 1, 2012).

6 THE BRAZILIAN PATENT OFFICE AS A SOURCE OF PROBLEMS

As the Federal Agency in charge of examining and granting patents, the Brazilian Patent and Trademark Office (INPI) is necessarily a major player in the IP system. Some indicators, however, may signify that this agency is at this stage a part of the problem.

The filing of patent applications has increased significantly since the amended Industrial Property Code entered into force, while the number of examiners available to adequately perform the examination has not grown accordingly. In 2006, 13,160 applications were received increasing to 19,471 in 2010. The number of patents granted has also grown, but at a lower rate, from 2,785 to 3,620.[16]

Consider the situation in 2010:

(a) Some 163,000 patent applications were awaiting examination;[17]
(b) In that year the agency received circa 28,000 filings of all kinds, examined almost 20,000 applications and granted 3,620 patents;
(c) The PTO had 273 patent examiners in all areas, whereas demand required at least 300 examiners.[18]

By 2011, the *expected* period for examination of a patent was on average 8.3 years.[19] From this situation three scenarios may arise:[20]

---

16 Data found at http://www.inpi.gov.br/images/stories/downloads/pdf/INPI_Relatorio_Comunicacao.pdf (accessed August 1, 2012).

17 Data obtained from the document of the Federal Prosecutor Office, http://ccr3.pgr.mpf.gov.br/institucional/grupos-de-trabalho/mercado-de-capitais/planejamento_estrategico/diagnostico_inpi-final (accessed August 1, 2012. This document indicates a backlog of 154,000 in 2009. Taking into account the non-examined applications filed in 2010, the backlog was then 164,000. Further data obtained at http://cit.ifg.edu.br/index.php/component/content/article/42-geral/164-resolver-backlog-de-patentes-e-prioridade-do-inpi; and http://www.andef.com.br/eventos/cipiagri2011/palestras/LianeLage.pdf (both accessed February 2012).

18 This was the number indicated by the Court of Accounts of the Republic as adequate staffing. In late 2012, a new public competition was authorized to increase the Brazilian PTO staff to the indicated levels. The process of incorporation will take some months to materialize.

19 According to the Federal Prosecutor Office's document, the backlog was 10.35 years in 2008 and 10.25 years in 2009.

20 For such scenarios and other considerations, see J. G. S. Silva and S. Borschiver, "Critérios para a avaliação dos sistemas patentários", *Revista da ABPI*, January/February 2009, p. 30 at p. 41.

(a) The PTO chooses to shorten the time allowed for examination of each patent, without increasing the number of examiners. In this case, the quality of the examination will be compromised since the examiner will not have time to do the research necessary to assess novelty and inventive activity in the case of a patent (PI) and novelty and inventive step in the case of the utility model patent (MU);
(b) The PTO chooses not to increase the number of examiners nor to compromise the quality of the examination. In this case the backlog will continue to grow;
(c) The PTO chooses to increase the number of examiners and their expertise in each area, choosing also to create a more efficient system of assessment and administration of the examination of these patents.

Situation (a), where examination is performed poorly, without the quality of research required for granting a patent, particularly with respect to verifying the novelty and inventive activity in the case of inventions – and novelty and inventive act in the case of utility models, will result in weak patents. These patents would be easy targets for administrative proceedings for nullity and judicial action or declaration of nullity.[21]

For investors, foreign or domestic, this means increased uncertainty.

In situation (b), investors will experience considerable economic and legal uncertainty, since investments and even marketing of the product or process subject to the patent frequently occur before its granting.

This uncertainty is two-pronged: once granted, the effects of the patent in Brazil are retroactive, essentially going back to the date of the publication of the filed application. Therefore, third parties will take considerable risks when assessing the impact of the new patent on their manufacturing, as the content of the claims in the issued patent may vary from what was included in its initial filing.

Furthermore, Brazilian law assures a minimum term of ten years post-grant (seven years for utility models) when the PTO is responsible for the delay. Therefore, the economic effect of the backlog is increased deterrence towards third parties, affecting competition. Many observers indicate that for this reason the backlog is not fiercely opposed by the major international players.

---

[21] A Federal court procedure for invalidation of patents is, as a rule, much faster than the overextended BrPTO examination (in the last six years a trial and appellate court examination could be obtained in a period as short as 18 months), and the court may issue an immediate order suspending the patent against which an invalidity suit was brought.

In the case of patents abandoned because of delay in examination and loss of interest in protection, the negative scenario for Brazil is no different, considering the arguable withdrawal of investments in production and marketing of products and processes in the country, especially in this case by local players.

Option (c) is, we believe, the most appropriate solution to the problem, affording more quality patents granted in the country. As would be expected,the strategic plans of the PTO indicate this to be the preferred option, as discussed below.

By early 2011, PTO indicated its intent to solve the backlog issue by 2015. The agency intends to achieve this goal and grant quality patents in a maximum of four years from the date of deposit.

In September 2011,the President of the PTO announced a set of measures designed to achieve such goals:

- Increased operational efficiency of the patent examination sector with the creation of an electronic system for patent applications.
- Hiring more examiners with master's and doctoral degrees for the specific areas of examination.
- Updating the guidelines and procedures for the examination of patents.
- Ongoing training and development of patent examiners.
- Directing most of the national applications to the PCT system whenever possible.
- Automatically eliminating formally unsuitable applications through the electronic filing system.
- Giving priority to examination of applications for areas considered strategic to the economic and technological development of the country.
- Increasing technical cooperation with other patent offices, aiming at the internationalization of examinations.
- Strengthening the system of subsidy to technical examination and post-award as a way to grant patents with higher quality and greater legal certainty.
- Providing information and proposing changes to the PCT system to increase the quality of technical information (international search and examination) offered by the international authorities to national and regional offices of patents.
- Revision of the rules of the Directorate of Patents; in particular, those aspects related to processing applications for patents and patent applications for utility model, strongly differentiating the two procedures.

The Report of the Federal Controller Court of September 21, 2011 (At 39/2011), however, does not consider this target to be attainable:

> In terms of productivity, we have that, in 2009, the PTO had 223 patent examiners working in the area of granting patents, according to the Statistical Bulletin of the PTO. These 223 examiners, in turn, were able to assess 15,077 cases in 2009, leading to a per capita production of 68 cases per examiner/year. In turn, in 2010 the number of examiners increased to 273, and these were able to assess 19,471 cases, representing 71 cases per examiner/year.
>
> For this reason, in the simulations . . . for the years 2010 and 2011 an average of 70 cases per examiner/year was considered as an indicator of productivity. The BrPTO report takes as a premise that productivity would increase to 80 cases per examiner/year for the years 2012 to 2015 as a result of the measures of "Project Backlog Solution Patent." This increased productivity is also quite optimistic, representing a growth of approximately 15% in the productivity of patent examination, and it is known that it takes an average of three years for new examiners to reach the productivity levels of the most experienced.
>
> Clearly, therefore, [the BrPTO] assumes a too optimistic scenario for its purpose of reducing until 2015 the procedures for the granting of patents to a delay of less than four years. This finding, however, belies the measures that have been taken by the PTO to control the backlog of patents. The Federal Government should, as far as possible, grant the PTO the means necessary for it to increase its capacity to undertake patent examination.

7 BRAZILIAN PTO PATENT EXAMINER AS A RELEVANT PLAYER

In a recently published inquiry on the role of patent examiners in Mexico, Peru and Brazil,[22] the following facts about the Brazilian examiner are reported:

> Some of the interviewed examiners noted institutional changes in INPI's last two administrations. (. . .) However, a few subjects point to a relaxation of "rigor" in the exams, despite resistance by the more senior staff.
>
> Another interesting result related to institutional changes and continuity was that INPI's institutional culture is more influenced by EPO than by USPTO. On the other hand, a significant number of examiners declared that TRIPS had exerted little influence on the patent-exam process itself.
>
> In INPI's case, and this is of extreme relevance, the examiner's personal rate

[22] A. C. Castro, A. M. Pacón, and M. Desidério, "Varieties of Latin-American Patent Offices: Comparative Study of Practices and Procedures", in L. Burlamaqui, A. C. Castro, and R. Katte, *Knowledge Governance: Reasserting the Public Interest*, London, Anthem Press, 2012.

> of application acceptance appears to vary greatly and is normally low, around 25 percent, with considerable variation according to patent class.

The same study reports the main problem found at the PTO:

> The main problem found is the physical infrastructure and the high level of backlog in patent examinations.

8 PATENTS VERSUS PVP: SOME FURTHER CONSIDERATIONS

As mentioned above, an interesting comparison could be made between the Brazilian patent system and its PVP counterpart. As has been seen, most PVPs are granted in Brazil to local entities; a considerable number of registrations are issued to the Federal Research agency Embrapa.[23]

Embrapa's success was due to a "focused" approach, which meant addressing specific problems caused by local issues (e.g., climate, soil) or sanitary concerns that allowed the development of varieties suited to the *cerrado* and the "boom" in grain production.

The cost of new technologies to local users is a further consideration. According to academic studies on the effect of the introduction of the 1997 statute, the impact of PVP on specific crops did not entail a significant cost increase for farmers. This was apparently due to the significant presence of farmer cooperative research units, which do not operate on a royalty-return rationale, and also to the ample availability of protected varieties supplied by informal sources or non-protected varieties of market-acceptable products.

However, particularly during 2012, farmers from the southern states fought fiercely in court against a set of Monsanto patents and plant varieties on account of high royalties and denial of breeders' rights.[24] It seems, therefore, that the different impact of patents and PVPs could be attributed to the right holder's policy and not to the nature of the IP right.

It must be noted that most such PVPs issued to local breeders are not abstract IP rights, but correspond to actually produced varieties. The efficiency of regional innovation has allowed Brazilian institutions to shine, contrary to the global trend in which foreign holders prevail. Plant

---

[23] Borges Barbosa and Lessa, "The New Brazilian Government Draft Law on Plant Varieties".

[24] See http://www.conjur.com.br/2012-abr-16/liminar-proibe-monsanto-cobrar-royalties-soja-suspensa.

varieties developed locally have accounted for most of the Brazilian grain market.

Embrapa alone was responsible for 44% of recommended soy varieties for the 2007/08 crop. Brazilian institutions jointly accounted for 72% of the same.

According to the USDA,[25] success factors in Brazilian plant variety research were:

> (. . .) First, substantially underutilized, but highly viable land remains available for agricultural production.
>
> Second, a strong domestic demand from a large, increasingly urbanized population is bolstered by an outlook for steady per capita income growth.
>
> Third, rapidly growing domestic poultry and pork sectors represent a robust source of demand for grains and protein meals.
>
> Finally, an extensive national agricultural research network that already has a proven track record, especially with soybeans, of successful varietal development and adaptation to tropical conditions.

In recent years, Embrapa's relations with multinational enterprises acting in the Brazilian marketplace have been, if anything, most amicable. The frequent joint R&D efforts are testament to a clearly collaborative (and not contentious) approach. In the initial years of the present Federal administration, Embrapa's attitude towards its multinational competitors was met with acerbic criticism from some leading members of the ruling Workers' Party (which despite its name is not a conventional leftist political organization).

9 THE REEXAMINATION OF THE BIOTECHNOLOGY BALANCE OF INTERESTS

As indicated above, the 1996 Brazilian patent statute has addressed conflicting interests. Chemical and pharmaceutical patents were not only provided for as mandated by TRIPS (some nine years before such an obligation was mandatory for developing countries), but patents already published were accepted whenever issued abroad. On the other hand, biotech inventions were covered by a quite restrictive set of provisions.[26]

---

[25] Schnepf et al., "Agriculture in Brazil and Argentina: Developments and Prospects for Major Field Crops".

[26] D. Borges Barbosa and K. Grau-Kuntz, "Exceptions, Limitations and Exclusions to Patent Rights – South America", SSRN, January 3, 2011, http://ssrn.com/abstract=1734269 or http://dx.doi.org/10.2139/ssrn.1734269.

Sixteen years after the law was issued, an extensive appraisal of such policy is afoot:[27]

> The call for private rights to innovations appears to go hand in hand with a concern to make scientific and technological commons available in the long term against a backdrop of global competition in the field of biotechnology. There is sometimes convergence between the positions of researchers, entrepreneurs and the State on this question.
>
> Public-sector researchers wish to see common rights restricted to Brazilian researchers and their private-sector (or indeed foreign) partners. Companies are aware of the interest of creating partnerships with universities that have significant human resources and tools that are frequently expensive.
>
> The shared aim, which resonates with the desire of the States to develop national research and industry, is thus to benefit from each other's innovations and face up to those foreign stakeholders with which no partnerships exist.
>
> Brazil is currently seeking to restructure these bundles of rights on nature-based innovations as part of legislative reforms that are in all likelihood imminent. In the political, scientific and industrial circles in question, the debate currently comes down to the following question: is an absence of patentability of naturally occurring life forms compatible with development of the biotechnology sector?
>
> If Brazil allows IPRs on natural elements in the near future, the question will then become the following: in what circumstances will the appropriation of innovations and natural elements through patents make it possible to develop the national biotechnology sector, and how will this redefine relations between the public and private benefits of biodiversity? ABS is not simply an issue when it comes to North-South relations on the international scene: it may also unite or divide within a single nation.

10 THE REEXAMINATION OF PATENTS AND CHANGING LOCAL INTERESTS

A highly disputed aspect of the current Brazilian patent system is the double examination of pharmaceutical filings by the PTO and ANVISA (the agency of the Ministry of Health equivalent to the US FDA).[28] Some authors have indicated that this mechanism could help to correct the recurrent governance problem of patent offices which they allege tend to favor the interests of patent holders, even to the detriment of other societal

---

[27] Filoche, "Biodiversity Fetishism and Biotechnology Promises in Brazil: From Policy Contradictions to Legal Adjustments", pp. 133–54.

[28] For a description of such joint examination, see D. Borges Barbosa, "O papel da ANVISA na concessão de patentes", June 2009, www.denisbarbosa.addr.com/arquivos/novidades/papelanvisa.pdf.

interests.[29] As might be expected, the controversy has been led by foreign patent holders, who account for almost all pharmaceutical filings.

However, recently some local players have apparently changed sides on this issue. ANVISA's action, previously applauded by local firms, has apparently lost some fans. A 2011 study by Shadlen has indicated that this new positioning may reflect an overall reassessment by at least some stakeholders of the whole patent system:[30]

> As indicated, new policy instruments include an array of financial incentives and rewards designed to encourage public and private R&D, patenting, licensing, and university–industry linkages. Actors have responded to these incentives.
>
> From 2000 to 2005, private sector R&D expenditures relative to sales (turnover) has increased by 211 percent, resident patent applications have increased by 48 percent, and Brazilians' international, peer-reviewed, scientific publications have increased by 89 percent.
>
> Again, by international standards Brazil's scores on such science, technology, and innovation indicators are low, but what is most important for a dynamic and political approach to coalitional change are the changes over time: growth in innovation-related investments and capabilities yield enlarged constituencies for policies that reward such activities.

11 PATENTS IN BRAZIL: NO CLEAR ROOM TO MANEUVER

Since adoption of the 1996 Brazilian patent law new institutional and private players have entered the field. Some domestic interests that 16 years ago were manifestly against a stronger patent system have repositioned themselves. A more balanced institutional environment (especially GIPI and the specialized court system), research success in some areas, and enhanced interest in innovation through government incentives are some of the possible reasons for such change.

Notwithstanding, patent filings are mostly from foreign sources at a rate much higher than the world average. The growth of local filings is less than for global filings which seems to signal that increased interest in the

---

29 P. Drahos, *The Global Governance of Knowledge: Patent Offices and their Clients*, Cambridge, Cambridge University Press, 2010, p. 249: "From a social welfare point of view this Brazilian model is one way in which developing countries can improve the quality of examination in a sector of vital national interests."

30 Shadlen, "The Political Contradictions of Incremental Innovation: Lessons from Pharmaceutical Patent Examination in Brazil".

patent system has not been effective. Therefore, the definition of a long-term national interest with regard to the patent system remains elusive.

Some final considerations:

In connection with biotechnology, and especially bio-generics, there is recent but not yet fully developed support for a less defensive design of the patent system.[31] Regarding plant varieties and, more generally, agricultural technologies, Embrapa and the Ministry of Agriculture have been lobbying for an enhanced Plant Variety Regime that has been actively opposed by farmer and NGO interests.

In the pharmaceutical and other research fields, the federal government started in 2012 a new federally sponsored entity (modeled after Embrapa) to bring to new areas the success achieved in the agricultural area. For the amount of resources involved, the use of the purchasing power of the federal government may also be an important tool for upgrading local demand for new patents.

BIBLIOGRAPHY

Aviani, D., http://www.sbmp.org.br/6congresso/wp-content/uploads/2011/08/1.-Daniela-Aviani-Panorama-Atual-no-Brasil.pdf (accessed August 1, 2012).

Borges Barbosa, D., "Counting Ten for TRIPS: Author Rights and Access to Information – A Cockroach's View of Encroachment", November 4, 2005, SSRN, http://ssrn.com/abstract=842564.

Borges Barbosa, D., "O papel da ANVISA na concessão de patentes", June 2009, www.denisbarbosa.addr.com/arquivos/novidades/papelanvisa.pdf.

Borges Barbosa, D., "TRIPS art. 7 and 8, FTAs and Trademarks", March 9, 2006, SSRN, http://ssrn.com/abstract=889107.

Borges Barbosa, D. and Grau-Kuntz, K., "Exceptions, Limitations and Exclusions to Patent Rights – South America", SSRN, January 3, 2011, http://ssrn.com/abstract=1734269 or http://dx.doi.org/10.2139/ssrn.1734269.

Borges Barbosa, D. and Lessa, M., "The New Brazilian Government Draft Law on Plant Varieties (Or. . . 'How a Developing Country May Want to Enhance IP Protection Because It May Actually Need It')", SSRN, June 6, 2009, http://ssrn.com/abstract=1415406.

Carvalho, N. P. de, *200 Anos do Sistema Brasileiro de Patentes: O Alvará de 28 de Abril de 1809*, Rio de Janeiro, Lumen Juris, 2009.

Carvalho, N. P. de, *A Estrutura dos Sistemas de Patentes e de Marcas – Passado, Presente e Futuro*, Rio de Janeiro, Lumen Juris, 2009.

Castro, A. C., Pacón, A. M., and Desidério, M., "Varieties of Latin-American Patent

[31] See generally, Filoche, "Biodiversity Fetishism and Biotechnology Promises in Brazil: From Policy Contradictions to Legal Adjustments". Notable in this context in the creation of a trade association of local firms interested in bio-generics, Farmabrasil.

Offices: Comparative Study of Practices and Procedures", in L. Burlamaqui, A. C. Castro, and R. Katte, *Knowledge Governance: Reasserting the Public Interest*, London, Anthem Press, 2012.
Drahos, P., *The Global Governance of Knowledge: Patent Offices and their Clients*, Cambridge, Cambridge University Press, 2010.
Filoche, G., "Biodiversity Fetishism and Biotechnology Promises in Brazil: From Policy Contradictions to Legal Adjustments", *The Journal of World Intellectual Property*, vol. 15, no. 2, 2012, pp. 133–54.
Malavota, L. M., *A construção do sistema de patentes no Brasil: um olhar histórico*, 1st edn, Rio de Janeiro, Lumen Juris, vol. 1, 2011.
Schnepf, R. et al., "Agriculture in Brazil and Argentina: Developments and Prospects for Major Field Crops", Agriculture and Trade Report No. WRS013, Economic Research Service, USDA, 85 (2001) at 61, http://www.ers.usda.gov/publications/wrs013 (accessed May 28, 2009).
Shadlen, K. C., "The Political Contradictions of Incremental Innovation: Lessons from Pharmaceutical Patent Examination in Brazil", *Politics & Society*, vol. 39, 2011, p. 143, originally published online April 5, 2011, http://pas.sagepub.com/content/39/2/143.
Silva, J. G. S. and Borschiver, S., "Critérios para a avaliação dos sistemas patentários", *Revista da ABPI*, January/February 2009.
UN Department of Economic and Social Affairs, "The Role of Patents in the Transfer of Technology to Developing Countries at 5", UN Doc. E/3861/Rev. 1, UN Sales No. 65.II.B.1, 1964.

Websites

http://www.wipo.int
http://www.inpi.gov.br
http://ccr3.pgr.mpf.gov.br
http://cit.ifg.edu.br
http://www.andef.com.br
http://www.conjur.com.br

China

9. Evolution of the patent system in China

Wei Zhuang

1 INTRODUCTION

China's stunning economic performance over the past three decades has largely relied on its manufacturing competitive advantage which is to a great extent based on cheap labour, low-cost resources and extensive environmental pollution.[1] In order to achieve sustainable economic growth, the Chinese government seeks to transform itself from a global manufacturing hub to an innovation engine by 2020. The issuance of the landmark document titled 'The National Outline for Medium and Long Term Science and Technology Development Planning (2006–2020)' (hereafter 'the MLP') has mapped out such a transition. The MLP aims to enhance indigenous innovation capabilities through a variety of policies and measures, including financial and taxation policies encouraging technological innovation at the enterprise level and safeguarding the interests of intellectual property rights (IPRs) owners.[2] Despite the recent patent explosion in China, it remains to be seen precisely what effects these policies will have on China's technological progress.

1.1 A Patent Boom in China

China has experienced a boom in both patent filings and patents in recent years. Published patent applications from China's patent office have risen by an average of 16.7 per cent annually from 171,000 in 2006 to nearly

---

[1] K. Ma, Minister, National Development and Reform Commission, 'The 11th Five-Year Plan: Targets, Paths and Policy Orientation', Gov.cn, Chinese government's official web portal, 19 March 2006, http://english.gov.cn/2006-03/23/content_234832.htm.

[2] State Council of the People's Republic of China, 'The National Outline for Medium and Long Term Science and Technology Development Planning (2006–2020)', *Guofa* (the State Council issue), no. 44, 2005.

314,000 in 2010.[3] Out of all patents filed in China, the percentage of domestic applications rose to nearly 73 per cent in 2010 from less than 52 per cent in 2006, suggesting that Chinese entities have outpaced foreign companies in the patent surge.[4] A closer look at the patent data seems to confirm this view. According to the Annual Report of China Valid Patent 2011 (Excerpt), China had a total of 2,739,906 valid patents by the end of 2011.[5] Valid invention patents totalled 696,939, an increase of 23.4 per cent compared with the year 2010.[6] Invention patents developed by domestic companies accounted for 52 per cent of the total in 2011, while the ratio was just 1 percent in 2001.[7]

The growth in patent applications and patents in China has been strongly encouraged by the strengthening of patent protection and innovation policies. It is highly likely that this trend will continue. As part of its 12th Five-Year Plan (2011–15) for National Economic and Social Development, China has set itself very ambitious goals in terms of R&D expenditure and invention patents. China is attempting to raise its R&D expenditure to 2.2 per cent as a proportion of GDP and is aiming for 3.3 invention patents for every 10,000 head of population by 2015.[8]

1.2 The Patent Quality Challenge Facing China

Yet, quantity is one thing, quality is quite another. Through analysis of a variety of patent statistics, the European Union Chamber of Commerce in China (EUCCC) finds that 'China's progress in patent quality lags behind its rates of patent filings'.[9] Under Chinese patent law, patent pro-

---

[3] C. Y. Lee, 'China Tops U.S, Japan to Become Top Patent Filer', Thomson Reuters 2011, 21 December 2011, http://www.reuters.com/article/2011/12/21/us-china-patents-idUSTRE7BK0LQ20111221.

[4] C. Y. Lee, 'China Tops U.S, Japan to Become Top Patent Filer'.

[5] State Intellectual Property Office of People's Republic of China (SIPO), 'Annual Report of China Valid Patent 2011 (Excerpt)', 05 July 2012, http://www.sipo.gov.cn/mtjj/2012/201207/t20120705_720265.html; these data include all three types of patents granted in China, namely, invention patent, utility model patent and design patent. Section 1.2 further clarifies this issue.

[6] SIPO, 'Annual Report of China Valid Patent 2011 (Excerpt)'.

[7] SIPO, 'Annual Report of China Valid Patent 2011 (Excerpt)'.The total inventory of Chinese invention patents outnumbered foreign-owned patents for the first time.

[8] Legislative Affairs Office of the State Council PRC, '12th Five-Year Plan (2011–2015) for National Economic and Social Development of P.R. China', 17 March 2011, http://www.chinalaw.gov.cn/article/xwzx/szkx/201103/20110300335435.shtml.

[9] D. Prud'homme, 'Dulling the Cutting-Edge: How Patent-Related Policies

tection is available in three forms: invention patent, utility model patent and design patent. The utility model and design patents generally contain small and incremental innovations and are not subject to substantive examination. By the end of 2011, utility models and designs accounted for 40.9 per cent and 33.7 per cent of the total valid patents in China, while the percentage of invention patents was relatively low at 25.4 per cent.[10] The composition of valid patents held by domestic patentees was even less balanced. Invention patents accounted for only 15.3 per cent, whereas utility models constituted 48.2 per cent and designs comprised 36.6 per cent.[11]

Furthermore, most of the invention patents in China have been accused of 'embodying little technological progress' and being 'driven mainly by incentives put in place by the Chinese government to encourage patenting directly'.[12] The average life span of invention patents awarded to domestic entities (around 6.9 years) is significantly lower than for foreign-owned invention patents in China (around 10.3 years).[13] Of invention patents owned by Chinese entities 54.3 per cent maintain validity for less than five years and only 4.8 per cent are in force for over ten years. In contrast, 84.8 per cent of foreign invention patents remain in force for over five years and 24.7 per cent remain valid for more than ten years.[14] The patents with longer life span generally embody higher levels of innovation and economic value. Few patent inventions owned by Chinese entities are at the frontier of world innovation. In 2010, only 0.6 per cent of US utility patents granted were owned by Chinese entities.[15] Worse still, foreign

---

and Practices Hamper Innovation in China', The European Union Chamber of Commerce in China, August 2012, http://www.euccc.com.cn/upload/media/media/27/patentstudy2012%5B766%5D.pdf, p. 5.

10 SIPO, 'Annual Report of China Valid Patent 2011 (Excerpt)'.

11 In contrast, the patents held by foreign firms were mainly invention patents, with the percentage being 79.1 per cent, while utility models and designs accounted for 2.4 per cent and 18.4 per cent; SIPO, 'Annual Report of China Valid Patent 2011 (Excerpt)'.

12 M. Eberhardt, C. Helmers and Z. Yu, 'Is the Dragon Learning to Fly? An Analysis of the Chinese Patent Explosion', CSAE Working Paper WPS/2011–15, 2011, p. 2.

13 The average life cycle of utility models owned by Chinese patentees is 4.1 years, with that of designs being 3.2 years, whereas the average life cycle of utility models filed by foreign entities is 5.9 years with that of designs being 6.3 years. SIPO, 'Annual Report of China Valid Patent 2011 (Excerpt)'.

14 SIPO, 'Annual Report of China Valid Patent 2011 (Excerpt)'.

15 J. Bessen, 'China is Not About to Out-innovate the U.S.', HBR Blog Network, 3 December 2010, http://blogs.hbr.org/cs/2010/12/china_is_not_about_to_out-inno.html.

firms generally do not file patents on their breakthrough inventions in China, further suggesting that China's patent ecosystem may be composed of few highest-quality patents.[16]

Moreover, China's patent portfolio in high-tech fields is particularly inadequate.[17] The sectoral composition of patents held by Chinese entities favours traditional sectors, including food, chemicals, civil engineering and medicine, whereas 'foreign investors still hold the advantage in high-tech industries, especially in optics, transportation, audio-visual technology, medical technology, semiconductors and engines'.[18]

On the whole, China has a patent quality problem. What policies and laws has China enacted to tackle the low patent quality issue? Making the patent system work does not necessarily lead to welfare efficiency.[19] What are the rules designed to address social welfare concerns specific to China? Before answering these questions, the chapter first studies the historical development of the Chinese patent system.

2 HISTORICAL DEVELOPMENT OF THE PATENT SYSTEM IN CHINA

The corresponding Chinese symbols for the concept of 'patent' are '专利' (zhuan li), merely meaning 'monopoly, or exclusive controlling advantage'.[20] The idea of a patent contradicts the Confucian principles ingrained in Chinese culture, emphasizing sharing and community commitment rather than individual profit. The patent system thus did not emerge in China in the way it did in Europe, even though China has enjoyed 'a remarkable history of technological and creative enterprise'[21] and 'the Chinese invented a number of items prior to their invention or use

16 Prud'homme, 'Dulling the Cutting-Edge: How Patent-Related Policies and Practices Hamper Innovation in China', p. 5.

17 SIPO, 'Annual Report of China Valid Patent 2011 (Excerpt)'.

18 X. Wang, 'Created in China, the Power of Invention Patents', *China Daily*, 29 February 2012, http://www.chinadaily.com.cn/cndy/2012–02/29/content_14716851.htm.

19 P. Drahos, 'The US, China and the G-77 in the Era of Responsive Patentability', Queen Mary, University of London, School of Law Legal Studies Research Paper, no. 105, 2012, p. 7.

20 C. Zheng and M. D. Pendleton, *Chinese Intellectual Property and Technology Transfer Law*, London, Sweet & Maxwell, 1987, p. 51.

21 J. R. Allison and L. Lin, 'The Evolution of Chinese Attitudes toward Property Rights in Invention and Discovery', *University of Pennsylvania Journal of International Economic Law*, vol. 20, no. 4, 1999, pp. 735– 91, at p.742.

in the West'.[22] Several attempts to transplant the Western patent system from the late 19th to the mid-20th century ultimately failed due to frequent wars, political turmoil, economic backwardness as well as technological underdevelopment.[23]

In the first three decades after the founding of the People's Republic of China (hereafter 'China') in 1949, the basic concepts and approaches to patents developed in a market economy were alien to a country which implemented a rigid centrally planned economy and instilled a collectivist ideology. During this period, all inventions were considered as State property; inventions could not be monopolized and all enterprises (both State owned and collectives) were free to make use of them as they considered fit.[24] Only at the end of 1978 when China decided to adopt 'Reform and Opening-up' policies, did the Chinese central authority start to consider the potential role of a workable patent system in attracting foreign technologies. As a progressive step forward to a market economy, 'socialist' China enacted its first patent law in 1984. As of today, Chinese patent law has been amended three times: in 1992, 2000 and 2008.

2.1 1979–1984: The Establishment of the Modern Patent Law in China

When it came to establishing the modern patent law, there were extensive debates in China as to whether a patent system developed in capitalist

---

[22] W. Shi, *Intellectual Property in the Global Trading System: EU-China Perspective*, Berlin and Heidelberg, Springer, 2008, p. 25. Shi further points out that the famous four great inventions, namely papermaking, typography, the compass, and gunpowder, have profoundly impacted the world's economy and the human culture.

[23] Zheng and Pendleton, *Chinese Intellectual Property and Technology Transfer Law*, pp. 51–2; according to Zheng, the first true statutory patent law in China, entitled Regulations to Promote Industrial Property, was enacted by the Emperor Guang Xu in 1898, during the Bourgeois Democratic Reform Movement. As the Reform failed in 1899, these Regulations existed as law for less than two months. The second patent law in Chinese history, entitled the Interim Regulations on Awards for Devices, was published by the Central Government of the Republic of China in 1912, i.e., the second year after the overthrow of the Qing Dynasty. Before 1944 a total of 692 patents were granted under these Regulations. Then in 1944, the Kuomintang Government in Chongqing published the Patent Law of the Republic of China. This was the third Chinese patent law. Few patents were granted under this law, i.e., on the mainland, before the People's Republic of China came into being.

[24] 'Regulations concerning Awards for Inventions, the State Council Promulgated', 3 November 1963, article 23, http://cpc.people.com.cn/GB/64184/64186/66672/4493654.html.

countries would suit or conform to the socialist nature of China and whether such a patent system would essentially benefit China's industry and science.[25] The wide technological gap between China and the Western countries, it was thought, might endanger China's domestic industry. Yet, whenever the Chinese authorities attempted to encourage foreign entities to transfer technologies to China, the latter were concerned about 'how the Chinese government would effectively protect their technologies'.[26] On the assumption that patent protection could be a factor in attracting foreign investment, China finally decided to introduce a 'modern' patent law in 1984. The Chinese Patent Law entered into force on 1 April 1985 and China joined the Paris Convention in the same year.

As a major exporter of technology to China in the early 1980s, Germany supported China in establishing its patent system, and thus the initial Chinese patent system was heavily influenced by German patent law.[27] It adopted a first-to-file principle, established a national patent office and provided patent protection to inventions, utility models and designs. The provisions in China's patent system, especially the procedures for granting invention patents, are similar to the then-West German patent system.[28] The utility model system in the Chinese Patent Law is also similar to that of Germany as neither the patent office of China nor Germany carry out substantial examination regarding the patentability of utility models.[29]

The Chinese Patent Law of 1984 included several provisions to address national needs. First, under Article 25 of the 1984 Chinese Patent Law, foods, beverages and condiments, and pharmaceutical products were

---

25 S. Guo, 'Some Remarks on the Third Revision Draft of the Chinese Patent Law', in W. Z. W. Pyrmont et al. (eds.), *Patents and Technological Progress in a Globalized World: Liber Amicorum Joseph Straus*, Berlin and Heidelberg, Springer, 1 edition, 2009, pp. 713–28, at p. 713; as most Chinese enterprises, research institutions and other organizations belong to the State, the exclusive right of a patent may not suit China.

26 Y. Sun, 'A Comparative Study of the Chinese Patent Law Practice–Part I: Obtaining a Chinese Patent', *Perspectives*, vol. 6, no. 4, 2005, pp. 9–17, at p. 9.

27 Sun, 'A Comparative Study of the Chinese Patent Law Practice–Part I: Obtaining a Chinese Patent', at p. 11. Due to its cold war strategy, the US had restricted exports of high-tech products to China. Therefore, before drafting its patent law, China mainly sent its technical staff to Germany and Japan to study their patents systems.

28 Zheng and Pendleton, *Chinese Intellectual Property and Technology Transfer Law*, pp. 56–64.

29 Zheng and Pendleton, *Chinese Intellectual Property and Technology Transfer Law*, p. 65.

excluded from patent protection because the Chinese government was afraid that 'patent protection would deprive parts of the population from an adequate supply of vital commodities at reasonable prices'.[30] Second, the scope for compulsory licences was quite broad under the 1984 Patent Law. Under Article 14, the State retained its power to permit the exploitation of patents held by Chinese individuals or collectively owned units.[31] Articles 51 and 52 obliged a patent holder to work the patents in China. If, three years after the date of the grant of a patent right, the patentee of an invention or utility model has failed, without any justified reason, to manufacture the patented product or use the patented process in China, the Patent Office might grant a compulsory licence upon request. Thus, the mere importation of patented products did not constitute 'working'. Finally, the 1984 Patent Law was characterized by weak patent protection. For instance, invention patents were protected for only 15 years and utility models and designs were protected for only five years, counted from the filing date of the application.[32] Innocent infringement was excluded from any legal liability.[33] Patent law enforcement was mainly a matter of administrative prosecution at the local level.[34]

2.2 1992: The First Amendment to the Chinese Patent Law

Largely due to the alleged deficiencies in its intellectual property law, in particular, the failure to provide product patents for chemicals,

---

30 P. Ganea and T. Pattloch, *Intellectual Property Law in China*, Max Planck Series on Asian Intellectual Property Law, edited by Heath Christopher, vol. 11, The Hague, Kluwer Law International, 2005, p. 6.

31 Patent Law of the People's Republic of China (hereafter, the 1984 Patent Law), adopted at the Fourth Meeting of the Standing Committee of the Sixth National People's Congress and promulgated by Order No. 11 of the People's Republic of China on 12 March 1984, and effective as of 1 April 1985, Article 14. This Article provides that 'if patents held by Chinese individuals or collectively owned entities are of great significance to the interests of the state or the public and need to be applied on an extended scale, the matter shall be handled by the relevant competent department of the State Council according to the provisions of the preceding paragraph, after reporting to the State Council and obtaining its approval'. The concern is that Chinese-foreign joint venture may be swept within the ambit of this provision.

32 The 1984 Patent Law, Article 45.

33 The 1984 Patent Law, Article 62 (2).

34 Ganea and Pattloch, *Intellectual Property Law in China*, p. 7; the authors also contended that the protection of process patents was limited to the mere right of using the process, whereas the products directly obtained from the process could be freely exploited.

including pharmaceuticals and agrochemicals, China was designated in 1991 as a 'Priority Foreign Country' under Section 301 of the amended Trade Act of 1974.[35] The threat of sanctions by the US and intense negotiations between China and the US Trade Representative (USTR) resulted in a Memorandum of Understanding on the protection of intellectual property (1992 MOU) in which China committed to revising its patent law.[36]

Pursuant to the 1992 MOU, China significantly changed its patent law. The 1992 Patent Law afforded protection to all chemical inventions, including pharmaceuticals and agricultural chemicals, whether products or processes.[37] The scope of protection of a patented process was extended to the product directly obtained by the patented process.[38] The protection term for invention patents was extended from 15 to 20 years, while that of utility model and design patents increased from five to ten years.[39] Furthermore, unauthorized importation of products which infringe on patents was prohibited.[40] Finally, the (sufficient) local working requirement was removed and the use of compulsory licences was severely restricted. Compulsory licences were allowed only in exceptional circumstances, such as refusal to deal, national emergency, public interest, or dependent patents.[41] A compulsory licence is neither exclusive nor

---

[35] D. Qiao, 'A Survey of Intellectual Property Issues in China–U.S. Trade Negotiations Under The Special 301 Provisions', *Pacific Rim Law & Policy Journal*, vol. 2, no. 2, 1993, pp. 259–88, at p. 276; The Act defines 'priority foreign countries' as 'those foreign countries (A) that have the most onerous or egregious acts, policies, or practices that (i) deny adequate and effective intellectual property rights, or (ii) deny fair and equitable market access to United States persons that rely upon intellectual property protection. . .'

[36] Memorandum of Understanding between the Government of the People's Republic of China and the Government of the United States of America on the Protection of Intellectual Property (MOU), 1992, http://tcc.export.gov/Trade_Agreements/All_Trade_Agreements/exp_005362.asp (accessed 19 October 2012).

[37] 1992 MOU, Article 1, para (1) (a).

[38] Patent Law of the People's Republic of China (1992 amendment), adopted on 4 September 1992, Standing Committee of the National People's Congress, Industrial Property, June 1993, Article 45, http://www.wipo.int/wipolex/en/text.jsp?file_id=138095.

[39] Patent Law of the People's Republic of China (1992 amendment), Article 11.

[40] Patent Law of the People's Republic of China (1992 amendment), Article 11; a new paragraph was added to the original Article 11, providing that 'After the grant of the patent right, except as otherwise provided for in the law, the patentee has the right to prevent any other person from importing. . .'

[41] Patent Law of the People's Republic of China (1992 amendment), Articles 51, 52 and 53.

transferable.[42] Other restrictions on the conditions included a reasonable exploitation fee and the possibility of judicial review.[43]

The first amendment of the Chinese Patent Law incorporated the key elements of the 1992 MOU and brought the level of patent protection closer to international standards. It solved some problems relating to patent protection that China was or would have been facing in multilateral trade negotiations and paved the way for China to accede to the Patent Cooperation Treaty (PCT).[44] China became a PCT Contracting State on 1 January 1994.

2.3 2000: The Second Amendment to the Chinese Patent Law

China officially became a Member of the World Trade Organization (WTO) on 11 December 2001. During its accession negotiations, China committed itself to bringing all of its intellectual property laws, including patent law, into compliance with the Agreement on Trade-Related Aspects of Intellectual Property Rights (the TRIPS Agreement). China was also forced to accept a number of TRIPS-plus obligations, namely on test data protection. The second amendment to the Chinese patent law, adopted on 25 August 2000 and entering into force on 1 July 2001, attempted to strengthen patent protection and provide effective enforcement, as required by the TRIPS Agreement.

The second amendment first strengthened the protection of patent rights by providing patent holders with new substantive rights, such as rights of 'offering for sale',[45] narrowing the scope of exceptions to infringement,[46] and further limiting the grounds for granting compulsory licences.[47] The

---

42 Patent Law of the People's Republic of China (1992 amendment), Article 56.

43 Patent Law of the People's Republic of China (1992 amendment), Articles 57 and 58.

44 Qiao, 'A Survey of Intellectual Property Issues in China–U.S. Trade Negotiations Under The Special 301 Provisions', pp. 259–88, at p. 287.

45 Patent Law of the People's Republic of China (2000 Amendment), Standing Committee of the National People's Congress, 25 August 2000, Article 11, http://www.wipo.int/wipolex/en/text.jsp?file_id=125983; it is noted that offering for sale only applies to invention and utility model patents but not to design patents.

46 Under Article 62 (2) of the 1992 Patent Law, use or sale of a patented product without knowledge of its having been made and sold without the authorization of the patentee shall not be considered as an infringement of a patent right; however, the 2000 amendment considered such use as infringement; see Article 63 of the 2000 Patent Law.

47 For example, in relation to dependent patents, Article 50 of the 2000 Patent

revision also improved enforcement procedures. In accordance with the TRIPS Agreement, Article 61 of the 2000 China Patent Law provides for provisional measures before litigation. Statutory guidelines on damage calculation by the People's Courts were provided in Article 60. Finally, in order to 'encourage technological inventions and fair competition among State-owned and non-state firms and institutions',[48] the amended law provided the same treatment in obtaining patent ownership rights and assigning patent rights.[49]

Similar to the 1992 amendment, this revision was a response to international pressure and it brought the Chinese patent law into closer conformity with the TRIPS requirements. These pro-patent amendments to some extent led to the patent boom in China. As Hu and Jefferson (2009) observed, patent applications and grants in China began their surge in 2000, although there was a small blip in 1993 after the first revision of the Chinese patent law.[50] The study also found that, prior to 2000, applications for invention patents had been growing by less than 10 per cent per year, while after 2000 the annual rate of growth for invention patent applications accelerated to 23 per cent.[51] Interestingly, the statistics indicated that the growth of foreign patent applications jumped from 12 per cent per year prior to 2000 to 23 per cent annually afterwards.[52]

Law stipulates that when an invention or utility model that is granted patent rights involves an *important* technical advance *of considerable economic significance* compared to the prior granted patent, and the exploitation of the later invention or utility model depends on the exploitation of the earlier patent (the new restrictions emphasized).

[48] 'Patent Law Revised to Better Protect Rights', *People's Daily*, 1 September 2000.

[49] Under Article 6 of the 1992 Patent Law, a state-owned entity only had patent holding rights; Article 10 provided that 'If a state-owned entity wishes to assign a right of patent application or a patent right, it must obtain the approval of the competent authorities at the next higher level'. The 2000 amendments eliminated such restrictions.

[50] A. G. Hu and H. G. Jefferson, 'A Great Wall of Patents: What is Behind China's Recent Patent Explosion?', *Journal of Development Economics*, vol. 90, 2009, pp. 57–68, at p. 59.

[51] Hu and Jefferson, 'A Great Wall of Patents: What is Behind China's Recent Patent Explosion?', p.59.

[52] Hu and Jefferson, 'A Great Wall of Patents: What is Behind China's Recent Patent Explosion?', p.59.

3 THE THIRD REVISION OF THE CHINESE PATENT LAW

With the explosion of patenting activity in China in the past few years, the protection of IPRs has increased in significance on the political agenda. The State Council issued the Outline of the National Intellectual Property Strategy (NIPS) in June 2008 which aims to improve 'China's capacity to create, utilize, protect and administer intellectual property, making China an innovative country'.[53] In response to this national strategy, China revised its patent law on 27 December 2008 for the third time.[54] Major changes in the third revision can be summarized as follows: first, encouraging indigenous innovation through strengthening patent protection, promoting patent disclosure and improving patent quality; second, facilitating the wide use of technology through, for example, codifying the prior art defence and redefining co-owners' rights; finally, in order to balance patent rights and public interest, the revision improved the compulsory licensing system, introduced disclosure rules for inventions relying on genetic resources, explicitly allowed parallel imports and introduced the Bolar exception.[55]

3.1 Enhancing Innovation Capability

Echoing the Outline of NIPS to build an innovative nation, for the first time China has included the enhancement of innovation capabilities as one of the legislative objectives of its patent law.[56] China's latest five-year plan (2011–15) emphasizes that China 'will strive to speed up the construction of an innovative country'.[57] Ensuring patent quality, strengthening patent

---

[53] State Council of the People's Republic of China, 'National Intellectual Property Strategy Outline', *Guofa* (the State Council issue), no. 18, 2008, http://www.gov.cn/gongbao/content/2008/content_1018942.htm.

[54] The Chinese Patent Law was revised on 27 December 2008 and came into force on 1 October 2009.

[55] EPO and MOFCOM, 'Third Revision of China's Patent Law: Legal Texts and Documents on the Drafting Process 2006–2008', EU-China IPR2, 2009, p. 4, http://www.lexisnexis.com/documents/pdf/20100211022732_large.pdf (accessed 30 October 2012); WTO, 'Trade Policy Review: China', WT/TPR/M/264/Add.1, Trade Policy Review Body of the WTO, 22 August 2012, p. 25.

[56] Patent Law of the People's Republic of China (2008 Amendment), Standing Committee of the National People's Congress, 27 December 2008, Article 1, http://www.wipo.int/wipolex/en/text.jsp?file_id=178664.

[57] Legislative Affairs Office of the State Council PRC (2011), '12th Five-Year Plan (2011–2015) for National Economic and Social Development of P.R. China'.

protection and making full use of patent information are considered essential for building up indigenous innovation capacity.[58]

3.1.1 Patentability standard raised

Under the previous Chinese patent law, the mere use or knowledge of an invention or a utility model outside China did not destroy novelty.[59] To improve patent quality, the 2008 Patent Law has adopted the more common 'absolute novelty' principle under which 'prior art' refers to any technology known to the public in China or abroad before the filing date.[60] This change may shut the door to 'patent hijacking',[61] and address the concern of 'junk patents'.[62]

Meanwhile, in order to raise the quality of design patents, the amendment extends the 'absolute novelty' requirements to patentable designs.[63] A design patent has to be significantly different from a prior design or combinations of the features of prior designs.[64] Additionally, patent protection is no longer available for two-dimensional designs of images, colours, or the combination of the two, which mainly serve as indicators.[65] After 1 October 2009 when the new patent law took effect, the threshold for design patents became higher and the number of 'junk' design patents was expected to be reduced.

---

58 SIPO, 'The National Patent Development Strategy (2011–2020)', 18 November 2010, http://www.sipo.gov.cn/ztzl/ndcs/zscqxcz/2011ipweek/tpstr2011/201104/t20110419_598974.html (accessed 29 January 2013); the Patent Strategy views the patent system as a fundamental system to encourage innovation; its strategic goals for 2015 include: first, the protection of patents will be significantly improved; second, a patent information service system will be established; and others; enhancing patent quality is one strategic focus.

59 The 2000 Patent Law, Article 22.

60 The 2008 Patent Law, Article 22.

61 'Patent hijacking' means the patenting in China of an invention that has been used or seen, e.g., at a trade fair, outside China; see Managing Intellectual Property, 'The Radical Third Amendment', 1 April 2009.

62 'Junk patents' are patents that do not warrant patent protections. When a 'junk patent' is asserted against an alleged infringer in a patent litigation in China, it will often be invalidated during the administrative patent re-examination procedure. Their existence not only negatively affects the quality of the patents granted in China but also causes the waste of judicial and administrative resources; W. Yang and A. Yen, 'The Dragon Gets New IP Claws: The Latest Amendments to the Chinese Patent Law', *Intellectual Property & Technology Law*, 2009, p. 8, http://www.ipo.org/AM/Template.cfm?Section=Patents&Template=/CM/ContentDisplay.cfm&ContentID=25439 (accessed 30 October 2012).

63 The 2008 Patent Law, Article 23.

64 The 2008 Patent Law, Article 23.

65 The 2008 Patent Law, Article 25.

3.1.2 Strengthening patent protection

Exclusive rights to offer for sale granted to design patentees Under the previous Chinese patent law, an offer for sale did not constitute infringement with respect to a design patent.[66] In order to enhance the level of design patent protection, Article 11 of the 2008 amendment has granted design patentees the right to exclude others from offering to sell.[67] This change enables design patent holders to pursue claims of infringement by advertisements, displaying in exhibitions or through other methods without permission.

Codification of pre-litigation evidence preservation Pre-litigation evidence preservation has been provided in the 2001 Judicial Interpretation, yet a party can only file an application for evidence preservation when enforcing a pre-litigation injunction to cease a patent infringement.[68] In order to prevent the accused infringer from destroying evidence before litigation, Article 67 of the 2008 Chinese Patent Law allows the patentee or interested party to file an independent application of evidence preservation. Due to this change, prosecuting patent infringements becomes much easier and the legitimate interests of patent holders can be protected more effectively.

Increased infringement damages In order to more effectively deter patent infringement, the 2008 amendment increased monetary damages. For the first time, the law explicitly stipulates that the damages shall include the patentee's reasonable expenses for taking actions against infringement.[69] The administrative penalty that may be imposed is increased from three to four times the illegal earnings, whereas the fine that may be imposed for the case in which there is no illegal gain has been increased from RMB 50,000 to RMB 200,000.[70] The 2008 Patent Law has codified statutory damages and doubled both the upper and lower

---

66 The 2000 Patent Law, Article 11.

67 The 2008 Patent Law, Article 11.

68 Questions Concerning the Application of Law to Pre-litigation Injunctions to Cease Patent Infringement Activities Several Provisions, Promulgated by the Supreme People's Court on 7 June 2001 and effective as of 1 July 2001, Article 16. It provides that 'when enforcing a pre-litigation injunction to cease a patent infringement, the People's Court may, based on the application of a party, additionally effect preservation of evidence with reference to Article 74 of the Civil Procedure Law'.

69 The 2008 Patent Law, Article 65.

70 The 2000 Patent Law, Articles 58 and 59; the 2008 Patent Law, Article 63.

limits of the amount.[71] These enhanced penalties for the act of patent infringement will better serve the interest of patent holders.

3.1.3 Facilitating dissemination of patent information

Dissemination of patent information is very important for stimulating innovation, reducing duplicative R&D activities, preventing the public from incautious infringement of patent rights, and ultimately promoting technological progress and economic and social development.[72] For the purpose of meeting the growing public demands for patent information, China decided to improve its patent information service. The 2008 amendment explicitly obliges the patent administration department under the State Council to 'release patent-related information in a complete, accurate and timely manner, and publish patent gazettes on a regular basis'.[73] The importance of patent information is further stressed by the National Patent Development Strategy (2011–20). According to the Strategy, China will establish a user-oriented, coordinated and cooperative patent information management and operational mechanism.[74] By 2015, a national patent data centre, five regional patent information service centres and 47 local patent information service centres are expected to be established.[75]

In addition to the amendments to the patent law, China has outlined in its 12th five-year plan priorities for the development of strategic emerging industries (SEIs) so as to achieve its innovation goals and transform its development pattern. The SEIs mainly cover seven areas: (1) energy-efficient, green technologies: (2) next-generation information technology; (3) pharmaceuticals and biotechnology; (4) high-end equipment manufacturing; (5) new energy; (6) new materials; and (7) new-energy vehicles.[76] The share of SEI's total added-value in its GDP is expected to increase from 3 per cent in 2010 to 8 per cent by 2015.[77]

---

[71] Under Article 65 of the 2008 Patent Law, the amount ranges from RMB 10,000 to RMB 1,000,000, while it was from RMB 5,000 to RMB 500,000 in the past.

[72] WIPO, 'Report by the Standing Committee on the Law of Patents, Fourteenth Session', SCP/14/10, Geneva, 11 October 2010, para. 156, http://www.wipo.int/edocs/mdocs/scp/en/scp_14/scp_14_10_prov_1.doc.

[73] The 2008 Patent Law, Article 21.

[74] SIPO, 'The National Patent Development Strategy (2011–2020)'.

[75] SIPO, 'The National Patent Development Strategy (2011–2020)'.

[76] Legislative Affairs Office of the State Council PRC (2011), '12th Five-Year Plan (2011–2015) for National Economic and Social Development of P.R. China'.

[77] Legislative Affairs Office of the State Council PRC (2011), '12th Five-Year Plan (2011–2015) for National Economic and Social Development of P.R. China'.

3.2 Promoting the Utilization of Patents

Utilization of IP has been identified by the Outline of NIPS as one of China's primary IP goals for the near future. The 2008 amendment attempted to facilitate the commercialization of patents through incorporating prior art as a defence to infringement, promoting the exploitation of co-owned patents and removing the approval requirement for transfer of patent rights from Chinese nationals to foreigners.

3.2.1 Adding provisions on prior art defence

In previous patent infringement cases, the defendant would have to try and invalidate the patent before the Patent Re-examination Board (PRB) and the Court had to wait until the PRB's declaration of the invalidity of the patent before deciding no infringement was found.[78] The whole process would take several years. Even if the accused infringer finally won the case, he would still suffer great losses in terms of time, money, market and reputation, which was unfair to those that utilized prior art or prior design.[79] The 2008 amendment adds a new provision stipulating that if the alleged infringer can prove the technology or design he exploits is prior art or prior design, the infringement claim shall be dismissed.[80] Notably, the absolute novelty principle, as discussed above, has expanded the scope of 'prior art' and 'prior design' and thus a prior art defence could be more frequently articulated. This new provision will help stop accusations in bad faith and accordingly promote technology utilization.

3.2.2 Encouraging the exploitation of co-owned patents

The previous Chinese Patent Law was silent on co-owners' rights. The 2008 amendment provided a new provision regarding the exploitation of jointly-owned patent clarifying that when the patent co-owners have not reached agreement, any of the co-owners is entitled to exploit the patent independently or grant non-exclusive licences to others to exploit the patent.[81] Such provisions prevent one of the co-owners from blocking the utilization of the patents rights arising from joint research efforts and ultimately promotes the exploitation and dissemination of the patented technologies.

---

[78] EPO and MOFCOM, 'Third Revision of China's Patent Law: Legal Texts and Documents on the Drafting Process 2006–2008', p. 153.

[79] EPO and MOFCOM, 'Third Revision of China's Patent Law: Legal Texts and Documents on the Drafting Process 2006–2008', p.62.

[80] The 2008 Patent Law, Article 62.

[81] The 2008 Patent Law, Article 15.

3.2.3 Removal of the approval requirement for technology transfer to foreigners

Under the 2000 Chinese Patent Law, any assignment of a patent or patent application from a Chinese entity to a foreigner needed to be approved by the competent authorities.[82] This requirement was inconsistent with the *Technology Export Regulations* under which only transfers relating to technology that is restricted for export requires approval from provincial branches of the Ministry of Commerce of the People's Republic of China (MOFCOM).[83] The approval requirement under the 2000 Patent Law makes transfer of Chinese patents to foreigners virtually impractical, in particular for non-restricted technologies which may comprise around 95 per cent of patentable inventions.[84] The 2008 amendment makes it clear that transfer of Chinese patents or patent applications to a foreign entity shall be subject to the provisions of relevant laws and administrative regulations.[85] Transfer of non-restricted patented technologies will no longer require prior approval.

3.3 Safeguarding Legitimate Rights and Interests of the Public and Preventing the Abuse of Patent Rights

Balancing the rights of patent holders and the public interest is another objective of the third Revision of the Chinese Patent Law. To address social welfare concerns, China incorporated the TRIPS flexibilities into its own law. In line with the relevant international treaties, China has improved the compulsory licensing system, incorporated mandatory disclosure of genetic resources, and broadened the scope of exception to patent infringements.

3.3.1 Improving the compulsory licensing system

The latest amendments to the Chinese patent law introduce more detailed compulsory licence provisions which are largely in line with the Paris

---

[82] The 2000 Patent Law, Article 10.

[83] Measures of the P.R. China for the Administration of the Technologies Prohibited or Restricted from Export, issued by the Ministry of Commerce and Ministry of Science and Technology, issued on 30 December 2001, entry into force on 1 January 2002, amended in 2009, http://www.wipo.int/wipolex/en/details.jsp?id=6587.

[84] L. Ng, D. Lau and T. Mak, *Highlights of the Third Amendments to the Chinese Patent Law*, Hong Kong, ONC Lawyers, 2009, p. 5, http://www.onc.hk/pub/oncfile/publication/ip/0902_en_3rd_amendment_to_chinese_patent_law.pdf.

[85] The 2008 Patent Law, Article 10.

Convention and the TRIPS Agreement. These amendments aim to balance the interests of patent holders and users and address social welfare concerns, in particular regarding public health priorities.

Echoing Article 31 (k) of the TRIPS Agreement, the 2008 amendment has included illegal monopolistic actions as a new ground for compulsory licensing.[86] The latest Measures for Compulsory Licensing of Patent Implementation (hereafter, 'the 2012 Measures') further clarify that such behaviour has to be determined to be anti-competitive under the law in an in-force judgment or determination by a judicial authority or an anti-monopoly law enforcement agency.[87] This new provision signals China's desire to promote fair competition among enterprises and shows its determination to combat the monopolistic behaviours of certain patentees. Additionally, in response to Article 31 (c) of the TRIPS Agreement, the 2008 Patent Law provides that in the case of semi-conductor technologies, a compulsory licence can only be granted on the basis of illegal monopoly or for the purpose of the public interest.[88]

The 2000 Patent Law permitted compulsory licences where an entity was unable to obtain a licence on reasonable terms and conditions within a reasonable period of time.[89] Under the current Patent Law, however, the failure of prior negotiation efforts is only a pre-condition for granting compulsory licences where the patentee has not (fully) exploited within the stipulated time or where there are blocking patents.[90]

The requirement to first make efforts to obtain authorization from the right holder is waived in an emergency or exceptional event of the State, or for the purposes of the public interest. The competent department under the State Council is entitled to recommend SIPO to grant a compulsory licence to exploit the patent.[91] However, application of the compulsory licensing system was unnecessarily limited to infectious diseases under the 2005 Measures for Implementing Compulsory Licensing of Patents Relating to Public Health Issues (the 2005 Measures).[92] The 2012 Measures have removed such restrictions and allow compulsory licensing

---

[86] The 2008 Patent Law, Article 48 (2).

[87] Measures for Compulsory Licensing of Patent Implementation, Order of the Director of the State Intellectual Property Office no. 64, 15 March 2012, Article 11, http://www.san-you.com/en/NewsInfo.asp?ID=528&TypeID=1.

[88] The 2008 Patent Law, Article 52.

[89] The 2000 Patent Law, Article 48.

[90] The 2008 Patent Law, Articles 48 (1), 51 and 54.

[91] Measures for Compulsory Licensing of Patent Implementation (2012), Article 6.

[92] Measures for Implementing Compulsory Licensing of Patents Relating to Public Health Issues, Order of the Director of the State Intellectual Property Office

of patented pharmaceuticals for any public health purposes. The competent authority is now entitled to permit compulsory licensing for a much wider range of pharmaceuticals.

In response to paragraph 6 of the Doha Declaration on the TRIPS Agreement and Public Health, the 2008 Amendment provides a new definitive statutory basis to compel compulsory licences for the benefit of public health. Under Article 50, the competent authority may grant a compulsory licence to manufacture the patented drugs and export them to the following countries and regions: least developed countries or regions; and developed or developing Members that express their wish to import such medicine through informing the WTO in accordance with relevant international treaties.[93]

Despite the fact that compulsory licensing has been available under the Chinese Patent Law since 1985, China has never granted a compulsory licence, even during the severe acute respiratory syndrome (SARS) outbreak in 2003. Recently, the Chinese public has been demanding compulsory licensing of drugs for hepatitis B, tuberculosis and AIDS. The latest amendments have paved the way for local manufacturing of generic drugs, making the system more compatible with the need to deal with public health crises. As one SIPO government official stated, if China were to begin granting compulsory licences, it would likely start with pharmaceutical patents.[94]

3.3.2 Compulsory disclosure rules for inventions relying on genetic resources

The Convention on Biological Diversity (CBD) requires that access to genetic resources shall follow the principles of state sovereignty, prior informed consent and benefits sharing,[95] and further prescribes that the patent system shall facilitate, rather than hinder, the protection of genetic resources.[96] Countries rich in genetic resources like India and Brazil, as well as industrialized countries such as Switzerland, Norway and Denmark, have introduced disclosure requirements in patent law to ensure that information on the provenance of claimed genetic resources

no. 37, 29 November 2005, Article 2, http://www.wipo.int/wipolex/en/details.jsp?id=6518.

93 Measures for Compulsory Licensing of Patent Implementation (2012), Article 7.

94 J. Ma, 'The Position of Compulsory Licensing in China', *Intellectual Property Magazine*, 2011, pp. 55–7, at p. 57.

95 Convention on Biological Diversity, United Nations, 1992, Article 15.

96 CBD, Article 16.

is provided.[97] As a country with abundant genetic resources, China has long been a victim of biopiracy. Genetic materials from wild soybeans, for instance, have been misappropriated by industrialized country companies to develop hybrids which are patented and exported to China again.[98] To address the issue of biopiracy, for the first time, China incorporated tough disclosure rules for inventions relying on genetic resources into its current patent law in line with the CBD.

Under the 2008 China Patent Law, for an invention based on genetic resources, the applicant is obliged to disclose the direct and original source of the genetic resources. If the applicant is not able to state the original source, it or he shall state the reasons.[99] Similar to the Andean Community and Costa Rica, China includes mandatory disclosure as one of the conditions for patentability.[100] No patent rights shall be granted for inventions that are accomplished by relying on genetic resources which are illegally obtained or utilized.[101] As SIPO explained, it is 'in the interest of China to follow the same practice of developing countries in an area where international treaties have always focused on the interest of developed countries'.[102]

The 2010 Implementation Rules define 'genetic resources' as the materials of actual or potential value which are obtained from human bodies, animals, plants and microorganisms and contain functional units of heredity.[103] 'Relying on genetic resources' refers to the use of the genetic function of the genetic resources.[104] Yet, the impact of these provisions

---

[97] T. Henninger, 'Disclosure Requirements in Patent Law and Related Measures: A Comparative Overview of Existing National and Regional Legislation on IP and Biodiversity', *Diálogo Centroamericano sobre medidas relacionadas con la biodiversidad y el sistema de PI*, Costa Rica, 17–19 November 2009, p. 3.

[98] J. Sun, 'Protection of Genetic Resources will be Incorporated into the Chinese Patent System', China's National People's Congress, 4 September 2008, http://www.npc.gov.cn/huiyi/lfzt/zlfxzaca/2008–09/04/content_1448160.htm.

[99] The 2008 Patent Law, Article 26.

[100] Henninger, 'Disclosure Requirements in Patent Law and Related Measures: A Comparative Overview of Existing National and Regional Legislation on IP and Biodiversity', p. 8.

[101] The 2008 Patent Law, Article 5.

[102] EPO and MOFCOM, 'Third Revision of China's Patent Law: Legal Texts and Documents on the Drafting Process 2006–2008', p. 5.

[103] Rules for the Implementation of the Patent Law of the People's Republic of China, Promulgated by Decree No. 306 of the State Council on 15 June 2001, revised for the second time on 9 January 2010, Article 26, http://www.wipo.int/wipolex/en/text.jsp?file_id=182267.

[104] Rules for the Implementation of the Patent Law of the People's Republic of China.

depends on what will constitute illegal acquisition and utilization. Biotechnology companies must comply with this new genetic disclosure requirement; otherwise, a Chinese patent will be rejected or invalidated. This is especially the case for applications originating from the US, Japan, Australia and some European countries where there is no equivalent mandatory disclosure requirement in their patent laws.[105]

3.3.3 Two newly added exceptions to patent infringement: parallel importation and Bolar exemption

Article 69 of the 2008 Patent Law provides a series of exemptions for acts that shall not be deemed to be patent infringement. Parallel imports and Bolar exemption are two newly added causes for non-infringements.

Parallel imports are explicitly permitted Under the TRIPS Agreement, WTO Member States are free to decide their positions in terms of the issue of exhaustion of IPRs.[106] The previous Chinese patent law was silent on the issues of parallel imports. The 2008 China Patent Law clearly provides that when a patented product or a product directly obtained by using the patented method is sold with the permission of the patentee, any other person using, offering to sell, selling or importing that product shall not be deemed infringing a patent.[107] This provision has confirmed the legality of parallel imports and thus introduced a regime of international exhaustion. No doubt, such international exhaustion will restrict the ability of the patent holders to charge higher prices in China than in other jurisdictions, as they will be vulnerable to being undercut by parallel importers.[108]

Bolar exception is introduced Bolar exception, first created in the US, deals with the use of an invention relating to a pharmaceutical product to conduct tests and obtain approval from a relevant authority, before the expiration of the patent, for commercialization of a generic version after the expiration of the patent.[109] This exception aims to balance the interests

---

[105] Henninger, 'Disclosure Requirements in Patent Law and Related Measures: A Comparative Overview of Existing National and Regional Legislation on IP and Biodiversity', p. 4.

[106] Agreement on Trade-Related Aspects of Intellectual Property Rights, WTO, 1994, Article 6; Declaration on the TRIPS Agreement and Public Health, Doha WTO Ministerial 2001, WT/MIN(01)/DEC/2, 14 November 2001, para (5) (d).

[107] The 2008 China Patent Law, Article 69 (1).

[108] Marks & Clerk China, 'The Third Amendment to the Chinese Patent Law', *China IP Briefing*, December 2009.

[109] C. M. Correa, *Intellectual Property Rights, the WTO and Developing*

of the patent holders and those of generic drug manufacturers by solving the problem of the lengthy regulatory approval time. The Bolar exemption has been adopted by many countries including the US, Canada, Japan and EU Members.

Following the international trend, the 2008 China Patent Law explicitly provides that manufacture, import or use of patented drugs or medical devices in order to provide necessary information for regulatory approval shall not be deemed as patent infringement.[110] This provision enables the generic manufacturers to start producing patented drugs or medical devices before patents expire for the referred to purposes only, but ultimately facilitating faster access to drugs or medical devices at a lower price.

It is noted, however, that in contradiction to the practice of some countries, China does not provide any balancing provisions, for example, patent term extension or a supplementary protection certificate, to compensate the patent holders for the restriction of their patent rights.[111] This system has been criticized as 'unbalanced' mainly by the originator pharmaceutical industry for being in favour of the generic industry and acting as a disincentive for investments in pharmaceutical research in China, but it is fully consistent with the TRIPS Agreement and with the practice in many countries, where no particular impact on such investment has been observed.[112] It is also to be noted that the WTO panel in the *Canada – Pharmaceutical Patents* case specially allowed a 'Bolar type' exception without patent term extension.[113]

Countries: the TRIPS Agreement and Policy Options, London and New York, Zed Books Ltd and Third World Network, 2000, p. 77.

[110] The 2008 China Patent Law, Article 69 (5).

[111] For instance, in the US, in exchange for the Bolar exception to exclusive patent rights, the patent term of the original drug can be extended up to five years; in EU Member countries, supplementary protection certificates were introduced to compensate for the long time needed to obtain regulatory approval of pharmaceutical products. See Drug Price Competition and Patent Term Restoration Act of 1984, PL 98–417, 24 September 1984; Council Regulation (EEC) No. 1768/92 of 18 June 1992 Concerning the Creation of a Supplementary Protection Certificate for Medicinal Products, *Official Journal* L 182, 2 July 1992 P.0001–005, at http://eur-lex.europa.eu/LexUriServ/LexUriServ.do?uri=CELEX:31992R1768:EN:HTML (accessed 31 January 2013).

[112] EPO and MOFCOM, 'Third Revision of China's Patent Law: Legal Texts and Documents on the Drafting Process 2006–2008', p. 163.

[113] Panel Report, Canada – Patent Protection of Pharmaceutical Products, WT/DS114/R, circulated 17 March 2000.

4 CONCLUSION

Compared to the earlier amendments, which were mainly driven by pressure from foreign investors and some WTO Members, the third revision of Chinese patent law was strongly driven by domestic demand for 'developing a strategy that balances IPRs, public interest and international obligations'.[114] Accordingly, instead of largely relying on legal transplants, this revision is mainly based on China's own development needs and its domestic experience in the past 20 years against the background of strengthening self-innovation capacity.[115]

Some changes, for instance, those dealing with genetic resources and the Bolar exception, have caused concern among industrial countries. Regarding the sanctions for failure to disclose the source of relevant genetic resources, the EUCCC argued that not granting the patent right might be unfair to the inventor who would usually not be the one breaching any regulation;[116] with respect to the Bolar exception, the relevant government authorities and some pharmaceutical companies from the EU, Japan and the US considered that the 'Bolar exception' would create an imbalance between public and private interests and thus suggested that the relevant drug patent term should be extended.[117] These views could be expected in light of the mercantile trade and investment perspectives of these countries.

However, changes have been carefully drawn up to establish a balance between private rights and public interest through, for example, providing greater legal certainty regarding patent rights and exceptions to patent infringement. Efforts have also been made to balance international obligations and specific domestic needs by including changes to safeguard Chinese national interests. Overall, the third revision to Chinese patent law has reflected the government's effort to promote domestic innovation and protect IP in accordance with international IP law. The effectiveness of such changes remains to be seen.

---

[114] EPO and MOFCOM, 'Third Revision of China's Patent Law: Legal Texts and Documents on the Drafting Process 2006–2008', p. 2.

[115] SIPO, '2008/SIPO Annual Report State Intellectual Property Office', PR. China, published by SIPO, 2009, http://english.sipo.gov.cn/laws/annualreports/AnnualReport2008/ (accessed 30 October 2012), p. 24.

[116] EPO and MOFCOM, 'Third Revision of China's Patent Law: Legal Texts and Documents on the Drafting Process 2006–2008', p. 156.

[117] EPO and MOFCOM, 'Third Revision of China's Patent Law: Legal Texts and Documents on the Drafting Process 2006–2008', p. 71.

REFERENCES

Agreement on Trade-Related Aspects of Intellectual Property Rights, WTO, 1994.

Allison, J. R. and Lin, L., 'The Evolution of Chinese Attitudes toward Property Rights in Invention and Discovery', *University of Pennsylvania Journal of International Economic Law*, vol. 20, no. 4, 1999.

Bessen, J., 'China is not about to out-innovate the U.S.', HBR Blog Network, 3 December 2010, http://blogs.hbr.org/cs/2010/12/china_is_not_about_to_out-inno.html.

Convention on Biological Diversity (CBD), United Nations, 1992.

Correa, C. M., *Intellectual Property Rights, the WTO and Developing Countries: the TRIPS Agreement and Policy Options*, London and New York, Zed Books Ltd and Third World Network, 2000.

Council Regulation (EEC) No. 1768/92 of 18 June 1992 Concerning the Creation of a Supplementary Protection Certificate for Medicinal Products, *Official Journal* L 182, 02 July 1992 P.0001–005, at http://eur-lex.europa.eu/LexUriServ/LexUriServ.do?uri=CELEX:31992R1768:EN:HTML (accessed 31 January 2013).

Declaration on the TRIPS Agreement and Public Health, Doha WTO Ministerial 2001, WT/MIN (01)/DEC/2, 14 November 2001.

Drahos, P., 'The US, China and the G-77 in the Era of Responsive Patentability', Queen Mary, University of London, School of Law Legal Studies Research Paper, No. 105, 2012.

Drug Price Competition and Patent Term Restoration Act of 1984, PL 98–417, 24 September 1984.

Eberhardt, M., Helmers, C. and Yu, Z., 'Is the Dragon Learning to Fly? An Analysis of the Chinese Patent Explosion', CSAE Working Paper WPS/2011–15, 2011.

EPO and MOFCOM, 'Third Revision of China's Patent Law: Legal Texts and Documents on the Drafting Process 2006–2008', EU-China IPR2, 2009, http://www.lexisnexis.com/documents/pdf/20100211022732_large.pdf (accessed 30 October 2012).

Ganea, P. and Pattloch, T., *Intellectual Property Law in China*, Max Planck Series on Asian Intellectual Property Law, edited by Heath Christopher, vol. 11, The Hague, Kluwer Law International, 2005.

Guo, S., 'Some Remarks on the Third Revision Draft of the Chinese Patent Law', in W. Z. W. Pyrmont et al. (eds.), *Patents and Technological Progress in a Globalized World: Liber Amicorum Joseph Straus*, Berlin and Heidelberg, Springer, 1st edition, 2009.

Henninger, T., 'Disclosure Requirements in Patent Law and Related Measures: A Comparative Overview of Existing National and Regional Legislation on IP and Biodiversity', Diálogo Centroamericano sobre medidas relacionadas con la biodiversidad y el sistema de PI, Costa Rica, 17–19 November 2009.

Hu, A. G. and Jefferson, G. H., 'A Great Wall of Patents: What is Behind China's Recent Patent Explosion?', *Journal of Development Economics*, vol. 90, 2009.

Lee, C.Y., 'China Tops U.S., Japan to Become Top Patent Filer', Thomson Reuters 2011, 21 December 2011, http://www.reuters.com/article/2011/12/21/us-china-patents-idUSTRE7BK0LQ20111221.

Legislative Affairs Office of the State Council P.R. China, '12th Five-Year Plan (2011–2015) for National Economic and Social Development of P.R. China', 17

March 2011, http://www.chinalaw.gov.cn/article/xwzx/szkx/201103/20110300335435.shtml.
Ma, J., 'The Position of Compulsory Licensing in China', *Intellectual Property Magazine*, November 2011.
Ma, K., Minister, National Development and Reform Commission, 'The 11th Five-Year Plan: Targets, Paths and Policy Orientation', Gov.cn, Chinese government's official web portal, 19 March 2006, http://english.gov.cn/2006–03/23/content_234832.htm.
Managing Intellectual Property, 'The Radical Third Amendment', 1 April 2009.
Marks & Clerk China, 'The Third Amendment to the Chinese Patent Law', *China IP Briefing*, December 2009.
Measures for Compulsory Licensing of Patent Implementation, Order of the Director of the State Intellectual Property Office No. 64, 15 March 2012, http://www.san-you.com/en/NewsInfo.asp?ID=528&TypeID=1.
Measures for Implementing Compulsory Licensing of Patents Relating to Public Health Issues, Order of the Director of the State Intellectual Property Office No. 37, 29 November 2005, http://www.wipo.int/wipolex/en/details.jsp?id=6518.
Measures of the P.R. China for the Administration of the Technologies Prohibited or Restricted from Export, issued by the Ministry of Commerce and Ministry of Science and Technology, issued on 30 December 2001, entry into force on 1 January 2002, amended in 2009, http://www.wipo.int/wipolex/en/details.jsp?id=6587.
Memorandum of Understanding between the Government of the People's Republic of China and the Government of the United States of America on the Protection of Intellectual Property, 1992, http://tcc.export.gov/Trade_Agreements/All_Trade_Agreements/exp_005362.asp (accessed 19 October 2012).
Ng, L., Lau, D. and Mak, T., *Highlights of the Third Amendments to the Chinese Patent Law*, Hong Kong, ONC Lawyers, 2009, http://www.onc.hk/pub/oncfile/publication/ip/0902_en_3rd_amendment_to_chinese_patent_law.pdf.
Panel Report, Canada – Patent Protection of Pharmaceutical Products, WT/DS114/R, circulated 17 March 2000.
Patent Law of the People's Republic of China (the 1984 Patent Law), adopted at the Fourth Meeting of the Standing Committee of the Sixth National People's Congress and promulgated by Order No. 11 of the People's Republic of China on 12 March 1984.
Patent Law of the People's Republic of China (1992 amendment), adopted on 4 September 1992, Standing Committee of the National People's Congress, Industrial Property, June 1993, http://www.wipo.int/wipolex/en/text.jsp?file_id=138095.
Patent Law of the People's Republic of China (2000 Amendment), Standing Committee of the National People's Congress, 25 August 2000, http://www.wipo.int/wipolex/en/text.jsp?file_id=125983.
Patent Law of the People's Republic of China (2008 Amendment), Standing Committee of the National People's Congress, 27 December 2008, http://www.wipo.int/wipolex/en/text.jsp?file_id=178664.
'Patent Law Revised to Better Protect Rights', *People's Daily*, 1 September 2000.
Prud'homme, D., 'Dulling the Cutting-Edge: How Patent-Related Policies and Practices Hamper Innovation in China', The European Union Chamber of Commerce in China, August 2012, http://www.euccc.com.cn/upload/media/media/27/patentstudy2012%5B766%5D.pdf.

Qiao, D., 'A Survey of Intellectual Property Issues in China-U.S. Trade Negotiations under The Special 301 Provisions', *Pacific Rim Law & Policy Journal*, vol. 2, no. 2, 1993.
Questions Concerning the Application of Law to Pre-litigation Injunctions to Cease Patent Infringement Activities Several Provisions, Promulgated by the Supreme People's Court on 7 June 2001 and effective as of 1 July 2001.
'Regulations concerning Awards for Inventions, the State Council Promulgated', 3 November 1963, http://cpc.people.com.cn/GB/64184/64186/66672/4493654.html.
Rules for the Implementation of the Patent Law of the People's Republic of China, Promulgated by Decree No. 306 of the State Council on 15 June 2001, revised for the second time on 9 January 2010, http://www.wipo.int/wipolex/en/text.jsp?file_id=182267.
Shi, W., *Intellectual Property in the Global Trading System: EU-China Perspective*, Springer, Berlin and Heidelberg, 2008.
SIPO, '2008/SIPO Annual Report State Intellectual Property Office', People's Republic of China, published by SIPO, 2009, http://english.sipo.gov.cn/laws/annualreports/AnnualReport2008/.
SIPO, 'Annual Report of China Valid Patent 2011 (Excerpt)', 5 July 2012, http://www.sipo.gov.cn/mtjj/2012/201207/t20120705_720265.html.
SIPO, 'The National Patent Development Strategy (2011–2020)', 18 November 2010, http://www.sipo.gov.cn/ztzl/ndcs/zscqxcz/2011ipweek/tpstr2011/201104/t20110419_598974.html.
State Council of the People's Republic of China, 'National Intellectual Property Strategy Outline', *Guofa* (the State Council issue), No. 18, 2008, http://www.gov.cn/gongbao/content/2008/content_1018942.htm.
State Intellectual Property Office of PRC (SIPO), 'Annual Report of China Valid Patent 2011 (Excerpt)', 5 July 2012, http://www.sipo.gov.cn/mtjj/2012/201207/t20120705_720265.html.
Sun, J., 'Protection of Genetic Resources will be Incorporated into the Chinese Patent System', China's National People's Congress, 4 September 2008, http://www.npc.gov.cn/huiyi/lfzt/zlfxzaca/2008–09/04/content_1448160.htm.
Sun, Y., 'A Comparative Study of the Chinese Patent Law Practice – Part I: Obtaining a Chinese Patent', *Perspectives*, vol. 6, no. 4, 2005.
Wang, X., 'Created in China, the Power of Invention Patents', *China Daily*, 29 February 2012, http://www.chinadaily.com.cn/cndy/2012–02/29/content_14716851.htm.
WIPO, 'Report by the Standing Committee on the Law of Patents, Fourteenth Session', SCP/14/10, Geneva, 11 October 2010, http://www.wipo.int/edocs/mdocs/scp/en/scp_14/scp_14_10_prov_1.doc.
WTO, 'Trade Policy Review: China', WT/TPR/M/264/Add.1, Trade Policy Review Body of the WTO, 22 August 2012.
Yang, W. and Yen, A., 'The Dragon Gets New IP Claws: The Latest Amendments to the Chinese Patent Law', *Intellectual Property & Technology Law*, 2009, http://www.ipo.org/AM/Template.cfm?Section=Patents&Template=/CM/ContentDisplay.cfm&ContentID=25439 (accessed 30 October 2012).
Zheng, C. and Pendleton, M. D., *Chinese Intellectual Property and Technology Transfer Law*, London, Sweet & Maxwell, 1987.

India

10. India in the world patent order

Rajeev Kher[1]

1 INTRODUCTION

According to the statistics circulated by the World Intellectual Property Organization (WIPO),[2] in the year 2010, the share of residents in global patent applications at all patent offices put together was estimated to be 37.9%.[3] The share was 39.5% for all patent grants.[4] In India, the share of residents in applications was only 21.2% and in grants 28.0%.[5] At the two extremes of the arc of grants of patents to residents were Italy (89.3%), France (88.7%) and Japan (84.1%) on the one hand and Canada (10.0%), Australia (8.1%) and Singapore (8.3%) on the other.[6]

Evidently, Indian engagement with the world in the case of patents tends to reflect the general trend seen in the case of lower and middle income countries. The WIPO data shows that, barring a few exceptions, the share of residents in these countries generally appears to be concentrated much below the average and tends to range between 9 to 30%.

The question that needs answering is whether the landscape has changed enough to accommodate a new set of rules for the patenting system. Should the rules be changed since the landscape needs to change to ensure that a better share of the innovation universe accrues to the developing countries?

---

1 These views are personal.

2 World Intellectual Property Organization (WIPO), 'World Intellectual Property Indicators – 2011 Edition', WIPO, Geneva, 2011, http://www.wipo.int/freepublications/en/intproperty/941/wipo_pub_941_2011.pdf,(accessed 23 March 2013).

3 WIPO, 'World Intellectual Property Indicators – 2011 Edition', p. 37.

4 WIPO, 'World Intellectual Property Indicators – 2011 Edition', p. 40.

5 WIPO, 'World Intellectual Property Indicators – 2011 Edition', pp. 43, 49.

6 WIPO, 'World Intellectual Property Indicators – 2011 Edition', p. 49.

This chapter shall seek to place India and its development story in perspective as regards the possible World Patent Order.

2 INDIA IN THE WORLD

India's engagement with the world through trade shows interesting features over time.

Figure 10.1 tells a great story of the impoverishment of a rich country over a period of two hundred years due to colonial exploitation, and this poor country trying to shake off the bondage of poverty and striving for growth in the 65 years that it has been an independent modern nation. It would be naïve to believe that absent colonial rule, India would have been the economic superpower today that it was a thousand years ago. Yet, most of the manifestations of colonial rule were visible in India, including its declining status in the world economy. In the post-Independence era we have seen India struggling to adopt models of economic development ranging from a tightly controlled socialistic pattern with state ownership of industries to a comparatively more liberalised model with state intervention limited substantially and a much larger share for the private sector in the economy. What is interesting in Figure 10.1 is the upturn, however small, that is visible over the last two decades. This upturn has also been accompanied by renewed interest on the part of her trading partners in the Indian economy. There has been a much greater degree of economic engagement with India in the last twenty years than was visible over the preceding forty. It can be reasonably concluded that this interest is directly related to the economic revival witnessed in India over the period.

If India is able to meet her development objectives of inclusive growth and high access to the resultant manifestations of this growth, then India would be a very interesting market to reach and do business in. Some estimates hint at the possibility of India outstripping most developed economies in size on both absolute and purchasing power bases by 2050. This gives India the ability to be listened to in the international arena of politics, economics and other such spheres of international engagement.

This interest has often been seen to be manifest also in the way India handles her intellectual property (IP) ecosystem. This includes not just IP legislation but also the attendant rules, as well as the efficiency or otherwise of the enforcement regime as it applies itself to the protection of IPRs of foreign entities. Some of this interest is negative, as was seen in the way the Special 301 Report of the USTR has consistently put India on its Priority Watch List for more than a decade and also makes observations

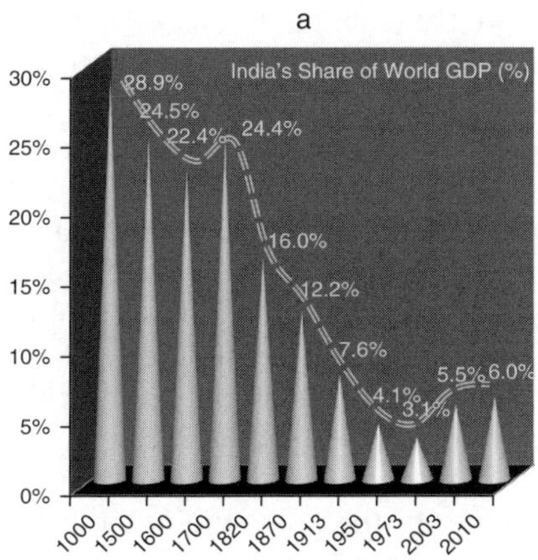

Source: Manas Chakravarty and Vatsala Kamat, 'India and China GDP: Trend During 1000–2014', *Livemint*, 3 January 2010, http://www.livemint.com/Money/tjnQtQuq545v3CaP4fPCkJ/India-and-China-GDP-trend-during-10002014.html.

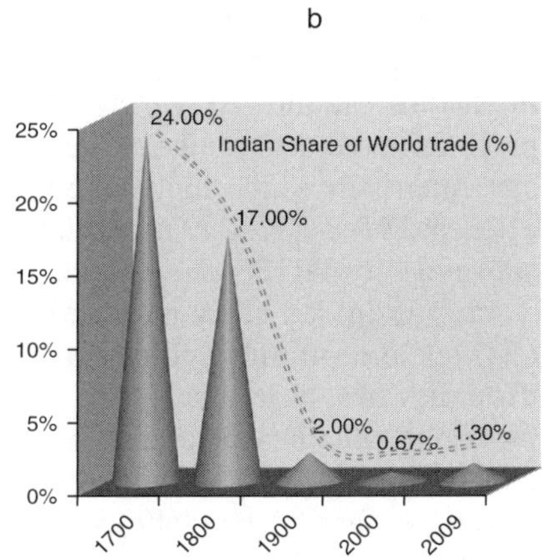

Source: Paul Kennedy, *The Rise and Fall of the Great Powers*, Random House, Inc., 1987, p. 149.

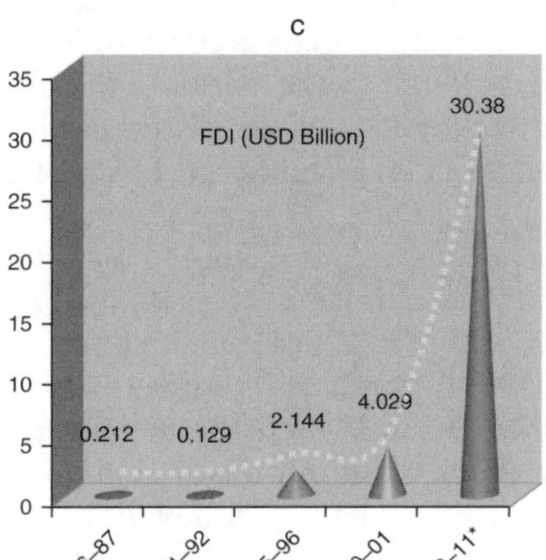

Source: UNCTAD.

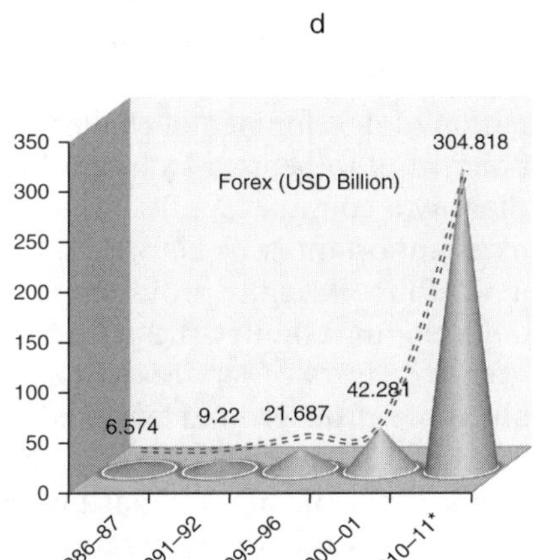

Source: http://portal.indiainfoline.com/datamonitor/Trade-and-Balance-of-Payments-Annually/Foreign-Exchange-Reserves.aspx.

Note: * Provisional.

Figure 10.1 India – certain trade-related indicators

on various facets of the Indian IP regime, to the extent that it feels US IPRs are put at risk.[7] Some of the comments also seem to carry a measure of implied threat and also seek to have India do more. At other times, trading partners have also sought to engage with India through bilateral trade agreements in which they have sought commitments towards protection of their IPRs. These commitments range from effective enforcement to substantially TRIPS-plus provisions on both legislation and enforcement.

Yet the Indian story is considerably tempered by the realities of, inter alia, socio-economic indicators of poverty, income inequalities, school dropout rates, lack of access to quality public health, availability of drinking water, the infrastructural constraints of electricity and road connectivity, and interregional imbalances. This is a clear indication of the tall order that India faces. The dichotomy is evident. On the one hand is the large GDP, a significant politico-economic profile that is building up, a high rate of savings, a major demographic dividend in the offing and, on the other, the difficult socio-economic indicators that are only too visible. The impact of such disparities is also to be seen in the multiple layers that the society has been sliced into. Thus, it is clear that there are multiple challenges before India and her people.

Among these challenges is one relating to the individualistic right of intellectual property. It is more relevant for a developing country to identify what its needs are and what it is being offered by the world. In this situation of developmental challenges, innovation is an extremely important policy tool to be used by a developing country. It is important to address the way a country handles innovation. I would like to emphasise that the most important issue before a developing society is not related to building a portfolio of legally protected IPRs and the technology it represents. For a developing country the greater challenge is that of ensuring an efficient way of delivery of services by being on the ball about how things are actually done at the ground level and how the processes work in such delivery. Thus, for a developing society the size of portfolio of private monopoly rights is not the most important indicator of the level of innovation. On the contrary the way innovation pervades society should be discernible in the distributive justice of the national income.

The vision of leaders helped develop a robust public sector in India in the 1960s and 1970s. Huge investments were made in scientific and technological infrastructure. Coupled with these a new ethos of innova-

---

7 Office of the United States Trade Representative, '2012 Special 301 Report', Washington, DC, April 2012, p. 35, http://www.ustr.gov/sites/default/files/2012%20Special%20301%20Report_0.pdf (accessed 23 March 2013).

tion developed in India which finds its roots in a scarcity-ridden society: 'Jugaad'. This term is not normally considered a very respectable term but on a practical basis it connotes the ability to find a way out of a difficult situation. One of the manifestations of this ability is found in the countryside of Central and Northern India where diesel water pump sets are put to multiple uses, one of them being to drive improvised goods vehicles which look like trucks used at the turn of the nineteenth century but made with even more rudimentary technology by local mechanics. There are no patents on this, no technology has been transferred, yet they exist. Such improvisations abound in the countryside and in small towns. For sure, this is not unique to India. This is the ground truth of innovation in a developing society where the focus is on delivery and where proprietary rights on innovation are not a concern. This is not to say that innovation is limited only to improvisation with the current state of the art. However, it is also a fact that in its attempt to attach a monetary incentive to innovation, the IP system might be ignoring the distributive justice essential during the development phase of any society.

3 THE WORLD ECONOMIC ORDER

We focus on the current situation of the world from the perspective of the rising role for developing countries. The most exciting position emerges from a motley group – BRICS. Discussion on this will appear later in the chapter.

It is likely that this story will be repeated in other countries which are similarly placed in the world economic order today. The most important aspect of this picture is that the mode of engagement with the rest of the world for these countries, jointly and severally, has undergone a paradigm shift. The first manifestation is their recognition of their market size as effective leverage in any trade negotiation. Secondly, trends in growth have been accompanied by substantial enhancement of technological capabilities and therefore of the ability to absorb as well as replicate sophisticated and cutting-edge technology in a large number of industries. These economies have also hit the crest of a demographic dividend almost in the manner of the baby boom of the 1950s and 1960s in the West. On the whole, these economies are also the new drivers of the world economy.

These features have given these and other similarly placed countries confidence to articulate their economic interests effectively in international forums. The way the stance of developing countries as a bloc has developed from the Uruguay Round to the Doha Development Agenda is an indicator of the way these countries now view their role in setting

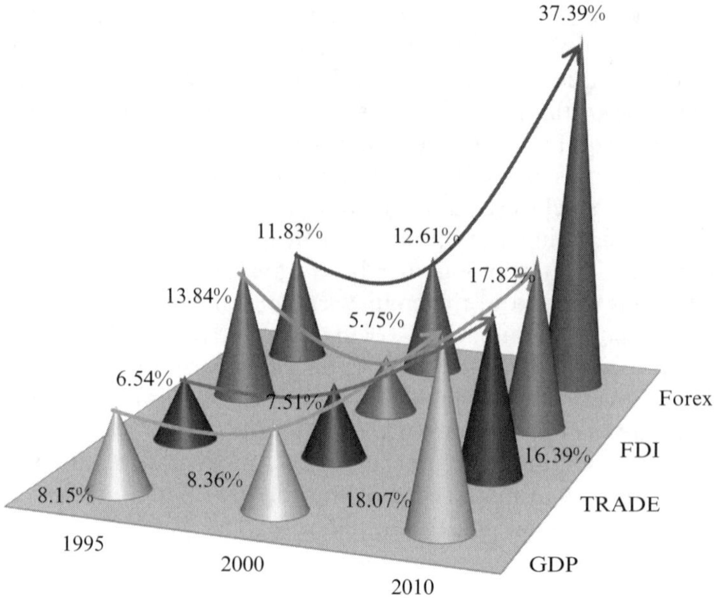

Source: The BRICS Report: A Study of Brazil, Russia, India, China, and South Africa with special focus on synergies and complementarities, Ministry of Finance, Government of India 2012, OUP, 2012.

Figure 10.2 BRICS over the years

the international agenda on trade and development. Where the Uruguay Round saw the developing world act as decision takers, not makers, the Doha process sees them emerging as agenda setters who will not go quietly into the night. The most important tool available for them has been the recognition of the power they can exercise via the size of the market they can offer to their trading partners. They have learnt how to leverage this power into effective negotiating stances at the WTO and beyond for political and economic gains. The way the new power dynamics are developing in the international politico-economic discourse it will not be easy for the developed world to continue to call the shots in the international arena as of yore.

Yet, the very same successful path of development seems to carry with it a possible threat to their trading partners since some of the developing countries are building capacity in exactly the same area of competitive advantage in which the developed world has held sway for more than a century, viz. technology. Thus, it would stand to reason that the maintenance of such comparative advantage in trade would require the technology gap to be maintained if not increased. This can be achieved by adopting one or more strategies contained in the broad categories of (a) enhanced innovation and (b) technology denial. Both these categories of strategies seek to use the international IP ecosystem to achieve their goals. While the first category would include offensive and defensive strategies, the latter would essentially be defensive. To give a simple example, the Bayh-Dole Act of the 1970s in the US was an offensive strategy to commercialise the fruits of government-funded research in the market through effective use of the IP system.[8] The efforts to create plurilateral instruments of IP protection such as the Anti-Counterfeiting Trading Agreement (ACTA) and the Trans-Pacific Partnership Agreement (TPPA) would fall into the second category. There is ample evidence of strategies under both categories being very much active in the de facto international IP regime today.

Having realised that the emerging economic realities would result in a new paradigm of trade and development and that the multilateral trade institutions were no longer the forum where economic dominance would be guaranteed, the 'plurilateralisation' of trade discourse was devised by developed countries as a strategy to maintain their dominance. While plurilateral agreements on government procurement and information technology existed, these were the result of the *ancien régime*. In fact, what we see is talk of a plurilateral agreement in services and expansion of the Information Technology Agreement. This can also be considered a tribute to the impact of developing countries in political and economic structures in the world.

4 INDIA'S ENGAGEMENT WITH MULTILATERAL PROCESSES IN THE FIELD OF IP

India has been a member of most of the important international conventions on IP such as the Paris Convention, the Berne Convention, the Universal Copyright Convention, etc.[9] In addition, India is a member of WIPO and most of the treaties governed by it. By virtue of being a founding member of the WTO, India is also a member of the TRIPS Agreement. However,

---

8 The University and Small Business Patent Procedure Act of 1980, 35 U.S.C. § 200–12.

9 World Intellectual Property Organization, 'Contracting Parties > India', WIPO, 2013, http://www.wipo.int/treaties/en/ShowResults.jsp?country_id=80C&start_year=ANY&end_year=ANY&search_what=C&treaty_all=ALL (accessed 23 March 2013).

this engagement with the international community regarding IP goes much beyond mere membership in the forums. As a responsible member of the international community, India has engaged effectively in almost all the negotiations related to international IP laws. Her interventions have been actively sought in most forums in support of or against many positions. India has made crucial contributions in the debates on the reform of the Patent Cooperation Treaty, the Substantive Patent Law Treaty, both at WIPO; the International Medical Products Anti-Counterfeiting Taskforce (IMPACT) related issues at the WHO; TRIPS-CBD (Convention on Biological Diversity) consistency issues; and the Nagoya Protocol. India was one of the active members of the negotiations that resulted in the Doha Declaration on the TRIPS Agreement and Public Health and paved the way for crucial amendments attempted in the agreement.

The global spectrum of intellectual property rights, particularly with respect to patents, has swung between one extreme of complete protection of creativity – reflected in low threshold of patentability, extended period of protection, strong enforcement with respect to violations, etc. – and the other extreme of a liberal environment – encouraging violation, low level of enforcement, copying – or high standards of patentability, limited period of protection and flexibilities drawn from TRIPS. TRIPS lays down the threshold of the international patent regime. Nations driven by so-called innovator concerns have tried to create a new global ecosystem in view of the low TRIPS threshold to safeguard their interests and lay down new levels of patent regimes. This can be seen in a largely diluted final version of ACTA and the TPPA (under negotiation at the time of writing). Yet another manifestation of this group's great concern to dominate was visible in a series of detentions of generic medicine consignments at some European airports a few years ago on the grounds of patent violation by exporters of medicines which were clearly destined for territories which neither had patent protection for those medicines, nor had they patent protection in their place of origin (India in this case). A strong aggression by India in the WTO in the form of a dispute led the European Union to modify its extant procedure and withdraw its relevant directives.[10] Yet another reflection of the conflict has been visible in the various patent law amendments pursued in some African countries based on an entirely misplaced understanding of the concept of territoriality and relevance of a patent in the industrial development of a country. These sets of examples

---

[10] World Trade Organization, 'European Union and a Member State – Seizure of Generic Drugs in Transit: Request for Consultations by India', WT/DS408/1, 19 May 2010, http://worldtradelaw.net/cr/ds408–1(cr).pdf.

clearly show the extreme conflict which existed between the two extreme sides of the spectrum. The debate continues unabated. There have been frequent attempts to confuse the issue of quality, safety and efficacy of medicines with breach of patent by often suggesting that generic medicines are a violation of patent rights, thereby misleading the proceedings in the WHO and broadly basing the aggression against developmental interest of developing countries in inter-governmental institutions such as the World Customs Organization, Interpol and WIPO.

4.1 Indian Patent System

The Indian Patent System has undergone three distinct phases. While it owes its origins to the British Patents regime that was the law of the land as the Indian Patents and Design Act of 1911, it was completely overhauled in 1970 based upon the recommendations of Justice N. Rajagopala Ayyangar whose report[11] was submitted to the Government of India in 1959. Much has been written and there has been great debate about this Report. Subsequently, in the context of the commitments made in the Uruguay Round, the Patent Act, 1970 was amended in 2005 to be in consonance with the TRIPS Agreement.

There appears to be reasonable cause to believe that the expansion and success of the generic drug industry in India is the direct result of the Patent Act, 1970 that resulted from this report. On the other hand it can also be argued by some that the 1970 law, which did not allow for product patents in the pharmaceutical industry, actually prevented India from developing a vibrant R&D ethos given that she had developed a large industrial base and had one of the largest pools of trained scientific manpower in the world. The jury is still out on the latter assertion. However, we need to give due credit to the vision of the author of the Report, who in 1959 had studied in detail the link between the level of technology in a country as underdeveloped as India and the need to provide access to cutting-edge art available in the rest of the world. After studying the patent laws of a large number of countries, some of which were developed countries at the time of writing of the Report, Justice Ayyangar stated the following:

> **Product claims for chemical substances not recommended; history of the law**
> 56. As regards inventions relating to chemical products and products produced by chemical processes, I am clearly of the view that the interests of the country would be best served by confining patentability to the processes by

[11] Justice N. Rajagopala Ayyangar, 'Report on the Revision of the Patents Law', September 1959.

which the products are obtained and to deny patents to the products either per se or in the qualified manner suggested in the bill.

57. The reasons for this recommendation are based on (1) history of the law relating to patents regarding chemical inventions in Europe during the past nearly 100 years and the lessons to be derived therefrom; (2) the experience of other countries somewhat similarly situated like India; and (3) the disadvantages to an underdeveloped country of permitting product claims for such inventions. . . .

Justice Ayyangar examined in detail the German, Dutch and English laws of the time and also saw the recurrence of the same theme in Austria, Brazil, Czechoslovakia, Holland, Hungary, Japan, Mexico, Norway, Poland, and the USSR. He also found the People's Republic of China had enacted a law that followed the USSR pattern in denying patents for chemical products while allowing processes to be patented.

What is evident is that the recommendation on process patents and not product patents for chemicals was not based on whims. Rather, the bases were the well-constructed patent regimes in many European countries that had grappled with the issue at their early stages of development and had moved on to a product patent regime only at a much later stage. The linkage between the level of development and the type of patent regime suitable to that stage is not an invention of India; rather it came from the same countries that were at the forefront of the upward harmonisation drive during the Uruguay Round at the WTO.

In the Indian context the laws on intellectual property and especially on patents are but tools of development. This philosophy also finds an echo in Articles 7 and 8[12] of TRIPS.

---

12 TRIPS Agreement

Article 7

Objectives

The protection and enforcement of intellectual property rights should contribute to the promotion of technological innovation and to the transfer and dissemination of technology, to the mutual advantage of producers and users of technological knowledge and in a manner conducive to social and economic welfare, and to a balance of rights and obligations.

Article 8

Principles

1. Members may, in formulating or amending their laws and regulations, adopt measures necessary to protect public health and nutrition, and to promote the public interest in sectors of vital importance to their socio-economic and tech-

Some observers have likened this approach to the now supposedly discredited 'infant industry argument' in the case of tariff protection that most countries provided for their fledgling industries in their early years of development. However, the logic of protection for new and developing industries at the early stages of development itself remains a viable and well-accepted logic in public policy even now. Thus, while certain commentators, with the benefit of hindsight, have commented adversely on the Indian patents law of the 1970s, there is no reason to believe with any degree of certainty that, absent such a law, innovation in India would have followed a different trajectory.

All this changed on account of the TRIPS Agreement. Article 27.1 of TRIPS required countries to necessarily provide for product patents in all fields of technology, including pharmaceuticals. TRIPS did allow countries like India a transition period of ten years to implement the necessary legislative changes to bring this about. This resulted in the Patents (Amendments) Act of 2005 which brought about the necessary changes in the Patents Act, 1970.[13] The passage of this piece of legislation was difficult and acrimonious to say the least. There had been very strong reservations against allowing product patents in the field of pharmaceuticals. A highly respected and eminent jurist and legal commentator described this type of patent as in clear violation of the Indian Constitution.[14] The

---

nological development, provided that such measures are consistent with the provisions of this Agreement.
2. Appropriate measures, provided that they are consistent with the provisions of this Agreement, may be needed to prevent the abuse of intellectual property rights by right holders or the resort to practices which unreasonably restrain trade or adversely affect the international transfer of technology.

[13] The Patents Act 1970, Controller General of Patents Designs and Trademarks [India], http://ipindia.nic.in/ipr/patent/patents.htm.

[14] 'To manufacture cheap outside, import and sell at any price in our market preventing by law indigenous producers is almost a definition of colonisation by a foreign power entering India, forbid Indians making the goods but offer a monopoly market. Why concede this dog-in-the-manger strategy? This is a textbook case of the violation of Article 19 (1) g and 19 (6) of the Constitution. This stratagem, if legislatively approved, is a shock and shame and proof of conquest by patent. Articles 14 (equal protection of the law), 19 (right to any trade or business) and 21 (right to life in good health) stand stultified if such glaring inequality between Indian products (denied patent) and foreign import of any commodity granted exclusive selling rights with no special benefit to the Indian consumer. This is gross inequality writ large, arbitrary, with no rational nexus to the wellbeing of "We, the People of India. . ." (Article 14). Similarly, Article 19 is unreasonably transgressed. To refuse the non-patentee the right to manufacture the same product, the restriction must be justified constitutionally by reasonable grounds relatable to

opposition to the legislation was so strong that the Government of India was forced to pass a Presidential decree by way of an Ordinance to meet its obligations under TRIPS on 1 January 2005. Later, after much debate both inside and outside the Parliament, the main Act came into existence and was notified on 5 April 2005. A quick reading of the Ordinance and the final law shows differences in a number of places, some of which are:

- New definitions of 'inventive step', 'new invention' and 'pharmaceutical substance' were deleted in the later version which became the law. The famous Section 3 (d) in its current form was a major development over the meagre addition of 'mere' ahead of 'new use' proposed in the Ordinance.
- There was a clear recognition that in the interregnum from 1995 until the coming of the Ordinance, there would have been considerable investment made by many companies in manufacturers in such products for which mail-box applications were pending and which might result in patents. For such cases, a reasonable royalty was allowed to the eventual patent holder.
- The scope of pre-grant opposition to a published patent application was considerably enhanced.
- The mechanism of 'compulsory licence' for supply to countries without adequate manufacturing capabilities in pharmaceuticals, as envisaged in paragraph 6 of the Doha Declaration on TRIPS and Public Health, was introduced.

The most contentious of these provisions has been that regarding the limitation on patentability imposed under Section 3 (d)[15] mentioned

---

public interest. For the surrender of a non-patentee's Article 19 rights, what is the substantial public interest for Indians? No other ground save that MNC Might is Right. And "the most unkindest cut of all" is that by the grant of patents on even agriculture, pharmaceuticals and essential items necessary for the life of the community, Article 21 – the right to life, health, shelter – is frustrated.'

Iyer, Justice V.K. Krishna, 'Human Health and Patent Law', *Frontline*, vol. 17, no. 21, 14–27 October 2000.

[15] Patents Act, 1970:

Section 3 – What are not inventions. –

The following are not inventions within the meaning of this Act, –

the mere discovery of a new form of a known substance which does not result in the enhancement of the known efficacy of that substance or the mere discovery of any new property or new use for a known substance or of the mere use of a known process, machine or apparatus unless such known process results in a new product or employs at least one new reactant.

above. The effort of the legislature has been to prevent that scourge of patent systems around the world, viz. 'evergreening'. On the face of it there cannot be any argument against a law that prevents evergreening. However, in India, this has adopted crucial hues because of the large market that India represents and the highly developed generic drugs industry in existence which can effectively produce legal generic versions of the patented products currently held by large multinational corporations. This amendment has been used to deny a number of patent applications in India. Additionally, a matter is currently at an advanced stage of argument before the Supreme Court in which action under this section has been challenged as inapplicable.[16]

Another recent development, which has attracted worldwide attention, is that of a compulsory licence granted under the provisions of the Indian law to an Indian manufacturer for a drug patented by a multinational

---

Explanation: For the purposes of this clause, salts, esters, ethers, polymorphs, metabolites, pure form, particle size, isomers, mixtures of isomers, complexes, combinations and other derivatives of known substance shall be considered to be the same substance, unless they differ significantly in properties with regard to efficacy;

16 In 1997, Novartis AG, a pharmaceutical company based in Switzerland, filed a patent application in the Chennai (Madras) Patent Controller's office for the beta-crystalline form of imatinib mesylate, brand name Glivec (Gleevec) on the ground that it invented the beta-crystalline salt form (imatinib mesylate) of the free base, imatinib. The Patent Controller in Chennai, in 2006, refused to grant Novartis a patent, on the grounds that the subject application lacked novelty, was obvious, and was not patentable under Section 3 (d) of the Patents Act, 1970. In June 2006, Novartis AG and its Indian subsidiary, Novartis India, filed a writ petition challenging the decision of the Patent Controller to refuse to grant Novartis a patent for the beta-crystalline form of its anticancer drug, imatinib mesylate, as well as the constitutional validity of Section 3 (d) that provided one of several grounds for rejecting its patent application. Novartis contended that since there was no clarity as to what constituted 'enhancement of efficacy' and 'significant enhancement of efficacy' as required by Section 3 (d), the law was vague and lent itself to arbitrary decisions by the Patent Controller. The Madras High Court dismissed Novartis' writ petition holding that the object of the Amending Act was to prevent '*evergreening*', to provide easy access to the citizens of this country to life-saving drugs and to discharge their Constitutional obligation of providing good health care to its citizens.

The order of the Patent controller was then appealed at the Intellectual Property Appellate Board (IPAB) which held that Novartis' alleged invention did not satisfy the test of Section 3 (d) in as much as Novartis did not provide data to show that the new form exhibited enhanced therapeutic efficacy over imatinib mesylate, the known substance. Novartis has approached the Supreme Court challenging the IPAB's interpretation and application of Section 3 (d) to its patent application.

company. It was found by the Controller General of Patents that the three conditions for grant of a compulsory licence as laid down in Section 84[17] of the Patents Act, 1970 were all met even though the licence could have been granted if only one of the conditions was met.

The Patents Act includes within its purview major flexibilities covering strict patentability conditions, exempted inventions, parallel importation, public non-commercial use, compulsory licensing under many conditions, including exports to least developed countries (LDCs), pre- and post-grant opposition, etc. In doing so, India has attempted to work within the overall ambit of the flexibilities allowed under the TRIPS Agreement as well as seeking to protect her prime national objective of achieving growth with equity by making access a crucial reference point of its legislation.

4.2 Is Domestic Innovation Stimulated by the System or is it Inhibited?

The moot question here is whether the patent law is vested with the responsibility of stimulating investment, or whether its existence is only to protect rights emanating from creativity and investment resulting in new knowledge.

While the underlying philosophy for any patent system is that patent protection is essential to maintain the virtuous cycle of creativity–reward–more creativity, empirical evidence on the existence of this causal relationship is not clear. Certain commentators are sceptical of giving deference to the patent system as the best solution to the problem of incentives.[18]

---

[17] **84. Compulsory licences**

(1) At any time after the expiration of three years from the date of the sealing of a patent, any person interested may make an application to the Controller for grant of compulsory licence on patent on any of the following grounds, namely:–
  (a) that the reasonable requirements of the public with respect to the patented invention have not been satisfied, or
  (b) that the patented invention is not available to the public at a reasonably affordable price, or
  (c) that the patented invention is not worked in the territory of India. . . .

[18] 'Fortunately, as economic studies have shown repeatedly, patents do not play a particularly important role in most fields of industrial innovation, and equally fortunately, those who advise industrial leaders in their journeys through the patent minefield are adept at negotiating solutions that in most instances avoid serious impediments to the pace of technological progress. It is nevertheless useful to assess the negatives and attempt to correct them through legislative or judicial action.'

F.M. Scherer, *Journal on Telecomm. & High Tech. L.*, vol. 7, 2009, pp. 167–216.

In this regard, the Report on the International Patent System prepared by the WIPO Secretariat finds '[i]nconclusive empirical evidence on patent strength and innovation relationship makes it difficult to draw any conclusion about the effectiveness of patent system to encourage R&D investments'.[19]

The European Patent Office (EPO) finds

> Now, due to the cumulative, multidisciplinary and collaborative innovation process, ownership of knowledge in many technical fields has become highly fragmented. That means that the use and diffusion of knowledge have become increasingly impeded, threatening the concept of new inventors 'standing on the shoulders of giants'. Even if this blockage is somewhat alleviated by the possibility of cross-licensing or the so-called research exemption on patented subject matter and 'fair use' exemptions in copyright law, that fundamental sharing of benefits offered by patents is under threat from modern IP ownership practices and enforcement of IPRs.[20]

This provides a reality check on the effectiveness of the existing patent system in fostering further innovation given that rights and obligations are in constant tension in any IPR regime.

Perhaps the answer can be found in the element of competition that results from the disclosure mandated under the law of patents. In an ideal world, if a knowledge holder were able to ensure that her knowledge would remain her secret and thus allow her to retain an incontestable lead over any competitor in the market, she would prefer such a lead in place of the limited period protection that a patent would provide. However, such secrecy is difficult to sustain even under laws related to undisclosed information as it cannot preclude reverse engineering. Thus, we can hypothesise that patent protection is a choice of the second-best option, which is exercised only when the knowledge holder is faced with the inevitable loss of secrecy due to disclosure norms, if her knowledge has to be commercialised. This contention leads us to a question as to whether the second-best choice can or should be made superior to maintaining total secrecy in terms of the extent of monopolistic protection it can provide to

---

19 World Intellectual Property Organization, Standing Committee on the Law of Patents, 'Report on the International Patent System', SCP/12/3 Rev., 20 June 2008, p. 9, http://www.wipo.int/edocs/mdocs/scp/en/scp_12/scp_12_3_rev.pdf (accessed 29 February 2012).

20 Shirin Elahi et al. (eds.), 'Scenarios for The Future: How Might IP Regimes Evolve by 2025? What Global Legitimacy Might Such Regimes Have?', European Patent Office, Munich, 2007, p. 29, http://documents.epo.org/projects/babylon/eponet.nsf/0/63A726D28B589B5BC12572DB00597683/$File/EPO_scenarios_bookmarked.pdf (accessed 29 February 2012).

the knowledge holder. The second question then would be whether such a statutorily protected monopoly over knowledge actually stimulates innovation. There is no conclusive economic evidence concerning this issue. Further, the implications of this for the scale of domestic innovation is not clear. Qian (2007), in a survey of 92 countries over the period 1978 to 2002, found

> National patent protection alone does not stimulate domestic innovation, as estimated by changes in citation-weighted U.S. patent awards, domestic R&D, and pharmaceutical industry exports. However, domestic innovation accelerates in countries with higher levels of economic development, educational attainment, and economic freedom. Additionally, there appears to be an optimal level of intellectual property rights regulation above which further enhancement reduces innovative activities.
>
> . . . In short, for countries that have relatively low levels of development, education, and market freedom, any potential benefits from additional innovation depend ultimately on domestic macroeconomic factors and require a substantial time-discount.[21]

This can be attributed to the fact that any patent system might be attempting to address too wide a spectrum of industries each with its own set of policy objectives, not necessarily related to promotion of innovation. In this regard, Bronwyn H. Hall states

> The evidence surveyed here also leads inexorably to the conclusion that a significant problem for policy makers is the heterogeneity of responses to the system, a heterogeneity that is firmly grounded in the heterogeneity of technology and its development. The debate presently taking place in the United States over patent reform highlights the problem: pharmaceutical firms, among others, find that the present system works well for them and are opposed to any changes designed to improve its operation for firms in 'complex' technology industries such as telecommunications and computing. ICT firms, on the other hand, seem to view the system as a necessary evil, requiring costly investments in patent portfolio building for defensive purpose while using other methods to secure returns to their own innovations. Many of these firms support reforms to the system that are designed to mitigate the problems which arise when a product contains many minor inventions and relies on a number of standards that may be covered by patents.[22]

---

[21] Yi Qian, 'Do Additional National Patent Laws Stimulate Domestic Innovation in a Global Patenting Environment: A Cross-Country Analysis of Pharmaceutical Patent Protection, 1978–2002', *Review of Economics and Statistics*, vol. 89, no. 3, August 2007, pp. 436, 450.

[22] Bronwyn H. Hall, 'Patents and Patent Policy', *Oxford Review of Economic Policy*, vol. 23, no. 4, December 2007, p 18, http://elsa.berkeley.edu/~bhhall/papers/BHH07_OxREP_patents.pdf (accessed 29 February 2012).

On the other hand, it has also been contended that import competition can stimulate innovation and product upgrading. Fernandes and Pauvnov (2010), studying the Chilean economy, came to the following conclusion:

> [These findings] suggest that increased exposure to imports can be beneficial for innovation outcomes. Moreover, we find that the mechanism driving this outcome is that firms react to the import pressure by innovating so as to differentiate their products as a way to escape competition. Our findings, therefore, point to the importance of competition policy more generally. In addition, our results indicate that easier access to imported inputs also has beneficial effects on innovation, which points to the importance of learning from trade in stimulating innovation. However, our evidence also suggests that such benefits only arise if the right conditions hold: it requires firms to dispose of skilled personnel and will occur mostly in industries whose attributes offer opportunities for such innovativeness. This implies that for the dynamic benefits of trade to materialize the framework conditions do matter.[23]

Further, there is evidence to the effect that the exception and limitations to patent law can also stimulate innovation. The WIPO Report cited above states:

> [35.] There is also ample evidence on the limitations of the patent system in encouraging innovation activities.

As it stands, there is no clear answer to these vexing questions. The efforts of national governments to find a best way forward within the context of various socio-economic considerations prevailing in the domestic economy is still very much a work in progress.

4.3 Patenting in India

Be that as it may, the Indian Patent law was amended with effect from 1 January 2005 to bring it in consonance with the commitments made at the WTO under the TRIPS Agreement. An interesting picture emerges from the patenting activity since then.

While the number of foreign patents granted in India was consistently higher through the period of 1999 to 2010, what was witnessed

---

[23] Ana Margarida Fernandes and Caroline Paunov, 'Does Trade Stimulate Innovation? Evidence from Firm-Product Data', Working Paper no. 286, OECD Development Centre, January 2010, p. 42, http://www.oecd.org/dataoecd/12/53/44457803.pdf (accessed 29 February 2012).

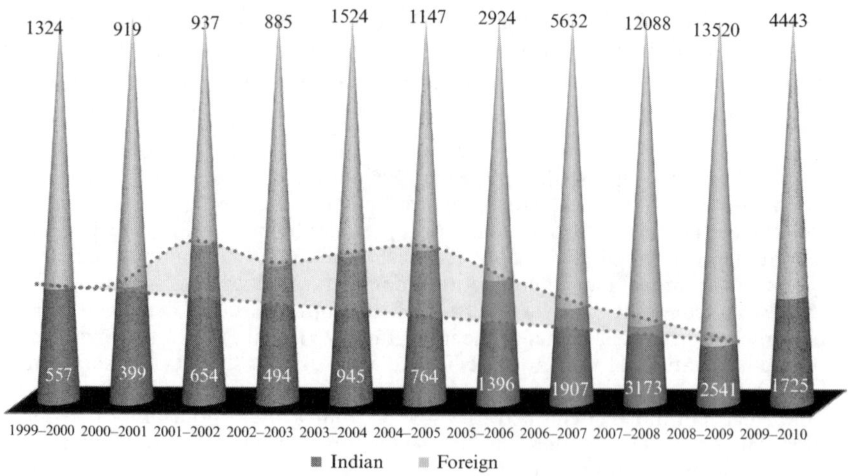

Source: Data from Indian Patent Office. The status of patents in force in India is not much better regarding Indian patents.

Figure 10.3 India – patents granted by nationality

was a spurt from 2005 to 2006. Not all of this can be explained by the mail-box. Since the information for 2009–10 is not complete, we may disregard that year to appreciate the trend. The second issue relates to the share of Indian patents in the total grant of patents. This can be seen to be declining until 2008–09. The recovery in 2009–10 appears aberrational.

What Figure 10.4 reveals is not only that the number of foreign patents in force in India is more than Indian patents in force by a factor of nearly five, but also that they exhibit an increasing trend at almost four times the rate of Indian patents.

A simple trend analysis of patents granted shows a similar picture. The trend shows that nearly four times more foreign patents than Indian patents are being granted in India.

If we shorten the period under consideration and remove the year 2009–10 as an aberrational year then the position becomes even more revealing:

Chaudhuri[24] found, rather disturbingly, 'the manufacturing and

[24] Sudip Chaudhuri, 'Multinationals and Monopolies: Pharmaceutical Industry in India after TRIPS', *Economic and Political Weekly*, vol. 47, no. 12, 24–30 March 2012, p. 46.

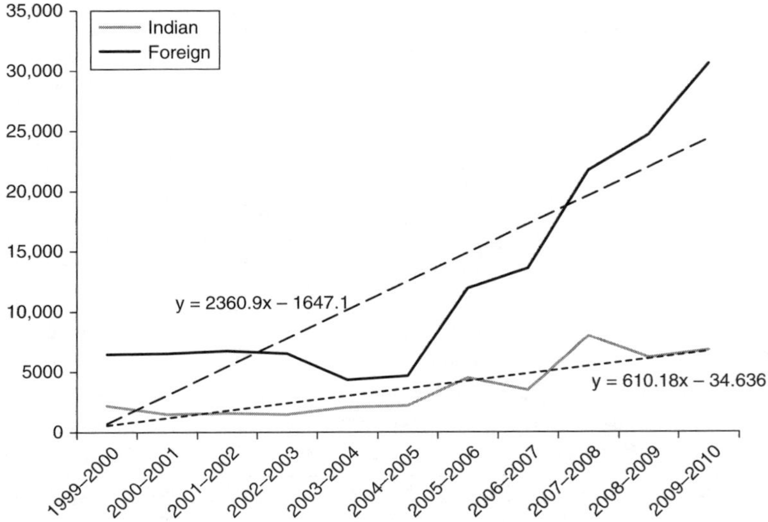

Source: Data from Indian Patent Office and author's calculations.

Figure 10.4 India – trends in patenting: patents in force

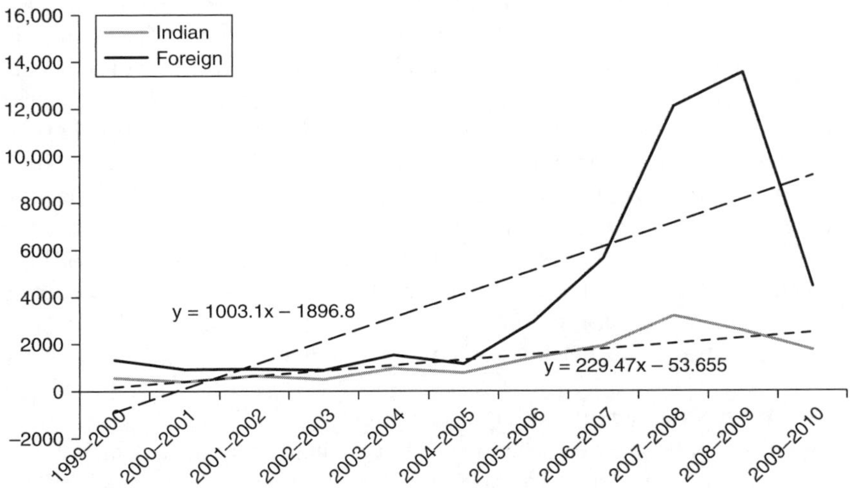

Source: Data from Indian Patent Office and Author's calculations.

Figure 10.5 India – trends in patenting: patents granted during 1999–2010

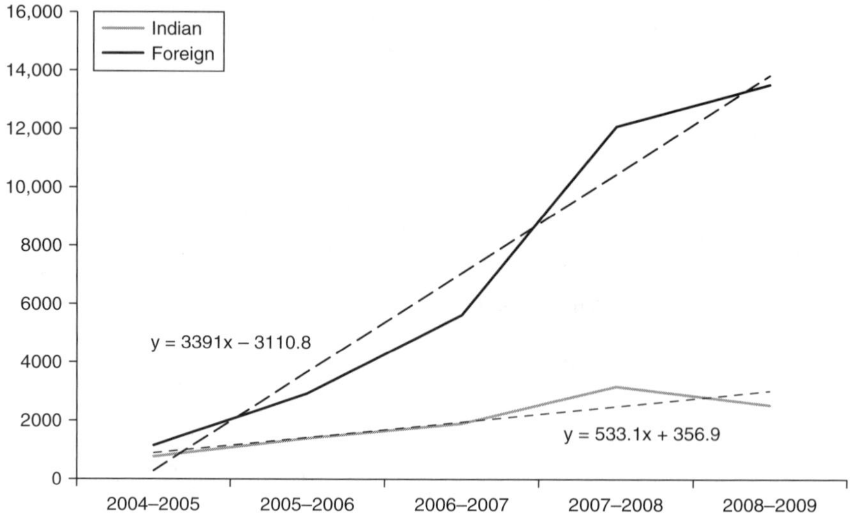

Source: Data from Indian Patent Office and author's calculations.

Figure 10.6 India – trends in patenting: patents granted during 2004–09

importing behaviour of the MNCs since the 1990s bear a close resemblance to that before the 1970s. Imports of high-priced finished formulations are expanding rapidly with manufacturing investments lagging far behind' in the pharmaceutical industry in India. He found that MNCs (multinational corporations) have increasingly reduced the local equity content in their Indian companies over the last ten years. He also found that, while their investment in new machinery has actually declined, the finished product content of their imports has been increasing steadily in the period. He concludes by saying, 'The manufacturing and importing behaviour since the 1990s bears a close resemblance to that before the 1970s. Imports of high priced finished formulations are expanding rapidly with manufacturing investments lagging far behind.'[25]

The questions that beg answers are:

- Who is the patent system in India serving?
- If the patent regime is being used overwhelmingly by foreign entities, would it be correct to state that the patent system in India has not

[25] Chaudhuri, 'Multinationals and Monopolies', p. 46.

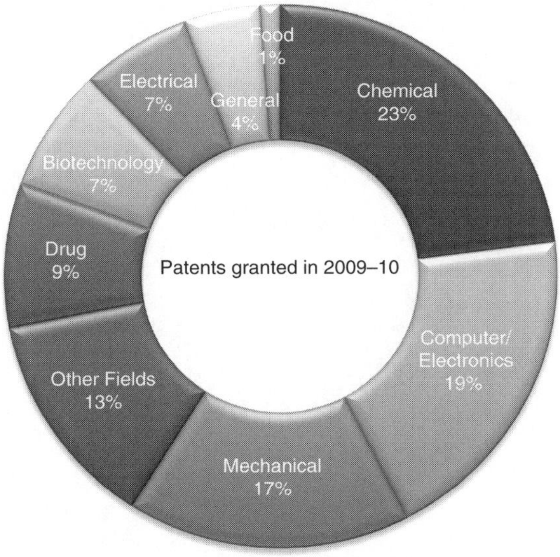

Source: Data from Indian Patent Office and author's calculations.

Figure 10.7 India – patents granted by class of product

been able to achieve one of the major objectives of IP protection – to stimulate innovation within the country?

- Why is the record of FDI in technology areas contradictory to the results that proponents of TRIPS Agreement patent rules suggested, viz. that FDI would follow?

The other aspect relates to the areas of patenting in India. The breakdown shown in Figure 10.7 is for the subject matter of patents.

Contrary to general understanding, a substantial quantum of patents granted pertains to sectors other than drugs and chemicals as well. In fact, if the total number of patents granted were to be broadly classified into two categories, viz. Chemical, Drug and Bio-sciences, etc. and Others, we would find that the latter category has more patents than what has generally been considered to be the mainstay of Indian patenting – drugs, chemicals and biosciences.

The Patent Office, unfortunately, does not reveal what was the share of residents and non-residents in these categories of patents granted. At the risk of making a grave error, if it were to be assumed that the general behaviour of resident patenting would have been similar to that of non-residents in India then it would be a different picture from what is

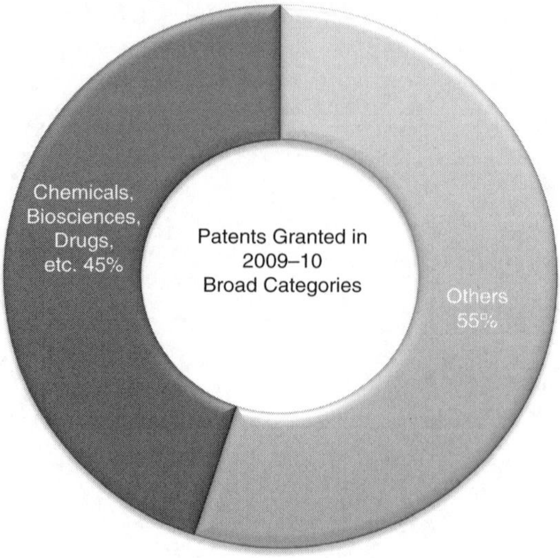

Source: Data from Indian Patent Office and author's calculations.

Figure 10.8 India – patents granted by class of product

generally known about the strength of innovation in the Indian industry, viz. Drugs, Chemicals and Bio-sciences.

We may well ask a question as to whether it would be appropriate to say that the patent ecosystem in India does not honour IPRs of foreign pharmaceutical companies when a large part of the resources of the Patent Office is deployed in doing just that.

4.4 India and the World of Patents

The Indian Patent Office has deployed considerable resources in handling the PCT National Phase applications. It is relevant to also see how much India has used the international patent system to its advantage. While in the year 2003 India was seen to have filed the largest number of PCT applications from among developing countries, the position obtaining currently is much different.

In terms of patents granted to Indian inventors by the USPTO and the EPO, the figures remain low whereas growth rates were erratic:

There are no trends as such discernible in Indians' patenting abroad, though the US appears a favoured destination overall.

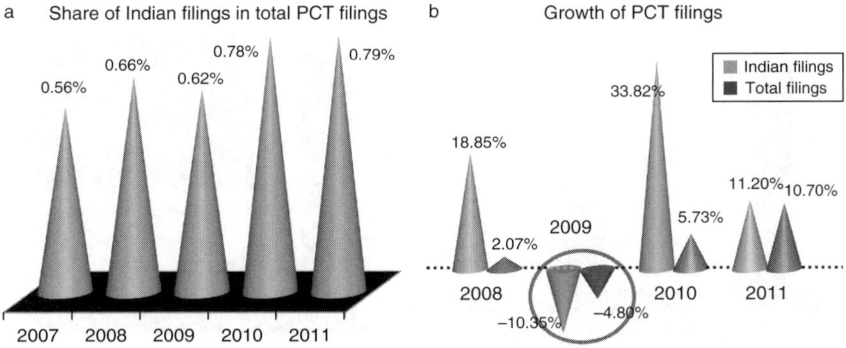

Source: WIPO.

Figure 10.9 India – PCT filings

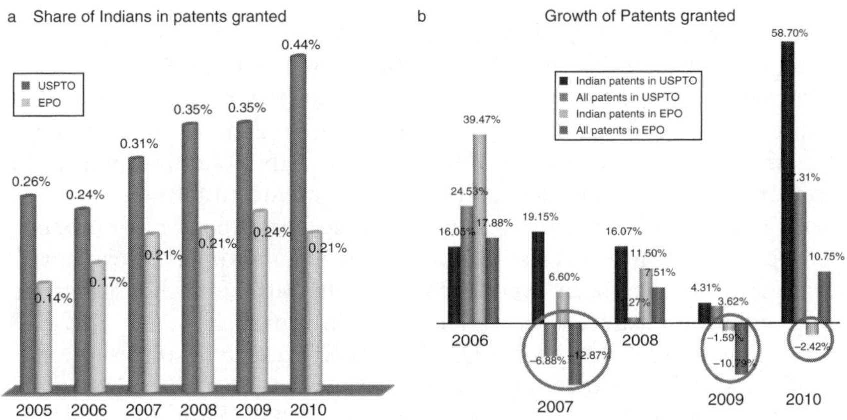

Source: EPO and USPTO.

Figure 10.10 India – share of Indian patents at USPTO and EPO

4.5 Can the Indian Patent Office Cope?

We also need to examine the status of the Indian Patent Office and its ability to handle the expectations of applicants both domestic and foreign. The first striking feature of the Patent Office in India is that it has four offices (Kolkata, Delhi, Mumbai and Chennai) spread over the country.

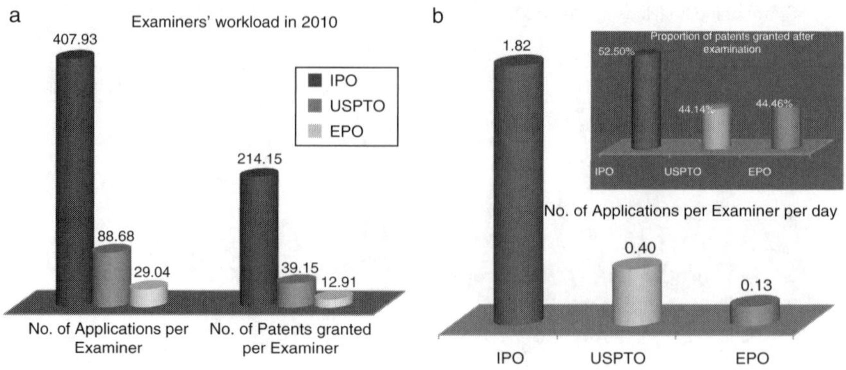

Source: Author's calculations based on USPTO, EPO and Indian Patent Office data.

Figure 10.11 India – patent examiners' workload compared to USPTO and EPO

Further, while the headquarters are at the Kolkata office, the Controller General of Patents has his office in Mumbai. Additionally, the Patent Information System is located at Nagpur. While the original intent was to ensure almost equal access to the Patent Office for all parts of the country, the subsequent modernisation of the Office and ability to file applications electronically has made such a structure redundant. In fact, this arrangement gives rise to difficulties in maintaining consistency of approaches between offices, influenced as they are by local conditions. A related risk, and one which has been experienced as well, is the tendency for forum shopping by applicants to find a more pliable approach.

The Patent Office has been upgrading its processes over the last decade. It offers search facilities and e-filing of applications. The applicant is also able to track the status of an application. What is not in doubt is the technological ability of the Office to handle the applications received. A piquant situation has emerged on account of the rapid expansion of the facilities not being matched by a similar expansion in human resource capacities. Today there are more 'controllers' or supervisors (79) than examiners (75) in the Patent Office.[26] A comparison of the performance of the examiners of IPO, USPTO and EPO is illustrative:

---

[26] Controller General of Patents Designs and Trademarks, 'Officers of Indian Patent Office', http://www.ipindia.nic.in/ipr/patent/patents.htm (accessed 25 March 2013).

It is evident not only that the workload of the Indian examiner is considerably more than that of her American and European counterparts, but also that, despite the supposedly higher standards of patenting adopted by India, it is comparatively easier to be granted a patent in India than in the other two jurisdictions. This fact can be indicative of two possibilities, not necessarily mutually exclusive – that the quality of examination in India might not be comparable with the best in the world and that there may be a tendency for the Indian examiner to accept examination results in other jurisdictions as a benchmark while conducting her own examination. Of course, most of the applications received from foreign applicants were in the manner of the national phase of PCT applications and hence would have had access to international search and examination reports. Yet, the latter conclusion appears to be more dangerous, the denial of patents to some of the blockbuster drugs of MNCs by the IPO notwithstanding. This is especially so since India has not only not joined the Patent Prosecution Highway (PPH)[27] initiative of many other patent offices, but also has been at the forefront of the efforts of WIPO to strongly oppose either the draft Substantive Patent Law Treaty or the proposed reforms to the PCT itself, which would allow for universal acceptance of examination reports from a number of Patent Offices, especially the Trilaterals.[28]

4.6 Capacity of the Legal System to Address Advances in Patent Law

Once decisions of the Patent Office are made, the matter enters the domain of the judiciary on appeal. The first appellate tribunal is the Intellectual Property Appellate Board working out of Chennai. Its constitution ensures a type of judicial oversight since the Chairman of the Board is invariably a person who has been at least a High Court Judge. The other members are a Vice-Chairman and technical members in the relevant IP areas of patents and trademarks.

The legal framework on IPRs has been criticised by certain trading

---

27 Under the PPH, an applicant receiving a determination from an office of first filing that certain or all claims in an application are allowable may request that the corresponding application filed at a second office be advanced, out of turn, for examination in respect of those allowable claims.

World Intellectual Property Organization, *Patent Cooperation Treaty [PCT] Newsletter*, No. 12/2009, December 2009, p. 1, http://www.wipo.int/edocs/pct ndocs/en/2009/pct_news_2009_12.pdf (accessed 25 March 2013).

28 A collective term used for the USPTO, the EPO and the Japanese Patent Office, who share information and examination results in their patenting activity, although they do not have the same patenting standards in absolute terms.

partners[29] and an oft-heard complaint relates to the inability of the judicial system to handle complex IP issues in the absence of specialisation. It would be inappropriate to make such judgments on the basis of a rather new patent law and its implementation in India. We need to remind ourselves that the judiciary the world over constantly updates itself on developments in the jurisprudence in any specific area. Judges have often used case laws in other jurisdictions to clarify and amplify their interpretation and understanding of municipal laws. India is no exception. Owing to its adoption of common law practices, it has recourse to a large body of jurisprudence in most fields, including that of IPRs. Thus, what cannot be faulted is the ability of the judiciary to apply the latest principles in the case of IP litigation. The National Judicial Academy at Bhopal also regularly conducts sessions on IPRs for lower judiciary as well as round-tables for High Court and Supreme Court Judges.

A special mention is necessary here of the demand to create a specialised set of courts to handle IP litigation. For a developing country like India, where the level of prosecution of IPRs is not all that high, devoting dedicated resources to such a structure within the judiciary is likely to have very high opportunity costs. Enforcement of IPRs is part of the overall universe of enforcement of laws in the country. Creating a separate wing in the enforcement superstructure dedicated to IP is neither cost effective nor expedient in a country beset with myriad other and perhaps more pressing social and economic concerns. In fact, some commentators have been known to say that such a system is more likely to be used by foreign rightholders than domestic, considering the number of patents being granted to foreigners.

Pendency of cases in Indian courts on patent issues has not been a major source of agitation among rightholders. What has agitated rightholders and users relates more to the law of patents and its use of exceptions than the inability of the courts to handle the issues. The position of the petitioner in the recent case of Novartis currently before the Supreme Court has undergone a complete makeover from its initial argument of the Indian law being counter to TRIPS, to its being *ultra vires* the Constitution, to the judgment of the High Court now being against the patent law itself.

Thus, it would be not only premature but also incorrect to consider

---

[29] Special 301 Report of the USTR for the year 2011 states, 'Nevertheless, India continues to have a weak legal framework, and ineffective overall IPR enforcement persists.' Office of the United States Trade Representative, '2011 Special 301 Report', USTR, Washington, DC, April 2011, p.28, http://www.ustr.gov/sites/default/files/2012%20Special%20301%20Report_0.pdf (accessed 25 March 2013).

the technical abilities of the Indian judiciary inadequate to handle patent litigation. However, this statement needs qualification in that there is likely to be a considerable increase in litigation on patent issues in the near future. The judiciary needs to be prepared both quantitatively and qualitatively for the expected increase.

4.7 Competition Law and IPRs in India

Another area of interest developing in India relates to the role of the Competition Act in addressing issues related to abuse of dominant position through IPRs. Currently, it is the IP laws of the country which address the inappropriate use of IPRs, by providing remedies within the provisions of the relevant laws. However, some matters have been aired before the Competition Commission related to abuse of dominant position in devising licensing conditions by the IPR holders. Thus, while the IP laws themselves set out the conditions for non-voluntary use of IP, the exact working of the contractual arrangements have been examined in certain cases by the Competition Commission. It is essential to state here that there is a history of antitrust law in India in the form of the Monopolies and Restrictive Practices Act, 1969[30] which viewed all monopolies as exploitative. Under the Competition Act, 2002,[31] which was notified in August 2009, the jurisprudence in this area has to develop in the context of this new law.

The Competition Commission, as established under the Act of 2002, has yet to develop its capacity for investigation to cover the entire expanse of anti-trust issues. However, the Commission achieved an 80.5% rate of disposal by the second year of its operation. The Commission has been in operation for only three years and has generally been known to deal with issues brought before it.

4.8 Is there a Political Economy of Patents?

During the twentieth century a country-divide between the owners and users of innovation and technology goods was quite evident. The developed countries had the technology goods and the developing and least developed countries did not. Hence, the latter group was only a user

---

[30] Ministry of Corporate Affairs [India], http://www.mca.gov.in/Ministry/actsbills/pdf/The_Monopolies_and_Restrictive_Trade_Practices_Act_1969.pdf (accessed 25 March 2013).

[31] Ministry of Corporate Affairs [India], http://www.mca.gov.in/Ministry/actsbills/pdf/The_competition_Act_2002.pdf (accessed 25 March 2013).

group. Owing to the monopoly positions of the rightholders, the latter group also had limited access to such goods, exemplified by monopoly prices or control over free dissemination. Under these conditions some countries wilfully and deliberately went for liberal IPR regimes. Some countries actively encouraged imitation even while being members of international agreements that did not allow such imitation. There were also instances, as in India, where strict conditions on patentability were deliberately adopted so as to facilitate access to modern and state-of-the-art technology.

All this changed with the advent of the TRIPS Agreement in 1995. Despite the period of moratorium given to developing countries as a whole, it was evident that the days of liberal access were a thing of the past. The entire access regime was to change and all countries were bound not only to recognise IPRs across borders in their laws through national treatment provisions, but also to enforce these rights within their jurisdictions. While there is sustained pressure to go beyond national treatment and seek international protection for nationally registered patents, such a system does not seem to have many takers.

The impact of the TRIPS Agreement took some time to settle down. The first reaction to the visible distortions in access regimes came in the form of the Doha Development Agenda and the Doha Declaration on TRIPS and Public Health and the introduction of certain specific flexibilities to address concerns in this regard. Further, reaction to the upped ante on higher levels of protection came in the form of the aggressively pushed development agenda at WIPO. Placing all negotiations at WIPO in the context of a development dimension was a defining moment in the international discourse on IPRs in general and of patents in particular. India was a strong supporter of this initiative of the group called 'Friends of Development'.[32] At the core of all these initiatives coming from the developing world has been the realisation therein that there was considerable scope for using liberal access to existing levels of technology to leapfrog into higher levels of technological sophistication and that this scope was being seriously undermined by the harmonisation of protection standards that TRIPS mandated.

Certain countries like India also developed effective strategies to play the TRIPS flexibilities to their full potential. A case in point is the controversial yet very much present Section 3 (d) discussed above. What is interesting is the comparatively much less noise about a similar exception in the

---

[32] World Trade Organization, Friends of Development Ministerial Declaration of 15 December 2011, WT/MIN(11)/17.

law of patents in the Philippines.[33] Evidently, the level of interest an exception like 3 (d) evinces in the case of India is proportionate to the size of the Indian market and the entities interested in accessing it. That this provision of the Indian law is under challenge from a multinational drug major is also understandable since this provision has the potential to prevent many patents in the pharmaceutical sector. The second interesting use of the flexibilities in India has been the recent compulsory licence discussed above. The relevant section of the Patents Act, 1970, viz. Section 84, has been in existence in its present form since 2005. This was the first use of the provision. The Controller General of Patents in a very elaborate decision justified his decision to grant compulsory licensing on grounds of affordability, availability and 'working' of patent. This decision was challenged in the Patent Appellate Body, which very recently upheld the decision on the grounds of affordability and availability.[34] One of the arguments on behalf of the appellants was that working of a patent did not necessarily include manufacturing within the country. Reports about the decision indicate that the Appellate Body did not give a conclusive finding on the aspect of 'working'. Thus, the jury is still out on the question of working. However, the Appellate Body has upheld the decision, clearly indicating strong support for any future initiative on compulsory licensing within the country. It is not, therefore, surprising that even before this decision there have been proposals under consideration by the government for fresh cases of compulsory licensing. The matter would not rest at this stage and would definitely go to the higher court. It also opens the possibility of such actions by other countries if the Indian action is upheld both nationally and internationally. This is extremely likely seeing that the developing

---

[33] Joint DOH-DTI-IPO-BFAD Administrative Order No. 2008–01
The Implementing Rules and Regulations of Republic Act 9502 otherwise known as the 'Universally Accessible Cheaper and Quality Medicines Act of 2008'

Rule 8. Patents.
Section 1. Non-Patentable Inventions. The following shall be excluded from patent protection:
(a) Discoveries; scientific theories; mathematical methods; and in the case of drugs and medicines: the mere discovery of a new form or new property of a known substance which does not result in the enhancement of the known efficacy of that substance, or the mere discovery of any new property or new use for a known substance or the mere use of a known process unless such known process results in a new product that employs at least one new reactant;

[34] Bayer Corporation v. Union of India, OA/35/2012/PT/MUM, Intellectual Property Appellate Board, Chennai, 4 March 2013, http://www.ipab.tn.nic.in/045–2013.htm.

country group as a whole tends to speak with a similar voice at all international forums as regards equitable access to medicines and to affordable public health. This would mark a new phase in assertiveness from these countries despite having been takers of most of international rule-making in the field of intellectual property rights. Developed countries have shown particular concern over the interpretation of the 'working of patents' as made by the Controller. The state of jurisprudence on the subject and the fact that the Controller has covered his decision with sound reasons on all the grounds possible under the relevant section indicate less likelihood of his decision being overturned by a judicial court.

This leads us to question if this regime that uses TRIPS flexibilities to the maximum is sustainable in the long run given the strong disincentive to research that it can create. Further, it would not be reasonable to presume that the world would be ready to accept liberal access as the new global paradigm on patents. Given that a high level of protection as required under the TRIPS was not likely to be jettisoned soon, developing countries would, sooner rather than later, need to seed their societies with domestically stimulated innovation. Whether this innovation comes out of a robust system of IPRs or out of alternate models of innovation or newer approaches[35] is a call that these countries would need to make.

---

[35] Some possible measures may be:
1. New innovation models such as:

Society Rewards – The society through its organs, such as the government, would reward creativity and thus would ensure repopulating of the 'Intellectual Commons' without restricting access to its use. The creativity-reward-more creativity cycle remains maintained without any monopoly rights being created. The risk is that rewards would be offered only to those products which are determined to be socially useful and thus would inhibit free-wheeling creativity that has been the source substantial technological and economic advancement over the years.

Open Source – A knowledge-sharing model that relies on the share-and-share-alike principle; has had some success over the years in certain specified areas such as software. A recent attempt has been made in the case of Open Source Drug Discovery (OSDD) in India. The results are still to be seen.

Compensatory Liability-based Models – This set of models, such as Reichman's Green Tulip Model, propounds the use of protected intellectual property without permission of the rightholder and then compensating the latter through a system of royalties.

2. Novel practices – In addition to these models certain practices can be adopted to ensure that the patent laws do not inhibit creativity or access such as:
   - Government supported system to pre-empt evergreening of patents; and

4.9 Type of Innovation Ecosystem India Needs

In the case of India, a robust system of IPRs, albeit with substantial use of exceptions, is already in place. Without taking sides in the rather interminable debate on IPRs and innovation, a few points can be made.

There is an emerging body of literature which has questioned the link between national patent protection and domestic innovation. In fact, domestic innovation seems to have a more direct relationship with higher levels of development, educational attainment, and degree of economic freedom. In fact, even now there is no clear evidence to show that the patent system stimulates creativity to the extent that is claimed. Thus, the moot question before a country like India is not whether innovation does take place without protection of law. After all most societies have elaborate systems of traditional knowledge which address local concerns with health, construction, education, etc. The question is not whether innovation takes place without protection of law or not – rather it is whether a culture of innovation can be sustained without protection of law. The ecosystem of IPRs has been in existence for a few centuries now. Considerable investment has been made in this ecosystem by most countries and societies.

It is not that India does not realise the importance of innovation in the country's aspiration for development. In fact, the Government of India constituted a National Innovation Council and declared the decade 2010–20 as the 'Decade of Innovation'.[36] The whole objective of the Council is to look at how innovation can be promoted and in the process how intellectual property is created.

However, the Government of India has recently started wide-ranging consultations on the need to introduce a system of utility models,

---

- Institutional arrangements for *systematic exploitation of out-of-patent technologies.*

3. International Cooperation – Developing countries can also develop international cooperation structures such as:
   - National and international cooperation on appropriateness of technology;
   - Strengthening institutional mechanism of transfer of technology including collective bargaining platforms within the country as well as on a South–South basis;
   - South–South cooperation in the form of technology pools. A beginning can be made using the BRICS platform.

[36] National Innovation Council, 'Introduction', Government of India, New Delhi, 2013, http://innovationcouncil.gov.in/index.php?option=com_content&view=article&id=26&Itemid=5 (accessed 25 March 2013).

including the conditions of protection thereof. The consultations are still on and there is no time frame that has been set for introduction of the necessary legislation in this regard. Some commentators have pointed out that any decision to adopt utility model protection with lower level patentability criteria would necessarily lead to a conclusion that innovation can take place only under an IPR system that rewards innovation monetarily, and that non-IP models of innovation such as collaborative research and Open Source Drug Discovery will not work.

It would be inappropriate not to include traditional knowledge (TK) within the ecosystem of both access and innovation. This is especially so in the context of the assertion that the IP system has not delivered on its claimed linkage between IP protection and development. It would be important to evaluate the indigenous systems of knowledge in existence since these systems carry with them a very important feature in the form of the ease of access that local communities have to the system in both physical and monetary terms. What does inhibit the system is the lack of intellectual and financial investment which would help build the body of knowledge through alternate methods of innovation and creativity. It needs to be recognised that the patent system is geared towards protecting such innovations as can be objectively assessed on the basis of well-structured criteria developed over a couple of centuries. To that extent, the modern patent system is a natural ally of the method of innovation it seeks to protect. As a corollary, it does not find itself effective in protecting any innovation emerging out of traditional knowledge. In view of its lacking many of the formal features of modern systems of innovation, the TK regime also does not lend itself to the system of protection that the patent system envisages. Thus, the challenge a country like India, which is extremely rich in TK, faces is that of developing a formal system of protection of its TK both domestically and internationally. The current state of play at WIPO in both the Inter-Governmental Committee (IGC) on Genetic Resource, Traditional Knowledge and Folklore (GRTKF) as well as the Standing Committee on Patents (SCP) regarding an international treaty for the protection of TK[37] and the draft Substantive Patent Law Treaty (SPLT),[38] respectively, is an example of the way the political economy of the linkage between the patent system and TK aspirations

[37] World Intellectual Property Organization, 'Intergovernmental Committee', WIPO, Geneva, 2013, http://www.wipo.int/tk/en/igc/ (accessed 25 March 2013) (listing most recent drafts of IGC's working documents).

[38] World Intellectual Property Organization, 'Draft Substantive Patent Law Treaty', WIPO, Geneva, 2013, http://www.wipo.int/patent-law/en/harmonization.htm, (accessed 25 March 2013).

operates. It is quite evident that progress on both the instruments had been tardy on account of hardball negotiations by two groups on either side of the development divide. For a period of time, it appeared that progress in one was predicated on progress in the other. However, now the scenario seems to be in favour of a treaty for TK while the SPLT process appears to be stagnant.

On the defensive side, countries like India have a more nuanced approach to prior informed consent (PIC). The logic of PIC seems to place much emphasis on clearly identifiable communities which hold the relevant TK. The history of the entire region of the Indian sub-continent has been one of migrations over long periods. With such movements of people, it would be difficult to pin a form of TK to a specifically identifiable and perhaps isolated community. Such communities do exist in India and they possess some elements of TK. However, a very large body of TK is shared between multiple communities and across various regions of the country. Further, there is a considerable body of formally codified, structured, recorded and documented traditional knowledge in traditional systems of medicine, cropping, plant varieties, irrigation and construction which does not lend itself easily to PIC and ABS. Under such conditions, there is in general no option but to ensure that patentability criteria are kept so high that such TK is not usurped through the patent route. The specific exception[39] under the Patents Act, 1970 seems to do the work quite succinctly and effectively by simply not allowing TK to be patented.

In addition, the Biological Diversity Act, 2000 also seeks to prevent misappropriation of genetic resources and associated traditional knowledge by specific prohibition on its export from the country. It regulates access to the biological resources of India.[40] It also very clearly provides restrictions

---

39 Patents Act, 1970

3. What are not inventions –
The following are not inventions within the meaning of this Act, –
(p) an invention which, in effect, is traditional knowledge or which is an aggregation or duplication of known properties of traditionally known component or components.

40 Biological Diversity Act, 2000

Section 3 (1)
No person referred to in sub-section (2) shall, without previous approval of the National Biodiversity Authority, obtain any biological resource occurring in India or knowledge associated thereto for research or for commercial utilization or for bio-survey and bio-utilization.

on transfer of biological resources outside the country.[41] Further, it specifically denies intellectual property rights on any biological resource *within or outside India* without approval of the competent authority.[42]

These are very strong defensive provisions. However, in the absence of a corresponding international law, these provisions remain bound to the domestic sphere only. There have been certain assertions made by India that many patents are regularly granted in many countries, especially of the West, which are based on biological resources originating from India. In an old civilisation such as India, it is very likely that any useful biological resource would have a body of associated traditional knowledge. Thus, misappropriation of biological resources is likely to also result in misappropriation of associated traditional knowledge.

India has accepted open source platforms as the mainstay of its governmental IT architecture. However, in reality this has not been entirely successful owing to a large number of issues, including those related to difficulty in accessing open source systems as compared with very easy but unauthorised availability of proprietary systems. This has resulted in a body of users who are now 'hooked' on to the proprietary systems, albeit obtained through piracy, and may not be able to migrate to other systems at this stage. This also makes them vulnerable to strong enforcement measures as well as making them dependent on the proprietary systems.

The present discussion has reached a point where an attempt can be made to state what might be a roadmap for India in the coming two decades as regards an approach to determining the contours of an IPRs ecosystem. Should it be to adopt an anti-IPR stance on the premise that the present international regime on IPRs militates against access to knowledge and technology and is essentially a denial regime? Should it

---

[41] Section 4:

> No person shall, without the previous approval of the National Biodiversity Authority, transfer the results of any research relating to any biological resources occurring in, or obtained from, India for monetary consideration or otherwise to any person who is not a citizen of India who is non-resident as defined in clause (30) of the Income-tax Act, 1961 or a body corporate or organization which is not registered or incorporated in India or which has any non-Indian participation in its share capital or management.

[42] Section 6:

> No person shall apply for any intellectual property right, by whatever name called, in or outside India for any invention based on any research or information on a biological resource obtained from India without obtaining the previous approval of the National Biodiversity Authority before making such application.

be to adopt a strong pro-IPR stance on the (equally tenuous?) premise that a strong IP regime stimulates creativity and innovation and would be helpful in encouraging domestic industry to innovate and gain access to the frontiers of technology? Should it be to go for a more practical route which allows for a degree of imitation, albeit without falling foul of the law?

As usual the likely path for India lies somewhere in between these vertices. It is certain that to make imitation a strategy to access technology is dangerous, essentially for two reasons, viz. that on the one hand it would open the country to international sanctions under WTO and other norms and on the other that it may cause complacence, inefficiency and general decline in innovative spirit. In this context the legal regime of IPRs in general and patents in particular would appear to have twin roles in stimulating innovation – to prevent undue barriers to access through 'evergreening' or 'thickets' and to ensure protection of IP created following due process of law by making enforcement of rights effective and efficient.

Given its growth and development trajectory, an emerging economy like India may at some point have to make a call on when to shift from seeking access to knowledge and technology by using the market or by flexibilities in international law, towards seeking an effective international regime preventing unauthorised imitation of its products. This may need to happen once India has built a self-sustaining ecosystem of innovation. This has happened in the past with many countries which are now developed[43] and is likely to happen to currently developing countries[44] as well. Like all questions regarding choice, this is also a choice of technique and

---

[43] US Congress, Office of Technology Assessment, *Intellectual Property Rights in an Age of Electronics and Information*, OTA-CIT-302 (Washington, DC: US Government Printing Office, April 1986) stated:

'Historically, there have been political tensions between nations whose role as producers of intellectual property allowed them greater access to such products, and nations that imported technology products, and had only limited access to them. When the United States was still a relatively young and developing country, for example, it refused to respect international intellectual property rights on the grounds that it was freely entitled to foreign works to further its social and economic development.'

[44] 'Focusing on the past decade, China has emerged as one of the fastest growing patent offices. Between 2001 and 2010, China experienced an average yearly growth rate of 22.6%, bringing its yearly patent applications from 63,450 in 2001 to 391,177 in 2010, to emerge as the second largest patent office. This is partly explained by China becoming the second largest economy in terms of GDP (gross domestic product) in 2010.'

World Intellectual Property Indicators – 2011 Edition, Section A: Patents, Utility Models and Microorganisms, pp. 39–40.

timing. There is unfortunately no fixed model which would determine the mode and time when this shift has to come about, if at all. In the interregnum, it would be appropriate for India not to lose the options that are currently available or that can be available through directed action.

Strategies on innovation and development have evolved in the developing countries in an interesting fashion over the last five or so years. Our assertion has been that in recognition of the increasing importance of developing countries as not only the drivers of growth in the world economy but also as major markets for goods and services, it has been possible for them to leverage their new purchasing power to demand and indeed wrest more market access for their own products. They have also been able to use this approach to ask for changes in the way the world perceives intellectual property. A case in point is the institution of a development agenda at WIPO under the leadership of developing countries.

In the domestic scenario another recognition has grown: that in case the desired level of innovation is not forthcoming from the innovator community in the private sector, then it would necessarily be incumbent upon the public sector to invest more in technologies to boost innovation to the levels necessary for the country. India has been engaged in developing strategies regarding public investments as well as encouraging venture capital in technological R&D to stimulate innovation in areas such as renewable energy, biotechnology, pharmaceuticals, etc.

Another area that has been attracting the attention of policy makers has been university research. While it is generally accepted that universities in most developed countries and in many developing countries have been at the forefront of extending frontiers of knowledge and developing new technologies, this has been wanting in India. There has been very little by way of incubation of technologies and their ultimate transfer to marketable products. The recent attempt to provide legislative support for such a process is a step in the right direction. This needs to be followed up in earnest. In the interregnum it may be appropriate to also identify certain institutions with the requisite capabilities to act as incubation centres of focussed technologies which can then be disseminated in the public interest outside the IP system.

In the international arena, it has been an interesting journey for developing countries from the heady days of the politically oriented Non-Aligned Movement (NAM) to more forceful articulation of individual economic interests through collective bargaining at trade and investment forums. Coalition building has been engaging the interest of developing countries on a variety of platforms such as climate-change negotiations, the Nagoya Protocol, the CBD, TRIPS Council, industrial products liberalisation and so on. There is reason to believe that this approach can be extended to research and development as well to exploit synergies in technological capabilities. There are indeed possibilities in developing technology pools through South–South technological cooperation. It has been a fact that most multilateral agreements and treaties have incorporated an agenda promoting technology and financial transfers from developed to developing countries. This agenda has been followed more in abeyance than in pursuance. This lays the ground for institutionalisation of a process and not just a legal enabling provision of transfer of technologies in areas of critical importance to developing countries at affordable prices. It can be readily seen that many developing countries have developed research capabilities of the highest level in certain specific sectors. There is no reason to believe that, unlike two decades ago when they were deficient in such capabilities, these countries cannot take a lead in conducting cutting-edge research in their own sectors of specialisation through focussed investment leading to the creation of a body of innovation. However, the fruits of such research can be shared between the countries participating in a programme of technology pools. This is not a new idea. In fact, more than a decade ago this idea had been debated but was not followed up due to the countries concerned being circumspect about the benefits that would accrue and the reliability of the process. They were also at that point in time not in a position to make the large investments necessary for establishing such research capabilities. However, now such capabilities have been in existence in some developing countries and there is no reason why these cannot be shared. There is no doubt that the formats necessary for such pools would be complex and would also have to contend with mutual competition in the same technology.

One set of recent developments of interest to the international community has been the efforts made by developing countries to raise awareness about access issues in general and in the context of intellectual property systems in particular, in other developing countries and especially in the least developed countries of Africa. It may be recalled that in the period 2006–08 there was a plethora of domestic laws either enacted or contemplated in many countries of Africa wherein the definition of patents – and indeed the resultant enforcement obligations – were defined in such wide terms that even local generic manufacturing would have been rendered impossible. In fact, some of these laws created extra-territorial reach for the patents of other countries by recognising them as valid instruments requiring protection in the country. This would have meant that these countries would provide patent protection to those products over which there were no granted patents in their jurisdictions. India had played a significant role in reaching out to some of the African governments to explain not only the import of these laws – especially the deleterious effects they might have on access to affordable healthcare—but also the possible violation of international arrangements on the territoriality of IP laws. These efforts contributed in some measure to the striking down of the Kenyan legislation by the Kenyan High Court, the withdrawal of the Ugandan bill placed for Presidential assent, the dropping of the draft Rwandan legislation and the stopping of the bill of the East African Community. This was also reflective of the fact that these governments were sensitive and cognisant enough of their national interests to withdraw from stated positions once the negative possibilities were brought to their notice. It also reflects positively on the coalitions that can be built between developing countries on issues of national importance within the countries. It may have been possible in the not too distant past for developed country trading partners or Western consultants to lead many developing and least developing countries into legislating on matters of interest to the former. It is almost impossible now to do so due to the increasing awareness of national priorities in the field of intellectual property.

Another example of the effectiveness of new coalitions has been the set of developments that took place in the WHO. IMPACT was briefly mentioned earlier. It may be recalled that the deep-seated IMPACT, which was essentially a platform to articulate the interests of patent holders in medicinal formulations against so-called counterfeiting and possibly directed at generic manufacturing, was removed from the WHO due to the persistent efforts of a group of developing countries. What this reflects is not only the increasing political-economic profile of these countries but also the better understanding of the long-term consequences of these provisions in international law. This is a far cry from the days of the 1990s and the early part of the 2000s. Now multilateral negotiations have much greater participation at much higher levels of sophistication from developing countries.

This discussion would be incomplete if I did not refer to ongoing negotiations on intellectual property under the India-EU broad-based trade agreement. These negotiations have generated phenomenal interest among civil society organisations, particularly on India's likely position on patent protection through provisions on patentability, patent linkage for marketing approvals, data exclusivity and border enforcement. To what extent India can leverage its market to ensure that these issues are settled in its interest is a matter for speculation. Globally, interesting developments have been taking place in the shape of negotiations on the Trans Pacific Partnership and the potential US-EU bilateral trade agreement, where new standards on intellectual property are being negotiated. Separately a Regional Comprehensive Economic Partnership (RCEP) is building up among the ASEAN and its six major trading partners (Japan, Korea, China, India,

Australia and New Zealand).[45] Are we seeing the emergence of a new club represented by these three formations in the global trading system? One perspective around these developments is a possible distribution of strengths on intellectual property and manufacturing among these groupings.

5 CONCLUSIONS

The examples that have been cited clearly indicate that developing countries have come of age as far as recognising and articulating their interests on multilateral platforms is concerned. While they have also come to realise that intellectual property policy can be used as a tool for development, they also have recognised that higher standards of IP protection is not a panacea for their access needs, be it of technology or affordable healthcare or of knowledge.

Development and IP can go hand in hand as long as development takes precedence in the policies of the country. Standards of IP protection cannot be the sole or even major indicator of development. What matters for a developing society is the quality and quantity of delivery of goods and services needed by the society.

It would also not be right to jettison all discourse on intellectual property from developing countries. In a country like India, there is clear evidence of there being two segments of industry. One segment is the one that operates cutting-edge technology and is completely integrated with the global value chain. This segment is most likely to support an IP value system which is akin to the value system on IP that exists in developed countries. On the other hand there is a much larger segment, perhaps in terms of volume and value of transactions, which is not yet integrated into a global system of manufacturing or trade. This segment needs to be protected as well. To address the needs of both these segments would require a new paradigm of innovation. The National Innovation Council has recognised this challenge. While it is still early days in the Council, they have set out to develop a roadmap on innovation for the country. The approaches to this challenge being debated include using a liability model for use of IP or a reward-based innovation regime as a viable alternative to innovation under an IP ecosystem.

---

45 Association of Southeast Asian Nations, 'ASEAN and FTA Partners Launch the World's Biggest Regional Free Trade Deal', *ASEAN Secretariat News*, 20 November 2012, http://www.asean.org/news/item/asean-and-fta-partners-launch-the-world-s-biggest-regional-free-trade-deal?category_id=27 (accessed 25 March 2013).

Russia

11. Russian trip to the TRIPS: Patent protection, innovation promotion and public health

Tetyana Payosova

1 INTRODUCTION

The end of 2011 was marked by the long-awaited approval of the Russian Federation's accession to the World Trade Organization (WTO), which means it is now bound by the covered agreements, including the Agreement on Trade-Related Aspects of Intellectual Property Rights (TRIPS Agreement). Although recognition and protection of intellectual property was not new to the Russian legal system, during the negotiations of accession conditions, Russia significantly changed its legislation on intellectual property protection, including patent legislation. At the beginning of 2012 amendments to the Chinese patent legislation and a decision of the Indian Patent Office led to a number of reactions by various stakeholders on compulsory licensing as a part of the TRIPS flexibilities. In this light this chapter firstly aims to analyze how the WTO accession affected patent protection in Russia and secondly, whether Russia would pursue a favorable approach towards compulsory licensing and make use of it following the practice of most of its BRICS partners (Brazil, South Africa, India and China) or choose its own way by encouraging local production drugs and promoting R&D in pharmaceutical sector.

This chapter starts with a brief overview of the patent protection regime in Russia, including a historical perspective and an introduction to the current situation in light of Russia's accession to the WTO. Further, it offers a brief presentation of the patent-related issues addressed in the accession process. The chapter concludes with a case-study analysis of the Russian patent protection and innovation policies in the pharmaceuticals sector in light of Russia's public obligation to ensure access to essential medicines.

2 BACK TO THE ROOTS: PATENT PROTECTION BEFORE THE RUSSIAN ACCESSION TO THE WTO

Russia is the largest country in the world in terms of its area, with a population of more than 140 million people as of 2012.[1] Its size and geographical location make it one of the most important political and economic powers in the world. Its market was and remains of interest both for foreign exporters and investors, and Russia's accession to the WTO played a crucial role in ensuring a level playing field with other major trading partners. In the late 1980s Russia started a rough and cumbersome transition from a Soviet economic model deeply rooted in Soviet society for over 60 years to a new market-based model. The reforms touched all spheres of economic, political and social life, including the protection of intellectual property.

2.1 Patent Protection in the Russian Empire

Unlike some developing countries, Russia has had a long history of granting protection to intellectual property dating back to the times of the Russian Empire. Patent protection for inventions, including pharmaceuticals, was no exception.[2] Patent protection in Russia stemmed from the system of feudal privileges. Granting protection for inventions before 1812 was exclusively subject to a decision of the tsar and not regulated by any specific law. A patent of that time was referred to as a privilege. The decision to enact specific legislation for the protection of inventions was based on a four-page report by the State Secretary of the Russian Empire, Mikhail Speranskiy, well-known throughout Europe for his negotiation

---

[1] US Department of State, "Background Note: Russia" (19 March 2012), http://www.state.gov/r/pa/ei/bgn/3183.htm (accessed 7 August 2012).

[2] In Russia, patent protection has existed since 1812 and was further developed in the Statute on Privileges for Inventions and Improvements as of 1896, which included the requirements of enablement and novelty, as well as an exclusive patent protection term of 15 years. In 1965 as part of the Soviet Union, Russia acceded to the Paris Convention and the first patent law of the independent Russian Federation was adopted in 1992. See on the history of Russian IP protection: Esprit Eugster, "Evolution and Enforcement of Intellectual Property Law in Russia", *Washington University Global Studies Law Review*, vol. 9, no. 1, 2010, p. 136; see also Joshua M. Green, "The Russian IPR Problem: How Accession to the WTO is Not the Magical Solution, Rather a Step in the Right Direction", *Intellectual Property Brief*, vol. 3, no. 2, 2011, pp. 58–60; Sergey Budylin and Yulia Osipova, "Total Upgrade: Intellectual Property Law Reform in Russia", *Columbia Journal of East European Law*, vol. 1, no. 1, 2007, pp. 17–23.

skills and in Russia for various progressive political and legal reforms. In this report he mentioned: "Every invention is a property of its inventor. There are only two ways to sustain this property: 1) secrecy and 2) its protection by the State. And since the first one is often not sufficient, the second should be used. This is where privileges stem from." (translation by the author). According to the General Law "On Privileges for Various Inventions and Discoveries in Arts and Crafts," privileges could be granted for three, five or ten years for both domestic and foreign inventions. The system of privileges provided for in the law of 1812 was amended several times in the 19th century, first and foremost to define more precisely the patentability criteria.[3] Between 1814 and 1833 only 72 privileges were issued, while during the period from 1833 to 1870 the number of granted privileges increased considerably and reached 1286. Only in 1870 did the new law introduce important amendments to the process of granting privileges. Namely, it changed a privilege into a certificate, which was no longer dependent on the subjective perception of state authorities as to the practicability of an invention, and instead was granted for every invention that complied with the criteria provided by law. The economic globalization trend at the end of the 19th century and a number of economic reforms in the Russian Empire attracted foreign investment, mainly from Germany and England, in the metallurgical, railway, coal and oil, electro-technical sectors of industry. Between 1896 and 1912, 23,238 privileges were issued, in the vast majority of cases (around 80%) to foreigners.[4]

2.2 The Soviet Period and its Dual Protection System

Following the revolution in 1917 almost all legislation was replaced or amended to reflect the new political order, where no private property was recognized. Consequently patents, confirming the exclusive rights of an inventor, also ceased to exist and were replaced by authorship certificates

---

[3] A. Pilenko, *Pravo izobretatelia: Privilegii na izobreteniya I ih zashchita v russkom I mezhdunarodnom prave: Istoriko-dogmaticheskoe issledovanie*, Kniga 1. Ocherk istorii privilegij na izobretenija (v sviazi s evoluciej doktriny) [The Right of the Inventor: Privileges for Inventions and their Protection in Russian and International Law] St. Petersburg, 1902, pp. 148–9, http://www.libertarium.ru/pilenko-patent (accessed 2 March 2013).

[4] See: A. Pavlovskiy (ed.), *Patentnoe Pravo v Rosii* [Patent Law in Russia], Moscow, Arbat-Inform, 2002, p. 248. The National Russian Library boasts a Collection of Privileges issued between 1865 and 1917. *See* [Foundation of Regulatory and Technical Documents], National Library of Russia, St. Petersburg, 2013, http://www.nlr.ru/coll/ofo/fonds_nttd/collections.html (accessed 2 March 2013).

(these, in fact, could be referred to as inventors' certificates, but Russian legislation used the "authorship" wording). The latter would recognize the authorship right of an inventor, as well as the right to remuneration, if his invention was used. Between 1924 and 1931 the system of patents was reintroduced and patents granted during the times of Russian Empire were recognized. Furthermore, the Patent Law of 1924 confirmed the exclusive rights of patent holders and established a 15-year term of patent protection. Drugs, as well as other substances obtained through chemical processes, were not patentable. The PRIS company (Patenting and Realization of Inventions) established in 1929 was entrusted with patenting inventions abroad and sales of licenses, as well as patenting foreign inventions in the Soviet Union.

After the enactment of the Decree of the Central Executive Committee of the USSR No. 3[5] in 1931, patents were recognized as an inefficient means of achieving socialistic aims. Although patents were not officially cancelled, certificates of authorship were reintroduced. According to this system an inventor would receive some remuneration as well as the right to benefits (e.g. additional vacations, privileged access to education, better accommodation etc.). Certificates of authorship were given for inventions made at work, and since most research activity indeed occurred within the walls of research institutes and departments, most inventions were covered exclusively by certificates and not by patents. The denial of exclusive rights to inventors was justified by the common beneficial use for the whole of Soviet society.[6] Importantly the Decree of 1931 also prohibited inventors from patenting their inventions abroad without specific permission from the central Soviet authorities. For several decades, no patents were filed and no licenses sold for Soviet inventions abroad. By 1939 PRIS was liquidated and its functions were subdivided between various state authorities. After World War II the need for and benefit from trading licenses became evident; and in the 1950s several licenses for the use of patents were sold and acquired by the Union-wide

[5] The decree is available in Russian. See [Decision of the CEC of the USSR N 3, SNK N 256 of 09.04.1931 for the Implementation of the Provisions on Inventions and Technical Improvements], [Russian Legal Portal], 2010, http://www.lawrussia.ru/texts/legal_861/doc861a657x339.htm (accessed 2 March 2013).

[6] Marina Portnova, "Ownership and Enforcement of Patent Rights in Russia: Protecting an Invention in the Existing Environment", *Indiana International and Comparative Law Review*, vol. 8, no. 1, 1997, pp. 506, 509–11, with a reference to Andrei A. Baev, "Recent Changes in Russian Intellectual Property Law and their Effect upon the Protection of Intellectual Property Rights in Russia", *Suffolk Transnational Law Review*, vol. 19, no. 1, 1996, p. 366.

export-import associations (in 1956 the Soviet Union licensed the use of its turbo-drill for oil wells to several companies, including an American company, Dresser).[7]

The Civil Code of the USSR of 1964 for the first time incorporated provisions on the protection of intellectual property into the Civil Code itself. Importantly, the USSR joined the Paris Convention for the Protection of Industrial Property in 1965, which led to further developments in Soviet patent legislation. In 1968 there followed its accession to the World Intellectual Property Organization (WIPO)[8] and in 1978 the ratification of the Patent Cooperation Treaty.[9] In the 1970s the Soviet Union enacted a number of legislative acts that introduced the parallel use of authorship certificates and patents, which was also reflected in the Civil Code provisions.[10] Inventions in the areas of food and pharmaceuticals would exclusively qualify for authorship certificates and not for patents.[11] In other sectors inventors (at least according to the law) were allowed to choose between patents and authorship certificates. However, in reality patents in the Soviet Union were granted almost exclusively to foreigners.[12] Furthermore, the legislation allowed for a kind of compulsory license in cases where patents were granted for inventions of special importance to the state and the patent holder would not agree to grant a license.[13] According to authorship certificates all exclusive rights related to an invention were transferred to the state (and its specialized agencies), whereas an inventor would have

---

[7] William C. Maurer, "Program to Develop Improved Downhole Drilling Motors: Semi-Annual Report", US Department of Energy, 1 November 1976, http://www.osti.gov/bridge/servlets/purl/6593677-bEpl8W/6593677.pdf (accessed 2 March 2013).

[8] WIPO Notification No. 6 Convention establishing the World Intellectual Property Organization. Ratification of the Convention by the Union of Soviet Socialist Republics, 18 December 1968.

[9] PCT Notification No. 16, Patent Cooperation Treaty. Ratification by the Union of Soviet Socialist Republics, 6 January 1978.

[10] Civil Code of the Union of Soviet Socialist Republics, 11 June 1964, Article 520.

[11] See: Decree of the Council of Ministers of the USSR as of 21 August 1973 No. 584, on the Regulation on Discoveries, Inventions and Rationalization Proposals, para. 25.

[12] Thomson Reuters, "Derwent World Patents Index Coverage: Soviet Union (SU)", Author, February 2013, http://ip-science.thomsonreuters.com/m/pdfs/dwpicovkinds/soviet_union.pdf (accessed 2 March 2013).

[13] Decree of the Council of Ministers of the USSR as of 21 August 1973 No. 584, on the Regulation on Discoveries, Inventions and Rationalization Proposals, para. 35.

the right to remuneration. Similarly to patent protection, the exclusive rights of the state based on the authorship certificate were limited to 15 years. Remuneration to an inventor depended on the savings or other positive effects resulting from the use of his/her invention.[14] The legislator differentiated between remuneration for inventions with a positive economic (saving) effect and without such an effect. For the former, remuneration was calculated based on the economic benefits achieved through the use of the invention at a rate of 2% from the overall annual economic benefit and paid for five years. The payments were made by the respective factories, institutes, or ministries making use of the invention.[15] Remuneration was capped at a maximum of 20,000 rubles for each invention.[16] The remuneration for inventions without saving effects was based on their overall positive effects, scope of application, substantive difference and the level of difficulty of the technical questions solved, and was determined by the head of the respective institute, agency or ministry.[17] Such a dual protection system existed in the Soviet Union until the end of the 1980s.[18]

The number of patent (authorship certificates) applications in the period from 1924 to 1980 in the Soviet Union varied considerably, mainly due to economic crisis and World War II. While in the 1920s the number of patent and authorship certificates applications was at least ten times less than in the US, by the post-war years it had doubled, and from 1964 till the late 1970s the Soviet Union led in patent applications, ahead of the United States and Japan.[19] Residents, most of whom worked for national research institutes, strongly supported and coordinated by the state, submitted the vast majority of applications.

---

[14] Civil Code of the Union of Soviet Socialist Republics, 11 June 1964, Article 521.

[15] Decree of the Council of Ministers of the USSR as of 21 August 1973 No. 584, on the Regulation on Discoveries, Inventions and rationalization proposals, para. 19.

[16] The official exchange rate set by the Soviet Union at that time was 0.8 rubles to one dollar.

[17] Guidelines for determination of remuneration rate for inventions and rationalization proposals, which do not create savings, Council of Ministers of the USSR, as of 15 January 1974.

[18] The Soviet model of certificates of authorship for inventions also spread to a number of communist countries, including China. *See* Peter Drahos, *The Global Governance of Knowledge. Patent Offices and their Clients*, Cambridge, Cambridge University Press, 2011, pp. 223–6.

[19] IP Statistics Prior to 1980s, WIPO official web-page, http://www.wipo.int/ipstats/en/statistics/patents/.

2.3 The Modern Period and Impact of Russia's WTO Accession Negotiations on Intellectual Property Protection

After the fall of the Soviet Union, Russia adopted several new laws for the regulation of intellectual property rights, including the Patent Law of 1992. This law was to a large extent based on international standards and reflected a transition to the market economy system.[20] However, the first version of the provisions of the Patent Law still contained a number of flaws inherited from the old system. Although the definition of patentability according to the Patent Law complied with internationally recognized criteria of patentability (an invention shall be new, involve an inventive step and be capable of industrial application), the definition of what is novel and inventive was not very clear.[21] This led to some enforcement problems, with the most notorious case involving a British company, Officescape.[22]

Russia applied for WTO membership three years after the fall of the Soviet Union – in 1994,[23] and although some voices predicted that it would join the organization by 1998, it took Russia another 14 years of negotiations to become the 156th WTO member. The protection of intellectual property rights was an important part of negotiations, but never became a real stumbling block to Russia's accession to the WTO. Back in

---

[20] Portnova, "Ownership and Enforcement of Patent Rights in Russia", pp. 511–17.

[21] Article 4 of the Patent Law of the Russian Federation No. 19-FZ, as of 23 September 1992 [available in Russian], http://base.consultant.ru/ (accessed 6 August 2012).

[22] Officescape is a British-owned company engaged in the installation of raised access flooring, a technology that was developed in the USA in the middle of the 20th century and became popular worldwide. In this case a Russian company (Department of New Technology, or DNT) had obtained a utility model patent in Russia for exactly the same flooring. Officescape had been active in this business in Russia for some years when the Russian DNT filed a lawsuit for patent infringement, which resulted in criminal proceedings. See an overview of this issue at John Bonar, "Someone's Stolen My Brand!", *Passport*, http://www.passportmagazine.ru/article/381/ (accessed 2 March 2013).

[23] The application for the accession of Russian Federation was received in 1993. *See* World Trade Organization, "Accession: Russian Federation", Geneva, Author, 2013, http://www.wto.org/english/thewto_e/acc_e/a1_russie_e.htm (accessed 2 March 2013). The Soviet Union joined neither the ITO negotiations nor the Tokyo Round trade negotiations, and only requested GATT (General Agreement on Trade and Tariffs) observer status in 1986. *See* Julia Selivanova, "Russia", in Patrick F.J. Macrory, Arthur F. Appleton, and Michael G. Plummer (eds.), *The World Trade Organization: Legal, Economic and Political Analysis*, vol. I, New York, Springer, 2005, p. 289 ff.

the 1990s, when the WTO accession became an issue in Russia, Rospatent, the Russian patent authority, conducted a study on the compatibility of Russian legislation with the TRIPS Agreement and came to the conclusion that in general there was no significant non-compliance.[24] However, the European Union and the United States, from the very beginning, expressed their concerns about the enforcement of intellectual property protection, including border measures and judicial review.[25] As in all accession negotiations, the main challenge was to reach an agreement with the most important and powerful trading partners, which would further determine specific conditions under which a country could join the WTO. The US played this crucial role in the formulation of Russia's commitments in the intellectual property sector.

A long-negotiated market access agreement between the Russian Federation and the United States was signed in November 2006 in Hanoi and contained a Side Letter on the implementation of legislation on intellectual property protection and enforcement.[26] The official memo noted: "The bilateral market access agreement also includes important provisions that will strengthen IPR protection in Russia. Under the terms of the agreement, Russia will take action, starting immediately, to address piracy and counterfeiting and further improve its laws on IPR protection and enforcement, both stated priorities of the Russian Government, which

---

[24] "Russia's Part IV Problems", *Managing Intellectual Property*, no. 173, 1 October 2007, pp. 48 ff.

[25] Christian L. Broadbent and Amanda M. McMillian, "Russia and the World Trade Organization: Will TRIPS be a Stumbling Block to Accession?", *Duke Journal of Comparative & International Law*, vol. 8, no. 2, 1998, pp. 519–62.

[26] Office of the United States Trade Representative, "United States, Russia Sign Bilateral WTO Market Access Agreement: Negotiations on WTO Membership Now Move to the Multilateral Phase", USTR, Washington, DC, 19 November 2006, http://www.ustr.gov/archive/Document_Library/Press_Releases/2006/November/United_States,_Russia_Sign_Bilateral_WTO_Market_Access_Agreement_Negotiations_on_WTO_Membership_Now_Move_to_the_Multilateral_Pha.html (accessed 2 March 2013). The actual provisions of the Agreement are not available for analysis, since its text was not made public, based on the exemption related to the foreign state information according to the Freedom of Information Act (FOIA); see a note by Steve Charnovitz on this matter: "USTR Refuses Public Disclosure of US-Russia Trade Agreement", *Public Citizen*, Washington, DC, 4 August 2009, http://citizen.typepad.com/eyesontrade/2009/08/ustr-refuses-public-disclosure-of-us-russia-trade-agreement.html (accessed 2 March 2013). The text of the Side Letter is available at the Office of the United States Trade Representative [USTR Side Letter], http://www.ustr.gov/archive/assets/World_Regions/Europe_Middle_East/Russia_the_NIS/asset_upload_file148_10011.pdf (accessed 2 March 2013).

has confirmed its commitment to implementing this agreement. The agreement also sets the stage for further progress on IPR issues in the ongoing multilateral negotiations."[27] Although the main focus of the bilateral discussions was, as is apparent from the Side Letter, the protection of copyright, the US was also concerned about the protection of undisclosed information and test data.[28] According to the Side Letter, the Russian Federation undertook an obligation to provide protection against unfair commercial use for undisclosed information submitted to obtain marketing approval from a regulatory agency (e.g. for registration and marketing approval of pharmaceuticals by a department of the Federal Service on Surveillance in Healthcare (Roszdravnadzor)) for at least six years, as a commitment to implementation of Article 39(3) of the TRIPS Agreement. The respective legislation was to be enacted by 1 June 2007.[29]

Driven by the negotiations with the US, in 2008 the Russian Federation enacted the most important changes in its intellectual property legislation since the fall of the Soviet Union – all the separate legislative acts dealing with various aspects of intellectual property (namely, 54 laws, decrees etc.) were codified in a new Part IV of the Civil Code of the Russian Federation (the Civil Code). The Civil Code addresses all types of intellectual property and sets the requirements for their recognition and enforcement.[30] This version of the Civil Code is currently in force and has been subjected so far only to minor amendments in 2011.[31]

After the conclusion of the Side Agreement with the US, the WTO accession negotiations continued. The main part related to intellectual property issues was completed by 2008, when Russian accession was already visible on Lake Léman's horizon. However, Russia temporarily

---

27 USTR Side Letter.

28 See also Office of the United States Trade Representative, "Results of Bilateral Negotiations of Russia's Accession to the World Trade Organization (WTO): Action on Critical IPR Issues", USTR, 19 November 2006, http://www.ustr.gov/archive/assets/Document_Library/Fact_Sheets/2006/asset_upload_file151_9980.pdf (accessed 2 March 2013).

29 USTR Side Letter.

30 *See* Adolf Dietz, "Incorporation of Patent Law into Part Four of the Russian Civil Code – a Structural Analysis", in W.P. zu Waldeck und Pyrmont et al. (eds.), *Patents and Technological Progress in a Globalized World*, MPI Studies on Intellectual Property, Competition and Tax Law, vol. 6, Berlin/Heidelberg, Springer, 2009, pp. 692–94. Specific issues on compulsory licenses and patent exemptions are outlined in the section on pharmaceuticals.

31 The list of amendments and a table of comparison of the two versions is available in Russian at http://base.consultant.ru/cons/cgi/online.cgi?req=doc;base=LAW;n=76298;div=LAW;dst=1000000007 (accessed 3 August 2012).

put a halt to the accession process due to its participation in the formation of a Customs Union with Belarus and Kazakhstan. At that time it submitted a suggestion that the negotiations should proceed together with its Customs Union partners, which would annul the bilateral trade deals that had been achieved. It was clear that in this way Russia tried to renegotiate more favorable accession conditions with several of the WTO Members with which it had negotiated accession terms back in the 1990s. After some time Russia withdrew its proposal regarding joint accession with the Customs Union partners and confirmed its aim to enter the WTO by the end of 2011. The final agreement with the US was achieved in 2010.[32] However, the US International Trade Commission reported the same year that the US still had concerns regarding the intellectual property sector and that Russia had not complied with its promises under the Side Letter.[33] Moreover, as of 2011, Russia was still on the Priority List of the United States Trade Representative (USTR) under Section 301 of the Omnibus Trade and Competitiveness Act, along with China, Algeria, Canada and Argentina.[34] This was mainly due to internet piracy and enforcement of intellectual property rights in general, as outlined in the USTR report. Although it did not mention any problems with the patent system specifically, this chapter will consider whether the reforms of the patent protection system have been sufficient.

Finally, the Ministerial Conference approved the Russian accession to the WTO on 16 December 2011. Thereupon Russia was granted 220 days to ratify the agreement. Thus, it had to become a full member of the WTO

---

[32] International Centre for Trade and Sustainable Development, "Russia Resolves Key Issues with US over WTO Accession", *Bridges Weekly Trade News Digest*, vol. 14, no. 34, 17 October 2010, http://ictsd.org/i/news/bridgesweekly/86158/ (accessed 3 March 2013).

[33] See Daniel Griswold and Douglas Petersen, "Trading with the Bear: Why Russia's Entry into the WTO Is in America's Interest", Cato Institute, *Free Trade Bulletin*, no. 46, 6 December 2011, http://www.cato.org/publications/free-trade-bulletin/trading-bear-why-russias-entry-wto-is-americas-interest (accessed 3 March 2013).

[34] The so-called Special 301 (the amended Section 301 of the Omnibus Trade Act) serves as the legal basis for the USTR to identify countries that do not have adequate and effective protection of intellectual property rights. *See* Theresa Beeby Lewis, "Patent Protection for the Pharmaceutical Industry: A Survey of the Patent Laws of Various Countries", *The International Lawyer*, vol. 30, 1996, p. 852. Russia was placed on a Watch List in 1995, and in 1997 on the Priority Watch List. *See* Robert C. Bird and Daniel R. Cahoy, "The Emerging BRIC Economies: Lessons from Intellectual Property Negotiation and Enforcement", *Northwestern Journal of Technology and Intellectual Property*, vol. 5, no. 3, 2007, p. 404.

by August 2012.[35] On 10 July 2012 the Russian Parliament, the Duma, ratified the Accession Protocol, witnessing strong domestic opposition reflected in 46% of votes being against accession. Thereafter, the Russian President, Vladimir Putin, signed the Protocol. This finalized the domestic ratification procedures and Russia became officially bound by the legal provisions of the WTO Agreements, including the TRIPS Agreement, when it deposited its instrument of acceptance at the WTO.[36]

3 PATENT PROTECTION AND RELATED ISSUES AS A PART OF RUSSIA'S WTO ACCESSION NEGOTIATIONS

As mentioned above, patent protection was already in place in Russia when it submitted its application for WTO membership. Also, during the course of negotiations, patent-related questions were not regarded as priority issues to be addressed in the intellectual property discussion as a whole. However, some WTO Members had at least three main concerns related to patent protection, which will be addressed in turn.

The first and the most obvious concern expressed by some WTO Members was about the discriminatory rates of patent fees based exclusively on the origin of an applicant. Rospatent, the Russian patent authority, differentiated between residents and non-residents, and applied to foreigners patent fees almost seven times higher than those to be paid by domestic applicants. Finally, a landmark decision of the Russian Supreme Arbitration Court in April 2012 has confirmed that these legal provisions shall not be applied.[37]

---

[35] *See* World Trade Organization, "Ministerial Conference Approves Russia's WTO Membership", Geneva, WTO, 16 December 2011, http://www.wto.org/english/news_e/news11_e/acc_rus_16dec11_e.htm (accessed 3 March 2013).

[36] Olga Dronina and Yekaterina Shokhina, "State Duma Ratifies the Protocol for Russia to Accede to the WTO", *Russia Beyond the Headlines*, 13 July 2012, http://rbth.ru/articles/2012/07/13/state_duma_ratifies_the_protocol_for_russia_to_accede_to_the_wto_16345.html (accessed 3 March 2013).

[37] Decision of the Supreme Arbitration Court of Russian Federation, 11 April 2012, No. BAC-308/12, available in Russian at online database http://base.consultant.ru. It should be noted that this decision was issued based on the non-compliance of the above-mentioned legal provisions with several international agreements. Firstly, the Court noted that the discriminatory legal provisions contravene an obligation of the Russian Federation under the Partnership Agreement Russia – EU (since the claimant was from the Czech Republic). Article 98 of this Agreement guarantees non-discriminatory access to judicial and other state

Another important concern was the enforcement of patent protection and the lack of specialized court(s) for patent litigation as one of the reasons for poor enforcement. Previously, the general civil courts and arbitration courts would hear cases of patent infringements. The judges in such courts lacked expertise and technical or scientific knowledge and did not always refer to expert opinions. The number of patent cases tried in the courts was low (especially cases involving a foreign party). Moreover, there was and still is no database of all court decisions, including cases on patents, which would allow a relatively easy analysis of existing practice, or at least ensure transparency.[38] The State Duma adopted the law on establishment of the Arbitration Court for intellectual property rights (the so-called Patent Court) on 23 November 2011. As of 2013 the new court will accept and consider claims both from legal entities and from individuals. Interestingly, it shall have jurisdiction over the decisions of federal executive authorities in relation to intellectual property rights and over disputes about granting or terminating legal protection for intellectual property rights with the exception of copyright. This court will also hear cases as a court of appeal. Following the German model there will be a differentiation between judges-lawyers and judges-patent experts, who will be involved in different types of cases.[39] The creation of the Patent Court is expected to considerably improve the enforcement of patent-related rights.

Apart from patent enforcement issues, some WTO Members were concerned about the protection of undisclosed information, including test data in Russia. Notably, this requirement, along with some others, was imposed on Russia as a part of TRIPS-plus conditions upon its accession

---

authorities for legal protection of rights, including intellectual property rights. Furthermore, the Court referred to Article 2 of the Paris Convention providing for the national treatment principle. Finally, the Court concluded that the TRIPS Agreement, as an intrinsic part of the WTO legal framework, provides for a principle of non-discrimination. In light of the accession to the WTO, the Government of the Russian Federation adopted a Resolution as of 15 September 2011 no. 781, which provides for the elimination of the categories "resident" and "non-resident" and the differentiation of patent fees rates based thereon. These amendments entered into force after the official accession of Russia to the WTO.

38 Portnova, "Ownership and Enforcement of Patent Rights in Russia", p. 532.

39 Federal Constitutional Law on Amendments of the Federal Constitutional Law "On Judicial System of the Russian Federation" and of the Federal Constitutional Law "On Arbitration Courts of the Russian Federation" due to the creation of the Court on Intellectual Property in the system of arbitration courts No. 4-FKZ as of 6 December 2011, available in Russian, http://base.garant.ru/12174909/5/#500 (accessed 5 August 2012).

to the WTO. Although the Civil Code of the Russian Federation and some other legislative acts provided for the protection of undisclosed information, concerns were expressed in particular about the test data submitted in requests for drug marketing approval by the Ministry of Health.[40] The Federal Law No. 61-FZ "On the Circulation of Drugs", as amended in 2010, provides in Article 18(6) for a six-year prohibition on the receipt, disclosure, and use for commercial purposes, and for state registration applications of drugs, of information on the results of preclinical and clinical studies of a drug submitted by the applicant (which also applies to generics, including an expedited or abbreviated registration procedure). Furthermore, during the six-year period, in order to register generics, applicants are required to submit the same information on the results of clinical studies as was required of the first registrant (i.e. the originator), as well as information establishing bioequivalence and effectiveness. This system provides enhanced protection to originator drugs in addition to patent protection. However, unlike in the US, Canada, Japan and China,[41] the Russian regulatory authorities are not required by law to take into account the patent status of the product for marketing approval of generics (no "linkage" requirement). Thus, it is possible that a drug, which includes an invention protected by a patent, can be granted marketing approval in Russia, and thus can enter a market infringing the exclusive rights of the patent holder.[42]

Finally, according to the Report of the Working Party for the Accession of Russian Federation, the above-mentioned patent-related concerns have been allayed by the outlined amendments to Russian legislation and the recommendations of the WTO Members have been satisfied so far.[43]

As mentioned above, the creation of the Customs Union also played an important role in Russia's WTO accession process. Since 2008, in parallel with the WTO accession negotiations, work on intellectual

---

[40] *Report of the Working Party on the Access of the Russian Federation to the World Trade Organization*, Working Party on the Accession of the Russian Federation, WTACCRUS/70, WT/MIN(11)/2, 17 November 2011, paras 1282–96.

[41] Hiroko Yamane, *Interpreting TRIPS: Globalisation of Intellectual Property Rights and Access to Medicines*, Oxford and Portland, OR, Hart Publishing, 2011, p. 299. Notably, there is no linkage requirement for marketing approval of pharmaceuticals in the EU. It is believed, however, that the expeditious court proceedings ensure the enforcement of patent-related rights.

[42] A patent holder can, however, claim his rights in the court proceedings, which may lead to the annulment of marketing approval.

[43] *Report of the Working Party on the Access of the Russian Federation to the World Trade Organization*, Working Party on the Accession of the Russian Federation, WTACCRUS/70, WT/MIN(11)/2, 17 November 2011, paras 1272–8.

property-related issues has been taken up within the framework of the Customs Union established in 2009.[44] Although the main achievement was the establishment of regional exhaustion for trademarks in the Customs Union according to the Agreement on Unified Principles of Regulation in the Sphere of Intellectual Property Rights Protection, signed in December 2010 and in force since 1 January 2012,[45] this Agreement also aims at harmonization of the legislation on intellectual property regulation and protection in the three participating countries. The potential consequence is that the Customs Union partners will follow in application of the high standards for intellectual property protection imposed on Russia by its membership in the WTO. However, as far as Russia is concerned, creation of the Customs Union will not affect its patent protection system.

4 PATENT PROTECTION IN RUSSIA AFTER THE ACCESSION TO THE WTO, INNOVATION POLICIES AND PUBLIC HEALTH

4.1 Public Health and Pharmaceutical Sector in Russia

Russia, like many other developing countries, faces the serious problem of maintaining public health of its population. The rates of some diseases, such as the human immunodeficiency virus/acquired immune deficiency syndrome (HIV/AIDS), have increased considerably over the last decade in Russia as well as in a number of neighboring Eastern European countries (from 0.57% HIV prevalence among adults in 2002 to 0.79% in 2011, which is at least twice as high as in Western Europe).[46] Similarly to the other countries, which are signatories of the Declaration of Commitment on HIV/AIDS of the United Nations General Assembly Special Session

---

[44] See the Official Web-Page of the Customs Union between Russia, Belarus and Kazakhstan. "On the Customs Union", The Eurasian Economic Commission, http://www.tsouz.ru/AboutETS/Pages/default.aspx (accessed 3 March 2013).

[45] "Customs Union Pact Affects Trademarks in Russia, Belarus and Kazakhstan", *Marques*, 14 June 2011, http://www.marques.org/class46/Default.asp?D_A=20110614 (accessed 3 March 2013). The text of the Agreement is available in Russian at: http://www.fas.gov.ru/international-partnership/common-economic-space/documents/documents_30693.html (accessed 6 August 2012).

[46] John Burn-Murdoch, "World AIDS Day 2012: How Have Rates of Infection and Transmission Changed?", *The Guardian*, 20 November 2012, http://www.guardian.co.uk/news/datablog/2012/nov/20/world-aids-day-hiv-prevalence-infection-transmission (accessed 3 March 2013). In 2012 the AIDS growth rate constituted 12.5% in comparison to 2011.

on HIV/AIDS (the UNGASS Declaration), Russia undertook a commitment to ensure universal access to antiretroviral treatment for its population.[47] However, according to the Joint United Nations Programme on HIV/AIDS (UNAIDS) statistics, only a minority of people (around 19%) with HIV have access to antiretroviral treatment.[48] Moreover, the Eastern European countries, like many other developing countries, face the problem of access to medicines related to the lack of an efficiently functioning health insurance system, which results in mainly out-of-pocket expenditures on drugs. This in turn significantly affects the affordability and accessibility of the necessary treatment.[49]

Although not very well publicized in Russia itself, the topic of access to essential drugs in the country was taken up in a special report of the World Bank back in 2009.[50] This report, which dealt mainly with the issue of prices for drugs, showed that since 2008 prices for originator drugs have increased by over 105%, partly due to the economic crisis, high inflation rates and sharp depreciation of Russian currency which followed. This also led to a decrease in sales, mostly due to the inability of the majority of the Russian population to purchase the needed medication.

The statistics on the Russian pharmaceutical sector provide some additional insights into the situation regarding access to drugs. Although the pharmaceutical sector in the Russian Federation is not comparable with the dimensions of the corresponding Indian sector,[51] it is rapidly growing, taking into consideration the population of the country and its recent development rates. As predicted by PriceWaterhouseCoopers, Russia, along with Brazil, China, India, Indonesia, Mexico and Turkey, will

---

47 UNAIDS, "Country Report of the Russian Federation on the Implementation of the Declaration of Commitment on HIV/AIDS", 2006, http://data.unaids.org/pub/Report/2006/2006_country_progress_report_russianfederation_en.pdf (accessed 3 March 2013).

48 UNAIDS Technical Brief 2011, "Doha+10 TRIPS Flexibilities and Access to Antiretroviral Therapy", UNAIDS, Geneva, November 2011, p. 23, http://www.unaids.org/en/media/unaids/contentassets/documents/unaidspublication/2011/JC2260_DOHA+10TRIPS_en.pdf (accessed 3 March 2013).

49 "The World Bank in Russia: Russian Economic Report", no. 19, World Bank, June 2009, p. 15, http://siteresources.worldbank.org/INTRUSSIANFEDERATION/Resources/305499–1245838520910/rer19-eng.pdf (accessed 4 March 2013).

50 *See* "The World Bank in Russia."

51 Bird and Cahoy, "The Emerging BRIC Economies", p. 415. The pharmaceuticals sector is the second largest sector in India after textiles. Russia is one of the main importers of Indian medicine along with Singapore, Kenya, the Netherlands and South Africa. Russia exports mainly to its neighboring countries.

represent 20% of the global sales of pharmaceuticals by 2020.[52] Currently, Russia is first and foremost an active importer,[53] which to a certain extent also affects the prices of pharmaceuticals.

In 2008 the Russian market for pharmaceuticals was dominated by foreign drugs, while domestic producers were supplying just 20% of the market share. One of the main explanations for this situation is that, during the time of the Soviet Union, Russia was responsible only for active ingredients for drugs, while drugs were produced in Ukraine and some other communist allies (e.g. Bulgaria and Poland).[54] However, during the last decade, the market share of domestic pharmaceuticals began to grow. In 2010 the Russian pharmaceutical market was already dominated by domestic drugs (64% of real sales volume, while foreign drugs were leading in terms of sales value at 76.5%). An even stronger position for the locally produced drugs is predicted in light of the construction of several pharmaceutical manufacturing plants by foreign companies in Russia. As for exports, there are currently only a few Russian companies selling pharmaceuticals abroad. Pharmstandart (active in the Commonwealth of Independent States (CIS) markets), Silma (known in the markets of Western Europe), Polisan (working in South-East Asia) and Pharmsyntes (whose medicine has received the status of an orphan drug in the US and is in its final stage of clinical testing to enable it to enter the American market) are among them. In 2010, the ten leading companies present on the Russian market were Pharmstandart, Sanofi-Avenis, Berlin-Chemie, Nycomed, Bayer, Gedeon Richter, Novartis, Servier, Pfizer and LEK DD. In total, following the increase in demand, the pharmaceutical market in Russia has achieved a significant growth rate (11%) alongside China's (23%) and Brazil's (20%) in 2010.[55]

---

[52] PriceWaterhouseCoopers, "Pharma 2020: The Vision", http://www.pwc.com/gx/en/pharma-life-sciences/pharma-2020/pharma-2020-vision-path.jhtml (accessed 5 August 2012).

[53] In 2007 exports of pharmaceuticals from Russia accounted for only 0.04% of global sales.

[54] Nikolay Bespalov, "Export Exit from Import Reality", *Customs Union – Independent Review*, 22 September 2011, http://www.customsunion.ru/info print/4759.html (accessed 4 March 2013). For a comparison of prices for medicines in Russia and some other developing countries *see* Floriane Reinaud, "Drug Prices in Brazil, Russia and Turkey: A Comparison of Trends in Three Emerging Pharmaceutical Markets", HIS Healthcare and Pharma Blog, 13 February 2012, http://healthcare.blogs.ihs.com/2012/02/13/drug-prices-in-brazil-russia-and-turkey-a-comparison-of-trends-in-three-emerging-pharmaceutical-markets/ (accessed 4 March 2013).

[55] All statistical information for 2010 is taken from the DSM Group Report,

4.2 Impact of Russia's Accession to the WTO on the Pharmaceutical Sector

After joining the WTO, Russia became bound by the minimum standards on intellectual property protection provided for in the TRIPS Agreement and by the TRIPS-plus obligations imposed as a result of the accession process. While there are a number of positive implications of the strong intellectual property system for Russia, as a developing country it still faces some social problems, which can be made worse by the enhancement of this system (for instance, in light of the public health vs. patents for pharmaceuticals debate).[56] The question of accessibility of drugs largely depends on their price in a given market, especially when we consider developing countries. So far, locally produced drugs in Russia are relatively cheap; however, their prices are predicted to rise in the next years. In order to ensure their competitiveness in a liberalized market, the Russian Federation, along with its Customs Union partners (Kazakhstan and Belarus), pursues a policy of harmonization of national standards with international good manufacturing practice (GMP) standards.[57] These costs, related to an urgent need for modernization of the outdated infrastructure, will consequently be reflected in the consumer price of drugs.

Import taxes on drugs and medical equipment in Russia and in the Customs Union as a whole were not high even before Russia's accession to the WTO (5–10%), and therefore are not likely to affect prices for foreign-produced drugs. Nor are price-increasing effects in the pharmaceutical sector likely in relation to compliance with the TRIPS provisions. As mentioned before, strong modern patent protection for pharmaceuticals (both products and processes) has existed in Russia since the beginning of the 1990s. Unlike China and Brazil, Russian legislation never included a local working requirement for patents.[58] Moreover, the first Patent Law of

---

"Russian Pharmaceutical Market 2010", DSM, Moscow, http://www.dsm.ru/content/file/1306924994.pdf (accessed 4 March 2013).

56 Patent protection of medicines can have both positive and negative implications for public health. See on this issue: Philippe Cullet, "Patents and Medicines: The Relationship between TRIPS and the Human Right to Health", *International Affairs*, vol. 79, no. 1, 2003, p. 143; and Adam McBeth, "Why Have No States Used the WTO Scheme for Compulsory Licensing of Essential Medicines?", *The New Zealand Yearbook of International Law*, vol. 3, 2006, p. 76.

57 Compliance with the GMP will be compulsory as of 1 January 2014. According to some estimations, only 15% of Russian pharma producers comply with GMP standards.

58 Xiaonhai Liu, "A Study on Patent Compulsory License System in China – with Particular Reference to the Drafted 3rd Amendment to the Patent Law

the Russian Federation of 1992 had a single enforcement exception for the patent protection of pharmaceuticals – namely, for pharmacies making one-time preparations on prescription.[59]

In pursuance of TRIPS-compliant patent protection, Russia, however, might find it attractive to resort to the TRIPS flexibilities, inter alia to compulsory licensing, in order to ensure secure supply and affordability of certain essential drugs for public health purposes.

4.3 Compulsory Licensing under the TRIPS Agreement

The TRIPS Agreement not only provides for stringent obligations on patent protection, but also allows certain flexibilities, giving a number of exceptions to the exclusivity of the patent-related rights. Article 31 of the TRIPS Agreement provides for compulsory licensing, i.e. a license to produce a patented invention without the permission of the right-holder, which can be granted: (a) where prior negotiations with the right-holder to obtain a voluntary license on reasonable commercial terms have failed within a reasonable period of time; whereas (b) the prior negotiations requirement can be waived in a situation of national emergency, other circumstances of extreme urgency or in cases of public non-commercial use[60] and (c) the scope and duration of the use under compulsory licensing shall be limited to the purpose for which it is authorized. In such cases of compulsory licensing the right-holder shall still be notified as soon as reasonably practicable (Art. 31(b)) and shall be paid adequate remuneration depending on a specific case (Art. 31(h)). Importantly, Article 31(f) of the TRIPS Agreement sets an additional requirement, that a compulsory license under

---

of the P.R. of China" in W.P. zu Waldeck und Pyrmont et al. (eds.), *Patents and Technological Progress in a Globalized World*, MPI Studies on Intellectual Property, Competition and Tax Law, vol. 6, Berlin/Heidelberg, Springer, 2009, p. 117. The local working requirement in Brazil even led to a complaint in the WTO by the US, which was settled at the stage of consultations. *See* Brazil – Measures Affecting Patent Protection, World Trade Organization, http://www.wto.org/english/tratop_e/dispu_e/cases_e/ds199_e.htm (accessed 4 March 2013).

59 Bird and Cahoy, "The Emerging BRIC Economies", p. 416. See Article 11 of the Patent Law of the Russian Federation, as amended in 2003.

60 According to the Decision of the General Council of 30 August 2003 on the Implementation of paragraph 6 of the Doha Declaration on the TRIPs Agreement and Public Health (WT/L/540), which introduced compulsory licensing for exports, some WTO Members have confirmed that they will use this system only in situations of national emergency or other situations of extreme urgency. So far 11 countries have submitted this voluntary waiver: Hong Kong, China, Israel, Korea, Kuwait, Macao China, Mexico, Qatar, Singapore, Chinese Taipei, Turkey, and United Arab Emirates.

this article shall be used predominantly to supply the domestic market, which could be interpreted as limiting exports of licensed medicines.[61]

In 2001 the WTO Ministerial Conference of the World Trade Organization adopted the Doha Declaration on the TRIPS Agreement and Public Health, reaffirming the above-mentioned flexibilities of the TRIPS Agreement. Paragraph 6 of the Declaration mandated the WTO General Council to address concerns about the use of the compulsory licensing mechanism under Article 31 of the TRIPS Agreement by countries without the capacity to produce the needed pharmaceuticals.[62] The Decision of the General Council on the Implementation of Paragraph 6 of the Doha Declaration followed in 2003. This Decision introduced a system whereby an exporting country could issue a compulsory patent license for the purposes of supplying a pharmaceutical product to an importing country or countries that lacks capacity to produce that product (upon fulfilling certain conditions).[63] Although the mechanism under the 2003 Decision has been used only once by Rwanda and Canada,[64] compulsary licensing remain a hot topic. The beginning of 2012 was marked by new examples of international practices on domestic compulsory licensing: the recently enacted Chinese regulation on compulsory licenses[65] and the

---

61 *See e.g.* Swarup Kumar, "Compulsory Licensing Provisions under TRIPS: A Study of Roche vs Natco Case in India vis-à-vis the Applicability of the Principle of Audi Alteram Partem", *ScriptEd*, vol. 7, no. 1, 2010, pp. 135–54. See, however, the Decision of the General Council of 30 August 2003 (WT/L/540).

62 See an extensive discussion of the Doha Declaration in Yamane, *Interpreting TRIPS*, pp. 304–18.

63 For a detailed analysis of the 2003 Decision, *see* Frederick M. Abbott, "The WTO Medicines Decision: World Pharmaceutical Trade and the Protection of Public Health", *American Journal of International Law*, vol. 99, 2005, p. 317; The Swedish National Board of Commerce, *The WTO Decision on Compulsory Licensing: Does it Enable Import of Medicines for Developing Countries with Grave Public Health Problems?*, Kommerskollegium 2008:2, http://www.kommers.se/upload/Analysarkiv/Arbetsområden/WTO/Handel%20och%20skydd%20för%20immateriella%20rättigheter%20-%20TRIPS/Rapport%20The_WTO_decision_on_compulsory_licensing.pdf (accessed 5 August 2012); for an analysis of the flaws of the existing compulsory licensing system, see: McBeth, "Why Have No States Used the WTO Scheme".

64 See: Kumar, "Compulsory Licensing Provisions under TRIPS", pp. 139–40. On the disadvantages of the Canadian legislation *see* Richard Elliott, "Pledges and Pitfalls: Canada's Legislation on Compulsory Licensing of Pharmaceuticals for Export", *International Journal of Intellectual Property Management*, vol. 1, no. 1–2, 2006, pp. 94–112.

65 For an overview of Chinese legislation on compulsory licensing, *see* Jason Ma, "The Position of Compulsory Licensing in China", *Intellectual Property Magazine*, November 2011, pp. 55–7. The amendments to the legislation on

recent decision of the Controller of the Indian Patent Office on the same issue.[66] Russia as a new WTO Member could, if necessary, use the compulsory license mechanism either predominantly for its domestic market in accordance with the Article 31 of the TRIPS Agreement, or under the Paragraph 6 mechanism foremost for exports to LDCs and other countries with inexistent or underdeveloped pharmaceutical manufacturing capacity, similarly to Canada - Rwanda example.[67] Therefore, it is worth examining the approach to compulsory licensing pursued so far by the Russian Government in light of its public health situation.

4.4 Compulsory Licensing in Russia

In light of the TRIPS flexibilities outlined above, the current patent legislation in Russia provides for three main exceptions, which are of importance for the pharmaceutical industry:

- one-time preparations by drug stores of medicines on prescription using the invention (Art. 1359(5) Civil Code of the Russian Federation);
- the use of patented inventions in situations of emergency (natural disasters, catastrophes or accidents) (Art. 1359(3) Civil Code of the Russian Federation);

compulsory licensing of 2012 also make compulsory licensing available for the production of generics for export; *see* Tan Ee Lyn, "China Changes Patent Law in Fight for Cheaper Drugs", *Reuters*, 8 June 2012, http://www.reuters.com/article/2012/06/08/us-china-medicines-patents-idUSBRE8570TY20120608 (accessed 4 March 2013).

66 International Center for Trade and Sustainable Development, "India Grants First Compulsory License to Generic Drug Producer", *Bridges Weekly Trade News Digest*, vol. 16, no. 10, 14 March 2012, http://ictsd.org/i/news/bridgesweekly/128236/ (accessed 4 March 2013).

67 So far Russia has not submitted any notifications according to the Decision of the General Council of 30 August 2003. It shall be noted that taking into account Russia's recent modernization strategies in the pharmaceutical sector it most likely would use the mechanism of the 2003 Decision as an exporting country, e.g. to supply essential medicine in the region, since paragraph 2(a)(ii) of the Decision of the General Council of 30 August 2003 stipulates that non-LDCs (least developed countries) can use this mechanism only if their manufacturing capacity is insufficient or non-existent for the product(s) in question. According to the Annex of this Decision, only LDCs are deemed per se to have insufficient or no manufacturing capacities in the pharmaceutical sector. For other countries it shall be considered, for the product(s) in question, whether there is no domestic manufacturing capacity in the pharmaceutical sector or whether the existing capacity is insufficient, apart from the one that is owned or controlled by the patent owner.

- the use of inventions without the consent of the patent holder, subject to immediate notification of the patent holder and followed by fair compensation for the purpose of security and defense upon a decision of the Government of the Russian Federation (however, this provision does not make explicit reference to public health) (Art. 1360 Civil Code of the Russian Federation).

None of the three exceptions is referred to as compulsory licensing; rather they are described as non-violation clauses.

Chapter IV of the Civil Code of the Russian Federation also provides for the possibility of issuing a compulsory license (Articles 1239, 1361, 1423). The Civil Code mentions two main grounds for compulsory licensing:

- the non-use (or insufficient use) of the patented invention, known already from the Paris Convention of 1883,[68] and
- a compulsory license for a dependent invention.

With respect to the first condition, the main question is what constitutes a sufficient use according to the requirements of Article 1361 of the Civil Code of the Russian Federation, since no court in the Russian Federation has yet interpreted this notion. To interpret this provision, practitioners refer to Article 1358 of the Civil Code of the Russian Federation dealing with the types of use of inventions and utility models. Accordingly, importation of such inventions produced abroad would already constitute a use and thus the "working" requirement under the Russian Civil Code does not amount to a local working requirement and does not discriminate between domestic and foreign patent holders.[69]

A compulsory license can be granted under the Civil Code only *by a court* as a result of litigation, and the court shall determine in its decision the terms and conditions of the compulsory license based on suggestions by the claimant.[70]

These compulsory licensing provisions (including the non-use clauses)

---

[68] Article 5A(2) of the Paris Convention for the Protection of Industrial Property (20 March 1883).

[69] An opposite opinion has been expressed by E.Y. Nikolaeva, "Discussion on the Issuance of a Compulsory License", 29 September 2011, http://www.1conc.ru/news/article-8300.htm (accessed 4 March 2013).

[70] Plenum of the Supreme Court of Russian Federation no. 5, Plenum of the High Arbitration Court of Russian Federation Nr. 29, Resolution as of March 26, 2009 on Certain Issues Arising due to Entering into Force of Part IV of the Civil Code of Russian Federation, http://mvf.klerk.ru/otvets/otv0103.htm (accessed 7 August 2012).

raised certain questions during the accession negotiations. However, Russia gave its assurance that the relevant provisions of its Civil Code have been amended to be in full compliance with Article 31 of the TRIPS Agreement.[71]

If we compare provisions on compulsory licensing in Russia with those in the BRICS and other countries, the former appear to be narrower. Firstly, Russian legislation still does not have specific provisions on compulsory licensing for public health reasons similar to the recent Chinese rules, which entered into force in May 2012, or the Ukrainian legislation of 2011.[72] Secondly, unlike Brazil, Thailand and recently India, Russia has not issued a single compulsory license on any of the grounds listed in the Civil Code Part IV. In this light the question to be answered is whether Russia, instead of compulsory licensing, should pursue some different policy to ensure access to essential drugs for its population.

4.5 East of West – Home is Best: Russia's Promotion of R&D and the Local Production of Pharmaceuticals

Over the last 15 years there has been a clear trend of a surge in patent applications in Russia, with an increase of 15,000 applications per year

---

[71] *Report of the Working Party*, para. 1274.

[72] The Law of Ukraine on the Amendments of the Law on Pharmaceuticals as of 3 November 2011 – amending Art. 30 of the above-mentioned law: "With the purpose of protection of public health in the course of registration of a drug the Cabinet of Ministers of Ukraine according to the law can allow to the designated person the use of patented invention (utility model), which is linked to the drug, without the consent of the patent owner". (According to the general rule, in order to register a drug in Ukraine an applicant has to submit a copy of the patent or license and the document that confirms the validity of the patent in Ukraine). Most probably this amendment, among others, has been included in response to the case of Hoffman la Roche v. Ministry of Health Protection and OLLMED International Inc. *See* Leonid Shilovskij and Alexander Braharnyk, "Legal Alliance", http://legalalliance.com.ua/rus/press/1807/ (in Ukrainian) (accessed 5 August 2012). The possibility of introducing this legal provision was discussed at a seminar organized by the UNDP on Intellectual Property Rights and Access to Essential Medicines: Challenges and Opportunities in Free Trade Agreement Negotiations, Multilateral Instruments and National Laws, held on 21–22 June 2010 in Kyiv, Ukraine. The presentations and background papers for this seminar are available at United Nations Development Programme, "Seminar: Intellectual Property Rights and Access to Essential Medicines: Challenges and Opportunities in Free Trade Agreement Negotiations, Multilateral Instruments and National Laws – 21–22 June 2010, Kyiv, Ukraine", Kyiv, UNDP, 2013, http://www.undp.org.ua/en/projects-list-all/989 (accessed 4 March 2013). Although the legislation is already in place, Ukraine, which joined the WTO in 2008, also did not have a single instance of compulsory licensing.

since the late 1990s, making Rospatent, Russia's patent office, one of the top twenty patent offices in the world.[73] In 2011 alone the number of patent applications in Russia witnessed a rise of 3% in comparison with 2010. There was also a substantial rise in patent applications by foreigners – 9.7% comparing the last two years; the overall share of non-resident applications in 2011 already amounted to 36%.[74] In 2011 Russia was sixth in the world in terms of granted patents, 32.2% of which were received by non-residents. This trend is to a large extent explained by the fact that the patent protection system became more transparent and reliable with WTO accession.

Russian applicants were active in 2011 in submitting patent applications to American (719) and Chinese (120) patent offices, as well as to the European Patent Office (168). Most non-resident applications in Russia stemmed from the US (3707), Germany (2302), Japan (1931) and France (1033), whereas 82% of these applications were submitted through the PCT system.[75]

The rise in patent applications in the late 1990s coincided with innovation promotion policies undertaken by the Russian Government. Projects to promote R&D at the universities, establishment of the status of Science City (Naukograd) in 2000, improvement of IP legislation (mentioned above), and the First Target Program in Innovation were the first steps in the innovation strategy for the future. In 2006 the Russian Federation created at OJSC "SEZ" in order to develop special economic zones, which in two years were established in St. Petersburg, Zelenograd, Dubna and Tomsk. In light of the Second Federal Target Program in Innovation 2007–12, three main technology-oriented state corporations were created: Rosnano, Rostechnologii and Rosatom. According to the recent OECD analysis on innovation policies, it is only since 2010 that Russia has been on the way to mature national innovation system. The Presidential initiative on the creation of a Russian equivalent to the US's DARPA, the creation of a technical platform and the initiative on the innovation center in Skolkovo (all in 2010) showed a clear interest and dedication on the part of the Russian Government to innovation promotion.[76]

---

73 World Intellectual Property Organization (WIPO), "World Intellectual Property Indicators – 2012 Edition", Geneva, WIPO, http://www.wipo.int/ipstats/en/wipi/index.html, p. 48 (accessed 4 March 2013).

74 WIPO, "World Intellectual Property Indicators – 2012 Edition".

75 WIPO, "World Intellectual Property Indicators – 2012 Edition", pp. 57–9.

76 Organisation for Economic Co-operation and Development (OECD), "OECD Reviews of Innovation Policy: Russian Federation 2011", OECD Publishing, 2011.

Innovation in most sectors of industry in Russia is still highly dependent on governmental spending. In 2008 production enterprises performed less than 9% of business expenditures on R&D.[77] Notwithstanding this, Russia has quite a good rate of 1.9 resident patent applications per R&D expenditures, which is above the average world rate (1.7). However, Russia still has rather a low rate of patent applications filed per billion dollars of GDP – only 12.8, in comparison with 26.6 in Switzerland, 41.8 in China and 100.7 in the Republic of Korea.[78]

The general policy on promoting innovation inside the country also touched the pharmaceutical sector. This was combined with the idea of encouraging local production of pharmaceuticals in order to ensure the security of their supply. In Russia, as in a number of developing countries with a sufficient level of technological development, there exists a belief that local production is a viable solution to ensure its population with the availability and accessibility (price-wise) of necessary drugs along with other expected positive economic effects.[79] And although it should be noted that there are a number of arguments against very active promotion of pure local production (including the increase of direct procurement costs, inability to supply all necessary drugs for the local population, etc.), its combination with R&D and some other policies may help to match local production with public health needs.[80]

Indeed, in 2009 the Russian Government tried to negotiate with GlaxoSmithKline a reduction of 15% in the price for the antiretroviral medication Combivir. However, Russia failed to agree on a deal and thus to ensure the affordability of this drug, even though Glaxo did agree to reduce the prices for some products on several Asian markets by 50%.[81] Unlike Brazil, which following a warning of its intention subsequently issued a compulsory license for a disputed pharmaceutical in similar negotiations,[82] Russia did not try to use this strategy in a similar situation. Instead, in addition to promoting local production by both domestic and

---

77 OECD, "OECD Reviews of Innovation Policy: Russian Federation 2011".

78 WIPO, "World Intellectual Property Indicators – 2012 Edition", pp. 77–8.

79 Yamane, *Interpreting TRIPS*, p. 278.

80 Frederick M. Abbott, "Trends in Local Production and Related Technology Transfer", prepared for the WHO Department of Public Health, Innovation and Intellectual Property, WHO 2011, pp. 6–9.

81 Shirley S. Wang, "Glaxo Says No to Russia on Cutting Price of HIV Drug", WSJ Health Blog, 12 June 2009, http://blogs.wsj.com/health/2009/06/12/glaxo-says-no-to-russia-on-cutting-price-of-hiv-drug/ (accessed 4 March 2013).

82 *See* Bruno Salama and Daniel Benoliel, "Pharmaceutical Patent Bargains: The Brazilian Experience", *Cardozo Journal of International and Comparative Law*, vol. 18, no. 3, 2010, pp. 633–86.

foreign companies, the Russian Government capped the prices for some 500 titles of drugs designated as essential. As of January 2008, Russia introduced a nationwide drug reimbursement program for population based on two main items:

- essential drug reimbursement subprogram (ONLS) – implemented at the regional level; and
- program for the procurement of expensive drugs for the treatment of very severe diseases (VZN) – at the federal level.[83]

To promote its local production strategy, in 2009 Russia adopted the Strategy for Development of the Pharma Industry by 2020, known as Pharma 2020. The strategy not only set the goal of increased domestic production of pharmaceuticals in order to ensure the medical safety of Russia in compliance with the list of strategic medication and vaccines, but also of increased exports of pharmaceuticals. In line with this strategy, the Russian Federation also adopted the List of Essential for Life and the Most Important Drugs (567 items – 16.4% of them produced only by domestic companies; 36.5% produced only by foreign companies, and 47.1% produced by both foreign and domestic companies), for which it pays additional wholesale and retail allowances ensuring their price support.[84] Moreover, the strategy established a mechanism of R&D support in order to localize the full cycle of drug development in Russia. Pharma 2020 also introduced a system of public procurement priority for local producers and provided for the encouragement of joint ventures with foreign companies.

This strategy is mainly financed by the Federal budget and it is foreseen that overall around USD 6 billion will be spent on the implementation of this strategy. The majority of planned expenditures will be directed at R&D projects, with lesser portions for education and infrastructure, and for transfer to GMP (around 15% each).

These measures have already resulted in increased interest by foreign pharmaceutical companies. Instead of using compulsory licensing, due to the specific characteristics of its pharmaceutical market, Russia is attracting more and more foreign companies to enhance cooperation, technology transfer and domestic production. Three major pharmaceutical companies

---

[83] "The structure of Medicines", *Clinical Pharmacy* [web journal], 4 November 2010, http://clinical-pharmacy.ru/article/808-struktura-sistemy-obespecheniya-lekarstvennymi-sredstvami.html (accessed 4 March 2013).

[84] "The List of Medicines Essential for Life Will Not Change in 2013", available in Russian, http://www.pharma.net.ua/ru/node/19021, accessed 6 August 2012.

have agreed to build manufacturing plants in the country: Teva, Novartis and AstraZeneca. In September 2011, Teva released information about an investment agreement for the construction of a manufacturing facility in Yaroslavl. A few months earlier Novartis announced its plan to construct a manufacturing plant in Novoorlovskaya Special Economic Zone in St. Petersburg, and AstraZeneca plans to build a new facility in Kaluga.[85] However, it is not only pharmaceutical companies from developed countries that are trying to get a share of the Russian market and of the newly created common market for the Customs Union. In March 2012, during the official talks in New Delhi, India proposed to create joint ventures between Indian and Russian pharmaceutical companies for the production of 500 various titles of drugs (mainly generics and strategic drugs), which will be destined not only for the Russian market, but also for the markets of Kazakhstan and Belarus – the other members of the Customs Union.[86] Similar strategies of domestic production support have developed in the whole region. Similarly to Russian Pharma 2020, Kazakhstan has adopted a National Program on Development of Pharmaceutical Industry for 2010–14, which among other things provides for sales contracts with local pharmaceutical companies (producing locally) for the purchase of pharmaceuticals through a single distributor.[87]

The recent Russian innovation strategy in general and its specific policies in the pharmaceutical sector signify that Russia has been actively pursuing the aim of becoming a regional leader in innovation. In the pharmaceutical sector, instead of taking recourse to compulsory licensing,[88] as one of

---

[85] "What are the Leading Pharmaceutical Companies Investing in Russia?", *The Pharmaceutical News*, 2013, http://thepharmaceutical-news.com/world-pharmaceutical-market-focus/russia-pharmaceutical-market (accessed 3 March 2013).

[86] "India Proposes Joint Venture to Make 500 Drugs in Russia", *The Hindu Business Line*, 27 March 2011, http://www.thehindubusinessline.com/industry-and-economy/article3251131.ece (accessed 4 March 2013).

[87] "Import-Export of Pharmaceuticals in the Republic of Kazakhstan", *Vidal*, 18 February 2011, http://www.vidal.kz/novosti/novosti_1444.html (in Russian) (accessed 4 March 2013).

[88] While in the case of India it was suggested that one of the reasons for India's reluctance to use compulsory licensing was the fear of a WTO challenge, Russia obviously did not want to bring an additional item into the accession negotiations. Since nothing suggests that Russia has rejected the application of compulsory licensing, nothing prevents it from using this mechanism in the future. On the Indian case see Sara Beth Myers, "A Healthy Solution for Patients and Patents: How India's Legal Victory against a Pharmaceutical Giant Reconciles Human Rights with Intellectual Property Rights", *Vanderbilt Journal of Entertainment & Technology Law*, vol. 10, no. 3, 2008, p. 786.

the flexibilities available under the TRIPS Agreement, Russia has chosen to put the emphasis on R&D and to strengthen its domestic production, which may in the near future change its profile from a pharmaceutical-importing to a pharmaceutical-exporting country. An additional price cap policy for essential medicines by the Russian Government will ensure that these essential drugs are increasingly accessible and affordable to the Russian population.

5 CONCLUSION

The 18-year-long process of Russia's accession to the WTO coincided with its transition to a new economic system and witnessed considerable changes in its intellectual property legislation. Although patent protection never posed a serious obstacle to its membership in the WTO, even the minor non-compliances have been dealt with. Russia addressed the possible effects of enhanced intellectual property protection on the pharmaceutical sector and on access to essential drugs through a nationwide sectoral strategy aimed on the one hand at the promotion of innovation and facilitation of domestic production of pharmaceuticals, and on the other hand establishing price caps for essential medicines to ensure their affordability. So far it has not shown any interest in the use of the compulsory licensing mechanism. The next few years will show whether Russian innovation policies in the pharmaceutical sector will ensure its leading market position in the region and at the same time will be enough to cope with public health concerns.

South Africa

12. Harmonizing the national policies for healthcare, pharmaceutical industry and intellectual property: The South African experience[1]

Andre Kudlinski

1 INTRODUCTION

Africa has a disproportionately high share of the world's infectious disease burden: 76% of HIV/AIDS, 88% of malaria, 38% of respiratory infections and 38% of diarrheal diseases. Sub-Saharan Africa, which is home to 11% of the global population, bears 24% of the global disease burden but commands less than 1% of the global health expenditure, according to "The Business of Health in Africa" report published by the International Finance Corporation in 2007.[2] The AIDS epidemic reduced life expectancy in countries such as South Africa, Kenya, Uganda, Botswana and Zimbabwe by 20 years, from 57–65 years in the 1980s to 37–45 years by the early to mid-2000s. One child out of every ten born in Angola, Mozambique, Zambia and the Democratic Republic of Congo (DRC) dies before reaching the age of 5, most of them of preventable diseases. Angola and Zimbabwe have the highest maternal mortality rate in the world.

Even with the recent economic revival, chiefly driven by the growing demand for oil, gas and minerals, only a few countries in Saharan and sub-Saharan Africa can afford the US$35–40 per person per year, considered by the World Health Organization (WHO) as the necessary

[1] The opinions, interpretations, comments and conclusions expressed in the chapter are entirely those of the author and do not necessarily represent the views of the South African Department of Trade and Industry.

[2] International Finance Corporation, "The Business of Health in Africa: Partnering with the Private Sector to Improve People's Lives", IFC, Washington, DC, 2007, http://www.unido.org/fileadmin/user_media/Services/PSD/BEP/IFC_HealthinAfrica_Final.pdf.

minimum to provide basic healthcare. On average, 50% of total health expenditure in the region is financed by out-of-pocket payments, a precarious situation bearing in mind that a large proportion of population in the region lives at or below the poverty line; this is further exacerbated by a high level of penetration of fake, counterfeit and sub-standard medicines. The HIV/AIDS, TB and malaria treatment programmes in most sub-Saharan African countries are financed almost entirely by aid provided by Western governments, UN agencies and non-governmental organizations (NGOs), with billions of dollars in international aid dispensed over the past decade. The financial contribution of local governments to these programmes is minimal – for example, over 60% of the malaria control programme in Kenya is financed by the Global Fund for AIDS, TB and Malaria (GFATM) and only 0.5% by the Kenyan government.[3]

Probably the greatest global health achievement in the past decade, despite all odds, has been the scale-up of treatment of HIV/AIDS. According to the 2012 UN AIDS global report, only 300,000 AIDS patients in the low- and middle-income countries (2.7% of those eligible) had access to antiretroviral (ARV) treatment in 2002. Within a decade, the number of patients receiving ARVs grew to 6.6 million by the end of 2010 (reaching 47% of the total eligible) and to more than 8 million by the end of 2011.

The cost of ARV treatment has become manageable thanks to a hundred-fold reduction of prices of the basic first-line ARV combination (AZT-d4T-NVP), from over US$10,000 per patient per year in 2000, to just US$100 in 2011. The latest world record for the lowest-cost ARV, US$126 (1,072 South African Rand) per patient per year for the first-line "3 in 1" ARV fixed-dosage combination TDF-EFV-FTC (a generic equivalent of Atripla ®) was set in the South African ARV tender in November 2012.[4]

These price reductions became possible as countries took better advantage of flexibilities built into international patent law. Production of generic ARVs, reverse-engineering of patented technologies and manufacture of active pharmaceutical ingredients (ARV APIs) started in Brazil

---

[3] Shahid Hasan and Wilberforce Wanyanga, "Pharmaceutical Sector Profile: Kenya", United Nations Industrial Development Organization, Vienna, 2010, p. 28, http://www.unido.org/fileadmin/user_media/Services/PSD/BEP/Kenya_Pharma%20Sector%20profile_TEGLO05015_Ebook.pdf.

[4] Khulekani Magubane and Tamar Kahn, "State to Introduce Three-in-One AIDS Pill", *Business Day*, 29 November 2012, http://www.bdlive.co.za/national/health/2012/11/29/state-to-introduce-three-in-one-aids-pill.

(AZT in 1991–4[5]) and during the following two decades grew exponentially in China and India. The cost of ARV APIs accounts for 50% to 75% of the cost of the generic ARV medicines. Research continues to optimize technologies of the "old" ARV APIs; a remarkable development has been the invention of a streamlined route of synthesis of efavirenz (EFV) which helped to bring down the price of generic EFV from US$1,000 per kg in mid-2008 to below US$200 per kg today.

While the manufacture of generic ARV APIs is limited to a handful of companies in China and India, there has been enormous proliferation of manufacturers – formulators of generic ARVs. Today, there are over 100 registered manufacturers of generic ARVs worldwide (most of them formulating finished-dosage ARVs from imported APIs) even in the least-developed countries such as Uganda.

Notwithstanding these achievements, it is too early to celebrate. 2.5 million people worldwide were newly infected with HIV in 2011,[6] i.e. 1.1 million more than the gain in global antiretroviral therapy (ART) coverage in the same year. *The Lancet* in its 15 December edition ("AIDS is not over")[7] warns that with the current level of international AIDS funding it will be impossible to sustain the necessary level of efforts when the need for resources peaks in 2015. Estimated US$22 billion to US$24 billion per year will be needed in 2015, but international AIDS funding has been stagnant at $8.2 billion per year since 2009.

There are more reasons for concern about the medium-to-long-term sustainability of the current system that warrant a call for radical rethinking and redesigning of the health-related patent system, the international health aid programmes, the national, regional and global industrial and economic policies.

The first problem is the concentration of manufacturing of generic pharmaceuticals for global aid programmes in India (medicines in finished-dosage form and APIs) and China (chiefly APIs and intermediates for API synthesis). India accounts for over 80% of supply of annual global procurement of ARVs, by volume. 93% of procurement of ARVs financed by the Global Fund in 2009–10 came from Indian generic companies. The

---

5 Matthew Flynn, "Public Production of Antiretroviral Medicines in Brazil 1990–2007", *Development and Change*, vol. 39, no. 4, 2008, pp. 513–36.

6 Joint United Nations Programme on HIV/AIDS (UNAIDS), "Global Report: UNAIDS Report on the Global AIDS Epidemic 2012", UNAIDS, Geneva, 2012, http://www.unaids.org/en/media/unaids/contentassets/documents/epidemiology/2012/gr2012/20121120_UNAIDS_Global_Report_2012_en.pdf.

7 Michel Sidibé, Peter Piot and Mark Dybul, "AIDS Is Not Over", *The Lancet*, vol. 380, no. 9859, 15 December 2012, pp. 2058–9.

majority of ARVs procured by the US PEPFAR also come from India.[8] India's ARV API production plants are to a large extent dependent on imports of intermediates from China. China and India jointly supply 90% to 95% of the global volume of generic ARV APIs. This raises concerns about the global security of supply of ARV APIs in case of natural disasters, political tensions etc.

The manufacture of ARV APIs is particularly "dirty", generating roughly 100 kg of toxic and hazardous waste per 1 kg of final product. Safe and environmentally acceptable disposal of the waste is costly. In July 2012, the Andhra Pradesh Pollution Control Board ordered the closure of 12 API plants, including those belonging to India's leading ARV API manufacturers Aurobindo and Hetero. Earlier, the US FDA issued Aurobindo with a warning letter regarding its environmental monitoring data in 2009–10.[9]

Such concerns are well justified. 90% to 95% of the world's supplies of crude beta-lactam antibiotics (penicillin and cephalosporin) are manufactured in China, while most of the subsequent chemical conversion to semi-synthetic antibiotics (ampicillin, amoxicillin etc.) is carried out in India. The manufacture of most antibiotics, which involves fermentation, generates vast quantities of chemical and biological waste. To reduce the level of pollution, the Chinese authorities ordered the temporary shutdown of many plants, including antibiotic factories, before and during the Beijing Olympic Games in 2008. This resulted in worldwide shortages of antibiotics, lasting about 3 months.

The second problem is the insufficient installed manufacturing capacity to meet the expected rise in demand for ARV APIs in 2015–17. According to data presented by the Clinton Health Access Initiative (CHAI),[10] the demand for generic tenofovir (TDF) will grow threefold (from 250 metric tons in 2011 to 750 tons in 2015), and for efavirenz (EFV) by 65% (from 600 tons in 2012 to 1,000 tons in 2015). The installed manufacturing capacities for TDF and EFV in 2011 were 370 and 750 tons, respectively.

---

[8] Joint United Nations Programme on HIV/AIDS (UNAIDS), "Doha+10: TRIPS Flexibilities and Access to Antiretroviral Therapy: Lessons for the Past, Opportunities for the Future", *UNAIDS*, Geneva, November 2011, p. 32, http://www.unaids.org/en/media/unaids/contentassets/documents/unaidspublication/2011/JC2260_DOHA+10TRIPS_en.pdf.

[9] Natalie Morrison, "Indian API Production Takes Hit as APPCB Shuts 12 Plants", in-PharmaTechnologist.com, 18 July 2012, http://www.in-pharmatechnologist.com/Regulatory-Safety/Indian-API-production-takes-hit-as-APPCB-shuts-12-plants.

[10] Meredith Moore, "ARV Market Update", Clinton Health Access Initiative [presentation], Thiruvantapuram, India, 28 September 2011.

Projections for required new capacities take into account a safety margin of 20% to factor for wastage, maintaining the buffer stock etc. A less critical shortage of nevirapine (NVP) also has been projected (about 100 tons, i.e. 15% of the existing capacity). There also is uncertainty regarding the demand for a new non-nucleoside reverse transcriptase inhibitor (NNRTI) rilpivirine (RIL) and whether or not and to what extent it might ease demand for EFV.

Investment in the manufacture of generic ARV APIs is becoming less and less attractive due to high capital outlay, long project cycles and shrinking profit margins. As an indication, the capital cost of the South African ARV API project ("Project Ketlaphela")[11] with a capacity of 500 tons/year is US$170 million (€140 million) and the project cycle is 36 months. It should be borne in mind that Project Ketlaphela will supply only 40% of the ARV API volumes needed for the South African domestic market when the demand peaks in 2016–17.

The third problem is the "crowding-out" of national pharmaceutical manufacturers by the donors (PEPFAR, The Global Fund, CHAI etc.) and in national tenders, due to competition with low-cost medicines imported from India. In the South African 2010–12 ARV tender, contracts awarded to South African manufacturers were not executed for several months until the entire allocation of the PEPFAR grant was exhausted (used entirely to pay for imported ARVs). When finally the Health Department at short notice issued delivery orders, there was a temporary acute shortage of ARVs in some parts of South Africa as the manufacturers scrambled to reactivate API import contracts and resume production. While large South African manufacturers can adapt to such a roller-coaster demand, absorb the losses and survive, the lack of concern for domestic manufacturers is devastating for smaller companies in less affluent countries, such as Zimbabwe, which often operate at 20% capacity utilization.[12]

The decimation of national pharmaceutical manufacturers due to competition with imports from India is not limited to ARVs: the South African company Aspen-Pharmacare mothballed its state-of-the art oral contraceptives plant in East London (the only such plant on the African continent) after losing the South African Health Department's family planning drugs tender in September 2011.

---

11 *Ketlaphela* means "I will survive" in Sotho.

12 Chris Chitemerere, "Pharmaceutical Sector Profile: Zimbabwe", United Nations Industrial Development Organization, Vienna, 2011, http://www.unido.org/fileadmin/user_media/Services/PSD/BEP/Zimbabwe_Pharma%20Sector%20Profile_032011_Ebook.pdf.

The fourth problem concerns the failure of the current health and economic aid programmes to bridge the technology gap between the African countries and the rest of the world and stimulate domestic production efforts. While millions of AIDS sufferers in developing countries have benefited from low-cost generic medicines, so far the dissemination of modern pharmaceutical technologies has benefited just a few countries, first and foremost India and China and to a much lesser extent Brazil and South Africa.

Strangely, a majority of developing countries that have been affected by this technology dependency appear to be doing little to address it. There is growing complacency among the health aid recipient countries and it appears that the earlier plans to gradually build domestic and regional manufacturing and R&D capabilities (announced at various declarations of the ministers of health of African countries) have been put on hold. This will only protract the problem and condemn the majority of African countries to perpetual dependence on foreign aid. The technology gap between Africa and the rest of the world has become massive. Progress in pharmaceutical technologies (especially in biologics and vaccines) in the last decade has been so rapid that the ability of the "third-tier" "pharmerging" countries (which include South Africa)[13] to absorb the transfer of modern technologies is often questioned.

While, admittedly, the poor state of many African economies is an important constraint on providing quality healthcare and investing in developing domestic manufacturing base, it is not an insurmountable barrier. This is emphasized in the Commission on Intellectual Property Rights, Innovation and Public Health (CIPIH) report[14] which cites the Cuban pharmaceutical biotech and national health system as an example.

---

[13] Tier 1 (China); Tier 2 (Brazil, Russia and India); Tier 3 (Venezuela,* Poland, Argentina, Turkey, Mexico, Vietnam, South Africa, Thailand, Indonesia, Romania, Egypt, Pakistan and Ukraine). David Campbell and Mandy Chui, "Pharmerging Shake-up: New Imperatives in a Redefined World", *IMS Health*, March 2010, p. 5, http://www.imshealth.com/ims/Global/Content/Insights/Featured%20Topics/Emerging%20Markets/Pharma_Shake-up_Imperatives.pdf. Countries are arranged in descending order of incremental pharmaceutical market value growth. (* The ranking of Venezuela is mainly attributed to unusual inflation and currency changes.)

[14] Commission on Intellectual Property Rights, Innovation and Public Health (CIPIH), "Public Health, Innovation and Intellectual Property Rights", World Health Organization, Geneva, April 2006, p. 2, http://www.who.int/intellectualproperty/documents/thereport/ENPublicHealthReport.pdf.

2 THE AFRICAN PHARMACEUTICAL SECTOR AND THE CONTINENT'S HEALTHCARE NEEDS

2.1 The State of Healthcare in Africa

Africa has a disproportionately high share of the world's infectious disease burden: 76% of HIV/AIDS, 88% of malaria, 38% of respiratory infections, 38% of diarrheal diseases, 97% of trypanosomiasis (sleeping sickness) and 35% of lymphatic filariasis (the cause of elephantiasis). The maternal mortality ratio is the highest in the world – for example 1,400 per 100,000 live births in Angola and 880 in Zimbabwe. Infant mortality rate is 116 per 1,000 live births in Angola, 108 in Mozambique, 103 in Zambia and 92 in the Democratic Republic of Congo (DRC).[15]

The sub-Saharan Africa, which is home to 11% of the global population, bears 24% of the global disease burden but commands less than 1% of the global health expenditure. Large parts of the African continent do not have the infrastructure and facilities necessary to provide minimum levels of health services. The continent and especially central and southern Africa also face a severe shortage of trained medical personnel.

The healthcare resource differences among countries in the sub-Saharan Africa are huge: the annual average per capita spending on healthcare ranges from US$610 in South Africa to US$18 in Zimbabwe and just US$1.30 in the DRC. Mozambique, a country with a population of 20.5 million has just 110 pharmacists (one per 200,000 population); the DRC (population 66 million) has 1,150 pharmacists (one per 65,000), compared with South Africa's 11,850 pharmacists (2.4 per 10,000 population).[16]

Chiefly due to the AIDS epidemics, the life expectancy at birth in countries such as South Africa, Kenya, Uganda, Botswana, Swaziland, Lesotho and Zimbabwe fell by 20 years, from 57–65 years in the 1980s to 37–45 years by the early to mid-2000s. Recently, the life expectancy in most of these countries has substantially improved.[17]

On the positive side, low-cost interventions such as the distribution of insecticide-impregnated mosquito nets have brought down the cases of malaria in children. Providing clean water and implementing the fortification of staple food with vitamins, iron and zinc have reduced the incidence

---

15 Southern African Development Community (SADC), "Pooled Procurement of Essential Medicines and Medical Supplies: Situational Analysis and Feasibility Study" [draft], September 2011, Boksburg-Johannesburg, South Africa, pp. 17–19.

16 SADC, "Pooled Procurement", pp. 11, 18.

17 "Historial Data Graphs per Year", *IndexMundi*, http://www.indexmundi.com/g/g.aspx?v=30&c=lt&l=en (using data from CIA World Factbook).

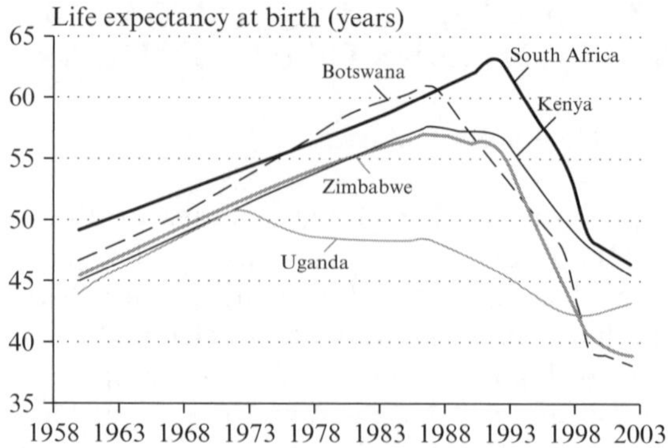

Source: World Bank, World Development Indicators, 2004.

Figure 12.1 Life expectancy at birth (years)

of cases of child underweight and micro-nutrient deficiency in Central, Eastern, Western and sub-Saharan Africa.[18]

2.2 The Pharmaceutical Sector in Africa

The African pharmaceutical market was estimated at US$10 billion in 2006. It is projected to grow to US$30 billion by 2016 and to US$45 billion by 2020, at a compounded annual growth rate (CAGR) of 10.6%, which is the same as South America's (10.5%) and second only to Asia-Pacific (12.5%), according to an IMS White Paper on the African Pharmaceutical Market.[19] The growth will be driven by the overall improvement of the African economies, population growth, a rapid rate of urbanization and a rising proportion of the middle class. The bulk of the growth in demand will be for medicines against communicable (infectious) and parasitic diseases (AIDS, TB, malaria etc.), but medicines to treat non-communicable

---

[18] Stephen S. Lim et al., "A Comparative Risk Assessment of Burden of Disease and Injury Attributable to 67 Risk Factors and Risk Factor Clusters in 21 Regions, 1990–2010: A Systemic Analysis for the Global Burden of Disease Study 2010", *The Lancet*, vol. 380, no. 9859, 15 December 2012.

[19] Ramya Logendra et al., "Africa: A Ripe Opportunity – Understanding the Pharmaceutical Market Opportunity and Developing Sustainable Business Models in Africa", IMS Health, 2012, http://www.imshealth.com/deployedfiles/ims/Global/Content/Insights/Featured%20Topics/Emerging%20Markets/IMS_Africa_Opportunity_Whitepaper.pdf.

and chronic diseases such as cardiovascular, cancer and diabetes are becoming a fast-growing segment (20%).

It must be borne in mind that the projected growth will be achieved from a very low base. By the end of 2020, Africa will account for just 3% to 3.5% of the global pharmaceutical market by value. For comparison, the global pharmaceutical market is projected to grow from US$990 billion in 2012 to US$1,140 billion by 2014, reaching US$1.3 trillion by 2020.[20]

The IMS report concedes that African markets are still poorly understood, information on medicine consumption is not systematically collected, resulting in fragmented and inconsistent data. While the donor funding is well documented, there are significant discrepancies in the estimates of the value of national pharmaceutical markets, domestic production, exports and imports.

At US$ 3.7 billion, South Africa's pharmaceutical market was the largest in Africa in 2011, followed by Egypt ($3.0 billion), Algeria ($2.8 billion), Nigeria ($1.8 billion), Morocco ($1.2 billion) and Kenya ($660 million) (all data at ex-factory prices). Most estimates of the national markets are consistent, but the IMS estimates of the Nigerian pharmaceutical market show a wide discrepancy with other reports such as UNIDO[21] (US$717 million by 2011), Business Monitor International (US$600 million in 2009), Frost and Sullivan (US$740 million in 2009) and the World Bank–International Finance Corporation "The Business of Health in Africa" report (US$506 million in 2006).

Aside from simple re-packaging operations, domestic manufacture of pharmaceuticals (formulation from imported APIs) is limited to South Africa, Egypt, Algeria, Tunisia, Morocco, Nigeria, Ghana, Kenya and Uganda. Three countries – South Africa, Egypt and Ghana – also have (albeit limited) API production. Vaccines are manufactured in Egypt, Senegal and South Africa. According to the African Development Bank, there were 129 pharmaceutical manufacturing plants in Africa in 2010.[22]

---

20 "Pharma 2020: The Vision", IMS Health, http://www.pwc.com/gx/en/pharma-life-sciences/pharma-2020/pharma-2020-vision-path.jhtml.

21 Charles Wambebe and Nelson Ochekpe, "Pharmaceutical Sector Profile: Nigeria", United Nations Industrial Development Organization (UNIDO), Vienna, 2011, p. 1, http://www.unido.org/fileadmin/user_media/Services/PSD/BEP/Nigeria_Pharma%20Sector%20Profile_032011_Ebook.pdf.

22 Feng Zhao, "Opportunities and Challenges: Africa Pharmaceutical Sector", Human Development Department, African Development Bank [presentation], 2011, p. 3, http://www.hha-online.org/hso/system/files/3zhao_pharmaceutical_sector__africa_value_for_money_tunis.pdf.

2.3 Plans to Increase Pharmaceutical Production in Africa

Low level of domestic production of pharmaceuticals, growing reliance on imports and donor programmes have been identified as the continent's strategic weakness in various declarations of the ministers of health of African countries. There are multiple challenges to viable domestic production in Africa, including the small size of most national pharmaceutical markets, the necessity to import most inputs such as active pharmaceutical ingredients, excipients, quality packaging material etc., competition with imports, difficult access to finance, unreliable supply of electric energy etc. With very few exceptions pharmaceutical plants in Africa have been unable to obtain accreditation by the US Food and Drug Administration (FDA);[23] this makes them not eligible to supply even their own national markets under the US government-financed programmes such as PEPFAR, USAID, Centre for Disease Control and Prevention (CDC) and the US President's Malaria Initiative (PMI).

Access to formulation technologies/know-how is not seen as a major challenge to the manufacturers of generic medicines. The least-developed counties also can take advantage of TRIPS exemptions.

So far, attempts to integrate the national markets – create a "critical mass" of regional pharmaceutical markets in Africa – have not been successful (for example, the 1996 PHARMESA project in the Common Market for Eastern and Southern Africa – COMESA – and the 2002 Economic Community of West African States – ECOWAS – regional Pharmaceutical Manufacturers Association projects).

The renewed market integration efforts include:

- the African Union Assembly Decision 55 taken at the Abuja summit in January 2005 which mandates COMESA member countries to support local production of generic medicines in Africa, and
- the East African Community's protocol on the movement of goods, labour, services, and capital which came into force on 1 July 2010.

Thus far, it is difficult to assess the impact of these developments on the intra-African trade in pharmaceuticals. Some reports show that the largest and most modern pharmaceutical plant in East Africa, Uganda's Quality

[23] In March 2005, Aspen-Pharmacare Oral Solid Dosage (OSD) facility in Port Elizabeth, South Africa became the first manufacturing site outside the USA to receive FDA approval for the supply of generic ARVs, including the "3 in 1" triple combination ARVs to the US market and for the US Government-sponsored aid programmes.

Chemical Industries Ltd (QCIL),[24] is operating at or below 50% capacity chiefly due to competition with low-cost ARV imports from Asia. QCIL received the WHO Good Manufacturing Practices (GMP) certification for its ARVs in 2010, which makes it eligible to export ARVs under the WHO-funded programmes.

Currently, there are three major transnational pharmaceutical projects in Africa: the SADC (Southern African Development Community[25]) Pharmaceutical Business Plan 2007–13,[26] the East African Community Regional Pharmaceutical Manufacturing Plan of Action 2012–16[27] and the African Union's Pharmaceutical Manufacturing Plan for Africa (PMPA). The PMPA Business Plan ("Business Plan for the Operationalization of the Pharmaceutical Manufacturing Plan for Africa – PMPA") that resulted from a strategic partnership between the African Union (AU) Commission and UNIDO was approved by the African Union Ministers of Health and subsequently endorsed by the African Heads of State at their Summit in July 2012. The business plan represents a framework for a comprehensive technical assistance programme offering solutions towards the creation of a commercially viable pharmaceutical industry on the African continent.

The SADC, the AUC–UNIDO and the EAC–UNIDO documents provide comprehensive health-related data for the member countries, a needs analysis, an analysis of strengths and weaknesses, opportunities and threats, including an assessment of differences in national patent laws and medicines regulatory systems among the SADC, EAC and AU member countries. In many countries pharmaceuticals, even those manufactured in Africa, are not exempt from customs duties and taxes. It appears that

---

24 Quality Chemical Industries Ltd (QCIL) plant in Kampala, Uganda, commissioned in 2006, is a joint venture of Cipla (India), the Government of Uganda and Quality Chemicals Ltd of Uganda. The plant manufactures solid-dosage ARVs (tablets and capsules) and anti-malaria drugs, artemesin-based combination therapies (ACTs).

25 SADC member states are: Angola, Botswana, the Democratic Republic of Congo (DRC), Lesotho, Malawi, Mauritius, Mozambique, Namibia, Seychelles, South Africa, Swaziland, Tanzania, Zambia and Zimbabwe. Madagascar's SADC membership has been suspended following a military coup d'état in that country.

26 Southern African Development Community, "SADC Pharmaceutical Business Plan 2007–2013", SADC Secretariat, 27 June 2007, http://www.unido.org/fileadmin/user_media/Services/PSD/BEP/SADC%20PHARMACEUTICAL%20BUSINESS%20PLAN%20-APPROVED%20PLAN.pdf.

27 East African Community, "East African Community Regional Pharmaceutical Manufacturing Plan of Action (2012–2016)", EAC Secretariat, Arusha, Tanzania, 2011, http://feapm.com/fileadmin/user_upload/pharma_marketing_plan_2011.pdf.

finding a practical solution to the financing of pooled procurement, making cross-border trade simple, reducing perverse incentives and corruption may be major obstacles to the implementation of the project.[28]

The latest round of the SADC conference on pooled procurement of essential medicines and medical supplies was held in Boksburg–Johannesburg, South Africa, from 17 to 19 September 2012. The focus of the SADC pooled procurement document[29] is on the prices and quality of medicines, with no reference to the regional and national production capabilities or the implementation of the 2005 Abuja Summit Decision 55. Also, strangely, there appears to be little or no synchronization between the SADC and the AU pharmaceutical projects.

2.4 The African Patent Office

Differences in the national patent laws of many African countries have been identified among obstacles to the integration of national pharmaceutical markets and pooled procurement of medicines. There are two transnational patent offices in Africa – the African Regional Intellectual Property Organization (ARIPO) for the Anglophone countries and Organisation Africaine de la Propriété Intellectuelle (OAPI) for the Francophone countries.

The recent plans of the African Union to establish the Pan-African Intellectual Property Organization (PAIPO) were greeted with mixed, mostly negative reactions.[30,31] According to the PAIPO draft statute, the organization would have sweeping policy-making powers and legal authority[32] but would not provide any meaningful capacity addition, such

---

[28] "Intra-African Barriers are Costly and Very Tedious", *Business Report*, 5 February 2013, http://www.iol.co.za/business/business-news/intra-african-barriers-are-costly-and-very-tedious-1.1464118.

[29] Southern African Development Community, "SADC Strategy for Pooled Procurement of Essential Medicines and Health Commodities", September 2012, Southern African Regional Programme on Access to Medicines and Diagnostics, http://www.sarpam.net/wp-content/uploads/2012/12/SADC-PP-Strategy-16–11–12-final-English.pdf.

[30] William New, "Move Toward New Pan-African IP Organisation Alarms Observers", Intellectual Property Watch, 27 September 2012, http://www.ip-watch.org/2012/09/27/move-toward-new-pan-african-ip-organisation-alarms-observers/.

[31] Brook K. Baker, "Intellectual Property Policy Incoherence at the African Union Threatens Access to Medicines – Proposed Pan-African IP Organization a Terrible Idea", Fix the Patent Laws, 27 September 2012, http://www.fixthepatentlaws.org/?p=438.

[32] African Union Scientific, Technical and Research Committee, "Final Draft Statute of the Pan-African Intellectual Property Organization (PAIPO)" docu-

as substantive examination of patent applications, to the ARIPO, OAPI and the national patent offices.

3 THE SOUTH AFRICAN HEALTHCARE SECTOR

South Africa, a country with a population of 50 million, has the largest and most sophisticated economy in Africa, with GDP of US$408 billion in 2011 (0.66% of the global economy). 8.5% of South Africa's GDP is spent on healthcare, divided roughly 50:50 between public and private healthcare. The private healthcare system caters for 8.3 million of South Africans (16% of the population) who can afford private medical insurance, and the public system for the remainder (42 million South Africans plus permanent residents). Healthcare spending per capita in the private sector was 11,150 South African Rand (ZAR) (US$1,530) in 2010 compared with ZAR 2,770 (US$380) in the public sector. There are major differences between the quality of care in the two sectors.

Plans are under way (a pilot phase started in 2012) to integrate the two systems into a single National Health Insurance (NHI) over a period of 14 years. Plans for the NHI were outlined in a government Green Paper published in August 2011.[33] Spending on the NHI, which would be in addition to the normal National Health budget (ZAR 84 billion in 2008/09), is projected to start at ZAR 125 billion in 2012 and gradually increase to ZAR 225 billion at 2010 prices (US$31 billion) in 2025.

Comprehensive information about the NHI, including the history of universal health coverage projects in South Africa and the world (the former going back to 1944), opinions of a broad spectrum of public health experts, the pros and cons and the consequences of the NHI for the South African economy and the pharmaceutical sector are posted on a website of the South Africa association of the R&D-based pharmaceutical industry, Innovative Medicines of South Africa (IMSA).[34] The NHI Green Paper proposes centralizing the procurement of essential healthcare goods, including pharmaceuticals, in a body reporting to the Minister of Health. It is envisaged that the NHI will sharply increase the demand for and

ment Ref No: AU/STRC/522, 2012, African Union, http://www.au.int/en/dp/hrst/sites/default/files/PAIPO%20Statute%20English.pdf.

[33] National Health Act (Act 61 of 2003): Policy on National Health Insurance, *Republic of South Africa Government Gazette*, vol. 554, no. 34523, 12 August 2011, http://www.doh.gov.za/docs/notices/2011/not34523.pdf.

[34] "National Health Insurance: Policy Briefs", Innovative Medicines of South Africa (IMSA), http://www.imsa.org.za/national-health-insurance/policy-briefs/.

the market share of generic medicines, to the detriment of branded and innovator products, posing a dilemma for the R&D-based pharmaceutical companies in South Africa as to whether or not to stay in the country.[35]

It will be interesting to see if the concerns of the US R&D-based companies will result in placing South Africa on the "Watch List" of the US PhRMA Submission 301. There is a precedent – for example, New Zealand was included in the 2000 US PhRMA submission to the USTR requesting to place the country on the "Special 301" Priority Watch List.

> . . .the policies of the New Zealand government, with regard to policies, practices and acts of the agencies setting the reimbursement price of medicines, act to largely deny market access for the American research-based pharmaceutical industry to the New Zealand market.

4 THE SOUTH AFRICAN PHARMACEUTICAL SECTOR

4.1 The Size and Structure of the South African Pharmaceutical Market

Mirroring the two-tier healthcare systems, the South African pharmaceutical market is divided into the public and private markets.

The South African pharmaceuticals market at ex-factory prices was ZAR 30 billion (US$3.7 billion) in 2011, forecast to reach US$4 billion in 2012. The public market, which is supplied by government tenders and donor programmes, accounts for 75% of volume and 35% of the market by value. The private market accounts for 65% of the market by value (ZAR 25 billion) and only 25% of the volume, reflecting a high share of branded and innovator (originator) products. Branded medicines accounted for 48% of the private market by value in 2011.[36]

Generics (including patent-protected ARVs manufactured under licence) make up the bulk of the tender market. The few exceptions where government procures branded products are vaccines, some ARVs (for example the protease inhibitor Kaletra ®) and some oncology medicines, due to non-availability of generic equivalents registered by the South African medicines regulatory authority. The growth of the tender market

---

35 "Will the NHI Benefit All?" *Business Live*, 13 May 2011, http://www.healthman.co.za/images/NHI%2013%20May%202011.pdf.

36 Jamie Clark, "SA Market: Good Fundamentals but Some Longer-Term Risks", Emerging EMEA/Healthcare, Bank of America–Merrill Lynch, 5 July 2012.

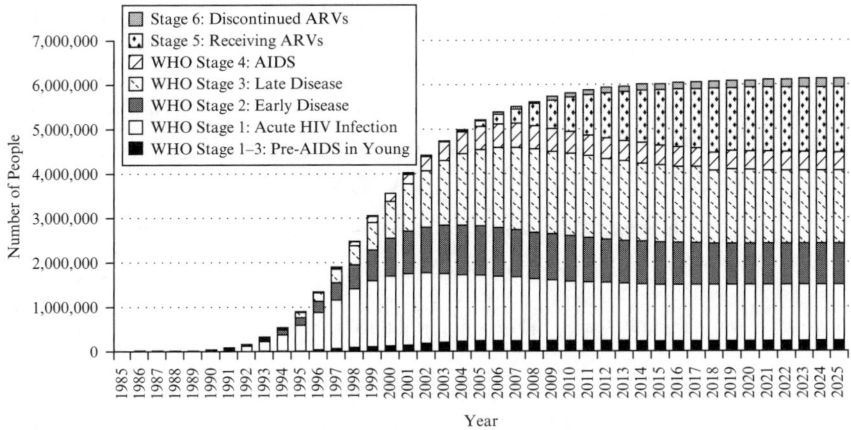

Source: The Actuarial Society of South Africa; ASSA2003 model: http://www.actuarialsociety.org.za/Models-274.aspx.

Figure 12.2 Staging of HIV infection in South Africa from 1985 to 2025, using the Actuarial Society of South Africa (ASSA) 2003 model with standard assumptions about treatment and interventions

has been mainly driven by ARVs: the latest two-year ARV tender (running from 1 January 2013 to 31 December 2014) is estimated to cost ZAR 5.9 billion (US$672 million at ZAR 8.80 to the US$) compared with ZAR 4.2 billion in the previous 2011–12 ARV tender.

Figure 12.2 shows the 2005 projections by the Actuarial Society of South Africa (ASSA) regarding the number of South Africans at various stages of HIV infection and AIDS until 2025.

The South African government provides antiretrovirals free of charge to all eligible South African citizens and permanent residents; the sharp rise in the number of patients is due to the dynamics of the AIDS epidemics and the recently (in 2011) changed criteria for eligibility, i.e. the commencement of ARV treatment, from the CD4 count of 200 (stage IV of AIDS) to CD4 of 350 (stage III).

It is generally expected that the earlier start of treatment (at CD4 of 350) will reduce the number of new infections (stage I) and, by slowing down the progress of the disease, swell the number of patients in Stages III and IV, i.e. the patients receiving ARVs.

With TB being the most common co-infection in AIDS patients, demand for anti-TB medicines is projected to grow proportionally to the number of ART patients. UN AIDS estimates that of the 5.7 million

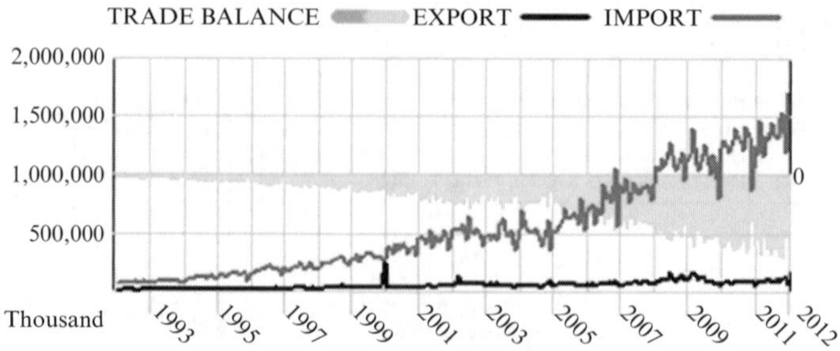

Source: Compilation based on DTI economic database http://tradestats.thedti.gov.za/.

Figure 12.3 Trade balance, exports and imports of pharmaceutical products (products classified under Customs Tariff Chapter 30), monthly value in thousands of current Rands (ZAR)

HIV-positive South Africans, 1.8 million will be co-infected with TB in their lifetime. The incidence of diagnosed TB cases in South Africa is 970 per 100,000 population, of whom 2% have multi-drug resistant TB (MDR TB). All medicines used in TB treatment in government programmes (including those against MDR TB) are off-patent generics.

4.2 The Pharmaceutical Sector in the South African Economy

South Africa accounts for just 0.4% of the global pharmaceutical market by value and less than 1% by volume. Antiretrovirals are the only segment of the market where South Africa is the world's no. 1 (25% of the world's developing countries' ARV market).

The pharmaceutical industry contributed 1.58% to South African GDP in the 2008/09 financial year. The manufacturing base comprised 26 companies (both domestic and foreign) operating 32 plants, ranging in size from micro, employing 20 people, to large, such as the Aspen-Pharmacare plant in Port Elizabeth, employing 2,500. The industry's total direct employment was 9,500 in 2009.

South Africa imports 65% of its demand for pharmaceuticals, by value, 90% to 95% of medical devices and 100% of medical diagnostics. Medical products (pharmaceuticals, medical devices and medical diagnostics) are the fifth largest contributor to South Africa's trade deficit. Figure 12.3 shows the fast-rising imports of pharmaceuticals, stagnant exports and deteriorating trade balance.

Pharmaceutical imports recorded under Customs Tariff Chapter 30 (excluding active pharmaceutical ingredients which are classified under

Chapter 29) were ZAR 15.96 billion in 2011, while exports were only ZAR 1.12 billion, leaving a negative trade balance of ZAR 14.84 billion. In 2010, the figures were ZAR 15.1 billion, 937 million and 14.15 billion, respectively.[37]

The major contributor to the imports burden are imports of innovator and branded products from Europe and the USA. There is little competition with the domestic industry in this market segment. India, which tops the list of importers, is the supplier of generic medicines and competes directly with the domestic industry. Imports of medicines in finished-dosage form (classified under Customs Tariff Heading 30.04) from India have been growing at 13% per annum, from ZAR 1.21 billion in 2008 to ZAR 1.85 billion in 2011.

For medicines in finished-dosage form, the ratio of South Africa's imports to exports is 20:1. The major export destinations for South African medicines outside Africa are the USA, Australia and France (countries with the world's highest regulatory requirements), while in Africa the major export markets are Kenya, Zambia and Zimbabwe. The deterioration of the economic situation in Zimbabwe is reflected in the declining share of South African pharmaceutical exports to this country, from an average of 50% in the 1990s to just 5% over the past 12 years.

Table 12.1 shows South Africa's top ten trading partners – exporters and importers of pharmaceuticals in finished-dosage form (excluding vaccines) in 2010.

South African imports and exports of pharmaceuticals in finished-dosage form (TH 30.04) in 2010

The absence of imports from the world's largest generic manufacturers and exporters (apart from India) such as Israel, Brazil and Thailand among the "top ten" is remarkable. With zero customs duties and marginal preferences in government tenders, the South African pharmaceutical market is open to unrestricted competition, the only barrier being the quality and the registration of the product and the manufacturer by the South African medicines regulatory authority. The trade statistics indicate that the prices of generic medicines in South Africa are too low to be attractive to exporters; in other words, the trade statistics provide evidence that South African generic manufacturers can compete against any country *except* India. An analysis of the awards of contracts in the South African Health Department pharmaceutical tenders yields the same observation.

---

37 The average exchange rate during these two years was ZAR 7.30/US$ in 2010 and ZAR 7.10/US$ in 2011.

Table 12.1 South African imports and exports of pharmaceuticals in finished-dosage form, 2010

Rank	IMPORTS		EXPORTS	
	Country	ZAR '000	Country	ZAR '000
1	India	1,539,012	USA	75,189
2	Germany	1,390,203	Kenya	60,829
3	France	1,315,370	Australia	37,581
4	USA	1,175,100	Zambia	36,930
5	Italy	1,136,979	France	34,103
6	UK	1,124,567	Mauritius	32,514
7	Switzerland	614,703	Zimbabwe	32,010
8	Sweden	464,981	Hong Kong, China	20,563
9	Ireland	449,560	Mozambique	17,373
10	Spain	361,750	UK	16,753
	Other	2,033,429	Other	207,452
	TOTAL	**11,605,654**	**TOTAL**	**571,297**

Source: DTI economic database http://tradestats.thedti.gov.za/

4.3 Can a Country Such as South Africa Have a Sustainable Pharmaceutical Industry?

A paper by Warren Kaplan and Richard Laing[38] challenges established policy dogmas linking domestic pharmaceutical production in developing countries with economic benefits, improved security of supply and better access to medicines. The authors argue that inevitably the cost of domestic production in medium-sized developing economies such as South Africa will be much higher vis-à-vis India, China and Brazil. The paper concludes that for many such countries domestic manufacture of medicines makes little economic sense and, in fact, pushing local production may even constrain access to medicines if the costs and economies of scale are disregarded by national policy-makers.

The authors tentatively suggest that, in order to become globally competitive as a manufacturer of pharmaceuticals, a country has to meet crite-

[38] Warren Kaplan and Richard Laing, "Local Production of Pharmaceuticals: Industrial Policy and Access to Medicines – An Overview of Key Concepts, Issues and Opportunities for Future Research", World Health Organization, The World Bank Human Development Network, Health, Nutrition, and Population Family (HNP), January 2005, http://www.who.int/medicines/technical_briefing/tbs/KaplanLocalProductionFinal5b15d.pdf.

ria such as GDP greater than U$100 billion, population (domestic market) of about 100 million, appropriate secondary and tertiary education base, UNIDO competitiveness index above 0.15 and a net positive pharmaceutical balance of trade.

South Africa fails to meet at least half of these criteria. Yet, defying the odds, the South African domestic pharmaceutical industry has been remarkably resilient and competitive despite its small size and operating in a challenging environment, including almost total dependence on imports of active pharmaceutical ingredients, having a domestic market that is not protected by customs duties, various barriers to entry to export markets, negligible preferences in domestic government tenders, impact of price control, regulatory delays affecting the launch of new products etc. Having survived massive closures of pharmaceutical plants from 1999 to 2003,[39] the industry recovery was boosted by investment by South Africa's two largest pharmaceutical companies, Aspen-Pharmacare and Adcock-Ingram, supported by government investment incentives. Aspen became the world's ninth largest generic manufacturer in 2011.

Many of the constraints identified by Kaplan and Laing, such as tensions between the objectives of health and industrial policies (the one prioritizing affordability and access to medicines and the other promoting growth of what is primarily a private sector and optimizing profits in order to attract investment) are valid from the South African perspective.

However, the cost of production and the prices should not be seen as the absolute measure of competitiveness or as the only determinant of the economic rationale of domestic manufacturing. This has been shown in a cost-benefit study conducted by the South African Industrial Development Corporation (IDC) in 2008 to determine the impact on the national economy of a ZAR 1 billion (US$135 million) pharmaceutical tender, and the maximum premium to be paid for domestically manufactured pharmaceuticals vis-à-vis the lowest-priced imports.[40]

The IDC study used an input-output model to measure the economy-wide impact, both direct and indirect, in terms of GDP, fixed investment,

---

[39] 37 pharmaceutical plants were closed in South Africa between 1999 and 2003, resulting in the loss of 40% of manufacturing capacity and a similar proportion of jobs.

[40] "Cost-benefit Analysis of Procuring Antiretrovirals from South African Manufacturers as Opposed to Foreign Producers", Industrial Development Corporation, Sandton, South Africa, February 2008 (not published, copy available for academic research).

employment creation, income and government revenue generation, capital utilization, national balance of payments and trade balance.

The study concluded that, as long as a price premium paid to domestic manufacturers did not exceed 32.5%, the overall benefits to the national economy and the resulting additional tax revenue would exceed the cost of the price premium to the State.

At first glance, expectations of such a price premium may appear excessive and protectionist. However, Article XXIII of the 1994 WTO Agreement on Government Procurement (GPA)[41] identifies the exceptions the parties may apply to their own procurement when imposing or enforcing measures necessary to protect, among other things, public health. In any case, South Africa, like the majority of developing countries, is not a signatory of the GPA and is free to use government procurement as an industrial policy tool.

In practice, the price premium for domestic manufacturers in the South African government's pharmaceutical tenders has never exceeded 9%. The recent amendments to the preferential procurement regulations, in force since December 2011, took away the price premium and replaced it with a provision for possible "designation", exclusively for domestic manufacturers, of tenders and products by the Minister of Trade and Industry.[42]

South Africa's measures promoting domestic industry have been moderate – as a comparison, in December 2010 Brazil promulgated its new Federal Public Procurement Law No. 12.349/2010 allowing price preferences of up to 25% for domestic manufacturers in government procurement[43] (on top of existing import duties which range from 15% to 17% for pharmaceuticals).

---

41 Agreement on Government Procurement (GPA) signed in Marrakesh in April 1994 as part of an agreement establishing the WTO as a successor of the GATT. The GPA is plurilateral, which means that, unlike the multilateral WTO agreements, WTO member countries are not obliged to join it. "Agreement of Government Procurement", *World Trade Organization*, http://www.wto.org/english/docs_e/legal_e/gpr-94_01_e.htm.

42 Preferential Procurement Regulations, 2011, Notice R. 502, *Government Gazette*, Regulations Gazette No. 34350, 8 June 2011, http://www.info.gov.za/view/DownloadFileAction?id=147194.

43 Public Procurement Law (*Lei de Licitação*) No. 12.349/2010 (enacted 15 December 2010) – analysis in Tozzini Freire Advogados, "Brazil", in Global Legal Group, *The International Comparative Legal Guide to: Public Procurement 2011*, London, 2011, www.iclg.co.uk.

5 THE SOUTH AFRICAN PATENT SYSTEM

5.1 Survey of the South African Patent Law and Practice, Focusing on Aspects Pertinent to the Pharmaceutical Sector

A protracted legal battle between the South African government and 39 (initially 41) research-based multinational pharmaceutical companies represented by the Pharmaceutical Manufacturers Association of South Africa (PMA) over amendments to the South African medicines control act was making headlines all over the world from November 1997 to April 2001.[44] At the centre of the dispute were changes to the Medicines and Related Substances Control Act and specifically its Section 15C.[45] The research-based pharmaceutical industry alleged that language of Section 15C of the Act designed to give the Health Minister authority to authorize parallel importation of patented medicines into South Africa was contrary to the TRIPS Agreement.[46]

---

[44] The amendments to the Medicines and Related Substances were promulgated on 23 November 1997. The Pharmaceutical Manufacturers Association of South Africa (PMA) and the 39 companies involved in litigation against the South African Government withdrew the charges in April 2001. The Government undertook to (i) set up a task team with the pharmaceutical companies to cooperate on the drafting of regulations for the implementation of Section 15C and (ii) only to implement Section 15C in a manner which would be in accordance with South Africa's international obligations, including TRIPS.

[45] Section 15C awarded the Health Minister the power to:

> prescribe conditions for the supply of more affordable medicines in certain circumstances so as to protect the health of the public, and in particular may:
>
> (a) notwithstanding anything to the contrary contained in the Patents Act, 1978 (Act No. 57 of 1978), determine that the rights with regards to any medicine under a patent granted in the Republic shall not extend to acts in respect of such medicine which is being put into the market by the owner of the medicine, or with his or her consent.
>
> (b) prescribe the conditions on which any medicine which is identical in composition, meets the same quality standard and is intended to have the same proprietary name as that of another medicine already registered in the Republic, but which is imported by persons other than the person who is the holder of the registration certificate of the medicine already registered and which originates from any site of manufacture of the original manufacturer as approved by the Council in the prescribed manner, may be imported . . .

[46] The R&D industry argued that the TRIPS Agreement precluded such parallel importation. The R&D-based industry also alleged that Section 15C would more broadly allow the Health Minister to issue compulsory licences. South Africa's Patents Act already provided such authority to the Commissioner of Patents.

PMA also raised objections to Section 22F and G of the Act, which made provisions for the implementation of generic substitution and price control of medicines.

The US Trade Representative placed South Africa on the "Special 301" Watch List in May 1998. Following intense negotiations which, at some point, involved the Deputy President of South Africa Thabo Mbeki and his US counterpart Al Gore, in September 1999 the USA and South Africa reached an agreement resolving a looming trade dispute. South Africa was removed from the "Watch List" in December 1999.[47]

The case *PMA vs. the President of South Africa* has been extensively covered in numerous reports, analyses and dissertations. It is important to note that the provision of the Act allowing the Health Minister to authorize parallel importation has never been invoked in South Africa, nor has a compulsory licence for a pharmaceutical product ever been issued. South Africa has paid the price for being a trailblazer – the threat of US trade sanctions and possibly also the loss of foreign investment in the pharmaceutical industry.[48] However, the South African case and the subsequent mobilization of civil society worldwide paved the way for the November 2001 Doha Ministerial Declaration on TRIPS Agreement and Public Health, the successful ARV price reduction negotiations in Brazil and a series of voluntary licensing agreements for ARVs and other essential drugs for South African manufacturers.

In Brazil, negotiations over prices of ARVs between the Brazilian Ministry of Health and pharma companies, including Merck (MSD), Abbott, Bristol-Myers-Squibb (BMS), Gilead and Roche, took place between 2001 and 2003. Brazil skilfully used the threat of compulsory licensing as a negotiating tool, allowing it to successfully bargain for price reductions of up to 70%. The strong point for Brazil in these negotiations was the size of its pharmaceutical market and, most importantly, the capacity of its domestic sector (scientists and industry) to manufacture ARVs. The production of the first ARV (zidovudine, AZT) started in Brazil in 1993 and by 2001 the Brazilian industry was making seven

---

47 Robert L. Ostergard, Jr., "The Political Economy of the South Africa-United States Patent Dispute", *The Journal of World Intellectual Property*, vol. 2, no. 6, 2009, p. 875–88, www.robertostergard.us/research/pubs/jwip.pdf.

48 Some indication is given in the 2003 US PhRMA Submission 301 section on South Africa which states ". . .given the closure of 34 factories over the past two years – a direct result of the hostile business environment and Government's ambivalence towards patents". Pharmaceutical Research and Manufacturers of America (PhRMA), "PhRMA "Special 301" Submission", CPTech, 2003, p. 76, http://www.cptech.org/ip/health/phrma/301–03/2003-PhRMA-301.pdf.

ARVs, supplying 65% of the Brazilian Health Ministry AIDS treatment programme, by volume.[49]

South Africa did not have any of these advantages. Issuing compulsory licences was not the preferred solution for South Africa due to the lack of domestic reverse-engineering expertise. Recognizing this weakness, the Department of Trade and Industry supported negotiated solutions aimed at obtaining voluntary licences and technology transfers.

South Africa's first generic ARV was stavudine (d4T), manufactured by Aspen-Pharmacare under a voluntary licence from BMS. It was registered and launched in August 2003. Subsequently, voluntary licences for ARVs were granted on various terms, usually to a single licensee (Aspen or Adcock) and to restricted markets.

As the confidence of the licensors grew, the terms and conditions of the licences became more favourable. For example, in 2003 Eli Lilly signed a technology transfer contract with Aspen regarding the manufacture by Aspen of two off-patent MDR-TB drugs, capreomycin and cycloserine, for the global market. Eli Lilly provided the know-how, access to technical expertise and assistance to assure the quality and sustainability of the manufacturing processes. The unusual aspect of the deal was that the licensor (Eli Lilly) paid Aspen for the trouble of manufacturing the two drugs.

In February 2006 BMS signed a technology transfer agreement with Aspen, which included support for regulatory approval filings and a royalty-free licence to manufacture and sell BMS's new protease inhibitor atazanavir (Reyataz ®) in sub-Saharan Africa.[50] At the same time BMS signed a similar agreement with the Indian company, Emcure, for the Indian market.

5.2 Patents Act vs. the Competition Act

The practice of patent holders granting a voluntary licence to a single generic manufacturer was challenged by the Treatment Action Campaign (TAC), invoking the provisions of the competition legislation.

Two cases regarding patent-protected ARV were brought before the Competition Commission; the first of these, in 2002, by an AIDS sufferer Hazel Tau, trade union confederation COSATU and the TAC against

---

[49] Jillian Clare Cohen and Kristina M. Lybecker, "AIDS Policy and Pharmaceutical Patents: Brazil's Strategy to Safeguard Public Health", *The World Economy*, vol. 28, no. 2, 2005, pp. 211–30.

[50] "Bristol-Myers Squibb Seeks to Expand Access to its Most Recently Approved HIV/AIDS Medicine", Press release, Bristol-Myers Squibb, Princeton, NJ, 15 February 2006.

GlaxoSmithKline (GSK) and Boehringer-Ingelheim (Case no. 2002 Sep 226). The second, involving the AIDS Law Project representing the TAC against Merck, Sharp & Dohme (MSD), took place in 2007.

Ruling in the first case, the Commission concluded that GSK and Boehringer-Ingelheim had abused their market dominance and contravened several sections of the Competition Act, including charging excessive prices, refusing a competitor access to an "essential facility" and engaging in an exclusionary act.[51] GSK and Boehringer-Ingelheim denied all charges.

A settlement was reached separately with each of the defendants on 16 October 2003. Under the agreement, the matter was not referred to the Competition Tribunal for adjudication on the condition that GSK and Boehringer-Ingelheim issue multiple licences (GSK four, for zidovudine, lamivudine and the fixed-dosage combination Combivir ® and Boehringer-Ingelheim three for nevirapine) to generic manufacturers, permitting the manufacture in South Africa and importation of these ARVs. The agreements further allowed for the export of the ARVs manufactured in South Africa to all sub-Saharan African countries. The royalties were capped at 5% of net sales.

The 2007 case against Merck, Sharp & Dohme (MSD) focused on legal circumstances under which a rights' holder may be coerced to grant a licence to its competitors. MSD's patent for efavirenz (Stocrin ®, Sustiva ®) was valid until 2013. MSD granted a single licence for efavirenz to a South African company, Thembalami Pharmaceuticals, in July 2004. The plaintiff argued that MSD was "unlawfully refusing to license efavirenz on reasonable terms" and that a single licence was not sufficient to ensure generic competition and price reduction.

Mirroring the outcome of the earlier cases against GSK and Boehringer-Ingelheim, the MSD case was settled out of court in June 2007, with MSD agreeing to grant royalty-free multiple voluntary licences allowing the sale of the licensed efavirenz to the public and private sectors in South Africa and ten other southern African countries (Angola, Botswana, the DRC, Lesotho, Madagascar, Mauritius, Namibia, Seychelles, Swaziland and Zimbabwe).

Efavirenz remained the most expensive part of the first-line ARV treatment, even after the entry of multiple generic competition, accounting for a third of the cost of the 2008 South African ARV tender.

---

[51] Competition Commission, "GSK and BI Issue Anti-Retroviral Licenses", *Competition News*, March 2004, p. 1, http://www.compcom.co.za/assets/Uploads/AttachedFiles/MyDocuments/March-04-Newsletter.pdf.

From the author's perspective, the cases against GSK, Boehringer-Ingelheim and MSD were technically weak.

Firstly, the South African Competition Act (Act 89 of 1998) makes no express reference to the grant of a compulsory licence as a remedy for anti-competitive practices in respect of patented products or processes.

Secondly, Boehringer-Ingelheim argued that the investigation and the "guilty verdict" were technically defective, exposing contradictions with earlier pronouncements of the Competition Commission and showing that neither the plaintiff nor the Competition Commission officials were in a position to explain at which level of the Anatomical Therapeutic Classification (ATC) the alleged dominant position was assessed.

Boehringer-Ingelheim contended that the Competition Commission had assessed the market position of a single drug, nevirapine (Viramune ®) instead of, which is a standard international practice, the entire therapeutic class (in this case non-nucleotide reverse transcriptase inhibitors, NNRTIs). The defendant's market control position in South Africa with regard to Viramune at that time was 11% at the ATC-3 level and 33% at the ATC-4 level, neither of which was a "dominant position".[52]

Thirdly, the defendants maintained that the licensor is responsible for ensuring that the licensee has the capacity to maintain consistent quality of the product and that coercing them to dish out voluntary licences indiscriminately might impair the quality of the generic products.[53]

It should be borne in mind that at the time of the case *Hazel Tau and Others vs. GlaxoSmithKline and Boehringer Ingelheim*, ARVs were yet to become a standard treatment for AIDS in South Africa's public sector. South Africa also did not declare AIDS a public health emergency. The Operational Plan for Comprehensive HIV and AIDS Care, Management and Treatment for South Africa was adopted on 19 November 2003 and the first public sector ARV tender was awarded in mid-2004.[54]

---

[52] Information presented by Boehringer-Ingelheim during discussions with the South African Companies and Intellectual Property Registration Office (CIPRO) and the DTI, November 2003.

[53] GlaxoSmithKline (GSK) policy on granting voluntary licences was outlined in the GSK 2005 *Corporate Social Responsibility Report*: "Voluntary licences (VL) enable local manufacturers to produce and sell generic versions of our products. A decision to grant a VL depends on a number of factors including the severity of the HIV/AIDS epidemic in that country, local healthcare provision and the economic and manufacturing environment . . . . Selecting the most appropriate licensee is key. We need to be sure that the manufacturer will be able to provide a long-term supply of good-quality medicines and will implement safeguards to prevent the diversion of medicines to wealthier markets".

[54] Tender No. RT-71 2004 MF for the supply of ARVs from September 2004

Table 12.2 Boehringer-Ingelheim presentation to the DTI, in connections with a case before the competition commission in March 2004

Level	Class	Class name	Market control in S. Africa
ATC-1	J	Anti-infectives	
ATC-2	J / 5	Anti-viral, systemic	
ATC-3	J / 5 / C	Antiretrovirals for HIV therapy	Boehringer-Ingelheim: 11%
ATC-4	J / 5 / C / 1	NRTIs	Boehringer-Ingelheim: 0%
	J / 5 / C / 2	Protease Inhibitors (PIs)	Boehringer-Ingelheim: 0%
	J / 5 / C / 3	NNRTIs	B-I (Viramune ®): 33% MSD (Stocrin ®, EFV): 67%
ATC-5	J / 5 / C / 3 / 1	Nevirapine	B-I (Viramune ®): 100%

Note: ATC = Anatomical Therapeutic Classification.

5.3 Using the Competition Law to Achieve Price Reductions of Off-patent Drugs

Provisions of the South African Competition Act (Act 89 of 1998) were used effectively to persuade Bristol-Myers Squibb (BMS), a manufacturer of an off-patent antifungal drug amphotericin B (Fungizone ®)[55] to lower the price of the drug in South Africa. The AIDS Law Project, acting on behalf of the TAC and the South African HIV Clinicians' Society, approached BMS in February 2005 threatening to lodge an excessive pricing complaint with the Competition Commission, arguing that the drug was sold in Brazil for a fraction of the South African price. The matter was solved amicably within just a few weeks, at the end of April 2004, with BMS agreeing to reduce its prices by 80% and 85% for the public and the private sector respectively.

While amphotericin B was off-patent, BMS enjoyed a de facto monopoly in South Africa as a generic equivalent was not available.[56]

to August 2007. The South African domestic generic manufacturers won the bulk (80%) of the tender, by volume, despite modest price preferences, not exceeding 5%.

[55] Amphotericin B is a drug of choice to treat cryptococcal meningitis, a common opportunistic infection and a cause of death among AIDS sufferers in Africa.

[56] Tenu Avafia, Jonathan Berger, and Trudi Hartzenberg, "The Ability of Select Sub-Saharan African Countries to Utilise TRIPs Flexibilities and Competition Law to Ensure a Sustainable Supply of Essential Medicines: A Study

In conclusion, it appears that competition law can be used effectively to achieve substantial price reductions of both patent-protected and off-patent products. The powerful element of competition legislation is the possibility of imposing heavy penalties (in South Africa up to 10% of companies' annual sales). However, unlike in the case of patent legislation, there is little expertise and legal precedence in the developing countries as to how to apply competition legislation in support of national healthcare objectives. A heavy-handed intervention, especially if applied in a haphazard or wooden manner, may be counter-productive, prompting companies to divest or de-register their products.

5.4 Revision of the South African Intellectual Property Policy and Legislation

The cornerstone of South African intellectual property legislation is the Patents Act (Act 57 of 1978). South African patents are granted without substantive examination of patent applications, for 20 years from the date of publication of acceptance of the application in the Patent Journal, with no provision for extension. Generally, the patent may only be enforced nine months after grant.

A patent can only be challenged after it has been granted – there is no provision for pre-grant opposition. A patent may be challenged at any time after the grant, by any person, on the grounds that the invention was not new at the date of application or that it was obvious. The Patents Act (Chapter X – Articles 61 to 64) also specifies formal grounds on which a patent may be revoked, such as incomplete disclosure of the invention, insufficient clarity of the claims, fraudulent or false statement or misrepresentation in the application.

The Court of the Commissioner of Patents is the court of first instance in all patent-related matters in South Africa. The Court decision can be appealed, with leave, either to a provincial division of the High Court and thereafter to the Supreme Court of Appeal, or directly to the Supreme Court of Appeal.[57]

South Africa incorporated the "early working" Bolar-type provision

of Producing and Importing Countries", Trade Law Centre for Southern Africa, 2006, http://apps.who.int/medicinedocs/documents/s18249en/s18249en.pdf.

[57] The direct route to the Supreme Court of Appeal was used by Sanofi-Aventis in the recent case against Cipla regarding the anti-cancer drug docetaxel. Tamar Kahn, "Court Rules Public Interest Counts in Patent Fights", *Business Day*, 31 July 2012, http://www.bdlive.co.za/articles/2012/07/31/court-rules-public-interest-counts-in-patent-fights.

into the Patents Act in January 2003. The South African "Bolar Exception" is consistent with that of, for example, the USA and Canada, except that in South Africa it applies across all economic sectors, not only pharmaceutical, based on the principle of non-discrimination in any field of technology (Article 27 TRIPS). The passing of the "Bolar" provision prompted calls to establish a link between the patent registration office (the Companies and Intellectual Property Commission – CIPC) and the South African Medicines Regulatory Authority. Currently, the issuing of a regulatory approval does not involve the verification of the patent status of the drug and the IP rights of the applicant.

The peculiarities of the South African patent order are often dubbed as a "weak patent system with strong enforcement". The South African patent is intrinsically vulnerable as the grant of a patent does not guarantee that the invention is new or non-obvious, that the patent would be valid in other jurisdictions, that the patent cannot be revoked, or that the exploitation of the invention will not infringe on existing patents in South Africa or elsewhere.

The current round of revision of South African intellectual property policy and legislation started in May 2009 with the circulation of the Department of Trade and Industry's "Draft Policy on Intellectual Property of South Africa" for comments among stakeholders, including the pharmaceutical industry. So far (January 2013), the final version of the Draft Policy document has not been released for broad public consultation.

The overarching aim of the Draft Policy is to harmonize the intellectual property (IP) legislation with other pieces of legislation including:

- those dealing with access to healthcare, access to education, traditional knowledge, agriculture, biodiversity, publicly funded research, and with the new Consumer Protection Act, and
- the interface of the IP legislation and practice with the Customs and Excise regulations (including the treatment of the suspect fake, counterfeit and unauthorized generic copies of products in transit through South Africa).

Of special interest to the pharmaceutical industry is Chapter Five of the Draft IP Policy dealing with IP and public health policy and IP and competition, analysing possible provisions for compulsory licensing, systematic use of the clauses of the competition law in order to advance access to healthcare and as the means of promoting technology transfer.

There is growing pressure from NGOs, including Médecins Sans Frontières (MSF), AIDS Law Project and the TAC, which jointly launched the "Fix the Patent Laws" campaign,[58] demanding that the government exercise the TRIPS flexibilities to the maximum and critically examine the practice of unrestrained granting of South African patents for pharmaceutical products.

At the centre of the debate is whether or not South Africa has the capacity to undertake substantive examination of patent applications in a manner that would meet the world's best standards and at the same time not lead to a backlog of applications akin to those experienced with the registration of new medicines. The scale of difficulty is demonstrated by the fact that the South African patent registration office (CIPC) handles approximately 10,000 new patent applications per year.[59] The earlier-mentioned "Draft Policy on Intellectual Property of South Africa" does not offer a clear solution to the problem.

6 CONCLUSIONS

While the correlation between the wealth of countries and their national health indicators is indistinct for middle-income developing countries, without doubt poverty remains a key determining factor of the health status of people living in the least-developed countries. According to UN statistics,[60] least-developed countries are home to 880 million people, or 12% of the global population. 34 out of the global total of 49 least-developed countries are in Africa. Poverty is directly linked to major health risks such as poor sanitation and hygiene, grossly inadequate or non-existing access to health education, insufficient and improper nutrition, irrational beliefs, unhealthy living environment such as overcrowding, exposure to pathogenic micro-organisms residing in domesticated

---

58 "Fix the Patent Laws", Doctors Without Borders, http://www.msf.org.za/fix-the-patent-laws.

59 Based on the presentation of the South African Companies and Intellectual Property Commission (CIPC) to the Parliamentary Portfolio Committee on 29 November 2012. For the six-month period from April to September 2012, CIPC registered 4,953 new patent applications, and approved 22,700 patent renewal applications, 1,293 new industrial design applications and 18,192 new trademark applications.

60 "Least Developed Countries: About LDCs", United Nations Office of the High Representative for the Least Developed Countries, Landlocked Developing Countries and the Small Island Developing States, http://www.unohrlls.org/en/ldc/25/.

and wild animals – all this compounded by perpetual military conflicts triggering large-scale migration of people. There is a vicious circle: poverty predisposes people to ill health, and ill health perpetuates poverty.

In the least-developed African countries, the burden of disease caused by infectious diseases, maternal and perinatal conditions, and nutritional deficiencies represents 60% of the disease burden. The mobilization of the international community and billions of dollars in international aid have been critical in reducing the death toll due to AIDS, TB, and malaria in Africa over the past decade. Currently six million AIDS patients in Africa benefit from access to low-cost antiretroviral treatment. However, it appears that a broad category of diseases endemic in the tropics, dubbed "neglected diseases",[61] including viral, bacterial, parasitic and fungal infections, as well as acute respiratory infections and diarrheal diseases in children, has been receiving far less attention, R&D spending and financial support. The proposed solutions (such as those recommended in the report of the Commission on Intellectual Property Rights, Innovation and Public Health – CIPIH) do not seem to have induced an adequate positive response from pharmaceutical companies, governments and the donors.

The impact of intellectual property legislation on the health of people in the developing and least-developed countries has always generated considerable controversy. As pointed out by Judge Sir Hugh Laddie in the foreword to the CIPR report "Integrating Intellectual Property Rights and Development Policy Report", "for too long IPRs have been regarded as food for the rich countries and poison for poor countries". Notwithstanding some achievements such as the Doha Ministerial Declaration on Public Health and despite the continuing efforts of the WHO and individual governments, it appears that the parties remain as divided on this issue as ever.

South Africa played a crucial role in raising the level of the global debate on intellectual property and access to healthcare. While keeping provisions in the legislation, subordinating IP rights to access to healthcare, the South African government, recognizing the country's technology and economic limitations, encouraged voluntary licensing and technology cooperation. The pace of change was accelerated by the actions of civil society and NGOs, usually highly effective but sometimes controversial, starting in South Africa and spreading worldwide. The reduction in price

---

[61] The "neglected" diseases include those endemic in tropical zones and affecting the most disadvantaged populations – i.e. Chagas disease, African trypanosomiasis, onchocerciasis, leishmaniasis, schistosomiasis, leprosy, lymphatic filariasis, Dengue fever, Guinea worm, or blinding trachoma.

of ARVs became possible through a mix of public pressure and diplomatic efforts, leading to negotiated changes to international intellectual property laws and practice which unlocked reverse-engineering of patented technologies and large-scale production of generic ARVs and other essential medicines.

Most of the current health aid programmes such as PEPFAR, CHAI, GFATM, CDC and PMI focus on the most cost-effective provision of medicines. This has led to the concentration of manufacture of generic medicines in China and India. So far, these programmes have failed to bridge the technology gap between the African countries and the rest of the world, stimulate domestic production or start gradually to reduce the dependence of Africa on foreign aid.

> The protection and enforcement of intellectual property rights should contribute to the promotion of technological innovation and to the transfer and dissemination of technology, to the mutual advantage of producers and users of technological knowledge and in a manner conducive to social and economic welfare, and to a balance of rights and obligations (TRIPS Article 7).

Give a man a fish; you have fed him for today. Teach a man to fish; and you have fed him for a lifetime.

13. Patent law in emerging economies: South Africa

Yousuf A. Vawda

1 INTRODUCTION

This chapter reflects on the development of patent law and practice in South Africa. It commences with a description of the origins of the applicable regime; and proceeds to consider how the law has shaped the practice of the patent system, as well as the manner in which the courts have applied the law. It then explores the effects of this system on issues such as access, innovation, investment, and the industrial policy choices made by the democratic government; and considers proposed changes to the national intellectual property regime to best meet South Africa's developmental needs. Because the pricing of patent protected pharmaceuticals and its impact on public health has brought patents into sharp relief, this chapter includes a significant focus on pharmaceutical patents.

2 BACKGROUND TO PATENT LEGISLATION

South Africa has had a long history of patent legislation, dating back over a century and a half. As a former British colony, early patent legislation followed at least to some extent the corresponding legislation in force in Britain at the time. The legislatures in the four 'provinces' which pre-dated the Union of South Africa in 1910 all passed patent legislation in one form or another, the earliest being Act 17 of 1860 passed by the parliament of the Cape of Good Hope.[1] After the Union, the intellectual property laws of the erstwhile colonies and republics were consolidated and amended by the Patents, Designs, Trade Marks and Copyright Act 9 of 1916, which

[1] T. Burrell, *Burrell's South African Patent and Design Law*, Durban, Butterworths, 1999.

was based largely on British Patents Act 1907. Subsequently, Act 9 of 1916 was repealed and replaced by the Patents Act 37 of 1952 (modelled on the British Patents Act 1949) which was in turn repealed and replaced by the current Patents Act.[2]

In this post-Union era, South Africa acceded on 1 December 1947 to the Paris Convention for the Protection of Industrial Property of 20 March 1883, as revised on several occasions.

Other noteworthy developments include:

- The new South African Constitution, while containing a distinct property clause protecting property rights (section 25 of the Constitution of the Republic of South Africa, 1996) (the Constitution), does not afford intellectual property any special protection.
- South Africa became a member of the World Trade Organization (WTO) and hence a signatory to the Trade-Related Aspects of Intellectual Property Rights (TRIPS) Agreement on 1 January 1995[3] which required it to adopt national legislation and regulations to implement TRIPS. This was accomplished with the passage of the Intellectual Property Laws Amendment Act 38 of 1997.[4]
- South Africa became bound to the Patent Cooperation Treaty (PCT) on 16 March 1999.[5]
- Although South Africa falls within the 'catchment area' served by the African Regional Industrial Property Organisation (ARIPO) created on 9 December 1976,[6] for reasons related primarily to its apartheid history, it did not become a contracting party.

From the standpoint of the South African judiciary, the basic rationale underlying patent protection has been that it is desirable in the public interest that industrial techniques be developed and improved, requiring disclosure in exchange for a monopoly for its use, provided the invention is put into practice – the essential *quid pro quo* of intellectual property

---

2 Burrell, *Burrell's South African Patent and Design Law*.

3 World Trade Organization, http://www.wto.org/english/thewto_e/countries_e/south_africa_e.htm.

4 Burrell, *Burrell's South African Patent and Design Law*.

5 Companies and Intellectual Property Commission, Department of Trade and Industry, South Africa, http://www.cipro.co.za/products_services/patents_corptreaty.asp.

6 In terms of the Lusaka Agreement, http://www.wipo.int/wipolex/en/other_treaties/details.jsp?treaty_id=202.

theory. This notion was reiterated in decisions of the Supreme Court of Appeal (SCA).[7]

3 HOW DEVELOPED COUNTRIES INFLUENCE POLICIES AND PRACTICES INCLUDING THOSE OF THE JUDICIARY

In the first instance, as South African patent legislation is modelled primarily on its British precedents, the influence of the latter is paramount in terms of the provisions of the law, the practices of the patent office, and the jurisprudence of the courts. During the Dutch occupation of the Cape, the Estates-General in Netherlands granted monopolies for inventions. However, this influence did not endure, as 'Roman-Dutch law did not provide for more than the *ad hoc* grant of a monopoly'.[8] Secondly, there is an additional sphere of influence relating to the training provided to developing countries under the auspices of WIPO, as in the recent workshop on intellectual property enforcement.[9] Thirdly, the courts have increasingly drawn from the decisions of British courts in interpreting patent legislation.

South Africa has adopted a formal registration system for patent applications, and does not conduct substantive search and examinations. This means that the only way in which the validity of a patent may effectively be tested is when the matter comes before a court in infringement or revocation proceedings.

There is strong reliance on English law for many of its court decisions, such as those relating to the 'inventive step' requirement for patentability. For example, the SCA considered the issue of obviousness in the case of *Ensign-Bickford (South Africa) (Pty) Limited and Others v AECI Explosives and Chemicals Limited* 1998 BIP 271 (SCA) 281, and found that 'the objection based on a lack of inventiveness is one of long standing in our patent law'. The judgment followed the English decision of *Molnlycke AB and Another v Proctor & Gamble Limited and Others* 1994 RPC 49 (CA) 115, which set out a four-step enquiry in the application of the provisions of section 25 of the Patents Act as regards an inventive step.

---

[7] See e.g., *Syntheta (Pty) Ltd v Janssen Pharmaceutica NV & Another* 1999 (1) SA 85 SCA.

[8] H. Klopper et al., *Law of Intellectual Property in South Africa*, LexisNexis, South Africa, 2011.

[9] Regional Workshop on the Enforcement of IP Rights for the Judiciary and Law Enforcement Officials, Lusaka, Zambia, July 2012.

Applying this approach, the SCA arrived at the conclusion that the step claimed as inventive did not go beyond the state of the art, and that the solution devised would have been obvious to a person skilled in the art.

Also in reliance on English precedent, in *Stauffer Chemical Co & Stauffer Chemical (SA) (Pty) Ltd & FBC Agrochemicals (Pty) Ltd v Safsan Marketing & Distribution Co (Pty) Ltd & Chemtrade (Pty) Ltd v Kempton Produce Supply (Pty) Ltd* 1983 BP 140 149D–150D, the requirements for a temporary interdict (injunction) in infringement claims were set out. The court stated that the whole case needed to be considered, including the prospects of success in the main action, the balance of prejudice and whether an award of damages would afford an applicant an adequate remedy.[10]

4 IF DIFFERENCES EXIST, WHAT GOVERNMENT POLICIES ARE BEHIND THEM?

4.1 Traditional Knowledge

One distinguishing feature from developed countries lies in the treatment of traditional knowledge. Although there has been considerable attention to the potential role of intellectual property (IP) protection in hindering access to various health care-related commodities, such as generic medicines, recent legislative attention has focused on the issue of protecting traditional knowledge. The IP Laws Amendment Bill, 2010, which has not as yet been passed, seeks to protect

> the different species of traditional intellectual property and geographical indications . . . establish a national council to advise . . . on traditional intellectual property . . . (and) a national trust fund to facilitate the commercialisation of traditional intellectual property and the application of income generated to the benefit of indigenous communities.[11]

The aim of this legislation is to prevent exploitation of traditional knowledge, benefit indigenous communities and, in the case of traditional medicines, prevent biopiracy. It intends to do so through existing forms of intellectual property legislation such as trademarks, copyrights,

---

[10] For an application of these principles, and the applicability of foreign law in these circumstances, see the discussion below on the case of *Aventis v Cipla*.

[11] Memorandum on the Objects of the Bill of the Intellectual Property Laws Amendment Bill 8 of 2010.

geographical indications, designs and patents. The Bill was processed through the parliamentary committees, including opportunities for public comment. It encountered resistance from civil society, which argued that existing intellectual property law 'is not the most suitable avenue for protecting traditional knowledge' since it 'does not pay adequate regard to the communities' ability to regulate the use of traditional knowledge through customary law and practices'.[12]

4.2 Jurisprudence

Other discernible differences emanate from the imperative to interpret all South African legislation in terms of the Constitution. The courts are increasingly being asked to interpret and apply patent and other laws through the 'prism' of a human rights-based approach. One recent instance involving a patent dispute related to the 'Docetaxel' drug.[13] While essentially a dispute as to whether a holder of a pharmaceutical patent can obtain an interdict against an alleged infringer, this was a significant test case for the extent to which courts are required to apply broad constitutional principles (in this instance, the right of access to health care services and medicines) in intellectual property disputes.

The disputed patent related to a composition of unpatented products which, when combined, facilitate the intravenous administration of docetaxel, a treatment for cancer. The holder of the patent (Aventis Pharma SA) maintained that the generic manufacturer (Cipla Life Sciences) had infringed its patent by registering and commencing the manufacture and marketing of a cheaper version of the medicine. Cipla countered that the patent is invalid on account of ambiguity and lack of novelty and inventive step, essential requirements for patentability under South African law. A major complication is that the South African patents office does not conduct substantive examinations as to the merits of each patent application, nor is there any opportunity for an interested party to oppose such applications. Thus the court proceedings presented a first opportunity for any tribunal to consider the substantive merits of the docetaxel patent.

In its submissions, the *amicus* Treatment Action Campaign (TAC) argued that the provisions of the Patents Act must be interpreted in a manner consistent with the Constitution and the rights of the patent

---

[12] W.J. Du Plessis 'Protection of Traditional Knowledge in South Africa: Does the "Commons" provide a Solution?', 2011, http://ssrn.com/abstract=1997992.

[13] *Aventis Pharma SA and Others v Cipla Life Sciences and Others* (Treatment Action Campaign (TAC) intervening as *amicus curiae*) (138/12) [2012] ZASCA 108 (26 July 2012).

holder need to be balanced with those of persons requiring, but unable to afford, the relevant medication. Secondly, when considering the requirement of 'balance of convenience' in interdict proceedings which potentially threaten the right to access medicines, the party requesting the interdict must prove that its grant will not harm the public interest. Thirdly, while the evidence to enable the court to assess whether the rights of cancer patients would be harmed was inadequate, on the available information on the record, the interdict-seeker failed to discharge its onus of proof. And finally, it argued that, in line with courts in the USA and India, the court must assess whether a satisfactory alternative remedy (such as damages) is available to the party seeking an interdict.

In its judgment (handed down by the Supreme Court of Appeal on 26 July 2012), the Court accepted TAC's argument that the broader public interest, and not merely those of the litigating parties, ought to be considered when determining the balance of convenience in interdict proceedings, citing both South African and US case law.[14] However, it concluded that the public interest would not be served by denying an interdict on the facts of this case. It noted that Cipla's opposition was based on commercial considerations, namely, its need to establish a presence in the generics market. Furthermore, it noted that there was no evidence before it that Aventis could not continue to meet the demand for the medicine, nor was Cipla able to demonstrate that its product offered either superior medicinal benefits, or more than a marginal saving on the cost of its generic version of docetaxel in relation to Aventis' generic version (marketed as Docetere). And finally, it held that there would be no material disruption of medicine supply to patients should the interdict be granted.

While making a concession to the consideration of the public interest when determining the balance of convenience, the judgment was not unexpected given the constraints imposed by the legislation and the mindset of the judiciary. The court took a rather narrow view on the question of awarding damages (royalties) should the patent ultimately be found to be valid, holding that this would be tantamount to granting a compulsory licence. This approach is out of step with other jurisdictions such as India and the USA.

The decision once again exposes the weaknesses of the current system. It vindicates the call by civil society to amend South Africa's patent laws

---

14 *EBay Inc. v Mercexchange* L.L.C. 547 US 388 (2006) 392 in which 'the United States Supreme Court affirmed that the ordinary requirements in that country for the grant of a permanent injunction – which include demonstrating that "the public interest would not be disserved" by an injunction – applied as much to injunctions against patent infringement'.

to specify and properly apply strict standards of novelty and inventive step through a substantive examination of the merits of an application (including recourse to opposition procedures), and to prioritise the public interest in disputes concerning life-saving medicines.[15] It also highlights the perversity stemming from the ability of patent holders to frustrate generic competition, and hence access to cheaper medicines, by introducing their own generic versions when such a threat is imminent. No interrogation was undertaken as to the motives of Aventis (in the same manner that Cipla's commercial motives were foregrounded) in registering and marketing Docetere only at the stage that Cipla was on the verge of launching a generic docetaxel, and the long-term impact of such practices on accessibility and affordability of medicines.

5 THE EXTENT TO WHICH PATENT POLICIES ADOPTED HAVE BEEN EFFECTIVE IN CURING DEFECTS FOUND IN MATURE SYSTEMS

5.1 General

The foregoing discussion demonstrates that the patent regime in South Africa has mostly reproduced the problems existent in some of the more mature systems, namely, the proliferation of low quality patents, and decisions of the courts have similarly failed to uphold high standards of protecting only genuine innovations. Furthermore, the patent system has failed to incentivise local innovative capability, has advantaged foreign inventors, and in the context of pharmaceutical patents, poses a potential threat to the availability of accessible, affordable essential medicines.

5.2 Implications for Access, Innovation and Investment

This discussion raises the critical question: what implications do the existing patent law and practice have for access to essential goods, for the prospects for local innovation, and for the need to attract foreign direct investment (FDI) into the country?

Many of these issues were canvassed in a recent study of five developing countries – Argentina, Brazil, Colombia, India and South Africa – in

---

15 Treatment Action Campaign et al., 'Why South Africa Should Examine Pharmaceutical Patents', 2012, http://www.tac.org.za/community/files/file/WhySAneedsanexaminationsystem.pdf.

relation to pharmaceutical patents.[16] The study concluded that despite a decrease in the number of new chemical entities for pharmaceuticals, patents on products and processes covering minor, incremental innovations abounded. This proliferation of 'evergreening' pharmaceutical patents has the potential to block generic competition and thus limit access to medicines. The study found no evidence that such a patenting environment necessarily supported local innovators. The opposite was found to be the case – foreign companies were the overwhelming beneficiaries of lax patenting and examining standards. The report also suggests that applying well-defined patentability standards could obviate the need to issue compulsory licences – a highly contentious and politically fraught measure, to which developed countries are intractably opposed.

In the case of South Africa, the following observations were made:

- The patent office granted some 2442 pharmaceutical patents in a single year (2008).
- This is due primarily to the fact that there is no substantive examination of patent applications.
- There is an inordinately large volume of 'weak' patents, and more than half of the studied patents were based on '"Markush claims", namely, claims that include a general formulae with multiple options that allow for the protection, under a single patent, of up to several millions of molecules'.[17]
- The validity of patents can only be tested when infringement or revocation proceedings are brought before court. However, the volume of such litigation is miniscule (a mere seven such cases were litigated for the period 2003–08).
- Even so, courts are applying a low standard of patentability, as evidenced by the case of *Pfizer & Ano v CiplaMedpro & Ors* 2005 BIP 1, where the court refused to revoke a patent, ruling that a besylate salt was unexpected, constituted an advance on the state of the art, and thus represented an inventive step.
- Only 16 pharmaceutical patents (1% of the total granted during 2008) were granted to South African inventors, the main beneficiaries being the USA and UK companies holding 49% and 10%, respectively, of granted patents.[18]

---

[16] C. M. Correa, 'Pharmaceutical Innovation, Incremental Patenting and Compulsory Licensing', South Centre, 2011.

[17] Correa, 'Pharmaceutical Innovation, Incremental Patenting and Compulsory Licensing'.

[18] Y. A. Vawda, 'Pharmaceutical Innovation, Incremental Patenting and

Other South African studies have arrived at similar conclusions. In one instance, it was 'found that the current intellectual property rights regime not only fails to support the objectives of the national innovation system but also that it facilitates exploitation by foreign interests and creates substantial social costs'.[19] The authors suggest that the registration system employed in South Africa, one of the cheapest patenting regimes in the world, opens the doors to frivolous and useless patents being granted. It 'increases uncertainty, increases search and monitoring costs by interested patentees and makes more difficult the dissemination of prior art by useful or real inventions'.[20] Furthermore, it creates an 'asymmetry' which disadvantages local innovators, as foreign inventors are able to file their patents in South Africa cheaply, with local inventors finding the costs of protecting their inventions abroad prohibitively expensive.[21] Using a sampling approach they conclude, most tellingly, that had an examining system been utilised, more than 80% of current applications at the patent office would not have been granted.[22]

Several commentators have canvassed the effect of strong intellectual property rights protection on economic development.[23] Increased IP protection appears to have little effect in the developing country context. Qian suggests that 'domestic innovation accelerates in countries with higher levels of economic development, educational attainment, and economic freedom'.[24] Lerner surveyed patent laws in over 60 countries, and con-

---

Compulsory Licensing Country Case Study: South Africa', 2011, http://www.tac.org.za/userfiles/file/Vawda%20SA%20patenting.pdf.

[19] A. Pouris and A. Pouris, 'Patents and Economic Development in South Africa: Managing Intellectual Property Rights', *South African Journal of Science*, November/December, 2011, 107.

[20] Pouris and Pouris, 'Patents and Economic Development in South Africa: Managing Intellectual Property Rights'.

[21] Pouris and Pouris, 'Patents and Economic Development in South Africa: Managing Intellectual Property Rights'.

[22] Pouris and Pouris, 'Patents and Economic Development in South Africa: Managing Intellectual Property Rights'.

[23] E. K. Maskus, 'Intellectual Property Rights in the Global Economy', Institute for International Economics, 2000; J. Lerner, 'Patent Protection and Innovation over 150 Years', 2002, http://www.epip.eu/papers/20030424/epip/papers/cd/papers_speakers/Lerner_Paper_EPIP_210403.pdf; P. Moser, 'How Do Patent Laws Influence Innovation? Evidence from Nineteenth Century World Fairs' National Bureau of Economic Research Working Paper No. w9909, 2002.

[24] Y. Qian, 'Do National Patent Laws Stimulate Domestic Innovation in a Global Patenting Environment?: A Cross-Country Analysis of Pharmaceutical Patent Protection 1978–2002', *Review of Economics and Statistics*, August 2007, 89(3), 436–453.

cluded that strengthening patent rights resulted in an increase in filings from foreign applicants, with no effect on filings by local inventors.[25] In similar vein, a more recent study involving over 72 countries concluded that 'to date, there is no robust empirical evidence that stronger patent rights indeed stimulate growth'.[26]

Another key consideration is the correlation of IP protection with FDI. While there are no available studies of the impact of the IP system on the inflow of investments into the country, Kaplan argues that South Africa has attracted far less FDI than other countries whose IPR system appears to offer potential foreign investors weaker protection.[27] The correlation between strong IP protection and FDI is yet to be established.

6 ARE GOVERNMENT POLICIES A COMPONENT OF NATIONAL DEVELOPMENT STRATEGY (SUCH AS CATCHING UP IN THE TECHNOLOGY SPHERE, OR BASED ON LONG-TERM CONSIDERATIONS)?

6.1 Draft New IP Policy

Although a new intellectual property policy was to be released for public comment by the Department of Trade and Industry (DTI) in July 2012, this has not happened. An early draft has been circulated to certain interest groups.[28] This draft proceeds on the basis that, while South Africa needs to align its policy and legislation to international treaties and norms, they must be consonant with the developmental stage appropriate to this country. The objectives of the policy are therefore, *inter alia*: to develop a legal IP framework to empower all strata of citizens; to provide a conducive environment for economic opportunities; to apply alongside other government policies to contribute to development; to interface with

---

25 Lerner, 'Patent Protection and Innovation over 150 Years'.

26 A. G. Z. Hu and I. P. L. Png, 'Patent Rights and Economic Growth: Evidence from Cross-Country Panels of Manufacturing Industries', 2010, http://www.wipo.int/edocs/mdocs/mdocs/en/wipo_ip_econ_ge_5_10/wipo_ip_econ_ge_5_10_ref_huandpng.pdf.

27 D. Kaplan, 'Intellectual Property Rights and Innovation in South Africa: A Framework', *The Economics of Intellectual Property in South Africa*, WIPO, 2009.

28 Department of Trade and Industry, 'Draft Policy on Intellectual Property of South Africa: A Policy Framework', unpublished 2012.

related new emerging issues; and to improve and strengthen enforcement.[29] The draft is presented in 17 chapters and only those sections which relate to both patents and public health are discussed here.

- Chapter 1 focuses on the four main types of IP (trademarks, copyright, patents and designs). It includes recommendations to amend legislation to incorporate the flexibilities available in the Doha Declaration on the TRIPS Agreement and Public Health of 14 November 2001;[30] incentive schemes in areas of IP that advance developmental goals, such as poverty alleviation and health; and the necessity for competition law to be applied to patent law where there is over-concentration, dominance or abuse by IP holders. It argues against 'general blanket data protection' of information submitted to regulators, as this would frustrate generic entry. Interestingly, the document identifies the need to explore alternatives to IP, such as subsidies or prize funds, but does not develop this theme further.
- Chapter 2 deals with IP and its impact on public health. It recommends the use of compulsory licences and parallel importation; that IP, competition and trade policies should to be in harmony with health policy objectives; the inclusion of provisions for entry of generic competition; and stricter rules to apply to patenting.
- Chapter 5 deals with competition, public policy, compulsory licensing and technology transfer. It warns that trade and investment treaties pose the danger of undermining sovereignty, and recommends against adopting the World Intellectual Property Organization (WIPO) Roadmap seeking a harmonised patent regime, which could lead to policy compromises for the country.
- Chapter 8 deals with institutional capacity. It recommends that the country's meagre resources not be used for IP administration (presumably enforcement); and that it adopt a multifaceted approach for the registration of patents (a combination of the depository and examination systems).
- Chapter 9 deals with the international architecture of IP, and recommends that the Department of Trade and Industry 'cautiously filter advices' coming from developed countries and institutions such as WTO and WIPO; and that South Africa not enter trade agreements

[29] Department of Trade and Industry, 'Draft Policy on Intellectual Property of South Africa: A Policy Framework'.

[30] World Trade Organization, *Declaration on the TRIPS Agreement and Public Health*, 14 November 2001, http://www.wto.org/english/thewto_e/minist_e/min01_e/mindecl_trips_e.htm.

that undermine the exceptions and flexibilities it is entitled to, or which are TRIPS-plus.

- Chapter 10 deals with IP and development, and recommends the implementation of the Doha Development Agenda; reconciling IP and competition policy; proposes increased incentives for technology transfer; increased funding to promote indigenous scientific and technological capability; and that South Africa does not support the 'global enforcement and harmonisation of patent' agendas.
- Chapter 15 deals with enforcement of IP, and proffers a 'bare minimum' obligations approach, and resistance to TRIPS-plus requirements in policy, law, and trade agreements.

6.2 Industrial Policy Developments

The government's recently announced Industrial Policy Action Plan (IPAP) seeks to achieve several core objectives: to diversify the economy; create employment; promote industrialisation; and to move towards a knowledge economy.[31]

Within this context, South Africa's total pharmaceutical market was estimated to be worth R27.9 billion (US$3.85 billion) in 2010, and is expected to grow at a compound annual growth rate of 22% between 2010 and 2013. The value of contracts awarded under pharmaceutical tenders between 2009 and 2011 was on average R6 billion per year, with an additional R1.2 billion for vaccines. Presently these items are sourced from both innovator and generic companies, both foreign and local, according to the Department of Health.[32]

In terms of the IPAP, it is intended that between 70% and 80% of medicines procurement will be earmarked for domestic manufacturers. One of its key strategies is to promote the domestic production of active pharmaceutical ingredients for antiretrovirals (ARVs), which, it is anticipated, will reduce the current trade deficit, reduce the dependence on imports, and be accomplished by injecting advanced technology into local industry through technology transfer and investment partnerships with leading foreign companies.[33] This will doubtless impact on suppliers who hold patents on vital products, and, unless licensing arrangements can be

---

[31] Department of Trade & Industry, *Industrial Policy Action Plan (IPAP) 2012/13 – 2104/15 15* (2012).

[32] Department of Health, *Medicines Procurement Reform in the Public Sector* (2010).

[33] Department of Trade & Industry, *Industrial Policy Action Plan (IPAP) 2012/13 – 2104/15.*

arrived at, will require the issuing of compulsory licences in appropriate cases.

7 THE EXTENT TO WHICH THE DIFFERENT POLICIES ARE DESIGNED TO ADDRESS SOCIAL WELFARE CONCERNS SPECIFIC TO SOUTH AFRICA

7.1 Competition Act

The Competition Act 89 of 1998, promulgated after the advent of democracy, reflects the development tenor that the new government is seeking to introduce in business and social relations. It seeks a framework 'balancing the interests of workers, owners and consumers' and is 'focused on development' (Preamble to the Act), and aims to 'advance the social and economic welfare of South Africans' (section 2(c) of the Act).

Few regulatory bodies in South Africa have captured the public imagination as the Competition Commission has done. Not surprisingly, it is perceived as the 'saviour' of the consumer in combating rampant price increases in commodities such as food, fuel, medicines and other health services. In the past decade, it has investigated and sanctioned such diverse entities as the Association of Pretoria Attorneys, the South African Airways, Tiger Brands, Adcock Ingram and Sasol, and has imposed penalties for cartel behaviour ranging from R223 000 on the Association of Pretoria Attorneys, to R250 million on Sasol.[34]

While most of these investigations have concentrated on collusive behaviour on the part of the corporate sector which is prohibited by law (in terms of section 4 of the Competition Act No. 89 of 1998), it has increasingly also turned its attention to anti-competitive practices in the area of medicines pricing premised on patent protection.

South Africa has not, to date, issued a single compulsory licence in respect of a pharmaceutical product,[35] but the access to medicines movement notched its biggest price reductions for ARVs through negotiated voluntary licences with companies such as GlaxoSmithKline,

[34] L. Blignaut, J. Balkin and L. du Plessis, 'Zero Tolerance Displayed for Cartel Contraventions', Legalbrief TODAY, 8 June 2009, http://www.legalbrief.co.za/article.php?story=20090608171550274.

[35] Vawda, 'Pharmaceutical Innovation, Incremental Patenting and Compulsory Licensing Country Case Study: South Africa'.

BoehringerIngelheim and Merck. These licences followed successful complaints to the Competition Commission, which made findings of excessive pricing and other anti-competitive conduct on the part of the drug manufacturers.[36]

7.2 Draft IP Policy

As stated above, the draft new IP policy addresses the developmental aspects of patent reform, including recommendations to employ the use of compulsory licensing and parallel importation in furtherance of public health objectives in line with the Doha Declaration. It also promotes the application of competition law and policy to counter the failures of the patent system, such as where there is over-concentration of ownership and control, or dominance or abuse by IP holders. It is opposed to a 'general blanket data protection' of information in the hands of the regulator, as this will frustrate generic entry.

In dealing with the impact of IP on public health,[37] it promotes the use of TRIPS flexibilities; advocates for significant public funding for research and development into diseases of the poor; and argues for greater alignment of trade and health policy objectives.

These provisions constitute a significant attempt to reform, in particular, patent law and, generally, IP policy to serve all sectors of South African society.

8 CONCLUSION

How does South Africa compare with other emerging economies, such as India, Brazil and Thailand?

Although South Africa and India share the history of a common colonial power, their respective systems could not have been more different. While India, post-independence, excluded the patenting of pharmaceutical products through the Indian Patents Act, 1970, and embarked on 'redesigning a colonial institution',[38] South Africa preserved the colonially entrenched legislation, and retained a form-based registration system for

---

[36] *Hazel Tau & Others v GlaxoSmithKline & Boehringer Ingelheim* (Competition Commission) Case No. 2002 Sep 226; and *Treatment Action Campaign v MSD (Pty) Ltd & Another* November 2007.

[37] Chapter 2 of the Draft Policy.

[38] P. Drahos, 'The Jewel in the Crown: India's Patent Office and Patent-Based Innovation' in C. Arup and W. van Caenegem, *Intellectual Property Policy Reform:*

patents. Such an industrially driven policy choice by Indian legislators opened the door to a robust generic pharmaceutical manufacturing industry, and the resultant availability of affordable medicines. Later, when required to become fully TRIPS-compliant, they incorporated many of the TRIPS flexibilities in the Patents (Amendment) Act, 2005, notably strong patentability standards to prevent 'evergreening' of pharmaceutical products, provisions for opposition to patent applications and compulsory licences, among others.

Secondly, although South African legislation contains provisions for compulsory licences which pre-date TRIPS, it has not to date issued a single licence on a pharmaceutical product. Thailand, on the other hand, has demonstrated great success on this count. Since 2006, in perhaps the most far-reaching attempt by any developing country, the Thai government has issued seven compulsory licences and government use orders in respect of several drugs, ranging from antiretrovirals to medicines to treat heart disease and cancer, after attempts to lower drug prices had failed. This had the effect of considerably reducing drug prices. It achieved these results despite tremendous pressure from the US Administration and the pharmaceutical industry.[39]

Brazil's Industrial Property Law of 1996 contains provisions for the issuing of compulsory licences for abuse of patents, including failure to work locally. For over ten years, Brazil had effectively used the threat of compulsory licensing to negotiate significant discounts on patented medicines from pharmaceutical companies. As the government had not actually issued any licences, this strategy gradually began to lose its effectiveness, with the result that the discounts were increasingly becoming insignificant. Thus, when negotiations with the manufacturer of the antiretroviral drug *efavirenz* ground to a halt, the Brazilian government issued, in May 2007, a compulsory licence for import and for the local manufacture of generic versions of the drug. This has had the effect of reducing the price by almost one-third.[40]

African countries seeking to reform their patent laws confront many challenges, including the recently resurrected proposal by the African

Fostering Innovation and Ddevelopment, Cheltenham, UK and Northampton, MA, USA, Edward Elgar, 2009.

39 Open Society Institute, *Playing by the Rules: Using Intellectual Property Law and Policy to Improve Access to Essential Medicines*, 2008.

40 R. Reis et al., 'Access to Medicines and Intellectual Property in Brazil: A Civil Society Experience', in V. Terto Jr, R. Reis and C. Pimenta, *Intellectual Property Rights and Access to ARV Medicines: Civil Society Resistance in the Global South*, Brazilian Interdisciplinary AIDS Association, 2009.

Union to establish a Pan-African Intellectual Property Organisation,[41] which seeks to elevate IP standards above existing levels. This initiative has been justifiably criticised for pursuing an 'IP maximalist agenda'.[42] The Ministers meeting in Brazzaville in November 2012 resolved to defer the item in order to undertake further consultations.

Finally, as is the position with most developing and emerging economies, South Africa is buffeted by the twin forces of 'harmonisation', represented by treaty and trade obligations to keep up with the developed world, and the requirement to 'catch up' in terms of its technological, legislative and policy prowess. This will require the political will and commitment of its leaders to proceed with, among others, the process of patent law reform, and for leaders of the developed world to not, as Chang pithily states, 'kick away the ladder'.[43]

---

41 African Union, *Final Draft Statute of the Pan-African Intellectual Property Organisation (PAIPO)*, 2012, http://www.au.int/fr/sites/default/files/PAIPO%20 Statute%20English.pdf.

42 Intellectual Property Watch, 'Move Toward New Pan-African IP Organisation Alarms Observers', 2012, http://www.ip-watch.org/2012/09/27/ move-toward-new-pan-african-ip-organisation-alarms-observers/.

43 H. J. Chang, *Bad Samaritans: The Myth of Free Trade and the Secret History of Capitalism*, New York, Bloomsbury Press, 2008.

PART IV

ASEAN

14. Patents and the emerging markets of Asia: ASEAN and Thailand

Jakkrit Kuanpoth

1 INTRODUCTION

The Association of Southeast Asian Nations (ASEAN) consists of ten countries, which are diverse in size and level of social and economic development. It comprises the world's richest (i.e. Singapore and Brunei) and poorest countries (i.e. Cambodia, Laos and Myanmar). ASEAN's integration into the globalized world economy has required its members to work towards transforming the pattern of their economic development and collaboration in order to enable their businesses to compete internationally. One initiative that member countries of ASEAN have recently taken is to form an ASEAN economic community that will progressively liberalize trade and investment in the region. This forging of a European-style single market will necessitate the harmonization of some elements of intellectual property (IP) law and policy so as to ensure that the protection and enforcement of IP rights do not result in the creation of barriers to regional trade.

The purpose of this chapter is to examine ASEAN regional economic integration and discuss the role IP plays in the integration process. The chapter also intends to survey the current developments of IP law and policy within ASEAN and to examine the IP infrastructures and institutions of ASEAN members. The aim is to determine the readiness for the ASEAN economic community and to outline what is required for the protection and promotion of domestic creations and innovations of those countries. It first discusses IP integration within ASEAN and the IP norm-setting process under the free trade agreement that ASEAN signed with Australia and New Zealand. The chapter then examines the institutional capacities and resources of Thailand with regard to the administration of IP laws and the enforcement of IP rights. It argues that the country has already adopted IP legislation providing strong protection, but it lacks the necessary human and technical capacity to maximize benefits provided by IP. For ASEAN to be an effective economic community, technical assistance must be provided to help the developing member countries. This assistance should be directed towards the development of human resources and IP infrastructures in order to facilitate the use of IP as a tool for national economic development and integration in ASEAN.

2 ASEAN IP INTEGRATION

In 2003, ASEAN reached an agreement to establish by 2020 an ASEAN Economic Community (AEC). Four years later, ASEAN leaders adopted the AEC Blueprint bringing the deadline for completion of the ASEAN Community forward to 2015. The 2003 Agreement establishing the AEC envisages the conversion of ASEAN into a legal entity as a regional economic community and the transformation of ten ASEAN countries into a single market. The resulting single market means that goods, services, investments, capital and skilled labour will move freely among all the member countries. The AEC Blueprint committed member countries to work towards removing tariff and non-tariff barriers to trade and services as well as to harmonize and standardize trade and customs requirements. It is envisaged that the ASEAN single market will stimulate trade between member states and 'will boost the development of production networks in the region and enhance ASEAN's capacity to serve as a global production centre to better meet the demands of the global supply chain'.[1]

In order to achieve the aim of economic integration, collaboration policies on IP must be established. Like the European Union (EU), ASEAN has expressed its intention to promote collaboration on IP issues. It is agreed that IP rights granted by member states must not act as a barrier to the movement of goods across national borders.[2] In 1995, the leaders of the member nations signed the ASEAN Framework Agreement on Intellectual Property Collaboration establishing the ASEAN Working Group on Intellectual Property Collaboration (AWGIPC). The AWGIPC acts as an IP consultative body and has played a key role in promoting regional collaboration on IP-related matters within ASEAN since 1996.

---

[1] ASEAN Secretariat, 'ASEAN Economic Community Handbook for Business', ASEAN Secretariat, Jakarta, 2011, p. xiii, http://www.scribd.com/doc/97536042/29/ASEAN-Collaboration-in-Intellectual-Property-Rights (accessed 13 July 2012).

[2] A. Adcock and C. Gautier, 'ASEAN: The Impact of Free Trade on IP', *Managing Intellectual Property*, 1 November 2010, http://www.managingip.com/Article/2710652/ASEAN-The-impact-of-free-trade-on-IP.html (accessed 13 July 2012).

It has held a number of workshops, seminars and symposia on various IP subjects. It has also worked to form strong networks among member countries' government officials.

The work of AWGIPC has been guided by the ASEAN IP Right Action Plan 2004–10, the ASEAN IP Right Action Plan 2011–15, and the ASEAN Economic Blueprint. These action plans and the economic blueprint were adopted in order to identify the end goals of the AEC and to set out the roles of IP in the AEC process.[3] They aim to achieve the following strategic goals on IP: (1) balancing the IP system for registration and enforcement, including establishing a regional filing system for designs; (2) accession to international agreements regarding designs, patents and trade marks; (3) enhancing IP awareness at all levels; (4) upholding active regional participation in the international IP community through consultations and information exchanges among national enforcement agencies on IP protection; (5) promoting capacity building for government officers, as well as regional collaboration on IP issues such as traditional knowledge, genetic resources and traditional cultural expressions.[4]

Two important works have been initiated by AWGIPC: (1) the establishment of the ASEAN Patent Examination Collaboration Program (ASPEC) and (2) the introduction of the ASEAN IP Portal. The ASPEC was operationalized in 2009. It provides accelerated patent examination procedures for corresponding applications filed in participating member countries. The patent offices of ASEAN countries have agreed to share information and allow examiners in another office to reuse their search and examination results.[5] The patent office of a member country is not obliged to follow the search and examination results of another country's patent office, but they can use the results if they wish to. Each country's office will decide separately whether to grant or reject an application on the basis of that country's own interests. All ASEAN members, excluding Brunei and Myanmar, have participated in the ASPEC. The other IP programme is called the ASEAN IP Portal, which is scheduled to enter into operation in 2012. The programme will establish a single web-based

---

3 ASEAN Secretariat, 'ASEAN Economic Community Handbook for Business', ASEAN Secretariat, Jakarta, 2011, p. xiii, http://www.scribd.com/doc/97536042/29/ASEAN-Collaboration-in-Intellectual-Property-Rights, (accessed 13 July 2012).

4 Department of Intellectual Property, *Annual Report*, Department of Intellectual Property, Bangkok, 2011.

5 ASEAN Secretariat, 'ASEAN Intellectual Property Right Action Plan 2004–2010', ASEAN Secretariat, Jakarta, http://www.asean.org/news/item/asean-intellectual-property-right-action-plan-2004–2010 (accessed 13 July 2012).

database providing information in relation to ASEAN's progress and achievements on IP matters. Member countries' patent offices will be responsible for updating, managing and maintaining the database.

These arrangements aim to increase the efficiency of IP administration and reduce the costs of implementing IP laws. It is interesting to note that ASEAN does not envisage establishing a 'unitary' regional IP system, whereby effective enforcement of IP rights is ensured throughout the ASEAN territory. IP rights are still issued or granted by competent national authorities, and national courts still have jurisdiction to determine infringement and validity of IP rights. The planned regional arrangements for IP protection may only be regarded as the beginning of a regional patent system if ASEAN deepens its economic integration towards a single economy.

The severe problem in creating a unitary IP system faced by ASEAN relates to the political dynamics in each member country. ASEAN has faced similar obstacles to those faced by the EU when trying to create a single IP system. Some ASEAN members appear unwilling to amend their national laws to assimilate to Western standards. Some aim to advance their own national interest in the ASEAN IP systems by preserving their national languages and national IP office, and some are demanding that they become the location for the central IP office.

In addition, the deeper the integration process amongst ASEAN members, the more developmental and technological gaps among its members appear. Among ASEAN nations, there is an obvious disparity in institutional capacity and skilled human resources among national IP offices. It is believed that regional policies like ASPEC and the IP Portal will help to bridge the gaps with less need to invest in physical infrastructure at each office. The AWGIPC also plans to accede to international IP treaties in order to strengthen institutional capacity and cross-border cooperation. It is expected that ASEAN as a group will join the following international agreements in the near future: the Hague Agreement Concerning the International Deposit of Industrial Designs, the Patent Cooperation Treaty (PCT), and the Protocol Relating to the Madrid Agreement Concerning the International Registration of Marks.

3 FREE TRADE AGREEMENT: ASEAN–AUSTRALIA–NEW ZEALAND FTA

Apart from ASEAN's economic integration, individual ASEAN members have negotiated and implemented bilateral free trade agreements (FTA) with other countries and regions. Such agreements include but are not limited to: the Singapore–United States FTA, Japan–Thailand Economic Partnership Agreement, Japan–Malaysia Economic Partnership Agreement, etc. ASEAN as a group has also signed FTAs with some countries, including Australia, New Zealand, Korea, China, Japan and India. It is currently negotiating an FTA with the EU. The only FTA concluded by ASEAN with trade partners that contains IP commitments is the ASEAN–Australia–New Zealand Free Trade Agreement (AANZFTA). The details of IP obligations under the Agreement are now examined.[6]

AANZFTA was signed in 2009, and entered into force on 1 January 2010. The Agreement is quite comprehensive and wide in scope, covering various issues, including trade in goods and services, competition, e-commerce, investment, and IP. It generally aims to maximize market access and harmonize trade rules for exports of goods and services and investments between the two regions.[7] It reduces and eliminates duties and other non-tariff barriers in all participating countries and provides for government-to-government and investor-state dispute settlement mechanisms. This allows investors to take action against governments that fail to treat investments in accordance with the standards of the AANZFTA. Chapter 13 of the AANZFTA contains a number of specific obligations on the protection of IP rights. Most of the IP obligations build on the parties' existing rights and obligations under the World Trade Organization Agreement on Trade-Related Aspects of Intellectual Property Rights (TRIPS) with the goals of reinforcing TRIPS obligations and achieving a higher level of IP protection beyond the TRIPS standards.[8]

3.1 Patents, Trade Marks and Copyright

No AANZFTA provision specifically mentions patents. The Agreement only requires its parties to adhere to non-TRIPS patent treaties, including

---

6 J. Kuanpoth, 'Intellectual Property in ASEAN–Australia–New Zealand FTA', Tilleke and Gibbins Informed Counsel Bangkok, http://www.tilleke.com/resources/intellectual-property-asean%E2%80%93australia%E2%80%93new-zealand-fta (accessed 20 July 2012). See also D. Rocco and A. Caruso, 'Prosperity in Co-operation: The ASEAN-Australia-New Zealand Free Trade Agreement (AANZFTA)', *Journal of World Investment and Trade*, vol. 11, no. 2, 2010, pp. 197–226.

7 K. Heydon and S. Woolcock, *The Rise of Bilateralism: Comparing American, European and Asian Approaches to Preferential Trade Agreements*, Tokyo, United Nations University Press, 2009.

8 Mondaq Business Briefing, 'Intellectual Property in ASEAN-Australia-New Zealand FTA (AANFTA)', HighBeam Research, 29 February 2012, http://www.highbeam.com/doc/1G1–281702305.html (accessed 20 July 2012).

the PCT, the Patent Law Treaty, and the Budapest Treaty on the International Recognition of the Deposit of Microorganisms for the Purposes of Patent Procedure (1977). ASEAN members, most of which are not parties to the Budapest Treaty, are encouraged to seek accession to the multilateral patent convention. Accession to the Budapest Treaty would facilitate the patent-granting process for biotechnology. It was envisaged that the incorporation of a substantive PCT provision would establish a system of international filing of patent applications and would lead to better coordination of international patent information among ASEAN members. However, one criticism is that participation in the PCT will increase patent applications and will make developing countries' patent offices more dependent on the larger offices.[9] Accession to the PCT will also extend time periods for requesting a patent (i.e. from the 12-month priority date for patent applications under the Paris Convention to up to 30 months under the PCT).[10] With all the parties' seeking accession to and implementation of the World Intellectual Property Organization (WIPO) Patent Law Treaty, the AANZFTA will harmonize certain aspects of patent formalities, such as the requirements for filing a patent application, procedures for obtaining and maintaining patents, and other patent procedures.

The IP chapter also contains a number of specific obligations on protection of trade marks, geographical indications (GIs), and copyright. The provision on trade marks and GIs simply requires parties to make available on internet databases all pending and registered trade mark rights in their respective jurisdictions. The AANZFTA, in line with Australia and New Zealand's position in multilateral trade negotiations, relies on trade marks and passing off for GI protection. It also requires each party to protect trade marks that predate, in its jurisdiction, GIs.[11] The demand for the protection of GIs under existing laws governing trade marks and passing off could have significant implications for some ASEAN countries.

It may be noted that some countries implement their obligations under

---

[9] See P. Drahos, *The Global Governance of Knowledge: Patent Offices and their Clients*, Cambridge, Cambridge University Press, 2010.

[10] WIPO, 'PCT Applicant's Guide – International Phase', WIPO, Geneva, 2012, http://www.wipo.int/pct/en/guide/ipindex.html#TopOfPage (accessed 22 July 2012).

[11] Australian Government Department of Foreign Affairs and Trade, 'Agreement Establishing the ASEAN-Australia-New Zealand Free Trade Area', 2009, Chapter 13, Article 7, http://www.dfat.gov.au/fta/aanzfta/aanzfta.PDF (accessed 15 March 2013).

the WTO TRIPS Agreement by using trade mark law or using laws related to business practices to protect GIs as in the case of the United States, the United Kingdom and Australia. Many other countries, including France, the EU, India and Thailand, choose to adopt a *sui generis* legislation uniquely tailored to apply to specific subjects like GIs.[12] The *sui generis* GIs have much wider potential applications than trade marks and the prevention of unfair competitive practices. For developing countries with different production structures and natural endowments, the broader protection of GIs may constitute one of the most important categories of intellectual property, as reflected in the case of Thailand where the protection of GIs has recently received greater interest from its government. The increasing significance of GIs for Thailand stems from the fact that the country has abundant producers of all kinds of natural and agricultural products and of handicrafts as originating in a region or locality in the country. The protection of a name or sign used on certain products which corresponds to a specific geographical location or origin could be a significant factor contributing to economic development and for the promotion of the country's export.[13] While Australia and New Zealand gain when GIs are protected as trade marks, the use of trade marks for GIs may inhibit the attempts of some ASEAN countries, notably Thailand, which has enacted comprehensive *sui generis* legislation on the protection of GIs, to extend the protection of wines and spirits to all products, and to use GIs as a tool for the promotion of their quality products.[14]

For copyright protection, TRIPS requires criminal proceedings to take place in cases of wilful copyright piracy for commercial advantage or financial gain. The AANZFTA extends this obligation to cases where a person wilfully commits a significant infringement of copyright that is not committed for commercial advantage or financial gain, but which has a 'substantial prejudicial impact' on the owner of the copyright. Each party is also required to foster the establishment of appropriate bodies for

---

12 N.S. Gopalakrishnan, P.S. Nair and A.K. Babu, 'Exploring the Relationship between Geographical Indications and Traditional Knowledge: An Analysis of the Legal Tools for the Protection of Geographical Indications in Asia', ICTSD Working Paper, Geneva, 2007, http://www.iprsonline.org/ictsd/docs/Gopaletal%20-%20GIs&TK.pdf (accessed 15 March 2013).

13 For the extent of the discussion on the socio-economic implications of GI protection in Thailand see J. Kuanpoth and D. Robinson, 'Geographical Indications Protection: The Case of Thailand and Jasmine Rice', *Intellectual Property Quarterly*, vol. 3, 2009, pp. 288–310.

14 See World Trade Organization, 'Agreement on Trade-related Aspects of Intellectual Property Rights [TRIPS]', 1994, Articles 23 and 24, http://www.wto.org/english/docs_e/legal_e/27-trips.pdf (accessed 15 March 2013).

the collective management of copyright. They must also encourage such bodies to operate in a manner that is efficient, publicly transparent, and accountable to their members.[15] This establishment could be useful for a number of participating countries that are looking at better exploiting their cultural industries.

The AANZFTA parties have agreed to increase the level of protection for digital technologies by providing adequate legal protection and effective legal remedies against circumvention of effective technological measures that authors and related rights holders apply to protect their content. Effective legal remedies against circumvention of technological measures are already part of Australia's and New Zealand's legislation, but they have not been incorporated in the legislation of most ASEAN countries. This obligation will persuade ASEAN countries to reform their existing copyright regime by extending the conventional economic rights of the author to the right to use and distribute circumventing devices. This will enable copyright owners to extend control over access to and distribution of digital works.

The AANZFTA provides a guarantee to software owners that not only will their copyrights over software be highly protected, but they will also have exclusive rights to sell their products to national government agencies. Under the AANZFTA, each party confirms its 'commitment to maintain appropriate laws, regulations and policies that make provisions for its central government agencies to use only legitimate computer software and to encourage its respective regional and local governments to maintain or adopt similar measures'.[16]

3.2 Protection of Genetic Resources, Traditional Knowledge, and Folklore

The AANZFTA recognizes the significance of protecting traditional knowledge and cultural property. It provides that 'each party may establish appropriate measures to protect genetic resources, traditional knowledge and folklore'.[17] The inclusion of these issues (which are still

---

[15] Australian Government Department of Foreign Affairs and Trade, 'Agreement Establishing the ASEAN-Australia-New Zealand Free Trade Area', 2009, Chapter 13, Article 5, http://www.dfat.gov.au/fta/aanzfta/aanzfta.PDF (accessed 15 March 2013).

[16] Australian Government Department of Foreign Affairs and Trade, 'Agreement Establishing the ASEAN-Australia-New Zealand Free Trade Area', 2009, Chapter 13, Article 6, http://www.dfat.gov.au/fta/aanzfta/aanzfta.PDF (accessed 15 March 2013).

[17] Australian Government Department of Foreign Affairs and Trade,

being discussed multilaterally) into this regional FTA is not surprising given that ASEAN, Australia and New Zealand are known for possessing great wealth in cultural and natural heritages. Although the AANZFTA explicitly acknowledges the importance of these subjects, it fails to ensure their protection in concrete ways. Its provision neither mentions specific forms of protection for these areas, nor refers to the Convention on Biological Diversity and the Food and Agriculture Organization (FAO) International Treaty on Plant and Genetic Resources for Food and Agriculture (ITPGRFA). Those are the most comprehensive regimes for the protection of genetic resources and traditional knowledge to date.

The AANZFTA's provision on genetic resources, traditional knowledge, and folklore seems to reflect the perspective of the parties that this issue is being negotiated in multilateral fora and should be kept that way. However, the FTA provisions seem contradictory. While the AANZFTA gives parties the freedom to establish their own system of traditional knowledge protection, it demands that each party seek accession to the International Union for the Protection of New Varieties of Plants (UPOV Convention) 1991. Some ASEAN countries, such as Thailand, Malaysia and Indonesia, have implemented *sui generis* systems for plant variety protection. Their national legislation has incorporated requirements relating to protection of local plant varieties,[18] obtaining and disclosing prior informed consent as well as the need to demonstrate equitable benefit sharing.[19] By acceding to UPOV 1991 as required by the AANZFTA, those ASEAN countries will no longer maintain the *sui generis* plant variety protection systems that offer rights for local communities, restrict access to genetic resources, and provide sharing of benefits derived from their valuable resources and traditional knowledge.

'Agreement Establishing the ASEAN-Australia-New Zealand Free Trade Area', 2009,Chapter 13, Article 8, http://www.dfat.gov.au/fta/aanzfta/aanzfta.PDF (accessed 15 March 2013).

[18] See Republic of Indonesia, 'Laws of Republic of Indonesia, No. 29 of 2000 on Plant Variety Protection', 2000, Article 7, http://www.wipo.int/wipolex/en/text.jsp?file_id=226832 (accessed 15 March 2013).

[19] See Parliament of Malaysia, 'Protection of New Plant Varieties Act 2004 (Act 634)', 2004, Section 12, http://www.wipo.int/wipolex/en/text.jsp?file_id=128880#P87_3293 (accessed 15 March 2013); Government of Thailand, 'The Plant Varieties Protection Act B.E. 2542 (1999)', 1999, Section 48, http://www.wipo.int/wipolex/en/text.jsp?file_id=129781 (accessed 15 March 2013).

4 COUNTRY CASE STUDY: THAILAND

4.1 Economy

Thailand was one of the fastest-growing economies in the late 1980s. In 1988 and 1989, the Thai economic growth rate reached a remarkable 11 per cent.[20] The country's high-growth economic boom during that period led many people to believe that Thailand had the resources to become a developed country with a high per capita income. However, the economic crisis that struck in the late 1990s brought Thailand back to earth. The economic bubble that had grown for almost a decade finally burst in 1997 with the crash of the property market and the plunge in the value of the baht. The crisis subsequently spread from Thailand to other countries and became the East Asian financial crisis. However, the Thai economy has recovered quickly from the crisis and renewed its growth.

Currently, Thailand is an emerging economy, with solid growth during 2000 to 2008 averaging more than 4 per cent per year. In 2010, Thailand enjoyed total gross domestic product (GDP) of US$580.3 billion.[21] It is presently ASEAN's second largest economy after Indonesia. It has the fourth highest per capita GDP in ASEAN after Singapore, Brunei and Malaysia. Agriculture makes up 10.4 per cent of the country's GDP, industry 45.6 per cent and services 44 per cent.[22] Thailand's major trading partners are the United States (10.9%), China (10.6%), and Japan (10.3%). The EU, other ASEAN countries, Australia and New Zealand are also significant trading partners. Thailand has always enjoyed a substantial trade surplus. As the 2010 figure shows, its exports were worth US$191.3 billion and imports were US$156.9 billion.[23] Primary destinations for Thai exports include the United States (10.9%), China (10.6%) and Japan (10.3%), and the major import partners are: Japan (18.7%), China (12.7%), Malaysia (6.4%), the United States (6.3%), United Arab Emirates (5%), Singapore (4.3%) and South Korea (4.1%).[24] The following are the

---

[20] National Economic and Social Development Board, *Annual Report*, Bangkok, National Economic and Social Development Board, 1991.

[21] Asian Info, *Thailand's Economy*, Bangkok, http://www.asianinfo.org/asianinfo/thailand/pro-economy.htm, (accessed 17 July 2012).

[22] Asian Info, *Thailand's Economy*, Bangkok, http://www.asianinfo.org/asianinfo/thailand/pro-economy.htm, (accessed 17 July 2012).

[23] Asian Info, *Thailand's Economy*, Bangkok, http://www.asianinfo.org/asianinfo/thailand/pro-economy.htm, (accessed 17 July 2012).

[24] Asian Info, *Thailand's Economy*, Bangkok, http://www.asianinfo.org/asianinfo/thailand/pro-economy.htm, (accessed 17 July 2012).

country's major export products: textiles, footwear, fishery products, rice, rubber, jewellery, automobiles, computer parts and electrical appliances. Capital goods, intermediate goods, raw materials, consumer goods and fuels are among Thailand's principal imports.

4.2 IP Law

Thailand is a party to the TRIPS Agreement and the Berne Convention. It joined the Paris Convention in August 2008, and subsequently ratified accession to the PCT in September 2009. It is currently considering joining the Madrid system for the international registration of trade marks. Currently, there are seven laws protecting IP rights in Thailand, including the Patent Act B.E. 2522 (1979), the Trade Marks Act B.E. 2534 (1991), the Copyright Act B.E. 2537 (1994), the Plant Variety Protection Act B.E. 2542 (1999), the Protection of Layout-Designs of Integrated Circuits Act B.E. 2543 (2000), the Trade Secrets Act B.E. 2545 (2002), and the Geographical Indications Protection Act B.E. 2546 (2003). Apart from law protecting internationally recognized IP rights, Thailand has adopted legislation protecting traditional knowledge in the field of medicines. The Traditional Medicine Act B.E. 2542 (1999), which is under the administration of the Ministry of Public Health, lays down conditions on access to herbal resources and protection of Thai traditional formulations. The law establishes proprietary rights allowing traditional healers to retain control over traditional medicinal knowledge through public registration.[25]

4.3 Research Policy and Technology Diffusion

The Thai government has financed a number of research programmes in universities, public research institutes and private companies in order to encourage the development of local technology. In spite of this effort, the country still has a relatively low level of science and technology. Thailand's research and development (R&D) expenditures are small compared to those of industrialized countries. The amount of research spending in Thailand in 2009 accounted for 0.12 per cent of national GDP,[26] which was smaller than that spent by Japan (3.4%), the United States (2.7%),

---

25 J. Kuanpoth, 'Thailand', in Heath, C. (ed.), *Intellectual Property Law in Asia*, The Hague, Kluwer Law, 2002, pp. 337–62.

26 Office of the National Research Council of Thailand, *Annual Report*, Bangkok, 2010.

Germany (2.5%), France (2%), Republic of Korea (1.8%) and China (1.4%).[27] Apart from its small R&D budget, Thailand also has a shortage of skilled scientists and engineers to undertake R&D. According to the 2007 World Bank statistics, in Thailand there were only 316 research personnel per million people, which is a small number compared to 5,409 in Japan, 4,673 in the United States, 3,525 in Germany, 3,593 in France, 4,672 in Republic of Korea, and 1,077 in China.[28]

4.4 Patent Office

In May 1992, the Department of Intellectual Property (DIP) was established in response to the growing significance of IP. It is in charge of the implementation of all IP laws in Thailand with the exception of the Plant Variety Protection Act B.E. 2542 (1999), which is administered by the Ministry of Agriculture. The DIP is a government agency within the Ministry of Commerce. Specific duties and responsibilities of the DIP include the following: (1) registering patents, trade marks and licensing of IP rights; (2) developing systems, patterns and means to protect IP; (3) promoting effective use of IP for the purposes of education, R&D, and commercialization; (4) studying, analysing and recommending policies on IP to the Thai government; etc.[29]

Establishing an effective patent system is a challenge for developing countries like Thailand. Like most developing-country patent offices, the Patent Office administered by the DIP does not have adequate skilled personnel and sufficient institutional capacity to perform necessary patent examination. Unlike the Trilateral Offices of the USPTO (United States Patent and Trademark Office), the EPO (European Patent Office) and the JPO (Japan Patent Office), the Thai Patent Office only employs a small number of patent examiners. There are currently 42 patent examiners at the Thai Patent Office. Although the DIP has increased the number of its patent examiners in recent years, from 24 in 2001 to 42 in 2010, this number is still too small to guarantee the quality and efficiency of patent examination. The situation is even worse considering the fact that only 17 out of a total of 42 examiners are involved in the examination of patent applications for invention in the fields of chemistry, biotechnology, phar-

---

[27] United Nations Educational Scientific and Cultural Organization, UNESCO Institute for Statistics, www.uis.unesco.org (accessed 20 July 2012).

[28] The World Bank, *Data: Researchers in R&D (per million people)*, http://data.worldbank.org/indicator/SP.POP.SCIE.RD.P6 (accessed 19 July 2012).

[29] Department of Intellectual Property, *Annual Report*, Department of Intellectual Property, Bangkok, 2011, p. 16.

maceuticals, and engineering. The rest are involved in examining applications for designs and petty patents.[30]

It has to be noted that the recruitment of experienced engineers and scientists by patent offices to examine increasingly complex applications is a serious problem in developing countries. In Thailand, for example, 11.9 per cent of the patent examiners currently employed by the DIP have a bachelor's degree in science and the remaining hold a degree in science at the master's level. The majority of the examiners have little experience in patent examination. Of the total, 35.7 per cent have between 10 and 15 years' experience and the rest have work experience of less than 10 years.[31]

Experienced patent examiners cannot be hired quickly in the labour market. The problem is more acute as the DIP is not a self-financing executive agency. Patent examiners at the DIP are hired on the government pay scale, which is uncompetitive with non-governmental jobs. For example, the starting salary of a patent examiner is THB 12,000 (approximately US$300) per month, while an examiner with 5–10 years of experience receives the maximum salary of THB 50,000 (approximately US$1,666) per month.[32] As a government department, the DIP enjoys less flexibility in its working and budget arrangements than its counterparts in some other ASEAN countries such as the Singaporean and Malaysian patent offices, which are now autonomous organizations. The DIP is still regarded as a source of income for the Thai government. Most of its income generated from application and maintenance fees must be remitted to the Revenue Department. It is unable to use the surplus income to provide pay incentives or bonuses for examiners. Because of this limitation, the Thai Patent Office has struggled to recruit competent examiners, and as a result it is unable to deal with dramatic increases in the number of applications.

4.5 Backlog of Applications and Incomplete Patent Documentation

Like Thailand, many countries do not have sufficient expertise to maintain a modern patent office with full capability for thorough technical examination in all fields. In recent years, patent offices around the world have been facing a patent backlog problem due to dramatic increases in

---

[30] Kenan Institute Asia, *Comparative Assessment Study of Patent and Trademark Offices in Southeast Asia*, Bangkok, Kenan Institute Asia, 2012.

[31] Kenan Institute Asia, *Comparative Assessment Study of Patent and Trademark Offices in Southeast Asia*, Bangkok, Kenan Institute Asia, 2012.

[32] Kenan Institute Asia, *Comparative Assessment Study of Patent and Trademark Offices in Southeast Asia*, Bangkok, Kenan Institute Asia, 2012.

the number of applications.[33] As a result, a number of patents being issued for inventions do not meet the patentability criteria. In the United States, for example, very few patent claims reach the trial phase, and 'about 30–35% of patents brought to trial are found invalid or unenforceable'.[34]

The problem of patent backlog for developing countries like Thailand has become even more acute due to the weak institutional capacity in patent administration. It has become obvious that the DIP has struggled to cope with the increasing volume of patent applications. From 2005 to 2010, the Thai Patent Office received approximately 10,000 patent applications each year. The majority of the applications were related to designs. Only about 15 per cent were applications for a patent on invention. The time between filing and obtaining a patent grant in Thailand is, on average, from 3 to 5 years. This can be much longer for applications in complex fields. It is estimated that the period taken to obtain a patent for invention in areas such as physics and biotechnology generally takes 5–9 years. The delay in issuing a patent results from the DIP's lack of examiners in those fields of technology.[35]

It is estimated that each examiner of the DIP must process an average of 254 applications per year at an approximate rate of one application for every working day.[36] In practice, the DIP's patent examiners, due to limited resources and facilities, give great weight to patent grants for the same invention in other countries. Because of this practice, a claimed invention that has been granted a patent by a foreign patent office, particularly that of a developed country that is considered more capable of thoroughly examining applications, is almost guaranteed a patent right in Thailand.

Thailand has attempted to increase the quality of the patents it grants and reduce the administrative burden on the patent office by seeking international collaboration. The DIP has outsourced the searching and

---

[33] London Economics, 'Economic Study on Patent Backlogs and a System of Mutual Recognition', Report submitted to the UK Intellectual Property Office, London, Intellectual Property Office, 2010, http://www.ipo.gov.uk/p-backlog-report.pdf (accessed 23 July 2012); The Royal Society, *Keeping Science Open: The Effects of Intellectual Property Policy on the Conduct of Science*, London, The Royal Society, 2003.

[34] F.M. Abbott, 'Managing the Hydra: The Herculean Task of Ensuring Access to Essential Medicines', in Maskus, K.E. and Reichman J.H. (eds.), *International Public Goods and Transfer of Technology under a Globalized Intellectual Property Regime*, Cambridge, Cambridge University Press, 2005, p. 408.

[35] Kenan Institute Asia, *Comparative Assessment Study of Patent and Trademark Offices in Southeast Asia*, Bangkok, Kenan Institute Asia, 2012.

[36] Kenan Institute Asia, *Comparative Assessment Study of Patent and Trademark Offices in Southeast Asia*, Bangkok, Kenan Institute Asia, 2012.

examination of patents to foreign patent offices, such as the Australian Patent Office, with additional fees incurred by applicants. While the outsourcing option provides relatively low-cost, high-quality examination, it has created a language problem, as the patent law of Thailand requires all applications to be drafted in Thai.

Patent databases and patent documentation provide a wealth of information for local scientists. In reality, the patent specifications provided by the applicant are generally a translation of the patent application filed in a foreign country by the same applicant. The DIP's patent examiners have faced difficulties dealing with the large number of translated documents. A number of patent applications filed in Thailand are generally technically incomplete and poorly translated, which makes it difficult for the examiners to read and understand the technical descriptions of the applications.

It is interesting to note that a specialized profession of patent attorneys does not exist in Thailand. The law is silent about what types of qualifications the patent representative has to possess. Attorneys at law are, therefore, the only ones qualified to represent clients in the prosecution of patent applications. Such attorneys generally are law graduates and most of them do not have a technical degree. In addition, they are not technically trained to be Western-style 'patent agents' or 'patent attorneys' because, in Thailand, there is no graduate school for the professional training of patent lawyers.

4.6 Patents and Access to Medicines

Patents on a minor, incremental innovation can have a dramatic impact on access to medicines when they are used to block affordable generic products. Thailand's experience with trying to provide access to drugs to its poor population highlights the difficulties a country can face when life-saving and essential medicines are protected by patents. In November 2006 and January 2007, the Thai Ministry of Public Health issued government use licences against patents over three medicines: (1) efavirenz, Merck's anti-HIV drug (branded 'Stocrin'); (2) lopinavir/ritonavir (branded 'Kaletra'), an ARV distributed by Abbott Laboratories; and (3) clopidogrel ('Plavix'), an anti-clotting drug sold by Sanofi-Aventis and BMS. In fact, the patents for these drugs should not have been granted in the first place as some of these drugs do not meet the requirements for patentability. Lopinavir/ritonavir or 'Kaletra' is a mere combination of two existing products, which should not be considered patentable 'as it does not show a new and non-obvious synergistic effect'.[37] The patent on Clopidogrel or 'Plavix' is a

[37] C.M. Correa, 'Pharmaceutical Innovation, Incremental Patenting and

composition of matter patent, with claims over the hydrogen sulfate salt of clopidogrel or a polymorph. This form of invention would probably not be deemed a patentable invention because 'polymorphs are not invented but constitute an inherent property of chemical compounds'. In addition, the polymorph claim should not be considered as involving an inventive step as it is 'obvious for a pharmaceutical manufacturer to find the most suitable polymorph for any particular drug'.[38] As already mentioned, the Thai Patent Office does not conduct a proper substantial examination but relies on the examination results of a corresponding application in another major patent office. If the DIP could become a modern patent office and had the capability to properly test the novelty and inventive step requirements, there would be no need for the Thai government to grant a compulsory licence in order to improve access to medicines for its population.

4.7 Specialized IP Court

In Thailand, a special court for IP was set up by the Act for the Establishment of and Procedure for Intellectual Property and International Trade Court B.E. 2539 (1997). At the same time, the Office of the Attorney General also established a special division to deal with litigation involving IP. The aim was to have a special court equipped with specialized expertise to handle cases pertaining to IP and international trade matters.[39] A quorum of the Intellectual Property and International Trade Court (IP&IT Court) comprises two career judges and an associate judge who is an expert in the relevant field. The Court has its own procedural rules, which can be issued by the Chief of Justice of the IP&IT Court, with the approval of the President of the Supreme Court. An appeal against a judg-

---

Compulsory Licensing', South Centre, Research Paper, 41, 2011, p. 20, http://www.southcentre.org/index.php?option=com_content&view=article&id=1601%3Apharmaceutical-innovation-incremental-patenting-and-compulsory-licensing&catid=41%3Ainnovation-technology-and-patent-policy&Itemid=67&lang=en (accessed 31 January 2013).

[38] C.M. Correa, 'Pharmaceutical Innovation, Incremental Patenting and Compulsory Licensing', South Centre, Research Paper, 41, 2011, p. 20, http://www.southcentre.org/index.php?option=com_content&view=article&id=1601%3Apharmaceutical-innovation-incremental-patenting-and-compulsory-licensing&catid=41%3Ainnovation-technology-and-patent-policy&Itemid=67&lang=en (accessed 31 January 2013).

[39] V. Ariyanuntaka, 'TRIPs and the Specialised Intellectual Property Court in Thailand', *International Review of Intellectual Property and Competition Law*, vol. 30, no. 4, 1999, pp. 360–76; S.H. Legomsky, *Specialized Justice*, Oxford, Oxford University Press, 1990.

ment of the Court is filed directly to the Supreme Court. A new procedural law was also adopted providing practical guidance on the conduct of proceedings in the specialist court. The new rule authorizes a use of deposition and affidavit by a foreign witness in lieu of hearing a witness residing overseas. A hearing of evidence by means of video-conferencing is also allowed, in order to facilitate the conduct of the trial. According to the Rules for Intellectual Property and International Trade Cases B.E. 2540 (1998), various enforcement measures are available, including a preventive injunction (i.e. an injunction granted to prevent IP infringement prior to instituting an action) and an *Anton Piller* order (i.e. an order granted to preserve relevant evidence concerning the alleged infringement). The changes in procedural law are expected to provide for a speedy, efficient and fair trial.

The establishment of a specialist IP court in Thailand came in response to the lack of judicial expertise and experience in IP, which was viewed as a major problem in handling contentious IP matters. Despite this effort, the IP&IT Court still does not have an adequate number of judges with in-depth knowledge and expertise in IP. Since the IP&IT Court is a specialized court under the general administration of justice, its career judges are under the rotation system imposed by the Judicial Commission of Thailand. IP&IT Court judges generally move from the Court to another court every two to three years in order to gain promotion. A judge who has developed IP knowledge and has learnt all aspects of IP&IT Court practice is difficult to replace with someone of the same level of knowledge and experience. There is no doubt that, unless the institutional deficiencies and lack of IP resources and expertise are addressed, the establishment of specialist courts will be of little benefit.

4.8 IP and Technical Assistance

The significance of IP technical assistance for developing countries is crucial. Like many other developing countries, Thailand receives technical assistance on IP from foreign agencies. Technical assistance is provided with the aim of improving Thailand's capacity to handle IP-related matters. The Thai agencies that are the major recipients of technical assistance are the IP&IT Court and the DIP.[40]

---

[40] J. Kuanpoth, 'Intellectual Property-Related Technical Assistance, Collaboration, and Capacity Building: The Thailand Experience', Paper Presented at ICTSD Dialogue on Technical Collaboration for IP Policy in Developing Countries, Geneva: International Centre on Trade and Sustainable Development, 2005.

Each year, the IP&IT Court receives a variety of technical assistance that comes from different foreign agencies. The following are examples of assistance provided to the Court:

- The United Kingdom: The British Council offers several scholarships for studying in the United Kingdom. It also funds seminars and conferences, and sponsors the visit of foreign resource persons.
- The United States: The US Embassy organizes meetings between American IP law experts and lawyers, and judges from the IP&IT Court, through teleconferences. This allows both sides to share experience and clarify certain issues. Each year, USAID funds IP&IT Court judges to attend international symposia in the United States. It also sponsors judges from Vietnam to train and share experience at the IP&IT Court.
- France: The INPI Division of the French Embassy sponsors French resource persons to travel to Thailand to share skills, experiences and their IP activities with Thai judges.
- Australia: Australia on several occasions has provided support for organizing IP seminars.
- Germany: One scholarship per year is granted for Thai judges to undertake research at the Max Planck Institute in Munich. The scholarship is for a 2–3 month stay in Germany.
- Japan: Japanese granting agencies, such as JETRO, JICA, and JAI, provide various forms of technical assistance to the Court, including funding seminars, offering field trips to Japan, and sponsoring Thai judges to train in Japan for 2–3 weeks. The IP&IT Court has also entered into technical collaboration with Japan's Waseda University to develop a database containing court decisions.
- Through the ECAP Project (EC–ASEAN Intellectual Property Rights Collaboration Program), the EU provides support to the Court, including funding seminars, conferences, and events promoting IP, sponsoring field trips and social events for judges, and providing funds to develop an IP database.

Being an agency responsible for IP-related matters makes the DIP more attractive to foreign technical assistance. The DIP engages in technical collaboration with foreign agencies at three levels: multilateral, regional and bilateral. Multilateral collaboration mostly involves the World Intellectual Property Organization and the World Trade Organization. The DIP also enters into regional collaboration with APEC and ASEAN members. It has also attracted significant bilateral assistance from Japan, the EU, the United States, Australia, Korea, China and individual members of APEC. Foreign aid generally appears in the form of academic and educational collaboration on IP-related issues. It also takes the form of assistance in drafting and amending IP laws, improving the operation of existing legislation, training personnel involved in handling IP applications, etc.

To date, the majority of technical collaboration provided to Thailand is related to the protection and enforcement of IP rights. Support provided to the DIP is mainly focused on IP enforcement with an emphasis on training police, judges, and officers in agencies responsible for enforcement. Some donor agencies see the benefits of assisting the DIP, as they expect that in return Thailand will have better enforcement. Some collaboration is also concentrated on amending existing and drafting new legislation to offer a higher level of protection. The influx of massive amounts of foreign technical assistance in IP may not be in the interests of a recipient country like Thailand since they have made significant improvements in their level of IP protection over the last two decades. What these countries urgently need is the knowledge and expertise necessary for the management and commercialization of IP, rather than enforcement. They also require support to raise awareness of the social, economic and development impact of IP and to identify the social and business impact of advanced technologies such as biotechnology, nanotechnology and information and communication technology.

5 CONCLUSION

The foregoing outlines the attempt by ASEAN to harmonize IP regulations in order to facilitate a single market. ASEAN members can be characterized by striking asymmetries in IP policies, different levels of legal, social and economic environments and administrative capacity. The chapter reflects that Thailand, an ASEAN member, is still struggling to improve its capacity to implement IP laws. While a middle-income country like Thailand is unable to develop an efficient IP system, there can be no doubt that less-developed ASEAN members will find it more difficult to operate IP regimes efficiently and at low cost.

While programmes initiated by ASEAN like ASPEC and the IP Portal should help to address the major problem of disparate capacities among member countries' IP offices, the ASEAN nations still require support in human resources development, capacity building, and policy and institutional improvements. Foreign donors should assist developing countries to promote the legal, commercial and economic exploitation of IP rights, and help young companies and emerging industries in the recipient country to commercialize their work or to find markets for their innovative products. Assistance is also needed in the restructuring and reorganization of national agencies, such as the national IP office, to facilitate the better management of IP, to improve the efficiency of the office, and to review the process for granting and repealing IP rights.

The members of ASEAN need to set up national IP strategies that identify each country's areas of strength and weakness. Remedies should be found for weak areas. The areas of strength should be further enhanced with a view to attaining a successful and efficient functioning of the IP system. They also need to promote a common, systematic approach to capacity development for the judiciary and legislative authorities, enabling them to keep abreast of worldwide developments in IP. In addition, the ASEAN countries need to address strategic and policy areas of IP, particularly the critical issues that matter to their interests, including access to medicines, access to knowledge, as well as the protection of traditional knowledge, GI, plant varieties and genetic resources.

REFERENCES

Abbott, F.M., 'Managing the Hydra: The Herculean Task of Ensuring Access to Essential Medicines', in Maskus, K.E. and Reichman J.H. (eds.), *International Public Goods and Transfer of Technology under a Globalized Intellectual Property Regime*, Cambridge, Cambridge University Press, 2005, pp. 393–424.

Adcock, A. and Gautier, C., 'ASEAN: The Impact of Free Trade on IP', *Managing Intellectual Property*, 1 November 2010, http://www.managingip.com/Article/2710652/ASEAN-The-impact-of-free-trade-on-IP.html (accessed 13 July 2012).

Ariyanuntaka, V., 'TRIPs and the Specialised Intellectual Property Court in Thailand', *International Review of Intellectual Property and Competition Law*, vol. 30, no. 4, 1999, pp. 360–76.

ASEAN Secretariat, 'ASEAN Economic Community Handbook for Business', ASEAN Secretariat, Jakarta, 2011, http://www.scribd.com/doc/97536042/29/ASEAN-Collaboration-in-Intellectual-Property-Rights (accessed 13 July 2012).

ASEAN Secretariat, 'ASEAN Intellectual Property Right Action Plan 2004–2010', ASEAN Secretariat, Jakarta, http://www.asean.org/news/item/asean-intellectual-property-right-action-plan-2004–2010 (accessed 13 July 2012).

Asian Info, *Thailand's Economy*, Bangkok, http://www.asianinfo.org/asianinfo/thailand/pro-economy.htm (accessed 17 July 2012).

Australian Government Department of Foreign Affairs and Trade, 'Agreement Establishing the ASEAN-Australia-New Zealand Free Trade Area', 2009, http://www.dfat.gov.au/fta/aanzfta/aanzfta.PDF (accessed 15 March 2013).

Correa, C.M., 'Pharmaceutical Innovation, Incremental Patenting and Compulsory Licensing', South Centre, Research Paper, 41, 2011, http://www.southcentre.org/index.php?option=com_content&view=article&id=1601%3Apharmaceutical-innovation-incremental-patenting-and-compulsory-licen

sing&catid=41%3Ainnovation-technology-and-patent-policy&Itemid=67&lang=en (accessed 31 January 2013).
Department of Intellectual Property, *Annual Report*, Department of Intellectual Property, Bangkok, 2011.
Drahos, P., *The Global Governance of Knowledge: Patent Offices and their Clients*, Cambridge, Cambridge University Press, 2010.
Gopalakrishnan, N.S., Nair, P.S., and Babu, A.K., 'Exploring the Relationship between Geographical Indications and Traditional Knowledge: An Analysis of the Legal Tools for the Protection of Geographical Indications in Asia', ICTSD Working Paper, Geneva, 2007, http://www.iprsonline.org/ictsd/docs/Gopaletal%20-%20GIs&TK.pdf (accessed 15 March 2013).
Government of Thailand, 'The Plant Varieties Protection Act B.E. 2542 (1999)', 1999, http://www.wipo.int/wipolex/en/text.jsp?file_id=129781 (accessed 15 March 2013).
Heydon, K. and Woolcock, S., *The Rise of Bilateralism: Comparing American, European and Asian Approaches to Preferential Trade Agreements*, Tokyo, United Nations University Press, 2009.
Kenan Institute Asia, *Comparative Assessment Study of Patent and Trademark Offices in Southeast Asia*, Bangkok, Kenan Institute Asia, 2012.
Kuanpoth, J., 'Intellectual Property in ASEAN–Australia–New Zealand FTA', Tilleke and Gibbins Informed Counsel Bangkok, http://www.tilleke.com/resources/intellectual-property-asean%E2%80%93australia%E2%80%93new-zealand-fta (accessed 20 July 2012).
Kuanpoth, J., 'Thailand', in Heath, C. (ed.), *Intellectual Property Law in Asia*, The Hague, Kluwer Law, 2002, pp. 337–62.
Kuanpoth, J., 'Intellectual Property-Related Technical Assistance, Collaboration, and Capacity Building: The Thailand Experience', Paper Presented at ICTSD Dialogue on Technical Collaboration for IP Policy in Developing Countries, Geneva: International Centre on Trade and Sustainable Development, 2005.
Kuanpoth, J. and Robinson, D., 'Geographical Indications Protection: The Case of Thailand and Jasmine Rice', *Intellectual Property Quarterly*, vol. 3, 2009, pp. 288–310.
Legomsky, S.H., *Specialized Justice*, Oxford, Oxford University Press, 1990.
London Economics, 'Economic Study on Patent Backlogs and a System of Mutual Recognition', Report submitted to the UK Intellectual Property Office, London, Intellectual Property Office, 2010, http://www.ipo.gov.uk/p-backlog-report.pdf (accessed 23 July 2012).
Mondaq Business Briefing, 'Intellectual Property in ASEAN-Australia-New Zealand FTA (AANFTA)', HighBeam Research, 29 February 2012, http://www.highbeam.com/doc/1G1-281702305.html (accessed 20 July 2012).
National Economic and Social Development Board, *Annual Report*, Bangkok, National Economic and Social Development Board, 1991.
Office of the National Research Council of Thailand, *Annual Report*, Bangkok, 2010.
Parliament of Malaysia, 'Protection of New Plant Varieties Act 2004 (Act 634)', 2004, http://www.wipo.int/wipolex/en/text.jsp?file_id=128880#P87_3293 (accessed 15 March 2013).
Republic of Indonesia, 'Laws of Republic of Indonesia, No. 29 of 2000 on Plant Variety Protection', 2000, http://www.wipo.int/wipolex/en/text.jsp?file_id=226832 (accessed 15 March 2013).

Rocco, D. and Caruso, A., 'Prosperity in Co-operation: The ASEAN-Australia-New Zealand Free Trade Agreement (AANZFTA)', *Journal of World Investment and Trade*, vol. 11, no. 2, 2010, pp. 197–226.

The Royal Society, Keeping Science Open: The Effects of Intellectual Property Policy on the Conduct of Science, London, The Royal Society, 2003.

The World Bank, *Data: Researchers in R&D (per million people)*, http://data.worldbank.org/indicator/SP.POP.SCIE.RD.P6 (accessed 19 July 2012).

United Nations Educational Scientific and Cultural Organization, UNESCO Institute for Statistics, www.uis.unesco.org (accessed 20 July 2012).

WIPO, 'PCT Applicant's Guide – International Phase', WIPO, Geneva, 2012, http://www.wipo.int/pct/en/guide/ipindex.html#TopOfPage (accessed 22 July 2012).

World Trade Organization, 'Agreement on Trade-related Aspects of Intellectual Property Rights [TRIPS]', 1994, http://www.wto.org/english/docs_e/legal_e/27-trips.pdf (accessed 15 March 2013).

PART V

The Middle East

15. IP policy and regulation in the Arab world: Changes, challenges and opportunities

Mohammed El Said

The Arab world is witnessing a wave of change unrivalled in modern times. Although the region has been subject to a variety of calamities during the past century, one unique feature about this current wave of change lies in its origins; a movement largely arising from within rather than due to foreign factors. To those acquainted with the politics of the region, it is clear that, although the 'Arab Spring' officially commenced with the Tunisian 'Jasmine Revolution' in the early days of 2010, the roots and origins of such a revolution pre-date that particular event by many decades.[1] Such change may be attributed to many factors including poverty, rising unemployment, youth neglect, lack of institutions and ever-growing corruption at the state level in many countries of the region. Although Arabs are yet to reap the fruits of the 'Spring', many hope that the movement initiated in the wake of such developments will in the long run trigger a modern day Arab 'renaissance' movement, a movement for which many Arabs have been longing for many centuries.

The same applies to the development of patent and other intellectual property laws in the Arab world. Originally imposed by colonial powers, these laws were developed under their mandate, and continued their evolution and development in the post-independence era in line with the interests of the key technology producers from the Western world.[2] Such a process intensified following the creation of the World Trade Organization (WTO) in 1995. This chapter will provide an overview of the levels of patent laws in the region, and will shed light on some of the

[1] Since then, Tunisia, Egypt, Libya and Yemen have witnessed regime change.

[2] R.L. Okediji, 'The International Relations of Intellectual Property: Narratives of Developing Country Participation in the Global Intellectual Property System', *Singapore Journal of International & Comparative Law*, 7, 2003, pp. 315–85.

challenges facing the region in this area. It will conclude with an overview of the options and opportunities available to countries of the region.

1 PATENT PROTECTION IN THE ARAB WORLD

Modern day patent protection in the Arab world dates back to the beginning of the nineteenth century when these countries were under the colonial rule of the British and French powers. For instance, the protection of patents in Morocco was governed by the first modern industrial property law in the country which was promulgated on 23 June 1916 by the French Protectorate, and subsequently by the specific law for the International Zone of Tangier which was promulgated in 1938. A similar situation may be found in Lebanon whereby patent protection was introduced in the country for the first time when the French authorities – under whose protectorate Lebanon was placed at the time – issued the Law Governing Commercial and Industrial Property by Resolution No. 2385/LR of 17 January 1924. In Jordan, and following the collapse of the Ottoman Empire and after Jordan had been placed under the British Mandate, new laws related to the protection of industrial property were introduced. According to this, patents and industrial design protection were subjected to Ottoman laws until 1924 when the Palestinian Patent Law was inaugurated by the British Mandate, which was also applied in Jordan. A similar pattern can also be found in other Arab states.

Little has changed since then. The conclusion of the Uruguay Round of trade negotiations in 1994 and the subsequent birth of the WTO and its Agreement on Trade-Related Aspects of Intellectual Property Rights (the TRIPS Agreement) prompted a large number of Arab countries to reform and upgrade their intellectual property and patent laws in accordance with the standards prescribed under the TRIPS Agreement. This resulted in a reduction in the considerable policy space which some of these countries enjoyed prior to joining the WTO. Efforts directed towards raising the levels of intellectual property protection (including patent protection) intensified during the early 2000s as a result of unilateral measures or through the signing by a number of Arab states of several bilateral free trade and/or association agreements with both the United States (US) and the European Union (EU). Such agreements resulted in a further reduction of policy space and the emergence of so-called TRIPS-plus protection regimes which contained provisions exceeding those standards prescribed under the TRIPS Agreement.[3]

---

[3] M. El Said, 'The Road From TRIPS-minus to TRIPS to TRIPS-plus:

Table 15.1 Arab countries according to their ties to trade agreements and intellectual property

Arab Non-Members in the WTO	Arab Members in the WTO	Arab signatories to a bilateral free trade agreement with the USA
Algeria	Jordan	Jordan
Iraq	UAE	Bahrain
Sudan	Bahrain	Morocco
Yemen	Djibouti	Oman
Lebanon	Kuwait	
Occupied Palestinian Territories	Morocco	
	Saudi Arabia	
Syria	Tunisia	
	Egypt	
	Mauritania	
	Qatar	
	Oman	

The Arab world is home to 22 economically diversified states.[4] By contrast, the region is home to some of the richest countries in the world in terms of per capita annual income rates, while at the same time being host to some of the poorest countries in the world.[5] Disparities in relation to development stage, education, unemployment and literacy levels are evident throughout the region.

This disparity is also evident when it comes to the regulation of intellectual property. More specifically, intellectual property and patent protection regimes in the region may be divided into three groups according to their stage of development and compliance with international norms (see Table 15.1 above).

The first group includes those states which are yet to accede to the

Implications of IPRs for the Arab World', *Journal of World Intellectual Property*, 8, 1, 2005, pp. 53–66.

[4] Algeria, Bahrain, Comoros, Djibouti, Egypt, Iraq, Jordan, Kuwait, Lebanon, Libya, Mauritania, Morocco, Qatar, Oman, Saudi Arabia, Somalia, Sudan, Syria, Tunisia, United Arab Emirates, Yemen, Palestinian Occupied Territories.

[5] For more on economic indicators for the region see UNDP, *Human Development Report 2011: Sustainability and Equity, A Better Future for All*, New York, UNDP, 2011, http://hdr.undp.org/en/media/HDR_2011_EN_Complete.pdf (accessed 15 March 2013); UNDP, *Arab Development Challenges Report 2011: Towards the Developmental State*, Cairo, UNDP, 2011.

WTO. The common feature of the patent protection regimes of the countries in this group lies in the wide policy space available to each country, particularly since the majority of these countries are officially classified as least-developed countries (LDCs).[6] The patent protection regime of this group of countries may be described as TRIPS-minus.

The second group of countries includes those which have already joined the WTO. As a result of this accession, these member states underwent a major reform of their patent protection regimes in order to bring them into conformity with the standards of the TRIPS Agreement. Accordingly, the patent protection regimes of these countries may be described as TRIPS-compliant.

The third group of countries includes those countries that incorporate extensive intellectual property and patent protection regimes which go beyond those levels prescribed under the TRIPS Agreement. Those TRIPS-plus regimes, as referred to by Drahos,[7] adopt high levels of intellectual property and patent protection as a result of acceding to a number of bilateral and plurilateral trade and intellectual property agreements. Examples of these include the US–Jordan and US–Bahrain FTAs in addition to Morocco's membership in the controversial Anti-Counterfeiting Trade Agreement (ACTA).

However, the above classification may not be so clear, and might even be misleading in certain cases. The case of Lebanon demonstrates this. Although the country is not a WTO member, the country's patent protection regime contains a number of provisions which are of a TRIPS-plus nature. For example, the EU–Lebanon Association Agreement stipulates that data exclusivity must be provided for a period of at least six years from the date of approval.[8] The country was also obligated to join several World Intellectual Property Organization (WIPO) treaties which fall

---

[6] Such as Yemen, Sudan and Somalia.

[7] P. Drahos, 'BITS and BIPS: Bilateralism in Intellectual Property', *Journal of World Intellectual Property*, 4, 2001, pp. 791–808.

[8] The EU–Lebanon AA, Annex V, Article 4, states:

> The Parties to this Agreement shall protect undisclosed information in accordance with Article 39 [of] TRIPS. The Parties shall prevent applicants for marketing approval for pharmaceuticals and agricultural chemical products from relying on or referring to undisclosed test or other undisclosed data submitted by prior applicants to the competent approval authorities of the respective Parties for a period, from the date of approval, of at *least six years*, except where approval is sought for original products, or unless the first applicant is adequately compensated [emphasis added].

See The European Free Trade Association, *Annex V Intellectual Property*,

outside the scope of the TRIPS Agreement. As the case of Lebanon shows, the demarcation line between these three groups of countries may not be so clear.

Regardless of the above classification, all countries in the region have experienced rising levels of patent protection over the past decade. The following section discusses some shared challenges impacting the patent protection regime in the Arab world.

2 THE MAIN CHALLENGES FACING THE ARAB WORLD IN THE AREA OF PATENT POLICY

The current legal framework of patent protection in the Arab world could be best described as problematic. It is evident that the current regime has failed to achieve its objective of triggering innovation and fostering creativity within the region. This is evidenced by its poor performance in terms of the various general indicators related to innovation, productivity and creativity. One only needs to have a look at the 2012 Global Innovation Index Ranking to realize the massive gap which separates the majority of countries in the region from the rest of the world.[9]

Not only has the current patent regime failed to achieve its objectives, it has become a burden on these countries in some areas. For instance, it has been observed that strengthened patent protection in the field of pharmaceuticals has resulted in increasing drug prices, thus limiting their availability in a number of countries in the region.[10] In this regard, a 2012 study by Abbott found that 'Delayed market entry of generics due to enhanced intellectual property protection is estimated to have cost Jordanian private consumers approximately 18 million U.S. dollars in 2004'.[11]

---

http://www.efta.int/free-trade/free-trade-agreements/lebanon/~/media/87E615BD9EDD4DD1B59A294E3AFB0333.pdf (accessed 15 March 2013).

[9] INSEAD and WIPO, *The Global Innovation Index 2012: Stronger Innovation Linkages for Global Growth*, Geneva, INSEAD and WIPO, 2012.

[10] See for instance on the case of Jordan in Oxfam International, *All Costs, No Benefits: How TRIPS-plus Intellectual Property Rights in the US–Jordan FTA Affect Access to Medicines*, Oxford, Oxfam, Briefing Note, March 2007. For more on the case of Morocco see G. Krikorian, 'Intellectual Property and Access to Medicines: Paradoxes in Moroccan Policy', in Shadlen, K. et al. (eds.), *Intellectual Property, Pharmaceuticals and Public Health Access to Drugs in Developing Countries*, Cheltenham, UK and Northampton, MA, USA, Edward Elgar, 2011, pp. 56–76.

[11] See R. Abbott et al., 'The Price of Medicines in Jordan: The Cost of Trade-Based Intellectual Property', *Journal of Generic Medicines*, 9, 2, 2012, pp. 75–85.

In this context, the question is what are the common characteristics and challenges facing the current patent protection regime in the region that make such a regime ineffective and burdensome? The following is a summary of some of these factors.

3 FIRST: UTILIZATION AND USE OF THE PATENT'S REGIME FLEXIBILITIES

One of the biggest challenges facing the Arab countries today is the integration and utilization of the flexibilities of the patent regime in line with their development plans and priorities. This, however, has a twofold dimension, one related to the incorporation of these flexibilities under the national legal regime, while the second relates to the actual use and implementation of these flexibilities in practice.

The patent regime includes a number of flexibilities which if properly utilized could mitigate its monopolistic impact. Examples of these include compulsory licensing, government use, discretion in defining the patentability criteria, pre- and post-grant opposition systems, parallel importation, in addition to various exemptions and exclusions from the scope of patentability. In order for these flexibilities to be fully operational, they should be incorporated into the national patent regime in a clear and explicit manner. To date, a large number of Arab states have failed to fully incorporate such flexibilities into their national patent regime. One example is Morocco's adoption of a national exhaustion regime, thus limiting the country's ability to utilize parallel importation from other countries.[12] In addition, the majority of Arab countries' patent regimes do not exclude second use from their patentability criteria, or fail to define such criteria strictly in accordance with their development plans and priorities.

On the other hand, the incorporation of these flexibilities alone under national law would have little impact if there was no will nor public awareness to put them into practise. Again the case of the Arab world unveils the lack of such will in utilizing these flexibilities. For instance, while a growing number of Asian, African and Latin American countries have resorted in recent years to issuing compulsory and government

---

[12] See G. Krikorian, 'Intellectual Property and Access to Medicines: Paradoxes in Moroccan Policy', in Shadlen, K. et al. (eds.), *Intellectual Property, Pharmaceuticals and Public Health Access to Drugs in Developing Countries*, Cheltenham, UK and Northampton, MA, USA, Edward Elgar, 2011, pp. 56–76.

use licenses to cater for the public health needs of their nationals, no Arab country has for the time being issued, or even attempted to issue, a compulsory license or government use.[13] Moreover, the majority of these countries do not have in place clear procedures or user friendly guidelines related to the issuance of compulsory and government use licenses.[14]

Even in those countries where the patent regime allows for parallel importation, little effort has been made thus far to facilitate the importation of cheaper medicines and goods into such countries. The same may be said in relation to pre- and post-grant opposition procedures where little use has been made of such flexibility by third parties. Furthermore, Egypt's 2002 Patent Law novel concept calling for the establishment of a Drug Stability Fund dedicated to health and development and supporting the stability of medicine, other than those prepared for export under an independent corporate personality in the country, is yet to come into force more than a decade from its inception under the national patent protection regime.[15]

---

[13] In accordance with this, the need to issue compulsory licenses in the Arab world stems from two main factors, high prices of medicines and health concerns. According to WHO, 'Egypt has a very high prevalence of hepatitis C virus (HCV) and a high morbidity and mortality from chronic liver disease, cirrhosis, and hepatocellular carcinoma. Approximately 20% of Egyptian blood donors are anti-HCV positive. Egypt has higher rates of HCV than neighbouring countries as well as other countries in the world with comparable socioeconomic conditions and hygienic standards for invasive medical, dental, or paramedical procedures. The strong homogeneity of HCV subtypes found in Egypt (mostly 4a) suggests an epidemic spread of HCV.' See World Health Organization, *Global Alert and Response (GAR), 2003*, http://www.who.int/csr/disease/hepatitis/whocdscsrlyo2003/en/index4.html (accessed 15 March 2013).

[14] M. El Said, *Public Health Related TRIPS-plus Provisions in Bilateral Trade Agreements: A Policy Guide for Negotiations and Implementers in the Eastern Mediterranean Region*, Cairo, WHO and ICTSD, 2012, at http://applications.emro.who.int/dsaf/dsa1081.pdf (accessed 15 March 2013).

[15] See WIPO, *Law on the Protection of Intellectual Property Rights*, Law No. 82, 2002, Article 18, http://www.wipo.int/wipolex/en/details.jsp?id=1301 (accessed 15 March 2013). The Article states that such a fund shall be governed by the Minister of Health and Population, for the purpose of achieving development in health and ensuring that medicine prices shall not be affected by variable conditions. The 2002 IPRs Law further provides that the President of the Republic shall issue a decision regulating the fund and specifying its resources. Such resources shall include contributions, which are approved by the State, from the Granting States and international governmental and non-governmental organization.

4 SECOND: THE RISE OF TRIPS-PLUS PROVISIONS AND AGREEMENTS

During the past decade, a large number of Arab countries acceded to a number of plurilateral and bilateral trade agreements containing various intellectual property standards that go beyond those stipulated under the TRIPS Agreement (TRIPS-plus Agreements). In the case of the Arab world, such agreements took different shapes, including bilateral Association Agreements (AA), Free Trade Agreements (FTAs) and Bilateral Investment Agreements (BITs).[16] Other countries such as Qatar and Morocco opted unilaterally to incorporate TRIPS-plus legislations and provisions under their national law.

The negative impact of these standards cannot be underestimated in the area of patent law. They often prolong the monopoly term granted to patents, restrict the grounds for the granting of compulsory licenses, limit parallel importation, restrict and prohibit opposition procedures, demand additional enforcement obligations, introduce data exclusivity protection, and reduce the country's ability to utilize other flexibilities available to it under the international protection regime. The end result is to diminish the country's ability to design its patent policy in accordance with its stage of development and citizens' needs.

Many examples may be provided in this area from the region. The US–Morocco FTA, for instance, under Article 15.9.4 obligates Morocco to adopt a national exhaustion regime, hence prohibiting parallel imports of patented products into the country. Article 15.9.4 of the US–Morocco FTA states that:

> Each Party shall provide that the exclusive right of the patent owner to prevent importation of a patented product, or a product that results from patented process, without the consent of the patent owner shall not be limited by the sale or distribution of that product outside its territory.[17]

On the other hand, some agreements prolong the patent term beyond 20 years. For instance, the US–Oman FTA, Article 15.8.7, provides:

---

[16] M. El Said, *The Development of Intellectual Property Protection in the Arab World*, Lewiston, ME, Edwin Mellen Press, 2008.

[17] 'A Party may limit application of this paragraph to cases where the patent owner has placed restrictions on import by contract or other means.' Office of the United States Trade Representative, *United States–Morocco Free Trade Agreement*, Article 15.9.4 footnote 9, 2004, http://www.ustr.gov/trade-agreements/free-trade-agreements/morocco-fta/final-text (accessed 15 March 2013).

> When a Party provides for the grant of a patent on the basis of a patent granted in another territory, that Party, at the request of the patent owner, shall adjust the term of a patent granted under such a procedure by a period equal to the period of the adjustment, if any, provided in respect of the patent granted in the other territory.[18]

The US–Jordan FTA includes some restrictions in relation to compulsory licensing. It limits the grounds upon which a compulsory license can be issued beyond those grounds specified under Article 31 of the TRIPS Agreement. It only permits compulsory licenses to: remedy anti-competitive practices, for public non-commercial use, for a 'national emergency', or in case of 'extreme urgency'. Furthermore, compulsory licenses can only be granted to government entities or legal entities operating under the government. These limitations, which are not required under the TRIPS Agreement, could undermine the government's ability to negotiate cheaper patented drugs or to promote competition by generic products that could reduce prices and increase the availability of medicines in the country.

Another example is related to data exclusivity. Data exclusivity provisions refer to a regime whereby, for a fixed period of time, national drug regulatory authorities prevent and block the registration files of an originator from being used to register a therapeutically equivalent generic version of that medicine unless the originator consents to that use. The generic manufacturer has to wait for data exclusivity to expire or bear the cost of re-conducting the clinical trials. For example, the United States FTA with Morocco stipulates that:

> If a Party requires, as a condition of approving the marketing of a new pharmaceutical and agricultural chemical product, a) the submission of safety and efficacy data, or b) evidence of prior approval of the product in another territory that requires such information, the Party shall not permit third parties not having the consent of the person providing the information to market a product on the basis of the approval granted to the person submitting such information for at *least five years for pharmaceutical products and ten years* for agricultural chemical products from the date of approval in the Party. For purposes of this paragraph, a new product is one that contains a new chemical entity that has not been previously approved in the Party [emphasis added].[19]

---

[18] Office of the United States Trade Representative, *United States–Oman Free Trade Agreement*, 2009 http://www.ustr.gov/trade-agreements/free-trade-agreements/oman-fta/final-text (accessed 15 March 2013).

[19] Office of the United States Trade Representative, *United States–Morocco Free Trade Agreement*, 2004, http://www.ustr.gov/trade-agreements/free-trade-agreements/morocco-fta/final-text (accessed 15 March 2013).

In addition to bilateral TRIPS-plus agreements, some countries have also joined a number of multilateral and plurilateral agreements which also include TRIPS-plus provisions. Morocco's signing of the controversial Anti-Counterfeiting Trade Agreement (ACTA) and other Arab countries' accession to some of WIPO's patent treaties are examples.

On the other hand, a number of Arab states unilaterally enacted some TRIPS-plus laws. One example is Qatar's 2011 Law on Intellectual Property Rights Border Measures. The new law prohibits the entrance of any products that infringe *any intellectual property rights* protected under the law in the country. Furthermore, the new law obliges the General Administration of Customs to take all measures required to prevent the entrance of infringing products into the country, when it has *prima facie* evidence that these products are in fact infringing the rights.[20] In addition, the law provides for significant penalties for entering any products infringing intellectual property rights; the criminal penalties are imprisonment not exceeding one year and/or fines not exceeding 10,000 Qatari Riyal (equivalent to USD 2750). This is in addition to the confiscation of the infringing products. Importantly, the law contains some TRIPS-plus provisions which may have a negative impact on public health and access to medicines. One of these is related to the scope of coverage of intellectual property rights under the law. According to Article 2, the entrance of any products that infringe *any intellectual property rights* protected under the law in Qatar shall be prohibited. Such coverage will extend to patents. Under the TRIPS Agreement, mandatory border measures undertaken by customs departments are confined to trademark counterfeiting and copyright piracy. In this regard, Article 51 of the TRIPS Agreement[21] states:

> Members shall, in conformity with the provisions set out below, adopt procedures[22] to enable a right holder, who has valid grounds for suspecting that the importation of *counterfeit trademark* or pirated *copyright goods*[23] may take

---

[20] The 2011 IP Border Measures Law, Article 2.

[21] World Trade Organization, 'Agreement on Trade-related Aspects of Intellectual Property Rights [TRIPS]', 1994, http://www.wto.org/english/docs_e/legal_e/27-trips.pdf (accessed 15 March 2013).

[22] Footnote 13 of this Article states that 'It is understood that there shall be no obligation to apply such procedures to imports of goods put on the market in another country by or with the consent of the right holder, or to goods in transit.

[23] Footnote 14 of this Article states that for the purposes of this Agreement:

> (a) 'counterfeit trademark goods' shall mean any goods, including packaging, bearing without authorization a trademark which is identical to the trademark validly registered in respect of such goods, or which cannot be distinguished in its essential aspects from such a trademark, and which thereby infringes the

> place, to lodge an application in writing with competent authorities, administrative or judicial, for the suspension by the customs authorities of the release into free circulation of such goods. Members may enable such an application to be made in respect of goods which involve other infringements of intellectual property rights, provided that the requirements of this Section are met. Members may also provide for corresponding procedures concerning the suspension by the customs authorities of the release of infringing goods destined for exportation from their territories [emphasis added].

As widely discussed elsewhere, TRIPS-plus border measures may have a negative impact on the free flow of generic medicines and may also create barriers to legitimate trade in medicines in the country.[24]

The implications of such TRIPS-plus agreements and provisions are grave and long lasting. The reduction of the policy space available to Arab countries will likely have a negative impact on the much-needed development plans of these countries, particularly in the areas of education, public health, knowledge creation and dissemination, in addition to technology transfer.

5 THIRD: LACK OF COORDINATION, AND FRAGMENTATION OF POLICY-MAKING

One common feature in the region is the evident lack of coordination between the various national departments and stakeholders operating in the area of intellectual property in general and patent policy and regulation more specifically. This is also reflective of the lack of a unified national development and/or innovation agendas for utilizing the patent regime to meet the priorities of each country and to facilitate transfer of technology and creation of knowledge. Examples of such fragmentation may be found in the cases of Egypt, Morocco and Jordan.

In the case of Egypt – one of the most influential Arab states on the regional and international scene with considerable intellectual property expertise and global participation – the fragmentation is clear. Egypt was

---

rights of the owner of the trademark in question under the law of the country of importation;

(b) 'pirated copyright goods' shall mean any goods which are copies made without the consent of the right holder or person duly authorized by the right holder in the country of production and which are made directly or indirectly from an article where the making of that copy would have constituted an infringement of a copyright or a related right under the law of the country of importation.

24 For more see M. El-Said and A. Kapczynski, *Access to Medicines: The Role of Intellectual Property Law and Policy*, New York, The Global Commission on HIV and the Law, UNDP, July 2012.

one of the few countries in the region where studies on the impact of the TRIPS Agreement were undertaken back in the 1990s. For instance, a 1996 UNDP study found that Egypt would need USD 98,000 to increase patent personnel and add equipment, USD 192,000 to strengthen the judicial framework, and USD 1,000,000 to train and develop custom authorities. The study also stated that these figures did not include the costs needed to seek and obtain technical assistance for the development of human resources in the country.[25] One member of Egypt's People's Assembly stated at the time that:[26]

> TRIPS' impact is catastrophic and [will cause] a crazy rise in prices of medicines especially that 83 per cent of medicine raw material is imported from abroad. Therefore, I demanded that the 200 medicines that have not be registered so far to be registered.

Although the debate about Egypt's accession to the TRIPS Agreement was undertaken in the Egyptian Parliament (with the involvement of the Ministry of Health and Population), there is little evidence to suggest that there was a systematic way of involving all the stakeholders concerned. The same applies to other negotiations regarding intellectual property obligations. To the contrary, when the debate ensued in the Egyptian Parliament as to whether the country should utilize the transition periods awarded to it as a result of its developing country status under the TRIPS Agreement, the Ministry of Health Population (surprisingly) and the Patent Office supported the position advocated by multinational pharmaceutical companies favoring the application of the TRIPS Agreement in Egypt with immediate effect. This was probably based on the belief that such an approach would attract foreign direct investment and ensure the country's international recognition for its intellectual property laws and regulations. In countering such a position, the local pharmaceutical industry feared foreign competition and the likely loss of its market share. In the end the latter position prevailed and the 2002 Law utilized the transition period available to the country until January 2005.[27]

Even today, there seems to be little coordination between the various

---

[25] UNCTAD, *The TRIPS Agreement and Developing Countries*, Geneva, United Nations Conference on Trade and Development, 1996, pp. 23–4.

[26] M.K. Quoita (Member of the People's Assembly), telephone interview with the EIPR, 20 October, in EIPR, *The TRIPS Agreement and Egypt's Responsibility to Protect the Right to Health*, Cairo, Right to Health Program Egyptian Initiative for Personal Rights, January 2005. The translation is as it appears in the original source.

[27] N. Al-Ali, 'The Egyptian Pharmaceutical Industry After TRIPS – A Practitioner's View', *Fordham International Law Journal*, 26, 2, 2002, pp. 295–6.

public authorities operating in this area in the country.[28] As Abdel Latif explains:[29]

> The fragmentation of national policymaking is particularly apparent in the area of IP, which comes under the jurisdiction of a myriad of government departments and agencies. In this regard, Law 82 of 2002 defines the responsibilities of different government departments in the area of IP. These include the Ministries of Trade and Industry for TRIPS and trademarks, Higher Education and Scientific Research for patents, Culture for copyright and Information and Communication Technology (ICT) for computer software. The Ministry of Justice has also been a central player in the drafting of IP legislation, and the Ministry of Foreign Affairs in international negotiations in WIPO in particular. This fragmentation is not specific to Egypt and is present in many countries including developed and developing countries.

The case of Morocco illustrates a similar pattern. In fact, several conflicting polices have been adopted in the country since the early 2000s, on the one hand, promoting public health and access to medicines, while raising the levels of intellectual property beyond those of the TRIPS Agreement, on the other. More specifically, the country implemented a number of initiatives aimed at preserving public health and access to medicines, while at the same time signing a number of TRIPS-plus agreements, including an FTA with the United States, and joining the highly controversial ACTA, leading some to go so far as to describe such an approach as 'paradoxical'.[30]

---

[28] As Salah explains, 'There is little coordination amongst government agencies at the policy making and strategic planning level, instead they compete with each other for government financial allocations. Moreover, the Ministry of Population and Health (MOHP), theoretically the national health policy maker has little control over national planning, manpower policy, and budgetary discretion. MOHP spending at the governorate level is not correlated with the infant mortality rates. In other words, the governorates with the higher infant mortality rates are not necessarily receiving higher per capita resources from the MOHP'. For more see H. Salah, 'Mapping of Healthcare Financing in Eastern Mediterranean Region', Arab Republic of Egypt, World Health Organization, 2007, p. 11.

[29] See A.A Latif, 'Egypt's Role in the A2K Movement: An Analysis of Positions and Policies', in Rizk, N. and Shaver, L. (eds.), *Access to Knowledge in Egypt: New Research on Intellectual Property, Innovation and Development*, London, Bloomsbury Academic, 2010, p. 48. For more on the case and other cases see B. Hossam and Rebecca Wright, 'Access to Medicines in Egypt: A Human Rights Approach to IP, Trade and Health', in Rizk, N. and Shaver, L. (eds.), *Access to Knowledge in Egypt: New Research on Intellectual Property, Innovation and Development*, London, Bloomsbury Academic, 2010, pp. 56–91.

[30] G. Krikorian, 'Intellectual Property and Access to Medicines: Paradoxes in Moroccan Policy', in Shadlen, K. et al. (eds.), *Intellectual Property, Pharmaceuticals*

Finally, there is the case of Jordan. With a heavily implicated TRIPS-plus patent protection regime and a worsening economic and financial crisis, the country has found it more difficult in recent years to attend to the needs of its patients through the provision of cheaper and more affordable medicines. Empirical research has already proved that the country's patients and public authorities are paying higher prices for medicines as a result of the country's FTA with the United States.[31] Preoccupied with public health priorities, the Ministry of Health through its Food and Drug Administration (JFDA) attempted to adopt a pro-public health approach through narrowly interpreting the intellectual property provisions of the FTA with the United States, thus allowing for the registration of more generics and restricting the registration of 'new uses' of known medicines. Such a position was contrary to that taken by the Ministry of Economy and Trade, which attempted to

and Public Health Access to Drugs in Developing Countries, Cheltenham, UK and Northampton, MA, USA, Edward Elgar, 2011, pp. 56–76. Furthermore, it was reported in 2010 that the OMPIC and the European Patent Office (EPO) signed an agreement on the validation of European patents in Morocco. Under this agreement – reported as the first of its kind – applicants will be able to validate their European patent applications and EPO-granted patents in Morocco, even though it is not a contracting state to the European Patent Convention (EPC) and does not have an extension agreement with the European Patent Organization. Applications and patents validated in Morocco will have the same legal effects as those in the EPO member states also designated by the applicant. European patents are currently valid in up to 40 European countries. Notably, it was also reported that the agreement will facilitate technology transfer between Europe and Morocco. It was not clear how such a goal would be achieved. For more see European Patent Office, *Euro-Moroccan Partnership to Benefit the Patent System*, http://www.epo.org/news-issues/press/releases/archive/2010/20101220.html (accessed 15 March 2013).

[31] For example, according to a 2007 Oxfam study, 'TRIPS-plus rules, particularly data exclusivity, independently prevent generic competition for 79 per cent of medicines launched by 21 multinational pharmaceutical companies since 2001. Additional expenditures for medicines with no generic competitor, as a result of enforcement of data exclusivity, were between $6.3m and $22.04m'. See Oxfam International, *All Costs, No Benefits: How TRIPS-plus Intellectual Property Rights in the US–Jordan FTA Affect Access to Medicines*, Oxford, Oxfam, Briefing Note, March 2007. More recently Abbott et al. found that 'from 1999 to 2004 there was a 17% increase in total annual expenditure for medicines in Jordan. When assessing originator medicines that were marketed in both 1999 and 2004, and for which there were generic equivalents, the weighted average price of originator medicines increased while the weighted average price of equivalent generic medicines decreased. Delayed market entry of generics due to enhanced intellectual property protection is estimated to have cost Jordanian private consumers approximately 18 million U.S. dollars in 2004'. See R. Abbott et al., 'The Price of Medicines in Jordan: The Cost of Trade-Based Intellectual Property', *Journal of Generic Medicines*, 9, 2, 2012, pp. 75–85.

influence the JFDA's stance to take a pro-protection approach as a result of United States pressure and fear of retaliation.[32]

The above examples also show the extent of the lack of transparency and access to information regarding intellectual property, trade policy and decision-making in the region. Once again, the US–Morocco FTA provides such an example. The negotiation of the agreement was strongly criticized by interested civil society groups in Morocco and internationally for being secretive and opaque. Although the government of Morocco organized meetings and provided information to interested parties, this only came after the agreement was signed. This, of course, cannot substitute for access to information and public participation in decision-making before the conclusion of a trade agreement. The same approach was also followed during the country's negotiation and signing of ACTA.

6 FOURTH: THE LACK OF CHECKS AND BALANCES

The proper functioning of the patent protection regime within any country has to have as a prerequisite the existence of a number of supporting tools and policies. The aim of these tools is the creation of an enabling functioning environment for the patent protection regime whereby the negative impact of legal patent monopoly is mitigated. Such tools may be referred to as 'checks and balances' and include wide policy options such as consumer protection laws, access to information laws, national research and development (R&D) strategies, social security schemes, health care insurance schemes, in addition to an active and independent judiciary, to name but a few. Until today, the majority of countries in the region have suffered greatly from the lack of these checks and balances.

The countries in the region have made little use of one important legal tool: competition laws and policies. The importance of this tool was righty acknowledged in the TRIPS Agreement itself, which provides member states with the right to curb intellectual property abuses and distortions through the use of competition law and policy.[33] The TRIPS Agreement

---

32 M. El Said, 'The Morning After: TRIPS-plus, FTAs and Wikileaks – Fresh Insights on the Implementation and Enforcement of IP Protection in Developing Countries', PIJIP Research Paper no. 2012–03, American University Washington College of Law, Washington, DC.

33 For example see World Trade Organization, 'Agreement on Trade-related Aspects of Intellectual Property Rights [TRIPS]', Articles 8.2, 31 and 40, 1994, http://www.wto.org/english/docs_e/legal_e/27-trips.pdf (accessed 15 March 2013).

therefore incorporates several provisions which may be used to enhance and institutionalize competition law and policy in member states in order to foster the flow of and dissemination of know-how and technology. In relation to intellectual property, countries have some discretion in determining how to incorporate the relevant competition provisions; they can either incorporate these under current patent protection law or under an independent legislative tool. Many countries in the Arab world today do not have adequate competition laws and provisions to deal with patent and intellectual property abuses.

However, the mere incorporation of competition provisions related to intellectual property abuses is not enough; there is a need to activate their use. The case of Egypt provides some valuable insights into such a process. In this regard, Article 23 of the 2002 IP Law provides that if the abuse of the patentee has been proven, or if it has been proven that he practiced the rights afforded by the patent in an anti-competitive manner, then a compulsory license shall be issued without need for negotiations, or the lapse of a certain period of time in negotiations, even when the compulsory license does not aim at meeting the needs of the domestic market.[34]

Indeed the above provision is extremely valuable and could serve as a model for other Arab and developing countries. However, the problem lies in practise and implementation. These have not been used thus far in curbing patent and intellectual property abuses.

---

[34] Notably, the Article refers to a number of such practises, including:

> Overpricing the products protected by a patent, or the discrimination among the clients in respect of the prices and the selling conditions thereof.
> Not supplying the market with the protected product, or providing it with unfair conditions.
> Ceasing the production of the protected commodity or producing such in a quantity that does not bring about the proportion between the productivity and the market needs.
> Acting or behaving in a way that has a negative effect on the freedom of competition, in accordance with the declared legal constraints.
> Practicing the rights entitled by law in a way that has a negative effect on the transfer of technology.

See WIPO, *Law on the Protection of Intellectual Property Rights*, Law No. 82, 2002, Article 18, http://www.wipo.int/wipolex/en/details.jsp?id=1301 (accessed 15 March 2013).

7 FIFTH: CAPACITY AND RESOURCES

As has been generally observed – and as may be the case for the majority of developing countries – technical and legal knowledge related to intellectual property protection in general and patent protection in particular are modest even among officials involved in the relevant activities in the Arab world.[35] An exception to this may be Egypt which does possess some capacity due to a number of historical factors.[36] Even today, the region still suffers from a lack of expertise and specialized capacity in this area.

Important too is the role of patent offices in the region. For a long time these offices have lacked financial resources and qualified personnel. Emphasis in recent years on the need for these offices to become financially autonomous is also placing these offices under additional pressure and prompting them to focus on issuing more patents in order to survive and fund their activities and operations. In recent research, Krikorian comments on the operations of the Moroccan Patent Office, stating:

> The policy of the Moroccan patent office (OMPIC)[37] is straightforward: the number of patents granted is a reflection of the efficiency of the office. The more patents it registers, the better a job it is doing – and the richer it becomes. The OMPIC does not have patent examiners. According to the former director, in 2006 patent requests were not numerous enough to justify employing examiners qualified in all the various technological fields. He also saw that it was very difficult for the Moroccan office to compete in terms of efficiency with the examining capacity of the European or US patent offices.[38]

---

35 M. El Said, 'The Morning After: TRIPS-plus, FTAs and Wikileaks – Fresh Insights on the Implementation and Enforcement of IP Protection in Developing Countries', PIJIP Research Paper no. 2012–03, American University Washington College of Law, Washington, DC.

36 As Abdel Latif explains, 'Egypt has been one of the active developing countries in global trade and IP deliberations. It has thus been able to harness the expertise acquired in this area at the multilateral level and use it in bilateral negotiations with developed-country partners. Second, because of the greater size of its domestic market and its economic as well as political weight, Egypt has had greater leverage in negotiations with developed countries toward refusing extensive TRIPS-plus obligations'. A.A. Latif, 'Egypt's Role in the A2K Movement: An Analysis of Positions and Policies', in Rizk, N. and Shaver, L. (eds.), *Access to Knowledge in Egypt: New Research on Intellectual Property, Innovation and Development*, London, Bloomsbury Academic, 2010, p. 39.

37 The Moroccan Industrial and Commercial Property Office (OMPIC), *OMPIC*, 2010, http://www.ompic.org.ma/pages_en_5.shtm.

38 G. Krikorian, 'Intellectual Property and Access to Medicines: Paradoxes in Moroccan Policy', in Shadlen, K. et al. (eds.), *Intellectual Property, Pharmaceuticals*

Countries in the region need to invest more in their national patent offices. These offices should be placed at the heart of national development and innovation agendas.[39] Governments should recruit additional specialized personnel and upgrade these offices' current technological, technical, human and financial abilities. Fundamentally, these offices should also focus more on improving the quality of patents granted rather than on their quantity.

Finally, although there has been increased emphasis on technical assistance, training programs and workshops arranged by many international agencies and institutions and directed towards the region,[40] more attention should be paid towards the type of technical assistance provided within this context. More should be done to provide technical assistance and training directed towards utilizing the flexibilities of the patent regime rather than merely focusing on enforcement and protection of intellectual property rights.

8 SIXTH: THE LACK OF A REGIONAL AND INTERNATIONAL AGENDA

As the above discussion indicates, the majority of countries in the region share similar problems related to their patent protection regime. Based on this, one would expect that it would be easier for these countries to increase regional cooperation and develop a unified international position on intellectual property issues. In practise, this is far from happening.

Historically, the participation of Arab countries in global intellectual property discussions has been weak and largely non-influential. Apart from Egypt, the majority of countries have been absent from intellectual property discussions or did not have a clear and unified position.

On the other hand, the majority of countries in the region found it more convenient to deal with intellectual property protection through bilateral

---

and Public Health Access to Drugs in Developing Countries, Cheltenham, UK and Northampton, MA, USA, Edward Elgar, 2011, p. 66.

[39] See P. Drahos, *The Global Governance of Knowledge: Patent Offices and their Clients*, Cambridge: Cambridge University Press, 2010.

[40] Many agencies and institutions are often active in providing technical advice and training for the region, including United States Agency for International Development (USAID), United States Trademark and Patent Office (USPTO), European Patent Office (EPO), World Intellectual Property Organization (WIPO), World Health Organization (WHO), United National Development Programme (UNDP), United Nations Conference on Trade and Development (UNCTAD) and so on.

trade agreements than to design an indigenous protection system pertinent to their national needs and priorities. Lack of national participation and the secretive and non-transparent nature of negotiations under these agreements provided such countries with a covering blanket to introduce heavy-handed patent protection regimes in exchange for concessions in certain trade areas and financial aid. This also restricted the ability of these countries to negotiate or formulate a unified stand in multilateral negotiations. Today, unlike other regional groupings such as the African Group or the Association of Southeast Asian Nations (ASEAN), the majority of Arab countries do not belong to one specific group and lack a unified global position in relation to intellectual property negotiations in various forums.

9 CONCLUSION

The recent changes in the region have prompted some Arab governments to reconsider their position as regards dealing with the demands of their citizens. Calls for greater accountability, transparency and participation in decision-making are today's headlines throughout the region. One area where the above demands should extend to is the regulation of intellectual property. Still, there are many challenges facing the Arab world today. While some countries are still in the middle of the spring itself (such as Syria and Yemen), for the majority, managing the post-spring transition phase remains the priority. At the heart of this turbulent phase is the need for security and economic stability.

More attention should be directed towards developing and protecting the intellectual property emanating from the region. However, this should take a rather non-conventional approach. Counties should select and invest in those areas where they have (or are able to develop) a comparative advantage. Increasing R&D investment in areas such as green technologies should empower rich Arab states to become producers of knowledge and technologies in these sectors. Qatar's pledge to increase research spending from 0.8% to a planned 2.8% of GDP is a step in the right direction.[41]

The Arab Spring could provide the much-needed momentum for such a process to commence. The need to deal with rising youth unemployment in the region should trigger an overall evaluation of the current patent protec-

---

41 'Islam and Science: The Road to Renewal', *The Economist*, 26 January 2013, http://www.economist.com/news/international/21570677-after-centuries-stagnation-science-making-comeback-islamic-world-road (accessed 15 March 2013).

tion regimes towards taking advantage of the flexibilities of such a regime in order to assist in the development needs and aspirations of these countries. There are already some signs of this. On 25 April, Yemen became only the second country in the Arab world to adopt a law on citizens' right to information.[42] A few years ago this would have been impossible. Indeed, change must come and come soon if the Arab world is to emerge and regain the global prominence it once held. The regulation of patents and intellectual property in general is likely to play an important role throughout such a process. Dealing with the challenges identified above is essential in this context. As a recent UNDP Report stated in relation to the region:[43]

> The movement for change that has spread through the socio-political landscape of the Arab region asks for new development pathways that give greater prominence to the interlocking issues of democratic governance, social justice and decent employment.

REFERENCES

Abbott, R. et al., 'The Price of Medicines in Jordan: The Cost of Trade-Based Intellectual Property', *Journal of Generic Medicines*, 9, 2, 2012, pp. 75–85.

Al-Ali, N., 'The Egyptian Pharmaceutical Industry After TRIPS – A Practitioner's View', *Fordham International Law Journal*, 26, 2, 2002, pp. 274–314.

Drahos, P., 'BITS and BIPS: Bilateralism in Intellectual Property', *Journal of World Intellectual Property*, 4, 2001, pp. 791–808.

EIPR, *The TRIPS Agreement and Egypt's Responsibility to Protect the Right to Health*, Cairo, Right to Health Program Egyptian Initiative for Personal Rights, January 2005.

El Said, M., 'The Morning After: TRIPS-plus, FTAs and Wikileaks – Fresh Insights on the Implementation and Enforcement of IP Protection in Developing Countries', PIJIP Research Paper no. 2012–03, American University Washington College of Law, Washington, DC.

El Said, M., 'The Road From TRIPS-minus to TRIPS to TRIPS-plus: Implications of IPRs for the Arab World', *Journal of World Intellectual Property*, 8, 1, 2005, pp. 53–66.

El Said, M., *Public Health Related TRIPS-plus Provisions in Bilateral Trade Agreements: A Policy Guide for Negotiations and Implementers in the Eastern Mediterranean Region*, Cairo, WHO and ICTSD, 2012, at http://applications.emro.who.int/dsaf/dsa1081.pdf (accessed 15 March 2013).

---

42 The essence of the access to information law is to allow citizens to demand information from government bodies. It includes clauses on the accountability of the relevant authorities to provide information in a timely manner in order to improve transparency. Of countries in the region only Jordan and Yemen now have such laws.

43 UNDP, *Arab Development Challenges Report 2011: Towards the Developmental State*, Cairo, UNDP, 2011.

El Said, M., *The Development of Intellectual Property Protection in the Arab World*, Lewiston, ME, Edwin Mellen Press, 2008.
El Said, M. and Kapczynski, A., *Access to Medicines: The Role of Intellectual Property Law and Policy*, New York, The Global Commission on HIV and the Law, UNDP, July 2012.
European Patent Office, *Euro-Moroccan Partnership to Benefit the Patent System*, http://www.epo.org/news-issues/press/releases/archive/2010/20101220.html (accessed 15 March 2013).
Hossam, B., and Wright, R., 'Access to Medicines in Egypt: A Human Rights Approach to IP, Trade and Health', in Rizk, N. and Shaver, L. (eds.), *Access to Knowledge in Egypt: New Research on Intellectual Property, Innovation and Development*, London, Bloomsbury Academic, 2010, pp. 56–91.
INSEAD, and WIPO, *The Global Innovation Index 2012: Stronger Innovation Linkages for Global Growth*, Geneva, INSEAD and WIPO, 2012.
Krikorian, G., 'Intellectual Property and Access to Medicines: Paradoxes in Moroccan Policy', in Shadlen, K. et al. (eds.), *Intellectual Property, Pharmaceuticals and Public Health Access to Drugs in Developing Countries*, Cheltenham, UK and Northampton, MA, USA, Edward Elgar, 2011, pp. 56–76.
Latif, A.A., 'Egypt's Role in the A2K Movement: An Analysis of Positions and Policies', in Rizk, N. and Shaver, L. (eds.), *Access to Knowledge in Egypt: New Research on Intellectual Property, Innovation and Development*, London, Bloomsbury Academic, 2010, pp. 16–55.
Office of the United States Trade Representative., *United States-Morocco Free Trade Agreement*, Article 15.9.4 footnote 9, 2004, http://www.ustr.gov/trade-agreements/free-trade-agreements/morocco-fta/final-text (accessed 15 March 2013).
Okediji, R.L., 'The International Relations of Intellectual Property: Narratives of Developing Country Participation in the Global Intellectual Property System', *Singapore Journal of International & Comparative Law*, 7, 2003, pp. 315–85.
Oxfam International., *All Costs, No Benefits: How TRIPS-plus Intellectual Property Rights in the US–Jordan FTA Affect Access to Medicines*, Oxford, Oxfam, Briefing Note, March 2007.
Salah, H., 'Mapping of Healthcare Financing in Eastern Mediterranean Region', Arab Republic of Egypt, World Health Organization, 2007.
The European Free Trade Association., *Annex V Intellectual Property*, http://www.efta.int/free-trade/free-trade-agreements/lebanon/~/media/87E615BD9EDD4DD1B59A294E3AFB0333.pdf (accessed 15 March 2013).
UNDP, *Arab Development Challenges Report 2011: Towards the Developmental State*, Cairo, UNDP, 2011.
UNDP, *Human Development Report 2011: Sustainability and Equity, A Better Future for All*, New York, UNDP, 2011, http://hdr.undp.org/en/media/HDR_2011_EN_Complete.pdf (accessed 15 March 2013).
WIPO, *Law on the Protection of Intellectual Property Rights*, Law No. 82, 2002, Article 18, http://www.wipo.int/wipolex/en/details.jsp?id=1301 (accessed 15 March 2013).
World Health Organization, *Global Alert and Response (GAR), 2003*, http://www.who.int/csr/disease/hepatitis/whocdscsrlyo2003/en/index4.html (accessed 15 March 2013).
World Trade Organization, 'Agreement on Trade-related Aspects of Intellectual Property Rights [TRIPS]', 1994, http://www.wto.org/english/docs_e/legal_e/27-trips.pdf (accessed 15 March 2013).

PART VI

The OECD response

Europe

16. The impact of emerging market patent systems on Europe: Awaiting 'The Rape of Europa'?

Geertrui Van Overwalle

1 INTRODUCTION

Once upon a time there was a Phoenician woman of high lineage, called Europa. Enchanted by her ravishing appearance, Zeus fell in love with her. Being audacious, Zeus conceived a plan to seduce and abduct her. He transformed himself into a tame, white bull and joined the herd that belonged to Europa's father. When Europa and her female attendants were gathering flowers, Europa spotted the bull. Frightened at first, she overcame her fear, caressed his flanks, and eventually got onto his back. Zeus seized the opportunity, ran into the sea and swam, with Europa on his back, to the island of Crete. There he revealed his true identity. Europa became the first Queen of Crete.

This wonderful Greek myth depicts the awakening love between Zeus and Europa. Does this myth also hold a message for the burgeoning relationship between Zeus, this time disguised as an Asian tiger, and Europe? And can the budding encounter between Zeus and Europe culminate in an intimate love story? Or is Europa on the edge of being raped again? Translated into more commonsensical parlance the question arises whether the spectacular patent surge from emerging markets, such as China and Korea, poses a threat to Europe. Is there reason to be worried about the significant breakaway from emerging markets towards Europe, and emerging markets[1] lavishly applying for European patents? The myth is unclear as to whether Zeus ultimately took Europa by force or 'seduced' her. The same ambiguity applies to the relationship between emerging markets and Europe.

[1] Emerging markets are generally considered to be nations with social or business activity in the process of rapid growth and industrialization. One can think of the BRIC countries (Brazil, Russia, India and China), as well as the MIKT countries (Mexico, Indonesia, South-Korea and Turkey).

The present chapter will look into the relationship between emerging markets and Europe in a twofold way. First, the chapter will discuss the question from a European perspective, and investigate what impact emerging market patents may have on Europe. Second, the chapter will briefly address the issue from the emerging market perspective, and examine how Europe may affect emerging market patent systems.

The chapter will conclude that the discussions about the current surge of emerging market patent filings reveal a fundamental tension between two different patent discourses: a more conventional/legal narrative employing patents as policy tools to stimulate innovation, and a more contemporary/economic approach looking at patents as market instruments. Only when both those discourses are taken into account, and measures are contemplated addressing those two facets of patents, can a meaningful response to the current emerging market patent tsunami be developed.

2 IMPACT OF EMERGING MARKET PATENT FILINGS ON EUROPE

In Europe, an invention can be protected with a European patent in up to 38 European countries on the basis of a single application and examination procedure.[2] It is possible to obtain a European patent for any invention which is new, involves an inventive step, is susceptible of industrial application (Article 52 (1) European Patent Convention (EPC)) and discloses the invention in a manner sufficiently clear and complete for it to be carried out by a person skilled in the art (Article 83 EPC). Once the patent is granted, the patent is broken up into a 'bundle' of national patents which are further subject to national legislation and, more particularly, to national regulations with regard to nullity and infringement. As of late, an inventor can also opt for a 'European patent with unitary effect' (previously known as a 'Community patent').[3] Such a European patent

---

[2] Convention on the Grant of European Patents (European Patent Convention) of 5 October 1973 as revised by the Act revising Article 63 EPC of 17 December 1991 and the Act revising the EPC of 29 November 2000. *See* European Patent Office, 'The European Patent Convention', 2011, http://www.epo.org/law-practice/legal-texts/html/epc/2010/e/ma1.html (accessed 9 February 2013). On the basis of the EPC the European Patent Office (EPO) was brought into being to deal with European patents (and European patents with unitary effect, see further).

[3] Regulation (EU) No. 1257/2012 of the European Parliament and of the Council of 17 December 2012, implementing enhanced cooperation in the area of the creation of unitary patent protection. Also see the Agreement on a

with unitary effect will not fall apart into a basket of national patents, but will operate as a single patent valid across the territory of 28 EU member states.[4]

At present, two trends can be observed in European patent filings. First, demand for European patents is on the rise again. In 2012, the European Patent Office (EPO) received 258,000 patent applications, representing a 5.7% increase over 2011 (244,000). In the same year, the EPO granted 65,700 patents, 5.8% more than in 2011 (62,115). This growth is part of a long-term evolution.[5] Second, the geographical distribution of patent applicants shows that emerging markets, such as China and Korea, are fuelling the growth in filings. In 2011 the share of the 38 EPO member states accounted for 38% of the total, and that of the US for 24% of all filings.[6] China had a share of 6.6% and Korea a share of 5.5% of all European filings.[7] In 2012, China and Korea contributed significantly to

---

Unified Patent Court, Brussels, 11 January 2013. For a critical analysis of the European patent with unitary effect, *see* H. Ullrich, 'Harmonising Patent Law: The Untameable Union Patent', in M.C. Janssens and G. Van Overwalle (eds.), *Harmonisation of European IP Law: From European Rules to Belgian Law and Practice – Contributions in Honour of Frank Gotzen*, Brussels, Bruylant-Larcier, 2012, pp. 243–94. *Also see* R.M. Hilty et al., 'The Unitary Patent Package: Twelve Reasons for Concern', Max Planck Institute for Intellectual Property and Competition Law, Munich, 2012, http://www.ip.mpg.de/files/pdf2/MPI-IP_Twelve-Reasons_2012-10-17_final3.pdf (accessed 9 February 2013).

[4] For Regulation (EU) No. 1257/2012 ministers of member states have decided to legislate, not among 28, but only among 25 participating member states – this is called 'enhanced cooperation'. This procedure is allowed by the EU Treaties in order to limit the risks of blocking when a consensus cannot be reached between all member states.

[5] *See* 'All-time High for Activities of the European Patent Office in 2012', European Patent Office, 17 January 2013, http://www.epo.org/news-issues/press/releases/archive/2013/20130117.html (accessed 9 February 2013). For detailed information on the 2011 filings, *see* 'Patent Filings – New Record at European Patent Office in 2011', European Patent Office, 17 January 2012, http://www.epo.org/news-issues/press/releases/archive/2012/20120117.html (accessed 9 February 2013). *Also see* the blog of EPO President Batistelli. B. Batistelli, '2011 Filings in Detail', Blog, 27 March 2012, http://blog.epo.org/the-epo/2011-filings-in-detail/ (accessed 9 February 2013).

[6] *See* 'Annual Report 2011 – Statistics and Trends', European Patent Office, 2012, http://www.epo.org/about-us/office/annual-report/2011/statistics-trends/key-trends.html (accessed 9 February 2013). For some more details, as well as some instructive diagrams, *see* 'Annual Report 2011 – European Patent Filings', European Patent Office, 2012, http://documents.epo.org/projects/babylon/eponet.nsf/0/8AA0C5EA5DB73EAEC12579C2002B829B/$File/European_patent_filings_en.pdf (accessed 9 February 2013).

[7] *See* 'Total European Filings in 2011', European Patent Office, 2012, http://

the growth of patent filings again, with China accounting for a share of 7.3% and Korea for a share of 5.5% of all European patent filings.[8]

The current increase in European patent filings from China and Korea has led to concerns about the operation of the European patent system. Even though recent statistics do not show a global increase in patent filings from all emerging markets (yet), the boom in patent filings from China and Korea has raised serious concerns about the effect of an upcoming growth in patent filings from emerging markets. First and foremost, the steady increase in patenting activity from emerging markets has intensified concerns relating to the quality of patents. Some critics have suggested that the explosion of patents might spur the grant of low quality patents.[9] A considerable increase in emerging market patent filings might contribute to worsening the situation. Second, the rise of emerging market patents has reinforced concerns about the potential negative effect of the proliferation of patents on further innovation and commercialization. Various scholars are already worried about the risk that an intense use of the patent system would create 'patent thickets':[10] dense webs of overlapping patents that a researcher or a company would have to hack its way through in order to actually develop and commercialize a new product.[11] The fear is expressed that in some circumstances exclusive property rights can block effective economic applications of assets, which in turn could lead to what has become known as the 'tragedy of the anti-commons',[12] a

---

documents.epo.org/projects/babylon/eponet.nsf/0/5D89B207FACB5EAEC1257988003EBCB6/$File/top_countries_2011.pdf (accessed 9 February 2013).

[8] *See* 'Top 50 Countries of Origin', European Patent Office, 17 January 2013, http://www.epo.org/news-issues/press/releases/archive/2013/20130117/countries.html (accessed 9 February 2013).

[9] Although it is generally accepted that the quality of EPO patents is higher than those of the USPTO and the Japanese Patent Office. *See* M. de Saint-Georges and B. van Pottelsberghe de la Potterie, 'A Quality Index for Patent Systems', ECARES [working paper], 2011, https://dipot.ulb.ac.be/dspace/bitstream/2013/87167/1/2011–010-DESAINTGEORGES_VANPOTTELSBERGHE-aquality.pdf (accessed 9 February 2013); B. Doern, *Global Change and Intellectual Property Agencies*, London, Pinter, 1999; B. Van Pottelsberghe de la Potterie, 'The Quality Factor in Patent Systems', *Industrial and Corporate Change*, vol. 20, no. 6, 2011, pp. 1755–93.

[10] C. Shapiro, 'Navigating the Patent Thicket: Cross Licenses, Patent Pools, and Standard Setting', in A. Jaffe, J. Lerner and S. Stern (eds.), *Innovation Policy and the Economy, Vol. I*, Cambridge, MA, MIT Press, 2001, pp. 119–50, http://haas.berkeley.edu/~shapiro/thicket.pdf (accessed 9 February 2013).

[11] F.M. Scherer, 'The Economics of Human Gene Patents', *Academic Medicine*, vol. 77, no. 12, 2002, pp. 1348–67.

[12] M.A. Heller and R. Eisenberg, 'Can Patents Deter Innovation? The

situation where multiple (overlapping) private property rights prevent the efficient combination of assets. A patent tsunami from emerging market companies accumulating and asserting European patent rights across Europe might aggravate that problem.

Examining the numeric explosion of the European patent system from a legal-governance angle, it becomes clear that the explosion of patent filings relates to the failure of the European patent legislator to deal with its regulatory function.[13] In order to stimulate innovation, inventors are given the opportunity to recoup their efforts and investments by way of an exclusionary right, a patent. Patent law establishes competent authorities and prescribes patentability criteria, formal requirements and granting procedures to attribute such rights. In doing so, patent law regulates two facets. On the one hand, patent law regulates the *vertical* relationship by regulating the granting procedure, enabling competent patent offices (public authority) to grant patents (to individuals or firms) in accordance with the criteria determined in the patent law/treaty. On the other hand, patent law governs the *horizontal* relationship by defining the contours of the right in the post-grant phase between the patent holder and the potential licensees and the public at large. Current European patent law appears to be largely inapt in fulfilling its regulatory function with respect to both the vertical (patent authorities – patent applicants) and the horizontal relationship (patent holders – potential licensees, general public).

Patent law's failure in the *vertical* relationship is illustrated by the general criticism of patent quality. Patent law's inaptitude to deal with the *horizontal* relationship is demonstrated by the patent thicket problem and

Anticommons in Biomedical Research', *Science*, vol. 280, no. 5364, 1998, p. 698; M.A. Heller, 'The Tragedy of the Anticommons: Property in the Transition from Marx to Markets', *Harvard Law Review*, vol. 111, 1998, p. 621.

[13] *See* G. Van Overwalle and E. Van Zimmeren, 'Functions and Limits Of Patent Law', in E. Claes, W. Devroe, and B. Keirsbilck (eds.), *Facing the Limits of the Law*, Berlin-Heidelberg, Springer, 2009, pp. 415–42. In this paper we analysed current trends in European patent law and practice in great depth. The expansion of the patent system in terms of numbers was one of the most visible trends. In an attempt to better understand the deeper roots of this (and other) trend(s) and the concerns to which it gives rise, we turned to an analytical model set forth by E. Claes, W. Devroe, and B. Keirsbilck, 'The Limits of the Law', in E. Claes, W. Devroe, and B. Keirsbilck (eds.), *Facing the Limits of the Law*, Berlin-Heidelberg, Springer, 2009, pp. 1–24, revolving around the objectives and functions of the law. Applying this analytical model to patent law clearly pointed out the limits of patent law. These limits related to the major functions (the regulatory function, the symbolic function and the function of providing legal guarantees) and the objectives of patent law. Current European patent law is largely unable to fulfil its major objectives and functions within the current social, political and economic context.

the lack of legal rules guiding patent holders in the exercise of their rights and exploitation endeavours. Patent law and competition law (in the EU member states) leave considerable freedom to patent owners to set up their own licensing agreements and exclusive licensing is not prohibited. The present emerging markets patent tsunami challenges the (vertical and horizontal) regulatory function of the European patent legislator even more.

Studying the recent increase in patenting from an economic perspective points to the development of a market for technology as a reason for the recent surge in patent filings.[14] The coming about of more patent applications is induced by strategic tactics to influence competitors' behaviour.[15] Patents provide companies with the opportunity to build a market advantage over their competitors in various ways. In particular, patents provide bargaining power that can be used to restrain the power of suppliers by owning key technology elements in another part of the value or technological chain,[16] to prevent the development of a particular market or technology (technology suppression), to guarantee freedom to invent, to secure freedom to operate, to prevent others from acquiring patent rights (defensive patenting), to create a technological smoke screen, etc.[17] A boom in emerging market patent filings may have far reaching effects on market dynamics in Europe. Innovative emerging market companies may apply for patents not only to acquire a return on investment or to extract rent, but to strengthen their strategic position in the market for technology.

Reflecting on this multi-layered analysis of the surge in patent filings reveals a tension between two distinct perspectives on patents. On the one hand, there is the reading – often set forth in legal documents and jurisprudence – of patents as *incentives to innovate*, with attention to the policy role of patents as a means of stimulating innovation and recouping investment. On the other hand, there is the – more economically oriented – observation that patents are used as *market* instruments, with a focus on the role of patents as bargaining power. European patent law has adopted the normative ideal of patents as incentives as its prevailing justification

---

[14] *See* D. Guellec and B. van Pottelsberghe de la Potterie, *The Economics of the European Patent System*, Oxford, Oxford University Press, 2007, p. 85. *Also see* J. Penin, 'Patents Versus ex post Rewards: A New Look', *Research Policy*, vol. 34, no. 5, 2005, pp. 641–56.

[15] *See* Guellec and van Pottelsberghe, *The Economics of the European Patent System*, p. 87.

[16] *See* Guellec and van Pottelsberghe, *The Economics of the European Patent System*, p. 85; M. Reitzig, 'Strategic Management of Intellectual Property', *MIT Sloan Management Review*, vol. 45, no. 3, 2004, pp. 35–40.

[17] *See* Guellec and van Pottelsberghe, *The Economics of the European Patent System*, p. 86.

for patent law. However, at present European patent law is not fully equipped to accommodate patents as market instruments and to respond to the role of patents in market dynamics.

An adequate response to the exponential increase in emerging market patent filings in Europe should take the form of a response empowering the control of conflicts between (local) industrialists and (foreign/emerging) industrialists, and guaranteeing the interests of genuine follow-on innovators/true originators, and between (local and foreign) industrialists and consumers and users.[18] Such a response has to take into account both the policy and the market aspect of patents. For an approach to be effective, it should not only address the *static* layer of patent law, and deal with patent requirements and the scope of rights,[19] but also take into account the *dynamic* effects of patents on the market place, and address issues of access to technology and licensing practices. Addressing the surge in emerging market patent filings on the static level, requires vitalizing the *vertical* regulatory function, and contemplating steps in the area of patent quality and breadth of claims (see Section 2.1.). Dealing with the increase of emerging market patents from a dynamic perspective requires optimizing the *horizontal* regulatory function of patent law, and consideration of measures in the area of patent exemptions and patent licensing (see Section 2.2.).

2.1 The Static Perspective: Revitalizing the *Vertical* Regulatory Function

The surge of patent filings from emerging markets is a wake-up call for the European patent legislator to sharpen its regulatory function. In an attempt to revitalize the *vertical* regulatory function, measures relating to patent quality and breadth of claims may be contemplated.

High quality patents *predominantly* refer to patents which describe an invention that is truly new, involves a real inventive step for the person skilled in the art and is industrially applicable.[20] The grant of high quality patents implies a rigorous review of prior art and strict application of the patentability criteria. The EPO has a very high perceived level of patent

---

18 *Cf.* F.M. Abbott, C.M. Correa and P. Drahos, 'Emerging Markets and the World Patent Order: The Forces of Change', Chapter 1 in this volume.

19 P. Drahos refers to those issues as 'narcoleptic discussion[s]'. *See* P. Drahos, 'The US, China and the G-77 in the Era of Responsive Patentability', *Queen Mary Journal of Intellectual Property*, vol. 2, no. 4, 2012, p. 316.

20 It is relevant to note that a distinction should be made between a strong/weak *patent* and a strong/weak patent *system*. In the current chapter, a strong patent system does not refer to a patent system aiming to attribute *many* patents, but rather to a patent system aiming to grant a *few high quality* patents.

quality.[21] At times, however, European patents have been granted for inventions with a (very) low level of inventive step.[22] As current quality assurance mechanisms seem not to suffice to guarantee high quality patents, additional measures might be taken to assist the EPO in coherently monitoring and applying the (high) inventive step criterion in its day-to-day practice. A review of the patent system in the light of patent quality may play an important role in attaining the principal objective of patent law and in strengthening the regulatory function.

Current quality assurance mechanisms focus mainly on patentability standards and procedural issues.[23] Thoughtful scholars have referred to some *additional* characteristics for assuring high quality patents. They claim that in order to guarantee the quality of patents, there also has to be relatively little uncertainty over the breadth of the patent claims, as well as over the question as to whether these claims are likely to be upheld in opposition or in legal proceedings after the grant of the patent.[24]

---

21 *See* the survey of corporate and private practice IP professionals conducted jointly by Thomson Reuters and Intellectual Asset Management (IAM). Intellectual Asset Management Magazine, 'Private Practice', 'In-house Counsel' [online graphs], http://documents.epo.org/projects/babylon/eponet.nsf/0/15D2798FB51DB1E4C12578BD003FE172/$File/IAM_extract_en.pdf (accessed 9 February 2013).

22 An illustrative example is the patent granted for a so-called sweet toy, better known under its trademark name 'Trolliburger', but there are ample other examples. As to the 'Trolliburger', *see* European Patent No. 0 349 841, granted 15 January 1992 to Mederer. *See in particular* claim 1: 'Sweet-toy, in particular a foamed sugar mass and fruit gum, characterised in that it consists of at least three individual layers (2, 3, 4), wherein the uppermost layer (2) and the bottom layer (3) consist in each case of a foamed sugar body which has a rounded shape with porous surface and a flat cross-section, and the intermediate layer (4) of which there is at least one, is formed as a substantially disc-shaped or rod-shaped fruit gum layer.

23 *See e.g.* European Patent Office, 'Handbook of Quality Procedures before the EPO', Author, 2012, http://www.epo.org/law-practice/legal-texts/handbook.html (accessed 9 February 2013). Witness the blog of EPO President B. Batistelli: 'Quality has always driven the EPO's policy, as only high-quality patents provide the legal certainty that makes them such a valuable tool for companies, individual inventors and third parties alike. The EPO continues to invest heavily in *boosting quality, especially by streamlining procedures and improving IT systems.* And this study shows that our efforts at establishing a quality-based patent system are paying off.' (Emphasis added.) B. Batistelli, 'EPO Again Tops Patent Quality List', Blog, 28 June 2011, http://www.epo.org/news-issues/news/2011/20110628.html (accessed 9 February 2013). *Also see* Van Pottelsberghe, 'The Quality Factor in Patent Systems'.

24 B.H. Hall et al., 'Prospects for Improving U.S. Patent Quality via Post-grant Opposition', UC Berkeley Working Papers, Department of Economics, Working Paper No. E03–329 (2003), 2–3. *Also see* J. Bessen and M.J. Meurer, *Patent Failure: How Judges, Bureaucrats, and Lawyers Put Innovators at Risk*, Princeton, NJ,

The EPO patent granting policy in the biotechnology area has raised wide concern about awarding very wide (too wide) claims. A few examples may illustrate this point. In plant biotechnology, a patent was granted in 1989 to Lubrizol Genetics, with patent claims for genetically modified 'plant cells'[25] and 'plants'.[26] The claims were awarded, notwithstanding the fact that the description disclosed transformation of only sunflower and tobacco.[27] Similar claims were granted for other genetic modification systems encompassing the whole plant kingdom, even though the experiments described in the patent specification were related to a few varieties of plants only, mostly potatoes, tomatoes, carrots, alfalfa, and/or sunflowers.[28] The application and grant of these plant patents gave rise to a great deal of EPO jurisprudence. However, the disputes mostly revolved around the eligibility of plants for patent protection[29] and hardly ever focused on the breadth of the claims at hand. Wide claims were also granted in the area of animal biotechnology. The most prominent example here is the patent granted for the Harvard onco-mouse, with claims for a 'non-human mammalian animal',[30] even though the description only disclosed experiments with mice.[31] The EPO Examining Division took the view that the claimed invention referred to all non-human mammalian animals, whereas the invention described in the examples had been performed only on mice.[32]

Princeton University Press, 2008, especially their analysis of and comments on 'fuzzy boundaries'. *See also* EPO Economic and Scientific Advisory Board, 'Report: Workshop on Patent Quality', European Patent Office, Munich, 7 May 2012, http://documents.epo.org/projects/babylon/eponot.nsf/0/ bbc8744dd3ff80b8c1257a69004 6953d/$FILE/workshop_patent_quality_en.pdf (accessed 9 February 2013).

25 *See* Claim 19 of European Patent No. 0 122 791 (B1), issued 29 March 1989.

26 *See id.* at Claim 20.

27 *See id.* at 8.

28 *See* Claim 4 of European Patent No. 0 120 515 (B1). *See also* Claim 19 of European Patent No. 0 126 546 (B1). *See also* European Patent No. 0 131 620 (B1) at 23. For a more detailed discussion, *see* G. Van Overwalle, *Octrooieerbaarheid Van Plantenbiotechnologische Uitvindingen [Patentability of Plant Biotechnological Inventions]*, Brussels, Bruylant, 1996, p. 739. *Also see* G. Van Overwalle, 'Policy Levers Tailoring Patent Law to Biotechnology: Comparing U.S. and European Approaches', *UC Irvine Law Review*, vol. 1, no. 2, 2011, pp. 435–517.

29 For details, *see* the references in the previous footnote and G. Van Overwalle, 'Biotechnology and Patents: Global Standards, European Approaches and National Accents', in D. Wüger and T. Cottier (eds.), *Genetic Engineering and the World Trade System*, Cambridge, Cambridge University Press, 2008, pp. 77 ff.

30 *See* Claim 19 of European Patent No. 0 169 672 (B1).

31 *See* European Patent No. 0 169 762 (B1) (filed 6 June 1985 and granted 13 May 1992).

32 Not convinced that a skilled person would be able to carry out the invention successfully on all other kinds of non-human mammals as it had been performed

Last but not least, in the area of human genetics, complaints about unreasonably broad and unclear formulated claims have been voiced as well.[33]

The EPO should give a wider echo to patent quality considerations, relating to the breadth of patent claims. A more restrictive application of scope of patent claims in relation to specific technologies should be contemplated.[34]

2.2 The Dynamic Perspective: Revitalizing the *Horizontal* Regulatory Function

The EPC primarily regulates the pre-grant phase, and the coming into existence of patent rights. After the centralized granting procedure, the European patent equals a bundle of national patents with respect to exploitation and enforcement. But national (patent and competition) law rarely contains rules relating to the post-grant phase, and the exercise of patent rights. Quite often, national jurisdictions do not include legal rules guiding patent holders in the exercise of their rights and their exploitation or licensing strategy, apart from a few measures to temper really extravagant behaviour, such as abuse of a dominant market position in competition law. Addressing the issue of emerging market patents does not only require thoughtful examination of pre-grant safeguards looking into the

---

on mice, the EPO Examining Division rightly refused the application, inter alia, on the ground that the claims were unrealistically broad. *See* Decision of the European Patent Office, Board of Appeal, Case T 19/90 (3 October 1990), OJ EPO 476 (1990), Reason 3.2. The EPO Technical Board of Appeal argued that the mere fact that a claim is broad is not in itself a ground for considering the application as not complying with the requirement for sufficient disclosure. Only if there are serious doubts, substantiated by verifiable facts, may an application be objected to for lack of sufficient disclosure. Reason 3.3.

33 I. Huys, N. Berthels, G. Matthijs and G. Van Overwalle, 'Legal Uncertainty in the Area of Genetic Diagnostic Testing', *Nature Biotechnology*, vol. 27, no. 10, 2009, pp. 903–09. *See also* I. Huys, G. Van Overwalle and G. Matthijs, 'Gene and Genetic Diagnostic Method Patent Claims: A Comparison under Current European and US Patent Law', *European Journal of Human Genetics*, vol. 19, no. 10, 2011, pp. 1104–07; I. Huys, G. Matthijs and G. Van Overwalle, 'The Fate and Future of Patents on Human Genes and Genetic Diagnostic Methods', *Nature Reviews Genetics*, vol. 13, no. 6, 2012, pp. 441–8.

34 Formally, patent law operates as a 'one size fits all system'. All inventions, irrespective of the technological field must satisfy the same patentability criteria. However, patent doctrine contains different industry-specific 'sub-cultures' of interpretation, even if not explicitly acknowledged. *See* D.L. Burk and M.A. Lemley, *The Patent Crisis and How the Courts Can Solve It*, Chicago and London, The University of Chicago Press, 2009. *See also* Van Overwalle, 'Policy Levers Tailoring Patent Law to Biotechnology', pp. 435–517.

grant of patents, but also demands careful consideration of the post-grant phase of patents and the effects of patents in the market place. Measures assisting patent law in strengthening the horizontal regulatory function of patent law, and helping to mitigate the effects of the surge in patents, may involve patent exemptions and patent licensing.

Amongst patent exceptions, the research exemption is a prominent legitimate limit to the exclusivity granted by patent rights. It is commonly accepted that a research exception can fuel follow-on innovation,[35] but might also mitigate 'patent thicket' problems[36] and solve refusals to license.[37] In the past, numerous papers and reports[38] have been published expressing concerns about the availability and scope of the research exception.[39] Also in Europe, doubt reigns when it comes to the exact scope of the research exemption. Even though the various national patent acts may well have a research exception, and exceptions go back to the same 'mother provision', the exact scope of the exception may differ from country to country due to subtle differences in the statutory text[40] and subsequent differing interpretations by national courts. For the new 'European patents with unitary effect', an EU-wide research exception has been formally adopted.[41] It remains to be seen to what extent this statutory exception will trigger a transparent and undisputable scope at the national level. A second-best option could be to attempt to harmonize existing national research exceptions, by developing a common understanding on the application of the research exception.[42]

---

35 K. Strandburg, 'What Does the Public Get? Experimental Use and the Patent Bargain', *Wisconsin Law Review*, vol. 2004, 2004, p. 81.

36 *See* Shapiro, 'Navigating the Patent Thicket: Cross Licenses, Patent Pools, and Standard Setting', p. 119.

37 *See* E. van Zimmeren and G. Van Overwalle, 'A False Sense of Security Offered by Zero-Price Liability Rules? Research Exceptions in the US, Europe and Japan in an Open Innovation Context', in R. Okediji and M. Bagley (eds.), *Global Perspectives on Patent Law*, Oxford, Oxford University Press, (forthcoming 2013).

38 *See* the references cited in van Zimmeren and Van Overwalle, 'A False Sense of Security Offered by Zero-Price Liability Rules?'

39 Most of these publications express particular concern about the potential hindering effects of patents on biomedical research and the applicability of research exceptions to so-called research tools.

40 For details, *see* van Zimmeren and Van Overwalle, 'A False Sense of Security Offered by Zero-Price Liability Rules?'

41 *See* Article 27 of the Agreement on a Unified Patent Court, Brussels, 11 January 2013, which stipulates: 'The rights conferred by a patent shall not extend to any of the following: [. . .] (b) acts done for experimental purposes relating to the subject matter of the patented invention'.

42 The various research exceptions should apply irrespective of the way the pat-

Patent law and competition law in the EU member states leave considerable freedom to patent owners to set up their own licensing agreements and exclusive licensing is not prohibited. Nevertheless, exclusivity may lead to blocking positions and may hamper follow-on innovation and access to technology. At present, two measures exist which might temper cases of *extreme* monopolistic licensing behaviour by patent holders: the compulsory licensing scheme in patent law[43] and the abuse of a dominant position provision in European competition law, which comes into play if the behaviour of a dominant company raises anti-competitive concerns.[44] Such tools, either internal or external to patent law, could be used to meet the growing concern regarding the hindering effects of patents. However, that might not suffice. Additional measures safeguarding follow-on innovation and access to technology, and, ultimately, safeguarding the objectives of social and economic welfare may well be necessary.[45]

3 IMPACT OF EUROPE ON EMERGING MARKET PATENT SYSTEMS

Complementary to the question of what impact emerging market patents have on Europe, the question arises as to how Europe can affect emerging market patent systems. A burning issue in this regard relates to the optimal patent architecture of emerging markets.

It is crystal clear that patent systems in general, and emerging patent systems in particular, should have relative autonomy in designing a system

---

ented subject matter has been put into operation (as a product or as a process) and irrespective of the place of the experiment (be it a public laboratory, hospital, university or private company). The exception should extend to non-commercial purposes and mixed non-commercial/commercial purposes, but should be restricted to early stage ('long distance to market') research. *See* van Zimmeren and Van Overwalle, 'A False Sense of Security Offered by Zero-Price Liability Rules?'

43 C. Correa, 'Pharmaceutical Innovation, Incremental Patenting and Compulsory Licensing', Research Paper 41, South Centre, Geneva, November 2011; E. Van Zimmeren and G. Van Overwalle, 'A Paper Tiger? Compulsory License Regimes for Public Health in Europe', *International Review of Intellectual Property and Competition Law*, vol. 42, no. 1, 2011, pp. 4–40.

44 *See* I. Govaere, *The Use and Abuse of Intellectual Property Rights in E.C. Law,* London and Toronto, Sweet & Maxwell, 1996. *See also* I. Govaere and H. Ullrich (eds.), *Intellectual Property, Market Power and the Public Interest*, Brussels, Peter Lang, 2008.

45 *See* in that regard: G. Van Overwalle, 'Fair Use – a Workable Concept in European Patent Law?', *in Compulsory Licensing – Practical Experiences and Ways Forward*, R. Hilty and K.C. Liu (eds.), in press.

which meets their local needs. Emerging market economies should be able to construct a patent system which balances diverse private and public interests, and to establish safeguards internal or external to patent law. However, it is not at all evident what exact shape emerging market patent systems should take. Should a patent system in emerging markets be modelled along European patent law and should European patent legislation be exported to emerging market countries? In other words, should a patent system be designed to support high quality innovation, supporting originators? Or should an emerging market patent system rather be moulded to accommodate incremental changes and to support assemblers? A patent regime based on a low inventive threshold 'could be functional to the predominantly incremental innovation path prevailing in developing countries, as patents might encourage minor innovations developed by domestic companies'.[46]

Authoritative international institutions, such as the World Bank, are quite firm in suggesting that patent institutions should accommodate high quality innovation. Governments should adopt 'rigorous criteria to assess patentability so as to prevent granting of patents that do not make a substantive technical contribution to the state of the art'.[47] Leading IP scholars follow that reasoning by saying that 'application of low standards does not promote local innovation, while it favours the deployment of aggressive patenting policies by foreign companies'[48] and that 'for a patent wealth maximisation strategy to succeed a country's innovation system must generate core technologies'.[49]

The current debate invites us to believe that the European patent system can stand as a model for emerging market economies. In line with our analysis above, the European patent system may well serve as an example for the establishment of patent regimes in emerging market economies *if, and only if*, a European patent system is transplanted with extensive attention to its vertical and horizontal regulatory functions. In particular, safeguards should be put in place guaranteeing patent quality and

---

46 C. Correa, 'Pharmaceutical Innovation, Incremental Patenting and Compulsory Licensing'. *See* note 43.

47 R. Newfarmer et al., 'Global Economic Prospects and the Developing Countries 2002: Making Trade Work for the World's Poor', The World Bank, Washington, DC, 2011, p. 30, http://siteresources.worldbank.org/INTPROSPECTS/Resources/334934–1322593305595/8287139–1327608053648/GEP2002Chap1.pdf (accessed 9 February 2013).

48 C. Correa, 'Pharmaceutical Innovation, Incremental Patenting and Compulsory Licensing'. *See* note 43.

49 P. Drahos, 'The US, China and the G-77'. *See* note 19.

restricted breadth of claims, accommodating a firm research exception and a compulsory licence regime, and establishing further measures to promote access to technology and to govern licensing. In other words, transplanting the European patent system may be contemplated, *on the condition* that an enhanced and strengthened European patent system is developed; in other words, *if* a European patent system 2.0 is put in place.

4 CONCLUDING REMARKS

Is Zeus, disguised as an Asian tiger, on his way to seduce Europa? Put differently, will the dramatic increase in emerging market patent filings lead to the takeover of Europe by new economies, such as China and Korea? There is no simple and straightforward answer to this question. The present chapter argues that finding an adequate response to the steep increase in emerging market patent filings in Europe requires us to challenge well-established ideas about the objectives of patent law. Next to the conventional narrative of patents as policy tools to stimulate innovation, the discourse on patents as market instruments should be recognized. Only when the European patent system takes into account both aspects of patents – the policy dimension and the market aspect – can measures be contemplated and operationalized which may help dam the emerging market patent tsunami, and control conflicts between (local) industrialists and (foreign/emerging) industrialists, and between (local and foreign) industrialists and consumers and users.

Japan

17. IP-based nation: Strategy of Japan

Yoshiyuki Tamura

1 WHAT IS THE "IP-BASED NATION"?

1.1 Japan Learning from the U.S.

In January 2013, the Intellectual Property Strategy Headquarters at the Japanese Prime Minister's Cabinet announced that it was planning to establish new "Intellectual Property Policy Visions" for Japan. The first draft was published in February 2013 and contained the Japanese government's intellectual property (IP) strategies for competing with emerging economies in the Far East Asia region. The document states that in order to achieve the same levels of availability of intellectual property protection in those countries with emerging economies as in Japan, several measures, such as sending the Japan Patent Office's examiners to other patent offices in the region to harmonize examination processes and cooperation with the World Intellectual Property Organization (WIPO) to enhance intellectual property protection in those countries, would be needed.[1] According to governmental officials, these IP Policy Visions are intended to envision Japan's intellectual property policy for the next decade. They take into account ten years' experience of the "IP-based nation" policy and set out the baselines for making a future for the "IP-based nation" Japan.[2]

In this chapter I will provide a historical overview of Japan's intellectual

[1] Intellectual Property Strategy Headquarters, "Koremade no Senmon-Chousakai, Working Group no Giron o Fumaeta Ronten-seiri(an), Kyousouryoku-kyouka, Kokusai-Hyoujunka-kanren" [Proposed Agenda Based on Discussions in Specialized Committee and Working Group (Draft)] at 6, http://www.kantei.go.jp/jp/singi/titeki2/tyousakai/contents_kyouka/seisakuvision/dai2/siryou01.pdf (accessed 17 April 2013).

[2] Intellectual Property Strategy Headquarters, "Chiteki-Zaisan Seisaku Vision Kentoh Working Group no Sechi ni-tuite" [About Establishment of Working Group on Intellectual Property Policy Visions], http://www.kantei.go.jp/jp/singi/titeki2/tyousakai/contents_kyouka/seisakuvision/dai1/sankou1.pdf (accessed 17 April 2013).

property legislation from the perspective of "trends for and the future of the IP-based nation". Firstly, I will describe how Japan has benefited from the experiences of the U.S. A decade has gone by since the phrase "IP-based nation" started being used as a national policy in Japan in 2002. It originated from the Japanese economy's long-lasting recession, the so-called "Lost Decade", which began in the 1990s, following the bursting of the bubble economy. It is undeniable that Japan's international competitiveness has recently been undergoing a slight decline as compared with historical levels, against the backdrop of pressures from newly industrialized nations, especially those in East Asia, such as China and Korea. Some aspects of this situation can be compared with that of the U.S. in the 1980s. In the 1980s, as the U.S. economy suffered from the pressures of Japan's rise, the Reagan administration announced, in rapid succession, measures for the reinforcement of intellectual property protection. Although it is not clear whether there is actually a causal relationship, it is nonetheless a fact that the U.S. economy, unlike during the recession of the 1980s, rebuilt itself in the 1990s and once again became a world leader. It was then that voices calling for Japan to learn from the U.S. began to be heard. This is usually the story told when explaining the term "IP-based nation".

The reason for strengthening intellectual property protection, especially patent protection, in Japan so that the Japanese economy would benefit

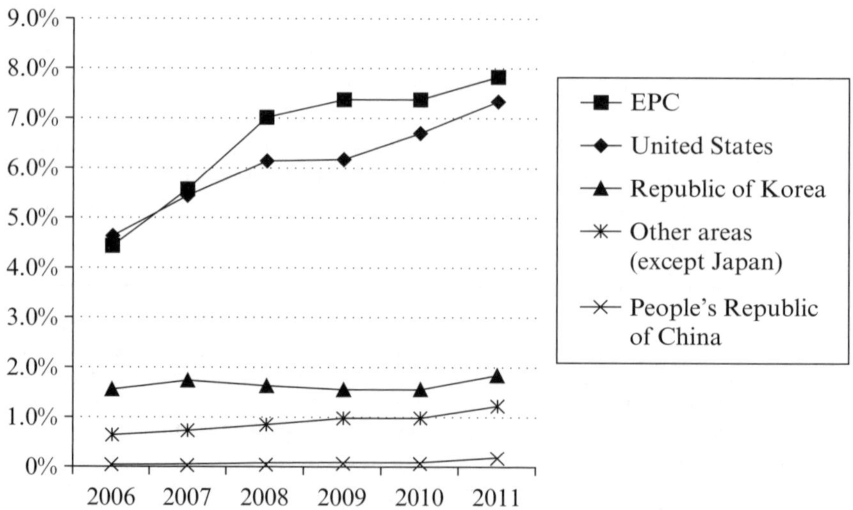

Figure 17.1 Ratio of foreign patent registrations to Japanese patents by nationality of applicant

Table 17.1 Ratio of foreign patent registrations to Japanese patents by nationality of applicant

	2006	2007	2008	2009	2010	2011
United States	4.6%	5.5%	6.2%	6.2%	6.7%	7.4%
EPC	4.5%	5.6%	7.0%	7.4%	7.4%	7.8%
Republic of Korea	1.6%	1.7%	1.6%	1.6%	1.6%	1.8%
People's Republic of China	0.0%	0.0%	0.1%	0.1%	0.1%	0.2%
Other areas (except Japan)	0.6%	0.7%	0.9%	1.0%	1.0%	1.2%

from it stems from the fact that the number of patent registrations for Korean and Chinese applicants in Japan is still quite small.[3] By strengthening patent protection, firms in Japan were thus expected to be better off within the Japanese market than those from other countries in East Asia.

1.2 Ultimate Objective of Intellectual Property Laws

I do not believe that the ultimate objective of intellectual property laws lies solely in the reinforcement of intellectual property rights. The ultimate objective is to encourage innovation and creative expression by providing a certain amount of protection for those intellectual property rights, and in turn, promoting the use of such intellectual property, and by doing so, to develop industries and cultures. I believe that this last part, in particular, is the ultimate objective. It is conceivable, then, that Japan's goal of becoming an "IP-based nation" is by no means a measure for enhancing intellectual property rights, but that the real point of the national policy is to achieve balanced protection. In other words, I believe that intellectual property legislation ought to cause the development of innovation by protecting intellectual property rights, while at the same time taking into consideration the promotion and convenient use of intellectual property, and by keeping an eye on both of the foregoing, as if they were the wheels of a car, so to speak. The following will be an attempt to arrive at an understanding of the recent trends for an IP-based nation from the perspective discussed above.

---

[3] Japan Patent Office, *Tokkyo Kyousei Nenji Houkukusho 2010* [Patent Administration Annual Report 2010], Tokyo, Japan Institute of Invention and Innovation, 2011, p. 25; Japan Patent Office, *Tokkyo Kyousei Nenji Houkukusho 2011* [Patent Administration Annual Report 2011], Tokyo, Japan Institute of Invention and Innovation, 2012, p. 17.

2 KOIZUMI CABINET'S "IP-BASED NATION"

2.1 Policy Speech – Enactment of the Intellectual Property Basic Act

An important trend in Japan's intellectual property legislation started in February 2002, when Prime Minister Junichiro Koizumi made a point of declaring in his policy speech that strategically protecting and using as intellectual property the results of research activities and creative endeavors, and thereby enhancing Japanese industries' international competitiveness, would become a national goal. This is the first time that intellectual property had been discussed in policy speeches.

Shortly after this policy speech was made, the Strategic Council on Intellectual Property was set up, which put together the Intellectual Property Policy Outline. At the same time, a law called the Intellectual Property Basic Act, which set forth an action program, was enacted.

2.2 Intellectual Property Strategy Headquarters and Intellectual Property Strategic Programs

Following the enforcement of the Intellectual Property Basic Act, the Intellectual Property Strategy Headquarters, an offshoot of the Strategic Council on Intellectual Property, was set up in 2003. In addition, the Secretariat of the Intellectual Property Strategy Headquarters was set up in the Cabinet Secretariat as the organ responsible for the administrative affairs of the Intellectual Property Strategy Headquarters. Since then the Secretariat has announced an Intellectual Property Strategic Program every year.

This is, in a sense, revolutionary in light of Japan's historical legislative formulation of intellectual property laws. Historically, each ministry and agency was in charge of its respective laws; that is, the Japan Patent Office was in charge of industrial property rights, such as the Patent Act, the Utility Model Act, the Design Act and the Trademark Act; the Ministry of Economy, Trade and Industry was in charge of the Unfair Competition Prevention Act; the Agency for Cultural Affairs was in charge of the Copyright Act; and the Ministry of Agriculture, Forestry and Fisheries was in charge of the Plant Variety Protection and Seed Act. In other words, each of the ministries and agencies was, in a way, separately formulating intellectual property laws, and issues relating to their multiple jurisdictions were resolved through negotiation between the ministries and agencies.

After the establishment of the Intellectual Property Strategy Headquarters, its Secretariat announces on a yearly basis the Intellectual Property Strategic Programs. These programs outline strategies for adopt-

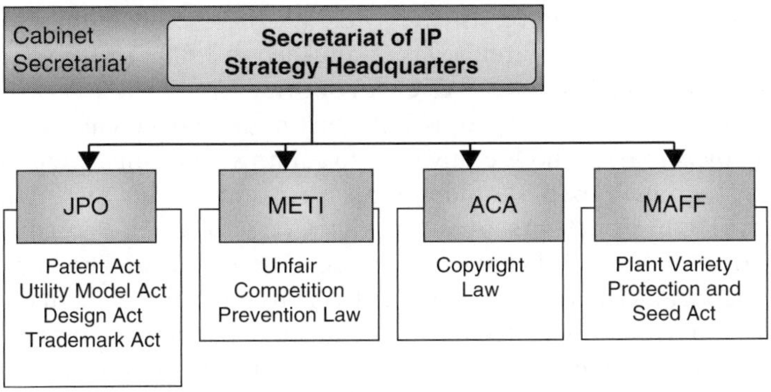

Figure 17.2 Structure of Intellectual Property Strategy Headquarters and related organizations

ing measures in the field of intellectual property protection in individual years. The concrete and final revisions of laws are still implemented by the ministries and agencies in charge.

2.3 Establishment of the Intellectual Property High Court

I believe that the biggest highlight of IP-based nation is the establishment of the Intellectual Property High Court.

With regard to lawsuits for the revocation of decisions made by the Japan Patent Office, the Tokyo High Court has always been the court of first instance with exclusive jurisdiction, and the Supreme Court has always been the court of second instance. This means that all lawsuits for the revocation of decisions made by the Japan Patent Office have been concentrated at and dealt with by the Tokyo High Court. The problem is that, with respect to cases regarding the infringement of intellectual property rights, district courts all over the country have had jurisdiction as the court of first instance, and high courts in eight different locations in the country have been acting as the court of second instance.

This approach had been recognized as being somewhat problematic, even before calls for an IP-based nation policy began to be heard. It was established in the 1996 amendment to the Code of Civil Procedure that the Tokyo District Court and the Osaka District Court would have concurrent jurisdiction with the usual district court of first instance over lawsuits regarding technical intellectual properties. However, this was a concurrent jurisdiction. For example, with regard to cases in Sapporo both the Tokyo District Court and the Sapporo District Court would have jurisdiction.

Under such circumstances, IP-based nation policy turned to the U.S.

court system for reference. In the U.S., an organ called the Court of Appeals for the Federal Circuit was established in 1982. This is referred to as the Federal Circuit or the CAFC, for short.

The CAFC has exclusive appellate jurisdiction over cases involving patent subject matter and is equivalent to Japan's high courts. Discussions arose as to how Japan should imitate this and set up an Intellectual Property High Court. As a result, the Code of Civil Procedure was amended in 2003 to designate the Tokyo District Court and the Osaka District Court as the courts of first instance to have exclusive jurisdiction over lawsuits relating to technical intellectual properties, patent rights and utility model rights, as well as lawsuits relating to computer program copyrights. In addition, the Tokyo High Court has become the sole court of second instance, and, as a result, jurisdiction over infringement lawsuits and lawsuits for the revocation of decisions made by the Japan Patent Office have become concentrated in the Tokyo High Court.

Next, non-technical claims, that is, lawsuits relating to the Trademark Act, the Unfair Competition Prevention Act, and the Copyright Act other than those lawsuits relating to computer programs, had historically been dealt with by district courts throughout the country. As a result of the amendment to the Code of Civil Procedure, the Tokyo District Court and the Osaka District Court were given concurrent jurisdiction as the courts of first instance. The district courts, however, also continue to have jurisdiction. Simply put, the situation improved one step from before. Therefore the changes made by the amendment were that technical intellectual property rights, such as patent rights, which were historically subject to concurrent jurisdiction, became subject to the exclusive jurisdiction of the Tokyo District Court and the Osaka District Court, and lawsuits in relation to other intellectual property rights are able to be filed anywhere, as was previously the case with patent rights and other technical intellectual property rights, but can now also be filed with the Tokyo District Court and the Osaka District Court.

Laying such groundwork, the Act for Establishment of the Intellectual Property High Court was enacted in 2004, under which it was determined that the Intellectual Property High Court should be established in April 2005 as a special branch of the Tokyo High Court. Although it is generally referred to solely as the Intellectual Property High Court, it is nonetheless a special branch of the Tokyo High Court. Therefore, despite the change in name, because the status of the jurisdictions of the courts are still in accordance with the 2003 amendment to the Code of Civil Procedure, I believe that the 2003 amendment to the Code of Civil Procedure was actually the bigger reform. In conclusion, the biggest reform that has occurred to the litigation of intellectual property disputes has been the concentration and unification of jurisdiction through the establishment of the Intellectual Property High Court in 2005 and the prior amendment to the Code of Civil Procedure in 2003.

The Intellectual Property High Court currently operates as four divisions, and if the judgments made by each of these divisions were to constantly differ, there would be no point in having a single Intellectual Property High Court. Therefore, a system referred to as "en banc (*dai-gōgi*)" was established, following the example set by the U.S. Court of Appeals for the Federal Circuit. Under this system, cases identified by the

Table 17.2 Ratio of IPHC judgments which found patents invalid with respect to the cases for revocation of the JPO decisions on invalidation trial

Year	2005	2006	2007	2008	2009	2010
Ratio of IPHC judgments which found patents invalid with respect to the cases for revocation of the JPO decisions on invalidation trial; (b−c+g)/(a−e)	58%	84%	80%	54%	50%	42%
(a) number of IPHC judgments with respect to the cases for revocation of the JPO decisions on invalidation trial	53	86	105	97	107	91
(b) number of judgments with respect to the JPO decisions which invalidated patents	31	65	75	55	66	39
(c) number of judgments revoking	6	3	10	15	21	12
(d) ratio; (c) / (b)	19%	4%	13%	27%	31%	30%
(e) number of judgments made due to the fact that correction of the patent claims had been allowed by the JPO	1	1	2	2	3	1
(f) number of judgments with respect to the JPO decisions which dismissed requests for invalidation	22	21	30	42	41	52
(g) number of judgments revoking	5	9	17	11	8	11
(h) ratio;(g) / (f)	22%	42%	56%	26%	19%	21%

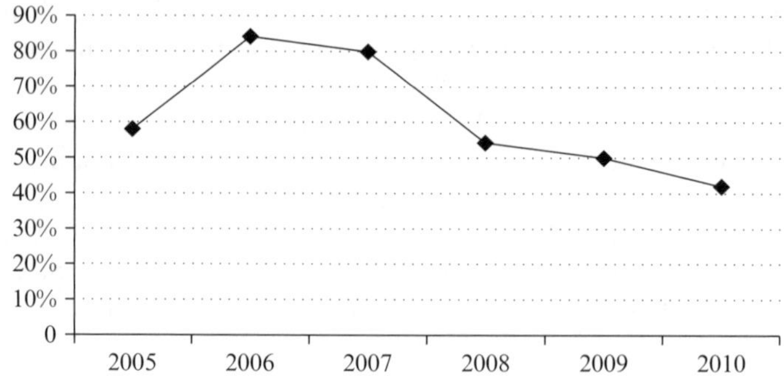

Figure 17.3 Ratio of IPHC judgments which found patents invalid with respect to the cases for revocation of the JPO decisions on invalidation trial

Intellectual Property High Court as significant cases relating to technical intellectual property rights are referred to as "en banc cases" and are tried by five judges representing the four divisions. The aim is to ensure consistency of judicial precedents within the Intellectual Property High Court.

It is hard to fully evaluate the effects of establishing the Intellectual Property High Court at the moment, since much has yet to be seen. Just to make a minor observation, right after its establishment, one could observe an anti-patent storm that raged at the Intellectual Property High Court for almost two years from 2006 to 2007. This was caused by the Japanese system of appointing judges, the main feature of which is the so-called "rotation" system of judges. It means that the judges are to be transferred from one court to another after a certain period of time. Coincidently, during the period of 2006 and 2007, the judges who had an anti-patent tendency were in the majority at the Intellectual Property High Court.

Recently, the anti-patent storm has calmed down somewhat. However, it should be noted that the Intellectual Property High Court has four divisions and the influence of the Chief Judge of each division on individual cases is enormous. The preferences of the four Chief Judges can be categorized by the three following types of preference: pro-patent, neutral and anti-patent. In 2010 there were huge tendency differences among the four divisions of Intellectual Property High Court.[4]

---

[4] A. Kawada and Y. Inoue, "Heisei 22 Nen ni okeru Tokkyo Shinketsu Torikeshi Soshou no Gaikyou" [Review of Recent Judgments of the Japanese IP-High Court in Appeal Cases against Decisions of the Japanese Patent Office], *Patent*, vol. 64, no. 3, 2011, p. 44.

Table 17.3 Inter-division differences in IPHC judgments which found patents invalid with respect to the cases for revocation of the JPO decisions on invalidation trial (2010)

Division	Patentee's favor	Patentee's disfavor	Ratio in patentee's favor
1st Div.	12	8	67%
2nd Div.	5	12	29%
3rd Div.	24	10	71%
4th Div	12	11	52%
Total	53	41	56%

From 2011 this diversification has been disappearing, presumably due to the transfer of judges through the "rotation" system.[5]

Table 17.4 Inter-division differences in IPHC judgments which found patents invalid with respect to the cases for revocation of the JPO decisions on invalidation trial (2011)

Division	Patentee's favor	Patentee's disfavor	Ratio in patentee's favor
1st Div.	5	1	83%
2nd Div.	15	11	58%
3rd Div.	15	14	52%
4th Div	20.4	9.6	68%
Total	55.4	35.6	61%

2.4 Evaluation

As discussed above, the accomplishments to date of "IP-based nation", the national strategy launched by the Koizumi Cabinet, can be summed up in the following three points: the establishment of the Secretariat of the Intellectual Property Strategy Headquarters, the implementation of Intellectual Property Strategic Programs, and the establishment of the Intellectual Property High Court. However, the trend in Japan's reinforcement of intellectual property protection actually started in the early 1990s, before the Koizumi Cabinet's "IP-based nation". In order to fully

[5] A. Kawada and Y. Inoue, "Heisei 23 Nen ni okeru Tokkyo Shinketsu Torikeshi Soshou no Gaikyou" [Review of Judgments of the Japanese IP-High Court in Appeal Cases against Decisions of the Japan Patent Office], *Patent*, vol. 65, no. 6, 2012, p. 89, 90.

evaluate Japan's intellectual property strategy, we also need to look at earlier events. Accordingly, I will be going back a little further in time for the purposes of the discussion hereafter.

3 HISTORY OF JAPAN'S LEGAL SYSTEM FOR INTELLECTUAL PROPERTY[6]

3.1 State of Japan's Intellectual Property Laws Prior to 1990[7]

Prior to 1990, Japan's protection of intellectual property laws, or what was referred to as industrial property laws at that time, was in fact among the weaker of those in the developed countries. This had been the case since the Meiji period, when protection for industrial property rights had been introduced due to external pressure and had been, in fact, requested as a condition for the abolishment of extraterritoriality applied to the citizens of some foreign countries who had been exempt from the jurisdiction of Japanese domestic law. During the 100-plus years from the Meiji period to the 1980s, Japan was more engaged in the development of domestic industries by imitating the most advanced technologies of foreign countries. This was based on the belief that leaving some room for imitation would better serve the purposes of national policies. Japan's approach was to fulfill the minimum level of obligations required to join treaties but not to provide further protection.

Even so, in 1959, the current Patent Act was enacted, and subsequently, from around the 1970s, due to the substantial advancement of Japan's own technology, amendments to the laws were made gradually in an attempt to transform Japan into a developed country in terms of intellectual property rights.

The first of these amendments was that of the Patent Act in 1975. With regard to chemical substances, for example, prior to the amendment patents were not granted to new chemical substances. Patents were granted only to the methods of creating such new chemical substances.

---

[6] N. Nakayama (ed.), *Tsūshōsangyō Seisakushi 11 Chitekizaisan Seisaku 1980–2000* [History of Trade and Industrial Policies 11, Intellectual Property Policies 1980–2000], Tokyo, Research Institute of Economy, Trade and Industry, 2011.

[7] See H. Odagiri, A. Goto and A. Sunami, "IPR and the Catch-Up Process in Japan", in Odagiri, H., Goto, A., Sunami, A., and Nelson, R.R. (eds.), *Intellectual Property Rights, Development, and Catch-Up: An International Comparative Study*, Oxford, Oxford University Press, 2010, pp. 95–129.

The 1975 amendment enabled patents to be granted to the chemical substances themselves.

In 1985, due to external pressure, as well as the development of Japan's own computer programming industry, it was determined that computer programs would be protected under the Copyright Act. At the time, there was a lot of controversy as to whether the Ministry of International Trade and Industry would take the initiative or the Agency for Cultural Affairs would take the initiative, and whether rights called "program rights" would be created or an amendment would be made to the Copyright Act. In the end, the Copyright Act was amended in 1985 in accordance with requests by the U.S., clarifying that computer programs would be protected as copyrighted works. Further, in the same year, Japan, together with the U.S., became the first countries in the world to establish an Act on the Circuit Layout of Semiconductor Integrated Circuits in order to protect the mask works of semiconductor chips.

The 1987 amendment to the Patent Act introduced "perfect multiple claims system" for the first time in Japan. Although even before the amendment the Japan Patent Office claimed that the 1975 amendment to the Japanese Patent Act had already introduced "multiple claims system" into Japanese patent law, the 1975 amendment had only permitted embodiment claims. Until 1987, applicants could not entirely cover related inventions in a single patent application. In the worst case scenario, they could not cover them even in multiple applications, because such applications could sometimes be rejected for being duplicative patent applications on the same invention. Since the enactment of the 1987 amendment applicants have therefore been able to enjoy full patent protection by utilizing the "perfect multiple claims system".

3.2 Overview of Measures Taken in the 1990s for the Reinforcement of Intellectual Property Protection

Of course, there continued to be various problems with the intellectual property rights protection system. For example in the 1980s an extremely serious problem remained with regard to the patent system, in that there were delays to or prolongation of examinations. A remedy to this problem was strongly pushed for, especially by the U.S., which criticized the process for taking as long as four or five years. At the time, the examinations alone took that amount of time and, where the examination resulted in a decision of refusal and an appeal against the decision was filed and rejected and proceeded to a lawsuit for the revocation of such an appeal decision, there were cases where the entire process easily took about ten years. Occasionally, there were cases that went on for so long that one had to wonder if winning the patent case after so much time would not be pointless. The U.S. had always regarded this as problematic, claiming that this was virtually the same as not protecting intellectual property rights.

Further, with regard to the scope of protection, Japan's courts at the time had a tendency to interpret claims in a fairly flexible manner, but did not, at least openly, acknowledge the Doctrine of Equivalents. It was said that asserting the Doctrine of Equivalents would, if anything, result in losing the lawsuit and that it would be a better litigation strategy to use the claim interpretation approach.

Moreover, with regard to damages, up until around 1990, the mainstream tendency was to calculate damages at a conservative level. Loss of profits was hardly ever acknowledged. There was also a tendency to not acknowledge the infringer's profits due to the difficulty of calculating such profits, or to not acknowledge reimbursement of infringer's profits unless the patent holder was working the relevant patent, and the amount of compensation equivalent to royalties was also only calculated at the market level rate for the industry. Therefore, it was said that it could, in fact, be more beneficial to commit an infringement.[8]

If we were to turn our eyes to the trademark system, we would find that the Trademark Act basically only protected trademarks of products and that service marks were not yet recognized as being subject to protection. Under the laws effective at that time, all service marks fell within the scope of the Unfair Competition Prevention Act and were not subject to the application of the Trademark Act. The Unfair Competition Prevention Act, at that time, consisted merely of six articles and, basically, the only article relating to intellectual property laws was the provision on the protection of well-known marks. The other provisions were on such matters as quality misconception and defamation. Also, restrictions on the use of trade secrets were not yet established in Japan in the 1980s, leaving trade secrets to be protectable only through contracts. As for protections against copies of a good's shape, the existence of such a thing had not even been contemplated.

Measures for the reinforcement of protection for various intellectual property rights finally began to be introduced, one after another, after the beginning of the 1990s. The Japan Patent Office took a great deal of trouble to reduce the delay in examination processes. These delays had been the subject of criticism during the Structural Impediments Initiative talks. The

---

[8] Y. Tamura, "Tokkyo-ken Shingai ni Taisuru Songai-baishō (1)–(4)" [Damages for Infringements of Patent Rights (1)–(4)], *Hōgaku Kyōkai Zasshi*, vol. 108, no. 6, 1991, pp. 7, 9 and 10; Y. Tamura, *Chiteki-zaisan-ken to Songai-baishō* [Damages for Patent Infringements], Tokyo, Koubundou, new edition, 2004.

Japan Patent Office started off by enacting the Act on Special Provisions for Procedures related to Industrial Property Rights in 1990 and then proceeding with the plan for paperless application documents, thereby succeeding in enhancing the efficiency of the examination processes. Further, at the time, applications for utility models were more common than those for patents and, in Japan, utility models were subject to a substantive examination system, which was one of the factors leading to the delay in examination processes. In 1993, the non-substantive examination system was adopted in order to lighten the burden of the Japan Patent Office. Countries which have adopted the utility model system include Germany and Japan, but do not include the U.S. The utility model systems are generally established by less technologically developed countries that have been required for various reasons to adopt industrial property laws and patent laws, based upon their perception that major patents are most likely to be monopolized by foreign companies and, therefore, that a special law on minor patents must be established in order to protect their domestic industries.

Various systems were also simplified in an attempt to increase the efficiency of administrative actions relating to examinations by reducing the back-and-forth required for amendment procedures as much as possible. Examples of this were restricting the period during which amendments to patent applications may be made and abolishing the trial system used in response to an examiner's ruling dismissing an amendment. As a result, by as early as 1995, the goal of becoming capable of issuing a first action within two years, that is, completing examinations within two years from the date on which the request for an examination was first made, was accomplished. As for the scope of the protection of patents and in respect to damages, various improvements were made through the formulation of judicial precedents and doctrines, primarily at the Tokyo District Court or the Tokyo High Court and, ultimately, the Supreme Court.

With regard to the Doctrine of Equivalents, the doctrine began to be squarely acknowledged by the Supreme Court in the very famous Ball Spline Bearing Case (Supreme Court ruling of February 24, 1998, Minshu, vol. 52, no. 1, p. 113 [Ball Spline Bearing]). Although the case was remanded on the grounds that it did not meet the necessary requirements, the Doctrine of Equivalents was established as a court precedent thereafter, due to the extremely detailed nature of the judge's opinion.[9] Of course,

[9] Y. Tamura, "Kintouron ni okeru Honshitsuteki Bubun no Youken no Igi (2-Kan) – Kintouron wa 'Shin no Hatsumei' wo Kyūsai Suru Seido ka?" [Significance of the Essential Part Requirement in the Doctrine of Equivalents (2-Final) – Is the Doctrine of Equivalents a System that will Rescue "True Investments"?], *Intellectual Property Law and Policy Journal*, vol. 22, 2009, pp. 55–85; Y. Tamura,

the number of rulings that actually acknowledge equivalency is limited. But I believe that it is significant that the requirements for the applicability of the Doctrine of Equivalents have been established.

Also with regard to damages, theoretical standards were implemented to raise the sums of damages, albeit only in the lower courts. For example, with regard to compensation equivalent to royalties, courts began to squarely propose to make compensation equivalent to royalties higher than the royalties payable pursuant to standard license agreements, based on the view that such sums should be in amounts appropriate to the damages paid by the infringers. I believe that the current approved rate is around 50% higher than the royalties payable pursuant to standard license agreements.

As for the reimbursement of an infringer's profits, although this area of law has undergone many changes, marginal profits (which are large profits that are not merely net profits) have come to be seen as reimbursable. Also, as a result of the 1998 or 1999 amendment to the Patent Act and subsequent court cases, presumptions have in many cases arisen with regard to the causal relationship of the loss of profits to the infringement, resulting in high levels of sums equivalent to royalties being received as compensation. The acknowledgment of infringers' profits and the recognition of the possibility of loss of profit compensation exceeding such amounts are also progressing. Consequently, I believe that the state of the law is no longer advantageous to infringers. Rather, I have become a little worried that there will be an increase, albeit not to the extent in the U.S., in situations in which third parties, in fear of becoming party to an infringement lawsuit and having to pay a significant amount of damages, are forced to pay royalties despite their belief that the scope of the protected patents might not extend to them or that the patents might later be proved invalid. It is necessary to keep an eye on the fact that third parties may become somewhat intimidated by this possibility.

Further, another important point is that, given the fact that patent rights are becoming more and more reinforced by judicial precedents and doctrines as discussed above, the actual patent rights, when reinforced to this extent, must in return be worthy of the reinforcement. The legal principle that aims to maintain such a balance is the one regarding the exercise of rights originating from patents that do not satisfy patentability requirements and therefore should be invalid. The historical understanding was that, even if there were grounds for invalidity with respect to a patent right, such as the lack of novelty, such a patent right remained valid

---

Tokkyohou No Riron [The Theory of Patent Law], Tokyo, Yuhikaku Publishing Co. Ltd., 2009, pp. 67–127.

until an invalidity decision had been finalized, and that administrative acts based on the right were tentatively valid. In practice, non-infringement judgments were, where possible, given with regard to patents with grounds for invalidity, using not only the theory of limitation to working examples (*Jisshirei Gentei-setsu*) but other various doctrines such as the theory of exclusion of publicly known technologies (*Kōchi Gijutsu Jogai-setsu*). The court practice in Japan since the Supreme Court was established under the former Constitution (*Daishin-in*), was for the court not to squarely state that a certain patent is invalid.

However, considering that the protection of patents is being widely reinforced, it would be unbalanced to allow the exercise of patent rights that should be invalid. I had been writing a thesis on how invalidity defenses should be acknowledged since around 1996,[10] and, in 2000, the Supreme Court ruled in the Kilby Patent Case (Supreme Court ruling of 11 April 2000, Minshu, vol. 54, no. 4, p. 1,368 [Semiconductor Equipment]) that the exercise of patent rights which will clearly be invalidated by an invalidation trial before the Japan Patent Office would in the future be deemed to be an abuse of rights and would therefore not be permitted.[11] Because the Kilby patent, an extremely famous patent relating to semiconductors, was the subject of this case, a defense sometimes referred to as the "Kilby Defense" was acknowledged.

Subsequently, in a 2004 amendment to the Patent Act, Article 104–3 was added to the Act, expressly setting forth that the court may, in infringement lawsuits, give a judgment admitting a patent invalidity defense. Although the text of the Article is somewhat difficult to interpret, it is ordinary court practice to interpret the Article as the court being able to judge that a patent is invalid, regardless of whether the invalidity is clear or not. I believe that it should be limited to cases where the invalidity is clear; however, actual court practice has progressed further from the Kilby Defense and judgments admitting an invalidity defense are being made boldly, including in cases where such invalidity is unclear.

The above is a discussion on patents, but there are also other examples, such as trademarks. Protection for service marks was adopted in 1991 and three-dimensional trademark protection was adopted in 1996. With regard to three-dimensional trademarks, in court cases following the adoption of the protection, there was a period of time in which attitudes regarding

---

10 Y. Tamura, *Kinouteki Chiteki-zaisan-hou no Riron* [The Functional Perspectives of Intellectual Property Law], Tokyo, Shinzansha Publisher Co. Ltd., 1996, pp. 58–137.

11 Y. Tamura, *Tokkyohou No Riron* [The Theory of Patent Law], Tokyo, Yuhikaku Publishing Co. Ltd., Tokyo, pp. 201–30.

the shapes of products were too strict, as represented by the Hiyoko Case (Intellectual Property High Court ruling of 29 November 2006, Hanji, no. 1950, p. 3).[12] However, unreasonable hurdles have been gradually reduced due to such judgments as that of the Intellectual Property High Court in the Coca-Cola Case (Intellectual Property High Court ruling of 29 May 2008, Hanji, no. 2006, p. 36 [Coca-Cola]).[13] Currently, three-dimensional trademarks other than the shapes of products are easily acknowledged.

As for the Unfair Competition Prevention Act, the Act underwent a complete revision in 1993. Firstly, in 1990, a provision relating to protection for trade secrets was set forth in the Unfair Competition Prevention Act. This is an extremely significant revision. The Ministry of International Trade and Industry, going with the flow of those times, set up the Intellectual Property Policy Office. However, unlike the Japan Patent Office, which is an external bureau, the Intellectual Property Policy Office was not in charge of many laws, so it was decided that the Intellectual Property Policy Office would be expanded and put in charge of the Unfair Competition Prevention Act. As a result, a complete revision was enacted in 1993, under which the Unfair Competition Prevention Act was expanded with regard to such matters as imitation of shapes of products and the protection of famous marks and other indications. A look at the cases pending before the courts today indicates that the most common cases relate to patents, followed by the Unfair Competition Prevention Act, the Copyright Act, and trademarks, in that order. The Unfair Competition Prevention Act is becoming a significant source of litigation.

4 CONCLUSION – FOR A TRUE "IP-BASED NATION"

Having taken a look, as we did above, we can see that, within the relatively long history of Japan's intellectual property legislation, Japan's intellectual property laws did not reach the minimum protection levels set forth in

---

[12] X. Liu, "Shouhin-nado no Rittai-teki Keijou ni Kansuru Shouhyouhou 3Jou 2Kou no Tekiyou – "HIYOKO" Rittai Shouhyou Touroku Shinketsu Torikesu Seikyu Jiken" [The Protection of Shapes as 3D Trademarks in Japan ("HIYOKO" Case, Intellectual Property High Court, 29 November 2006), *Intellectual Property Law and Policy Journal*, no. 16, 2007, pp. 311–44.

[13] Y. Tamura and X. Liu, "*Rittai Shouhyou no Touroku Youken nituite – 'Coca-Cola' Rittai Shouhyou Jiken*" [Registration of a 3D Trademark ("Coca-Cola" Case, Intellectual Property High Court, 29 May 2008)], *Intellectual Property Management*, vol. 58, no. 10/no. 11, 2008, pp. 1267–78/1393–404.

the Agreement on Trade-Related Aspects of Intellectual Property Rights (the "TRIPS Agreement") until recently – more specifically, the early 1990s when trade secret protection legislation (1990) and the service mark protection legislation (1991) were passed. In other words, it was not until immediately before the TRIPS Agreement was adopted in 1994 that Japan by and large reached TRIPS standards.[14]

Moreover, it was not until the late 1990s, when three-dimensional trademarks (1996) and the Doctrine of Equivalents (1998) were adopted and the system regarding damages for infringements was reformed, that Japan's level of protection of intellectual property rights exceeded the minimum level set forth in the TRIPS Agreement and Japan became a country with strong intellectual property protection.

That is to say, Japan, with its slogan of becoming an "IP-based nation", is, today, enjoying strong protection of intellectual property rights, but, up until very recently, Japan, with its weak protection of intellectual property rights, had been making efforts to catch up with and overtake the technologies of developed countries. To forget that and force other countries, including developing countries, to reach a level of intellectual property protection that even Japan could only reach in the 1990s (when it was the world's second largest economy), as if it were something that contributes to the development of industries and is the ethically logical thing to do, is, at least from a historical perspective, off the mark. Further, it is my belief that an understanding of such history indicates that we should, in thinking not only about foreign countries, but about the future of intellectual property legislation in Japan, proceed with systemic reforms only after deep consideration as to whether complete devotion to the enhancement of intellectual property rights really does lead to industrial development.

REFERENCES

Intellectual Property Strategy Headquarters, "Chiteki-Zaisan Seisaku Vision Kentoh Working Group no Sechi ni-tuite" [About Establishment of Working Group on Intellectual Property Policy Visions], http://www.kantei.go.jp/jp/singi/

---

14 The strategies adopted by Keidanren and MITI (Ministry of International Trade and Industry) for the TRIPS negotiations in the late 1980s were reportedly designed to elevate the level of intellectual property protection in developing countries on the one hand and to control and mitigate the impact of U.S. protectionism on overall negotiations. See H. Tohya, "TRIPs no Kyouyu Chishikika (Kanzen-Ban)" [Globalization of TRIPs as Consensual Knowledge: Structure, Process, and Actors], *Chiteki Zaisan Hohseisakugaku Kenkyu*, vol. 35, 2011, pp. 164–5.

titeki2/tyousakai/contents_kyouka/seisakuvision/dai1/sankou1.pdf (accessed 17 April 2013).
Intellectual Property Strategy Headquarters, "Koremade no Senmon-Chousakai, Working Group no Giron o Fumaeta Ronten-seiri(an), Kyousouryoku-kyouka, Kokusai-Hyoujunka-kanren" [Proposed Agenda Based on Discussions in Specialized Committee and Working Group (Draft)] at 6, http://www.kantei.go.jp/jp/singi/titeki2/tyousakai/contents_kyouka/seisakuvision/dai2/siryou01.pdf (accessed 17 April 2013).
Japan Patent Office, *Tokkyo Kyousei Nenji Houkukusho 2010* [Patent Administration Annual Report 2010], Tokyo, Japan Institute of Invention and Innovation, 2011.
Japan Patent Office, *Tokkyo Kyousei Nenji Houkukusho 2011* [Patent Administration Annual Report 2011], Tokyo, Japan Institute of Invention and Innovation, 2012.
Kawada, A. and Inoue, Y., "Heisei 22 Nen ni okeru Tokkyo Shinketsu Torikeshi Soshou no Gaikyou" [Review of Recent Judgments of the Japanese IP-High Court in Appeal Cases against Decisions of the Japanese Patent Office], *Patent*, vol. 64, no. 3, 2011.
Kawada, A. and Inoue, Y., "Heisei 23 Nen ni okeru Tokkyo Shinketsu Torikeshi Soshou no Gaikyou" [Review of Judgments of the Japanese IP-High Court in Appeal Cases against Decisions of the Japan Patent Office], *Patent*, vol. 65, no. 6, 2012.
Liu, X., "Shouhin-nado no Rittai-teki Keijou ni Kansuru Shouhyouhou 3Jou 2Kou no Tekiyou – 'HIYOKO' Rittai Shouhyou Touroku Shinketsu Torikesu Seikyu Jiken" [The Protection of Shapes as 3D Trademarks in Japan ("HIYOKO" Case, Intellectual Property High Court, 29 November 2006)], *Intellectual Property Law and Policy Journal*, no. 16, 2007, pp. 311–44.
Nakayama, N. (ed.), *Tsūshōsangyō Seisakushi 11 Chitekizaisan Seisaku 1980–2000* [History of Trade and Industrial Policies 11, Intellectual Property Policies 1980–2000], Tokyo, Research Institute of Economy, Trade and Industry, 2011.
Odagiri, H., Goto, A., and Sunami, A., "IPR and the Catch-Up Process in Japan", in Odagiri, H., Goto, A., Sunami, A., and Nelson, R.R. (eds.), *Intellectual Property Rights, Development, and Catch-Up: An International Comparative Study*, Oxford, Oxford University Press, 2010, pp. 95–129.
Tamura, Y., "Tokkyo- ken Shingai ni Taisuru Songai- baishō (1)–(4)" [Damages for Infringements of Patent Rights (1)–(4)], *Hōgaku Kyōkai Zasshi* vol. 108, no. 6, 1991, pp. 7, 9, 10.
Tamura, Y., "Kintouron ni okeru Honshitsuteki Bubun no Youken no Igi (2-Kan) – Kintouron wa 'Shin no Hatsumei' wo Kyūsai Suru Seido ka?" [Significance of the Essential Part Requirement in the Doctrine of Equivalents (2-Final) – Is the Doctrine of Equivalents a System that will Rescue "True Investments"?], *Intellectual Property Law and Policy Journal*, vol. 22, 2009, pp. 55–85.
Tamura, Y., *Kinouteki Chiteki-zaisan-hou no Riron* [The Functional Perspectives of Intellectual Property Law], Tokyo, Shinzansha Publisher Co. Ltd., 1996.
Tamura, Y., *Tokkyohou No Riron* [The Theory of Patent Law], Tokyo, Yuhikaku Publishing Co. Ltd., 2009.
Tamura, Y. and Liu, X., 'Rittai Shouhyou no Touroku Youken nituite – 'Coca-Cola' Rittai Shouhyou Jiken" [Registration of a 3D Trademark ("Coca-Cola" Case, Intellectual Property High Court, 29 May 2008)], *Intellectual Property Management*, vol. 58, nos. 10/11, 2008, pp. 1267–78/1393–404.

USA

18. The United States response to emerging technological powers

Frederick M. Abbott

1 INTRODUCTION

If knowledge were a global public good, the geographic location of innovative activity would not be a matter of national concern. Technology would diffuse without regard to national boundaries. Producers and consumers would take advantage of new ideas regardless of their source. But the success of industry has been closely linked to the innovation-component of goods and services[1] and the success of industry has been correlated with national economic growth, employment and standards of living.[2]

Over the past 10 to 15 years the world economy has been transformed by rapid development in a number of the larger developing countries, such as Brazil, China, India, Indonesia and South Africa. This transformation in some developing countries has brought with it profound changes. Increasing technical capacity in the emerging economy countries has placed pressure on wages in developed countries and hastened their shift from goods-based to service-based economies.[3] Competition for natural resources has become more intense as demand for them has risen. Financial markets have become increasingly interconnected, seemingly heightening risks. It is generally a time of stress in the global economy.

In such an environment, it is not surprising that national governments

---

1 Dating back at least to the "high technology" competition between the United States and Japan of the 1970–80s. See Laura D'Andrea Tyson, *Who's Bashing Whom: Trade Conflict in High Technology Industries*, Washington, DC, Institute for International Economics, 1992.

2 *See, e.g.*, "Engines of Growth: Manufacturing Industries in the U.S. Economy", U.S. Department of Commerce, Economics and Statistics Administration, Office of Business and Industrial Analysis, July 1995.

3 *See* Thomas Palley, "Rethinking Trade and Trade Policy: Gomory, Baumol, and Samuelson on Comparative Advantage", Public Policy Brief, No. 86, Levy Economics Institute of Bard College, 2006, regarding economic trends and political reaction to them.

are inclined to pursue "protective" or defensive technology agendas. Technology is perceived as an "asset". That asset is protected in two basic ways: (1) by physical and technical defenses, such as plant security guards and anti-cyber-attack software; and (2) by intellectual property legal barriers, such as patents. *The New York Times* has recently published a series of articles describing the threat to US industry from cyber-attacks originating from China,[4] following warnings from policy experts.[5] The US government is debating ever-stronger measures to address cyber-threats from abroad[6] and the Obama Administration has launched a "strategy on mitigating the theft of US trade secrets".[7] Cyber-security portends to be a growth industry worldwide.

On one level, cyber-security measures and patents are designed to protect against the same threat. Both types of security are intended to prevent unauthorized appropriation of valuable technology. But, the contexts are different. Cyber-security devices and physical protective measures are generally designed to function as a form of trade secret protection, keeping technology out of the hands of a competitor (whether private or military). Patents, on the other hand, exist because their owners wish to exploit technology in an environment where it will not remain secret. The purchaser of the patented product would otherwise be able to reverse engineer the technology, and to make and sell a competing product.

---

4 Nicole Perlroth, David E. Sanger and Michael S. Schmidt, "As Hacking Against U.S. Rises, Experts Try to Pin Down Motive", *New York Times*, 4 March 2013,http://www.nytimes.com/2013/03/04/us/us-weighs-risks-and-motives-of-hacking-by-china-or-iran.html (accessed 12 April 2013); David E. Sanger, David Barboza and Nicole Perlroth, "Chinese Army Unit Is Seen as Tied to Hacking Against U.S.", *New York Times*, 18 February 2013, http://www.nytimes.com/2013/02/19/technology/chinas-army-is-seen-as-tied-to-hacking-against-us.html (accessed 12 April 2013).

5 *See, e.g.*, Richard A. Clarke and Robert E. Knake, *Cyber War: The Next Threat to National Security and What to Do About It*, New York, NY, HarperCollins Publishers, 2010.

6 *See, e.g.,* David E. Sanger and Thom Shanker, "Broad Powers Seen for Obama in Cyberstrikes", *New York Times*, 3 February 2013, http://www.nytimes.com/2013/02/04/us/broad-powers-seen-for-obama-in-cyberstrikes.html?pagewanted=all (accessed 12 April 2013).

7 *See* Executive Office of the President, "Administration Strategy Mitigating the Theft of U.S. Trade Secrets", The White House, Washington, DC, Defense Security Service, February 2013, http://www.whitehouse.gov/sites/default/files/omb/IPEC/admin_strategy_on_mitigating_the_theft_of_u.s._trade_secrets.pdf (accessed 12 April 2013). In 2006 the United States ratified the Council of Europe Convention on Cybercrime, becoming a member 1 January 2007. *See* Declan McCullagh and Anne Broache, "Senate Ratifies Controversial Cybercrime Treaty", *CNET News*, 4 August 2006.

2 LEGAL BACKGROUND

2.1 US Section 337

The United States has long been attentive to technological competition from foreign nations. It has maintained legislation intended to prevent the importation of goods that would infringe upon patents in force in the United States.[8] Section 337 of the Tariff Act of 1930 began to be used significantly for IP claims against allegedly infringing imports in the late 1980s and was the subject of a GATT (General Agreement on Trade and Tariffs) dispute initiated by the EU, decided in 1989.[9] The GATT Panel found that, despite its seemingly neutral appearance, the version of Section 337 in force in 1989 was designed to discriminate against imported products by facilitating patent infringement claims against them (as compared with comparable claims involving products within the US domestic stream of commerce).

Section 337 continues to be actively used by holders of US patents in various industry sectors as a means to prevent entry of infringing goods into US commerce. Apple has invoked Section 337 against Samsung.[10] Pfizer has used Section 337 to obtain a global blocking order against imports of sildenafil citrate (Viagra).[11] In a Section 337 proceeding initiated by Fuji Photo, the Court of Appeals for the Federal Circuit ruled that parallel importation of patented products into the United States was unlawful.[12]

---

[8] *See* Frederick Abbott, Thomas Cottier, and Francis Gurry, *International Intellectual Property in an Integrated World Economy*, 2nd edn., New York, NY, Aspen Publishers, 2011, pp. 774–84.

[9] United States – Section 337 of the Tariff Act of 1930, Report by the Panel adopted on 7 November 1989 (L/6439–36S/345).

[10] *See* United States International Trade Commission, In the Matter of Certain Electronic Digital Media Devices and Components Thereof, Inv. No. 337-TA-796, 2 August 2011 (Complainant Apple Inc.; Respondent Samsung Electronics Co., Ltd., et al.).

[11] United States International Trade Commission, In the Matter of Certain Sildenafil or Any Pharmaceutically Acceptable Salt Thereof, Such as Sildenafil Citrate, and Products Containing Same, Inv. No. 337-TA-489, General Exclusion Order.

[12] *Jazz Photo v. ITC*, 264 F.3d 1094 (Fed. Cir. 2001). It is worth noting that this decision adopting national exhaustion for patents is *not* by the Supreme Court, and that the Supreme Court has adopted international exhaustion with respect to other IP rights. The United States follows a policy of international exhaustion with respect to copyright (*see Kirtsaeng v. John Wiley & Sons, Inc.*, US Supreme Court, Slip Opinion, No. 11–697, decided 19 March 2013), and a policy of international exhaustion for trademark (under a common control doctrine) (*see K Mart Corp. v. Cartier*, Inc., 486 U.S. 281 (1988).

2.2 The TRIPS Agreement

Section 337 addresses only importation. The United States made its first serious foray toward addressing appropriation of US technology outside its borders by placing negotiations on trade-related intellectual property rights in the GATT Uruguay Round mandate in 1986.[13] Shortly thereafter, Congress enacted Special 301 as part of 1988 amendments to the Trade Act of 1974, establishing a mechanism under which foreign countries might be placed on a special priority IP violators list, subjecting them to accelerated Section 301 trade remedy proceedings.[14] Following seven years of negotiation at the GATT, the WTO TRIPS Agreement emerged. The TRIPS Agreement established baseline substantive and enforcement standards for IP, as well as providing for dispute settlement with potential trade sanctions.[15]

During the Uruguay Round, the concern of the United States was basically with "outright copying" of US-developed technology by foreign enterprises. China was barely a blip on the economic radar screen. The Asian Tigers, including Taiwan, were becoming very adept at replicating US technology, but in the 1980s and early 1990s, these countries were not generating new technology on their own (though expatriates from these countries were helping to fuel the innovation boom in Silicon Valley).

3 THE EVOLVING INTERNATIONAL SCENE

3.1 The New Form of Competition

Today the character of the competitive innovation threat confronting the United States is shifting. China, India and Brazil are not yet generating

---

[13] This observation applies to civilian technologies. After World War II the United States led an effort among "Western" powers to prevent their military technologies from being acquired by Cold War adversaries. This included the creation of the Coordinating Committee for Multilateral Export Controls or "CoCom". *See, e.g.*, "CoCom", Wikipedia, http://en.wikipedia.org/wiki/COCOM (accessed 12 April 2013).

[14] Regarding enactment of Special 301 and its relation to the Uruguay Round TRIPS negotiations, see Frederick M. Abbott, "Protecting First World Assets in the Third World: Intellectual Property Negotiations in the GATT Multilateral Framework", *Vanderbilt Journal of Transnational Law*, vol. 22, no. 4, 1989, p. 689.

[15] As discussed later in this chapter, the United States incorporated an IP chapter in the North American Free Trade Agreement (NAFTA) (which entered into force on 1 January 1994) that largely reflected TRIPS Agreement rules.

innovative technologies at the same level as the United States, Germany and Japan, but it seems evident that the capacity-differential is narrowing.[16] In fact, given the ubiquity of the Internet and the development of educational systems in China, India and Brazil, it seems doubtful that elements of the US economy and political system that give it advantages in innovation capacity will persist. No one suggests that American inventors are inherently more intelligent or more capable than Chinese, Indian and Brazilian inventors. For the latter countries, it is a matter of addressing certain infrastructure factors.

American financial markets have been very successful at aggregating capital so that it can be invested in research and development. Private sector companies are supported for investing in innovation, a phenomenon that has been less common in developing countries. This, coupled with a relatively robust IP enforcement system, has supported the US innovation market. Moreover, up until now the university-level education system in the United States is better funded and enjoys qualitative advantages over university systems in China, India and Brazil.

But the alternative Chinese model of government aggregation of capital (and increasingly private market capital aggregation) seems to neutralize to a certain extent the historical investment-related advantages held by the United States. Chinese technological advancement does not appear to have been held back by its relatively weak patent enforcement system, and that system appears to become more robust as local enterprises participate in it. China is investing heavily in education, with a focus on the sciences. India has developed a university system devoted entirely to the pharmaceutical sector (the NIPERs system), experimenting with the concept of educational subject matter targeting.[17] Other emerging markets will no doubt invest in and improve their educational infrastructure as the importance of education to innovation becomes evident, including by reference to countries such as China. Such developments take time, but it seems reasonable to assume that something closer to parity will exist in education by 2020, at least with respect to China.

While the pace of the technology-capacity shift from the "industrialized West" to the emerging market countries can be debated, and it may not be clear which countries will lead among the emerging markets, the general fact of a shift does not appear open to debate. There is evidence

---

[16] As Wei Zhuang notes, in Chapter 9 in this volume, the rate of patenting by Chinese nationals has increased substantially, but there is some question at this early stage about the quality of those patents.

[17] *See, e.g.*, information at National Institute of Pharmaceutical Education and Research, Punjab, India, http://www.niper.gov.in/ (accessed 12 April 2013).

in international patent databases to confirm China's entry among the technological powers.[18] Even if China represents a "new Japan", and not a general trend among emerging economies, given the economic weight of China, the global innovation and technology balance is shifting.

3.2 Rethinking International Economics

Adam Smith, David Ricardo, et al., suggest to us that the growing technological strength of the emerging market countries benefits global economic welfare, as well as the economic welfare of the United States. Looked at solely from the standpoint of the United States, consumers have the benefit of new technology-based products from overseas. If those products arrive less expensively than comparable products developed and produced in the US, enterprises within the US should be shifting to other areas of R&D and production where they may have a comparative advantage. But, there does seem to be some question whether liberal trade theory works in the new technological environment, primarily because of a lack of substitute employment opportunities at comparable wages for displaced workers.[19] Smith and Ricardo may have overestimated the extent to which national economies can move workers into new jobs that pay comparable wages when there is a global oversupply of labor.[20] The ubiquity of information accessible through the Internet and its sub-networks, combined with the possibility of communicating globally at very low cost, is making it increasingly difficult for any particular country, including the United States, to assert an overwhelming human-capacity advantage in a specialized subject matter area. Specialized professional intellect is becoming less geography-specific.

As globalization seemed poised to "hollow out" the US economy, creating an embedded large gap between highly paid professional service providers and blue-collar hourly wage earners, the government has begun to pay more attention to improving the domestic manufacturing base and to "bringing jobs home". The financial crisis of 2007–09 forced labor unions to accept wage accommodations, while discovery of new ways to recover energy resources has improved the overall manufacturing climate. In this

---

[18] *See* Carsten Fink, Chapter 2 in this volume.

[19] *See* Palley, "Rethinking Trade and Trade Policy", referring to Paul Samuelson and others.

[20] Of course, it is rather difficult to know precisely why the US economy is not doing as well as it might in light of the economic downturn precipitated by the implosion of the housing market as a consequence of imprudent lending, leveraging and borrowing practices.

regard, the United States may be reaching a new equilibrium point where it is more competitive with the emerging markets, as wages and prices in the emerging markets provide less of an advantage, and as US manufacturers increase reliance on automated production processes. Nevertheless, concerns persist about long-term US competitiveness, and these concerns are reflected in the dialogue concerning intellectual property and innovation.

4 US RESPONSES TO GLOBAL COMPETITION

4.1 Digital and Other Integration of the US IP Framework

At least a part of the US reaction to the increasingly global character of the technology environment is to bring US law into closer alignment with the rest of the world. In 2011, Congress enacted the America Invents Act (AIA) that, among other things, moves the United States from a "first to invent" to a "first of file" inventor priority system, generally aligning it with other countries.[21] The AIA also removes vestiges of discrimination against foreign inventors relating to the form of publication or disclosure that may be used to anticipate prior art. The AIA introduces a significantly more robust post-grant opposition procedure that should be similar to that prevailing in Europe. All of these changes signal a policy interest in the United States of integrating its patent system with that of other countries, perhaps as a prerequisite to a push toward a "global patent".

The theory behind integrating the US patent system with practices in the rest of the world is that this will facilitate the efforts of US-based multinational companies to secure protection in other jurisdictions. Even for the largest multinational companies, the present global patent system is cumbersome and expensive. While as well-funded actors the multinationals may be better placed to take advantage of this inefficient system, it would appear that interests in securing wider geographic coverage have been determined to trump benefits from restricting the number of participants.

The United States has also been a leader in digitizing and facilitating applications for patents (and other registration-based IP rights).[22] This

---

21 Information concerning the America Invents Act and its implementation can be found at "AIA Resources", The United States Patent and Trademark Office, Alexandria, VA, http://www.uspto.gov/aia_implementation/resources.jsp (accessed 12 April 2013).

22 Patent tools are available at the US PTO website, at http://www.uspto.gov/patents/index.jsp, as are highly automated trademark application tools and databases, at http://www.uspto.gov/trademarks/index.jsp.

works to the benefit of smaller enterprises in the United States that are better able to cope with the complexities of the application process (even if still requiring the services of lawyers or patent agents).[23]

On the whole, US policymakers are encouraging US businesses and individuals to secure rights in innovation, branding, etc., across a wider geographic scope. This encouragement also extends to foreign-based businesses that benefit from facilitated application and registration processes. But, this is only one side of the coin.

4.2 Addressing "Unfair Competition"

There is a strong political current in the United States toward protection against what is portrayed as "unfair competition" from abroad, particularly from China. This is an extraordinarily complicated problem given that US enterprises have invested heavily in China, such that a significant part of the competition from China is in fact coming from US-based enterprises. This is one of the peculiar anomalies of the US economic relationship with China. US multinational business has poured investment into China knowing full well the gaps in its IP protection system, and with the Chinese government's interest in building up its national technological infrastructure self-evident.[24] To the extent that US business complains about the lack of sufficient IP protection in China, this has very largely been a self-inflicted cause for concern. For better or worse, there was no national government policy in the United States restraining US-based businesses from transferring their valuable technologies to China. Rather, the government pretended that sending trade diplomats to confer with Chinese authorities and accepting bilateral promises would somehow override domestic Chinese policy interests.[25] Why anyone might have thought this would transform Chinese domestic policy is baffling.

---

[23] *But see* Peter Drahos, *The Global Governance of Knowledge: Patent Offices and Their Clients*, Cambridge, UK, Cambridge University Press, 2010, noting that patents are issued predominantly to a relatively small group of large multinational corporations.

[24] *See, e.g.*, Frederick M. Abbott, "The Enduring Enigma of TRIPS: A Challenge for the World Economic System", *Journal of International Economic Law*, vol. 1, 1998, p. 508.

[25] US attempts to secure improved protection for its technology-based enterprises in China began shortly after China's opening to the West in the late 1980s with the conclusion of two bilateral IP agreements. See Abbott, Cottier, and Gurry, *International Intellectual Property in an Integrated World Economy*, pp. 730–44, and documents in Frederick Abbott, Thomas Cottier, and Francis Gurry, *The International Intellectual Property System: Commentary and Materials,*

Recently, concerns in the United States about losing technology to China have shifted toward Chinese cyber-incursions exploiting weaknesses in Internet security. This is a much different kind of threat than failure by the Chinese government to provide adequate IP protection in its own territory. This is a more aggressive form of exploitative behavior, and does not arise out of a deliberate decision by multinational enterprises to take advantage of China's market. It is entirely possible that the only real solution to cyber-incursion is an increase in US network security that may ultimately end up changing the character of the Internet itself. It may well be that Internet 1.0 is simply too open for its own good, and must give way to a more controlled Internet 2.0. It may be that there will be multiple internets. There is perhaps good reason to be skeptical about whether the problem of cyber-incursions can be addressed by legal rules any better than downloading of MP3 files (or the earliest security problems involving copying of software on floppy disks).

Patent law, however, addresses downstream behaviors in the sense that infringement actions are directed toward products (or services) that enter (or attempt to enter) the stream of commerce. In this regard, patents may represent at least a partial response to cyber-security threats because they may prevent resulting market competition from taking place. Whether patents can successfully perform this market-control response function is not entirely clear. But, whether they can or not, problems of cyber-security and problems of patent law enforcement are rather distinct. It is unlikely that the United States can deter cyber-crime by increasing patent law enforcement.

4.3 Bilateral Forums

The United States is finding it difficult to take China on within its own territory. But, it can perhaps better take on China, India and other emerging market countries by tilting the playing field further in favor of US-based multinational companies by establishing IP and other regulatory standards in third-country markets where they will compete with Chinese, Indian and other economic actors.

Part Two, The Hague, Kluwer Law International, 1999.The US secured significant IP-related concessions from China in its WTO accession protocol including, for example, agreement on providing marketing exclusivity for pharmaceutical products based on submission of regulatory data. The US finally brought WTO dispute settlement claims against China in 2007 for alleged IP-related enforcement failures (though none involving patents), but failed to assemble the kind of evidence that might have offered a chance for success. Abbott, Cottier, and Gurry, *International Intellectual Property in an Integrated World Economy*, pp. 731–44.

The United States concluded fairly shortly following the Uruguay Round negotiations that the WTO would not be the preferred arena for further negotiations regarding intellectual property, and shifted toward bilateral and regional negotiations.[26] So far, outside of Australia and South Korea, which are larger advanced economies,[27] US successes in this area have largely involved smaller developing countries that are unlikely to be exporters of high technology products that would compete with US products in the marketplace. Notably, Brazil, India and other major emerging market countries have been unwilling to enter into bilateral negotiations with the USA that are aimed at ratcheting up IP standards. India's negotiations with the EU for a bilateral Economic Partnership Agreement are well advanced. India has committed not to include TRIPS-plus IP standards, at least in the area of pharmaceuticals, though recent pronouncements call into question whether this commitment will be fulfilled.

The present book concerns patents, and this section will focus on the patent elements involved in US bilateral and regional agreements. In its template trade agreement, the United States seeks to fill a number of gaps left open in the TRIPS Agreement.[28] This includes requiring that animals not be excluded from patentability, that patents be allowed for new uses of known substances (including second medical indication patents), that patent term extension be authorized in cases of unreasonable delay by patent offices and that regulatory review exceptions be drafted narrowly. The template incorporates definitions for utility and sufficiency of disclosure.

Related to patents, at least regarding pharmaceuticals and agricultural chemical products, there are provisions operating to prevent the grant of marketing authorization during pendency of the patent, providing notice to the patent owner and the opportunity to intervene in the marketing approval process, including by obtaining an injunction. In addition, the

---

[26] For an account of forum shifting, see John Braithwaite and Peter Drahos, *Global Business Regulation*, Cambridge, UK, Cambridge University Press, 2000, ch. 24.

[27] South Korea presently enjoys GDP per capita rivaling those of the Western industrialized economies, and should be considered to have "emerged". South Korea, which was long chastised by the United States for failing to adequately protect US intellectual property, might provide an interesting case study for whether high IP standards are a good path to developmental success.

[28] *See generally*, Frederick M. Abbott, "Intellectual Property Provisions of Bilateral and Regional Trade Agreements in Light of U.S. Federal Law", UNCTAD–ICTSD Project on IPRs and Sustainable Development, Issue Paper No. 12, February 2006.

agreement template establishes a period (including extensions) of marketing exclusivity for pharmaceutical products during which the counterpart country agrees not to grant approval based on submission of regulatory data within any country party to the agreement.

The bilateral and regional agreements also allow for initiation of private investment disputes against host governments in alternative dispute resolution forums (such as ICSID). The agreements typically provide that the grant of compulsory patent licenses will not be considered illegal takings of property, provided that the rules of the TRIPS Agreement are followed. With recent filings by pharmaceutical companies against host governments whose courts have rendered decisions adverse to patent holder interests, such as a case recently initiated by Eli Lilly against the government of Canada,[29] the risks to governments and the public of incorporating such provisions in bilateral and regional agreements are becoming more apparent.

4.4 The EU-USA Bilateral

One of the more interesting recent developments that may qualify as a response by the United States and the EU toward heightened technological competition from emerging market countries is initiation of negotiations on a bilateral FTA between the EU and USA. The ostensible purpose of this bilateral is to address regulatory hurdles to the free movement of goods, including agricultural products, between these two geographical areas.[30] Although the United States will be negotiating on behalf of itself,

---

[29] *See* "Eli Lilly and Company v. Government of Canada", Foreign Affairs and International Trade Canada, Ottawa, ON, http://www.international.gc.ca/trade-agreements-accords-commerciaux/topics-domaines/disp-diff/eli.aspx?lang=eng&view=d (accessed 12 April 2013): "On November 7, 2012, Eli Lily and Company, a US-based corporation, served the Government of Canada with a Notice of Intent to Submit a Claim to Arbitration under NAFTA Chapter 11. Eli Lilly and Company is alleging that the invalidation of its Strattera pharmaceutical patent by Canada is inconsistent with Canada's commitments under NAFTA." Also, Notice of Intent to Submit a Claim to Arbitration Under NAFTA Chapter Eleven, Eli Lilly and Company, Disputing Investor, and The Government of Canada, Disputing Party, 7 November 2012.

[30] *See* White House, Office of the Press Secretary, "U.S., EU Announce Decision to Launch Negotiations on a Transatlantic Trade and Investment Partnership: Statement from United States President Barack Obama, European Council President Herman Van Rompuy and European Commission President José Manuel Barroso", Office of the United States Trade Representative, 13 February 2013, http://www.ustr.gov/about-us/press-office/press-releases/2013/february/statement-US-EU-Presidents (accessed 12 April 2013).

it is certainly foreseeable that Canada and Mexico as NAFTA countries will seek to be associated with the negotiations in some way.

Establishing new harmonized regulatory measures raises the prospect of establishing barriers or hurdles to market penetration by emerging market-based enterprises. South Africa's Ambassador to the WTO, Faisel Ismael, already has warned of the threat that these negotiations present to the multilateral trading system.[31]

Although there has been some discussion about establishing new "gold standards" of intellectual property protection in an EU-USA FTA,[32] there has been limited concrete discussion about what such gold standards might entail. Further to Article 4 of the TRIPS Agreement, whatever IP "benefits" or "concessions" are conferred on the parties to the agreement, these must be extended on an MFN (most favored nation) basis.

Because of legislative involvement in the drafting of domestic IP rules in both the US and EU, it seems doubtful that an FTA would be the basis for a material change in national IP laws. Still, the creation of a bilateral "super-bloc" between the US and EU that establishes new sets of regulatory compliance standards could act to inhibit growth in and competition from the emerging market countries.

There is a risk, of course, that the US and EU could overplay their hands and encourage emerging market countries to establish their own exclusionary frameworks.

4.5 Plurilateral Forums

The United States has also pursued plurilateral agreements in the form of the Anti-Counterfeiting Trade Agreement (ACTA) and the Trans-Pacific Partnership agreement (TPP). It appears that through these agreements the United States is attempting to build a "ring fence" around China and other emerging market countries in terms of high standards of IP protection.

This chapter does not explore the ACTA in-depth. The ACTA negotiations started out as a "high protection" vehicle for OECD businesses, but was diluted as the result of pushback from NGOs, developing countries and academics.[33] One area where ACTA negotiators were forced to retreat

---

[31] Daniel Pruzin, "South African Envoy Says Proposed U.S.-EU Trade Deal Threatens WTO System", *Bloomberg BNA WTO Reporter*, 25 February 2013.

[32] *See, e.g.*, Stephen Ezell, "Estimating the Potential Benefits of an EU-US Free Trade Agreement", The Information Technology and Innovation Foundation, Washington, DC, 14 March 2013, http://www2.itif.org/2013-estimating-potential-benefits-eu-us-fta.pdf (accessed 12 April 2013).

[33] A lesson to producers of "hard goods" such as pharmaceuticals and elec-

was in the field of patents when it became evident that the proposed rules would be inconsistent with US patent law and doctrine, including in the area of remedies. Because the US Congress had just completed significant revisions to the Patent Act through the America Invents Act, there was little chance that Congress would approve a plurilateral agreement that would approach patent law from a different perspective.

The TPP negotiations include proposals on intellectual property. The United States has proposed substantially enhanced protection for pharmaceutical originators. Under the US proposal, the TPP would incorporate patent/marketing approval linkage requirements, define a broad scope of patentable subject matter, specifically preclude adoption of a patentability requirement for new uses based on enhanced efficacy (repudiating India's Section 3(d)), as well as allowing pharmaceutical originators access to government decision-making regarding insurance reimbursement and pricing. The TPP would also include an investment chapter authorizing private to state third-party dispute settlement.

The US proposals for the TPP on patents, and particularly in the area pharmaceuticals, have received considerable pushback from other negotiating countries. Recent investor dispute actions based on alleged takings of intellectual property (e.g., the Phillip Morris claims against Australia's tobacco plain packaging, and the Eli Lilly claim against a patent invalidation by Canada's courts)[34] may have finally alerted governments to the risk of allowing such types of claims.

With respect to the intellectual property chapter of the TPP, the US is following its typical negotiating strategy which is – following initial pushback from other governments – to take the subject matter off the table until close to the end of the negotiations. If form holds, it will resubmit proposals very near to the end as a more or less "take it or leave it" proposition, forcing other negotiating parties to decide whether they are willing to abandon the entire deal over the IP issues. While this strategy has

tronic equipment from the ACTA negotiations may be to avoid including the entertainment industries within the same set of negotiations. Although one would like to think that the ACTA resistance was founded on concern for access to medicines and other socially important products, the major pushback and effective resistance seemed to come from European pirate parties and others interested in free access to digital entertainment.

[34] Regarding the Eli Lilly claim, *see* "Eli Lilly and Company v. Government of Canada". Documents regarding Australia's Tobacco Plain Packaging legislation can be found at "Investor-State Arbitration – Tobacco Plain Packaging", Australian Government Attorney-General's Department, Barton, ACT, http://www.ag.gov.au/Internationalrelations/InternationalLaw/Pages/Tobaccoplainpackaging.aspx (accessed 12 April 2013).

worked with smaller economy countries like Costa Rica and Colombia, it is not clear that it will work with Australia and Canada, but time will tell.

The curious thing about the US bilateral and plurilateral strategy is that it may no longer be an effective way to address the fundamental issue of innovation competition coming from countries such as China, India and Brazil. The latter countries may today begin to find it in their own interest to enter markets with stronger IP protection for their own goods and services, and not be so concerned with confronting higher standards. Particularly for China, the costs of litigation may no longer pose a significant hindrance to engaging in battles on the patent and IP fronts.

5 MEANINGFULLY ADDRESSING COMPETITION IN INNOVATION FROM EMERGING MARKETS

Over the coming decade it seems doubtful that the main preoccupation of IP policymakers in the United States will be over technology leakage to Chinese, Indian or Brazilian enterprises. Rather the concern will likely be how US companies can maintain competitive advantage in the technology arena. Outside the pharmaceutical sector where patents continue to play a meaningful role in allowing long-term recovery of R&D expenses as against relatively straightforward reverse engineering, recent studies have suggested that most competitive advantage comes from entering the market first with innovative products and successfully marketing them.[35] In a global environment in which access to basic technical skills is more widely shared, it may be that business management skills become as important as the ability to create new products.

Predictably, there will be two tracks of effort to maintain US competitive advantage in high technology products. The first will be "offensive" in terms of investing in innovation. Here the possibilities have been fairly well defined: (1) reliance on patent protection as a general incentive for investment in innovation; (2) government-targeted subsidization of R&D directed toward defined goals, including government commissioning of large-scale scientific infrastructure projects; (3) creative use of prize mechanisms; (4) providing fiscal and tax incentives toward establishment of R&D facilities, and; (5) subsidizing and encouraging scientific education and training.

The United States is already discovering that the patent system must be

---

[35] Stuart J.H. Graham et al., "High Technology Entrepreneurs and the Patent System: Results of the 2008 Berkeley Patent Survey", *Berkeley Technology Law Journal*, vol. 24, no. 4, 2009, pp. 255–327.

used judiciously as a stimulant for innovation because excessive patenting is liable to create roadblocks, particularly in fields such as computer software, standards and consumer electronic goods.[36] In this regard, one of the major challenges to the United States in meeting competition from emerging market innovators is to find the appropriate balance that rewards truly substantial advances in technology, but does not stifle more ordinary technical progress. Even then, given the acceleration in technology cycles, it might be that additional balancing is required, such as by decreasing the term of patents so as to reduce the roadblocks following innovation (or to adopt a system in which a period of exclusivity is followed by a mandatory licensing system).

In the current political environment in the United States there is a bias against government subsidization of new programs, including those that promise to advance science and industry, except insofar as the science relates to military application. Even the US space exploration program is moving toward a privatization model. Nonetheless, the success of the Airbus program in Europe and high-speed rail in China may give rise to some rethinking as to whether governments can successfully nurture technical progress.

As noted, there are other elements that would go into a program to advance US innovation as an "offensive" strategy. And, assuring that patent protection is available to US companies in foreign markets where competitors might emerge may be considered part of that strategy. In an environment where lead time to market is the key to commercial success, there remains a commercial advantage in increasing the time it takes for competitors to enter the market.

But, can and should patents be used as a means to deter Chinese, Indian, Brazilian and other emerging market enterprises from increasingly penetrating the lucrative US consumer market, or other foreign markets? In the late 1980s, US companies turned to Section 337 of the Trade Act of 1930 in efforts to forestall Japanese high-tech entry into the US market. Those efforts may have borne some fruit at the margins, but did little to affect the overall balance of trade. What they mainly did was to instruct Japanese companies regarding how to "game" the US economic system, resulting in quite sophisticated IP strategies followed by Japanese companies.

Today, at least in theory, US-based enterprises can limit import penetration of high technology products based on patents because

---

36 United States Department of Justice and Federal Trade Commission, "Antitrust Enforcement and Intellectual Property Rights: Promoting Innovation and Competition", April 2007.

US-based enterprises (and European and Japanese enterprises) are the preponderant owners of US patents.

Chinese enterprises have increased their patent filings in the United States, but not yet in very large numbers. However, it seems likely this will change as a reflection of the rapid increase in patenting within China, and use of the Patent Cooperation Treaty system. This raises the possibility that during the course of the next decade Chinese enterprises will begin to pursue infringement claims against companies based in the United States and against imports from rivals from other countries (and their own). How will the United States react? Will China be just another Japan doing business in the United States? Or, will Chinese enterprises be portrayed by policymakers as a threat to US economic and/or national security interests?

Part of the answer will depend on the extent to which China successfully transitions away from government ownership and/or control of industry. If US policymakers perceive Chinese inroads into the US market as part of a government program, the reaction is more likely to be hostile. If Chinese enterprises are legitimately private sector, this would seem to present less of a target for hostility because it would not be perceived as bolstering a foreign government with potential to affect national security interests. Finally, the role of the lawyers must be considered. Presumably Chinese users of the US patent system will be paying the fees of US lawyers and patent agents, and the legal community is fairly adept at protecting its sources of income.v

Index

Please note that 'IP' stands for 'Intellectual Property', while 'IPR' represents 'Intellectual Property Rights'.